THE PROVINCIALS

THE
PROVINCIALS

A Personal History of Jews in the South

ELI N. EVANS

ATHENEUM *NEW YORK*

1973

#2527

TO

Jennie and Eli

        Mutt and Sara

Isaac and Sadie

The Beginning

T H E wave of East European immigration to the United States from 1880 to 1920 contributed to a flowering of culture in an adopted land almost unparalleled in Jewish history. Uncaged from the Old World ghettos, children of the immigrants drank deeply from the wells of their new freedom, embracing every aspect of their chosen country. In their exuberance they caught the mood in the streets and the sounds of its people, and set it all to music or put it into words and translated it on stage and screen. Jewish artists gave voice to the American soul—composers and lyricists like Kern, Berlin, Gershwin, Bernstein and Oscar Hammerstein; writers like George S. Kaufman, Moss Hart, and Arthur Miller; entertainment moguls like Robert Sarnoff, Samuel Goldwyn, Louis B. Mayer, and the Warner brothers; giants of vaudeville and the movies like Al Jolson, Eddie Cantor, Danny Kaye, the Marx brothers, Fannie Brice, Jack Benny, and on and on.

Almost all of them began in the northeast, from center stage in New York, commanding applause and attention as definers of taste with such imagination and verve that no one ever bothered to look elsewhere. In the South especially, Jews languished as the provincials, the Jews of the periphery, not destined to triumph but just to survive—the dull, foolish relatives, subjects of condescension and pity, ignored, overlooked, and ridiculed, out on the rim where it didn't count—for the great Jewish drama in America was being played elsewhere. In the South, the Jews would slowly drift away from their urban roots to absorb regional

vii

characteristics and attitudes, though the immigrant influence would work its own paradox in the subconscious terminals of the mind. The deeper differences between Southern Jew and Southerner would keep them apart for at least two generations while the South itself shucked off its own version of the ghetto and joined mainstream America.

Three years ago, I chanced upon a yellowing typed manuscript, less than a hundred pages, that my grandmother Jennie Nachamson had dictated to one of her eight daughters during the last year of her life. The story told of the early days in Lithuania, the family debate to come to America, the first few years in a Baltimore slum, and, subsequently, of my grandparents' decision to gamble on the South. It was the story of raising a large Jewish family in the eastern North Carolina tobacco belt in the early 1900's; running stores in Dover, Kinston, and then Durham, North Carolina; and coping with the loneliness that plagues small-town Jews throughout the South. Jennie's story connected me with the life-force in my roots, and personalized the pain of the immigrant struggle. And she stirred the Southerner in me by revealing the wellsprings, a genesis far deeper than the Confederate ancestry the old families in Durham loved to brag about.

Still, I didn't intend to write this book until Willie Morris, then the editor of *Harper's* magazine, agreed to send me through the South in the summer of 1970 for a series of articles on Jews in the South. That trip became the catalyst for the book, though even the time away from the South had prepared me for it to some extent. Living in New York, I felt the Southern Jewish experience take on new dimensions. I walked the Lower East Side on Sundays, watched the Jews selling bagels and blouses out of small stalls on Delancey Street, and envisioned these same men in the South of the nineteenth century; I compared their sons on Long Island to the Jews I remembered in Durham.

To prepare for the trip, I read everything I could find on the history of Jews in the South and was startled to find how few books there were. The provincials—400,000 people scattered across eleven states—just didn't seem to interest Jewish writers and historians. Then I drove seven thousand miles that hot summer and, slowly, the terrain and the sounds began to churn up memories. Sometimes a few dozen miles took hours to drive because I stopped so often by the road to write down notes. In interviews, a chance remark or an expression, something unspoken, would set off a whole chain of recollections, until sometimes the notes I pondered over at night bore no resemblance to the conversations at all.

Dreams unfolded over a summer of self-discovery as I realized I was wandering in a web hundreds of years old. A cemetery in Charleston, a roadside history plaque in North Carolina, a plantation house in Louisiana, all bore traces of Jews since the earliest days of Southern history, struggling to find their place in the American South. Jews were not aliens in the promised land but blood-and-bones part of the South itself—Jewish Southerners, passing for white in that mysterious underland of America. Jennie's story was settling into context.

The quest for my own past, to find the hidden corners of my own life and expose them—not to claim common experience with all Jews in the South, just to lay my life out for others to react to—perhaps that would be the contribution. Suddenly, every memory was relevant—the boredom and the fears, the phantoms I fled from and the culture I embraced, the Southern Jesus all around me, roughneck whites looming large in nightmares, the easy intimacy of my home town, the tastes of barbecue and brunswick stew, the black maids who raised me, the gallant exaggerations of boyhood—I would now come back home, back to relive all those things I had left behind.

When the Southerner romanticizes his past, he thinks of the antebellum era—he looks back only a hundred years into what he thinks is an eternity. But my grandfather didn't romanticize the past that way. Things just weren't that great in Lithuania and Russia. He was a man more with his eyes on the future. He was doing better than his father did; his son would do better yet.

My father ran the family business successfully and tried, I always felt, to pass it on to his reluctant sons, though my brother and I rejected the stores and fled the South as many in our generation did. But Dad was more than just a man in his store—he was a citizen of his town as well. First elected mayor of Durham in 1950, he served six consecutive terms until 1962, straight through the toughest years of the civil rights movement. When so many Southern towns plunged into a dark reckoning, he worked behind the headlines to keep his part of the South out of the backwaters of violence. Neither the Klan mentality nor its more respectable counterpart, the White Citizens' Council, ever took charge in Durham, and part of the reason was his ability to reach into the texture of the town and tap its character. Durham brushed close to violence several times but successfully integrated its schools, hotels, and restaurants, always with crisis but never with disaster. But nobody writes about the towns that didn't blow up.

My mother is the oldest daughter of Jennie Nachamson, an extraordinary woman who, we were told, started the first Southern branch of Hadassah, the women's Zionist organization. In the middle of the Depression my father somehow found the money to send Jenny and my mother to Palestine to see the homeland. So my mother proudly called herself a Zionist all her life, traveling across the South for Hadassah in the forties, organizing in Jackson and Memphis and Birmingham during the roughest era of the struggle for Israel, risking denunciation as a radical, and facing ugly opposition from the older German Jewish families in the South who feared the repercussions of a Jewish state and fought it with ridicule or indifference.

I am not certain what it means to be both a Jew and a Southerner—to have inherited the Jewish longing for a homeland while being raised with the Southerner's sense of home. The conflict is deep in me—the Jew's involvement in history, his deep roots in the drama of man's struggle to understand deity and creation. But I respond to the Southerner's commitment to place, his loyalty to the land, to his own tortured history, to the strange bond beyond color that Southern blacks and whites discover when they come to know one another.

For this book, I have attempted to bare the soul of the Jewish South, to touch the subjective edges of the experience. Most of the interviews took place in the summer of 1970, though I returned to some states several times the following year as I focused my energies on certain people, events, and communities. None of my visits to the major cities were my first, for I had been bouncing from Atlanta to Charleston to New Orleans all my life, by virtue of those devices Southern mothers use to bring their sons into contact with Jewish girls.

I wanted to travel and just listen with an open ear to Southern Jews talk, in their own accents and idioms. I was determined to probe not only the Jews of all ages but the black ministers and militants, Klansmen and filling station attendants, farmers, churchwomen, and postmasters. For I was certain that Southern Jews were molded by the ethos they grew up in, and I wanted to reach for the nuances of the Southerner's attitudes toward the Jew he knew on Main Street as well as the chosen people he read about in the Bible. Southern writers overlooked this South—the South I loved and lived in—and the gap between the life I led and the South they wrote about always bothered me. The Jewish writers of the North, uptight and myopic, played stickball on the sidewalks for an extra generation in the cities, and they did not speak for me either. We were Jews; we were Southerners. I was never sure what either meant, nor how they came together.

That was the challenge of this book: to write it as I lived it and perceived it, not as prototypical of other Jewish Southerners (though I suspect that many will see shadows of themselves), but as one man's experience—my own boyhood, the trip in 1970, the history of the Jews in the region. Where it seemed appropriate, the names are fictitious. In most cases, they speak as I heard them.

Eli Nachamson Evans
Chapel Hill,
North Carolina
October 1, 1972

Contents

Contents

IV COMING OF AGE

V DISCRIMINATION

VI JEWS AND BLACKS

I

Tobacco Town Jews

ONE

An Inconsequential Town

D U R H A M as I recall it was an ordinary-looking town precisely divided into five pie-shaped sections, spreading out from Five Points, our "Times Square." Here five streets converged, and buses rumbled through all day, radiating in all directions so that a downtown shopper could climb on a bus home no matter where he lived. Every section had small pockets of black settlements, some no larger than three or four streets, but for the most part, the neighborhoods stayed to themselves, each with its own character.

First was Hayti (named after Haiti, I was always told, but pronounced "Hey-Tye"), where the Negroes lived alongside Fayetteville Street, lined with cheap grocery stores advertising catfish, fatback, and greens. The exotic store-front cults and the gypsy palmists added mystery to the neighborhood, while a lavish funeral home provided a touch of glamor, with its shiny hearse parked out front for advertising purposes. There were beer joints like Papa Jack's and the Bull City Sandwich Shop; little places like Pee Wee's Shoe Shop and the Two Guys' Cut-Rate Drug; and a movie theater featuring World War II films, with a homemade sign out front that said "White Section Inside." Middle class or poor, the blacks lived in Hayti. The beautiful homes of the North Carolina Mutual Insurance Company executives, who worked for "the largest Negro-owned company in the world," clustered on the paved streets around North Carolina College; on the next block, crumbling shanties lined the dirt streets. On every corner throughout stood the churches, some brick and manicured, others as

3

rundown as the congregation—St. Mark A.M.E. Zion Church, Fisher's United Memorial Holy Church, and the United House of Prayer for All People, "Bishop C. M. Grace, Founder."

Only the railroad tracks separated the working whites of East Durham from the blacks in Hayti—fifteen feet of parallel steel that might as well have been a gorge as deep as the Grand Canyon, except on Saturday nights when carloads of young whites might wheel through. The white millhands lived in clapboard dwellings with green shutters and small yards, their cars parked on the street because they didn't have garages. They too had churches on almost every corner, diners that advertised cold beer and grits and eggs, pool rooms, hardware stores, and Jimmie's Soda Shop, all surrounding the city softball field, where on most summer nights you could watch a girls' team or a Little League game, the name *Erwin Mills* or *Liggett & Myers* emblazoned on their jerseys.

West of Five Points, the red brick tobacco warehouses ringed the downtown, sometimes suffocating the city with the thick pungent odor of aging leaves, which we were conditioned to call "a rich aroma." Just beyond the factories and Durham High School, lived the middle class, in brick homes with postage stamp lawns that the young blacks mowed for a dollar. Most of the Jews who were not associated with Duke University lived here, though a few were audacious enough to try Hope Valley, even though they couldn't belong to the country club out there. The old Trinity College campus and the new Duke University provided a rolling green corridor to the Duke woods and the homes of the college administrators and the professors, puttering around in their azaleas on winding streets that valued a dogwood tree above all else.

Hope Valley was the home of the newly rich—the owners of the lumber companies and the corporation lawyers, the bank officials and the successful insurance salesmen, their white-columned or ranch-style homes surrounding the Hope Valley Country Club golf course. Any day you could see men in colorful outfits chipping up to a green out on the fairways. Their daughters were debutantes who entered the horse shows down in Pinehurst but mostly lolled around the pool at the club; the society page featured their wives during the Junior League fashion show.

The older rich lived in Forest Hills around a park that John Sprunt Hill had given to the city after he married the daughter of an American Tobacco Company executive and made his own for-

4

tune in banking and insurance. My parents' ambition had been to live in Forest Hills and they bought a lot there in 1939, across from the estate of Mary Duke Biddle. My father would take me there to walk around the trees where we were going to live some-day, on a hill as high as the Dukes lived on. During the war my mother would rip through *House Beautiful* and *Better Homes and Gardens*, tearing out pictures and ideas until she felt she knew exactly what she wanted—her "dream house." When we finally built it in 1950, it was the first split-level in town—so modern that the workmen brought their families out on Sunday to show them what unusual plastering and woodwork they had done that week. Even Mrs. Biddle ordered her limousine over for a look in, a triumph for the first Jewish family in Forest Hills. For our family 1950 was a special year—a new home and my father's first campaign for mayor of Durham.

My father always cared about his town, and it seemed that any time money had to be raised, Durham called on him. He was part of the generation that was too young for World War I and too old for World War II, the men left at home to carry the brunt of community work to buttress the war effort. He headed the Community Chest campaigns; he brought all the hostile political groups together to pass the bond issue for the new wings on the white and Negro hospitals; he twice headed the war bond campaign; and he even persuaded Judge Spears to serve as chairman of the United Jewish Appeal and raised $8,000 from the gentiles when other Jewish leaders in North Carolina were too timid to ask non-Jews for money.

In 1950, as the new president of the Merchant's Association, Dad was invited by the mayor to serve as one of the business representatives on the Citizens for Good Government Committee, a small group of leaders from the business community, labor, and the Negro political group who had formed to try to convince better candidates to run for local offices. Two days before the filing date for the spring election, the incumbent mayor received a federal appointment, and the key members of the committee began to cast around for a new candidate to replace him. Meeting followed meeting, but they could agree on no one. Finally, John Wheeler, the president of the Mechanics and Farmers' Bank and chairman of the Durham Committee on Negro Affairs, asked, "What about Mutt Evans?" John Stewart and Dan Martin, the other leaders of the

5

Negro organization at the meeting, said, "Evans helped build the Negro hospital and his store has been the only place where Negroes downtown can get something to eat or use a restroom." They also recalled that when he directed the Community Chest campaigns, he had been the first white ever to go into the Negro community to sit and eat with several hundred Negroes at their kick-off chicken dinner, a symbolic act in a Southern town in the 1940's.

My father was the only candidate that all the factions could agree on, but after the meeting the conservative members of the business group balked at endorsing anyone that the Negroes and labor trusted. They decided to run Judge James R. Patton against him, a canny corporation lawyer who had served as chairman of the Democratic Party in Durham until he was ousted by a new labor-Negro coalition several years before.

The newspapers announced the potential candidates, and some alarmed members of the Jewish community began calling my father to beg him not to run. They feared that if anything happened in the city, the whites would blame the Jews and that a divisive campaign might sink into an anti-Semitic slugfest that could cause racial unrest, threats to their business, and ugly incidents.

He decided to run anyway, on a platform of bringing the city together, but the "downtown crowd," of which he, ironically, was a leader, opposed him vigorously. As election day approached, *The Public Appeal*, a small local paper with a workingman's readership and run by vitriolic "Wimpy" Jones, published the fake Protocols of Zion, under a headline that suggested Durham was becoming part of a Jewish plot for world domination. When Joe Brady from New York, an old family friend whose father had been one of Buck Duke's cigarette rollers, sent a contribution, a whispering campaign started to the effect that Evans was the "puppet" of a group of wealthy New York Jews.

A minor candidate forced a first primary, and the results opened my father up to a new kind of attack. He had received overwhelming support from the black precincts, and ads began to appear in the paper asking, "Who will choose your city servants? The Political Bosses, the Negro Bloc? or . . . You!" and "What has Evans promised the Negro Bloc?"

The Public Appeal put it more directly in an article entitled "NAACP Aims," which said that the organization "through Com-

6

munist influence" sought "getting addressed in the white press as
Mr., Mrs., or Miss; picture publication, . . . their weddings and
social activities noted . . . the designation 'Negro' eliminated
from ALL court and public records . . . [so that] they can really
revel in all sorts of crime from rape to murder, and abolish all laws
which prohibit Negro children or youths from attending general
public schools and universities."

It was classic racial politics in the small-town South; my mother
worried about the personal threats, the obscene phone calls, and the
wildly scribbled letters. The week before the election the police set
up a twenty-four-hour watch on our house.

"Don't worry, Sara," my father tried to reassure her. "It's not
that serious. Just a precaution. Nobody means all that stuff and
nobody pays any attention to Wimpy. It's all just part of the
game."

"Politics blossoms like the dogwoods," they say each May, but
we didn't even notice the final afternoon of the campaign as my
father took me along with him from precinct to precinct to buck up
the people handing out the "Evans for Mayor" leaflets. At Hillside
High in Hayti the black poll workers greeted him excitedly, and one
of them secretly showed us the sample ballot being passed out to all
the black voters by the Durham Committee on Negro Affairs. I
beamed—"Evans" was circled in red.

But over in East Durham in the poor white districts, and out in
Hope Valley with the bankers and the businessmen, volunteers
pulled him aside so as not to offend the young boy with him, and
reported that the whispering campaign against him was working. I
picked up enough to understand. "It's rough out here, Mr. Evans, I
don't mind telling you."

My memory of that campaign rivets on a tissue-thin pink leaflet
showing a photograph of our new house just below big black
letters: "Do We Want a Goldberg or an Evans? What's the
Difference? They're All Alike."

The house . . . Would they do something to our house? Was
my father in danger from a campaign that he had told me would be
"fun"? Fear and ugliness engulfed my previous fantasies of adulation and victory. And then for the first time (a ridiculous thought
in retrospect), it hit me that people thought "Evans" didn't sound
like a Jewish name.

The man who printed the leaflets also did signs for our store and he had sneaked my father a copy. They would not be distributed, Dad explained, because there were decent people supporting his opponent, including the big lawyer Percy Reade, who had promised him that the leaflets would never leave the print shop.

My father believed that openness and pride were the best political means of combating anti-Semitism, so he printed on his posters: "Chairman, Statewide United Jewish Appeal Campaign" and "President, Beth-El Synagogue." "With our name," he explained, "we have to go out of our way to let people know. And besides, people down here respect church work."

So I remember my relief when the leaflet campaign was squelched. And I remember a secret thought too—I was glad that my name wasn't Goldberg.

As the campaign progressed, the opposition took ads charging that the candidates running on the new reform ticket my father headed were "the tools of the Negro bloc vote," and rumors began circulating that he had received campaign funds from "the New York Jews."

The Sunday before the election, two ministers from the largest Baptist churches preached sermons deploring the inclusion of racial and religious issues in the campaign, and said they personally intended to vote for Evans. The night before the election, Dad went on the radio and was introduced by Frank Hickman, the most popular professor in the Duke Divinity School, who said, "I want to introduce a friend of mine, a great humanitarian, and invite you to vote for him for mayor tomorrow." Dr. Hickman taught preaching to student ministers, and his voice reverberated with the righteousness of the hills of Judea.

Dad came on strong. "I ran to instill the same harmony in government affairs as we have had in civic affairs," he said to emphasize his chairmanship of two successful war bond campaigns. "If we are to attain unity in Durham, each individual must be judged on his merit alone, and we must stop arraying class against class, labor against management, race against race in a vicious cycle of resentment. If I am fortunate enough to go into office on May eighth, I will go as a representative of *all* the people, regardless of faith, creed, or position in life." Mom and I sat in the living room listening; she touched my arm as the band struck up "Marching along together, no one's gonna stop us now."

On election day, our black maid Zola voted early and Dad asked her at breakfast how things were going at the Hillside High precinct. She was so excited she could barely get it out. "Mister Evans, they's lined up from here to Jerusalem, and everybody's votin' for *you*."

We came back home in the late afternoon to sweat out the rest of the day with Gene Brooks, a crafty former state senator whose father had been one of the most progressive leaders in behalf of Negro education in the state. He was our family lawyer, political adviser, and campaign manager. Today, he had turned our living room into a command post with an extra phone to dramatize its new purpose, and both phones were jangling away.

"It's for you," he said, handing the phone to Dad.

Dad went pale listening and told the caller that he would talk to Gene and get right back to him. "He says there's a guy at the Fuller School precinct giving out razor blades to every voter and telling them to cut the Jew off the ticket."

Fuller School was a workingman's precinct where the struggling labor unions might sway a few poor white voters back from the reaction against any candidate with black support. Gene called Leslie Atkins, the controversial labor leader who had brought the Negroes into Democratic Party politics, put them in charge of their own precincts, and generally held the always frail Negro-labor coalition together. An hour later, Leslie called back.

"One of the boys took care of it," Gene said. And then with a puckish grin, he admitted, "They just slipped that fellow a bottle of liquor and he's finished for today—passed out."

The ballots were counted by hand, and at eleven o'clock Dad was far behind. Then the Hillside precinct came in: Evans 1,241 and Patton 64. Gene whooped, "I bet Jackie Robinson couldn't have done better." Then he added, "I wonder where those sixty-four votes came from. I'll have to get after somebody about that."

Pearson School, the other large Negro precinct, came rolling in at 833 to 29, and Dad was also doing well at the Duke University precincts where the "innylekchals," as Gene teasingly called them, were voting more heavily than usual.

When the radio announcer gave the final results in the mayor's race at 6,961 to 5,916, officially confirming the phoned reports from the precincts, Dad turned to my mother and kissed her. "I told you that it would all work out. How does it feel to be the first lady of Durham?"

Mother was heading for the kitchen to put some food on the

9

table for the few friends who might drop by when suddenly the door burst open and a gang of people from the Jewish community came thundering through, straight from an election night party at Hannah Hockfield's. Fifty or sixty strong, buzzing with excitement, kissing me and messing my hair, they went roaring through the kitchen and out to the dining room, like a starving army of locusts, and just as suddenly, they were gone, the table in the dining room stripped totally bare.

The next morning when the phone rang at breakfast, Zola answered with a resounding, "Mayor Evans' resee-*dense*," and Mother blushed at Dad across the table. Nobody had instructed Zola in the new greeting, but nobody ever corrected her either.

Dad served for twelve years, in six consecutive two-year terms, through the turbulent fifties when the Supreme Court jolted the South into responsibility and changed all the rules of living. He played the role of peacemaker, presiding over transition years until blacks would demand concessions as a human right and whites would yield as an economic and political necessity. He always tried to guide his town, pleading for respect for the law and the courts, seizing the openings, and bringing his slice of the South through the difficult times when whole corners of his universe were turning to demagogues and false prophets for comfort and defiance.

The South is filled with quiet heroes who worked skillfully behind the scenes, who understood the levers of change and did what was right because deep inside they knew that the South could go only one way. The literature of the South would focus on the confrontations and the failures, not on the plodding, indefatigable and unheralded work of the men in places where the passions did not explode, nor death and hatred spill out for the probing, eager lenses of the media. It seems so inconsequential in retrospect, but the story of the South is written in the first, faltering steps in a hundred "inconsequential" towns: my father would be proudest of the first Negro policeman and fireman, the moving of Negroes into supervisory positions in City Hall, and the years he hammered the City Council to set up the Urban Renewal Authority to build low-cost housing for the poor of both races, leading to the largest federal grant in the South at that time because Durham could claim to be a pioneer. He worked behind the scenes to settle the first lunch-counter demonstrations. ("Did the roof fall in today?" he

10

asked the reluctant manager of Woolworth's after they served a
Coke to their first black student.) He badgered the merchants to
hire Negro sales personnel, knowing that if all would move together, no one would be hurt and the community would be better
off. He always had respect for the other man's position, and would
talk and work while some leaders sought momentary advantage by
denouncing each other in emotional headlines.

There were the nasty fights on property taxes and garbage collection and fluoride in the city water. ("Mr. Mayor," the rasping
little old lady phone caller said, "I'm suing the city for damages
because the fluoride has turned my teeth green and is making my
heart palpitate," and he answered, "That's fine, ma'am, but we're
not putting it in for another month.") There were the victories,
like building the off-street parking garage and parking lots downtown to save it from drying up, ten years before others saw what
shopping centers and suburbs were going to do. Even at that, to
get the project launched Dad had to go out and sell the bonds
personally, and reduce the estimated costs for parking a car from
40 cents to 10 cents an hour (by selling the bonds to businesses
downtown, thus reducing the interest costs to the city).

There were some issues on which his Judaism influenced his
vote, like his support of the Sunday blue laws. "I didn't want people
saying a Jew didn't care about keeping Sundays holy," he said.
After his vote, the labor journal complimented his "respect for the
sacredness of the recognized Sabbath of most of Durham's citizens. . . . That kind of respect is worthy of only a true-blue
American. Oh, that such a spirit could prevail in the hearts of all
Protestants as well."

He had his brushes with the Ku Klux Klan, but he kept the
threatening letters and phone calls from his family; he never let
anyone know about the weekend he and my mother spent in a motel
because police informers had reported a bomb plot at a recent Klan
meeting. He liked telling about the quip of Billy Carmichael, the
vice-president of the University of North Carolina, that if "anybody
had told people that someday the Catholic vice-president of the
University and the Jewish Mayor of Durham would be on the same
platform, every sheet in the county would be riding by nightfall."

He never held a political grudge, because he believed that every
man had his reasons and that surely if a man disagreed on one
issue he might be with you on the next one. He was not doctrinaire

11

nor wedded to ideology, but believed in fairness and worked to resolve differences; he remained an optimist through the darkest times and once said to me when the streets were filled with demonstrators and the lines were hardening and the bitterness spreading, "I think we can crack this thing and have the first wide-open town for public accommodations in the South." He always held himself to the broadest vision: "We can't have a town where forty percent of the population is sullen and unhappy. We can be first and show the rest of the South how to do it." He conceived the simple idea of a human relations commission made up of leaders of both races as a permanent device to settle disputes and keep the races talking through any crisis, and letters came in from all over the South asking how to do it. It was old-fashioned—the love of a man for his home town; it was Southern—the loyalty of a man to place; it was Jewish—the commitment to rightness.

The Southern liberal of the fifties understood the mine field he lived in and how to pick his way through it. He knew that populism ran deep in the Southern soul and that the interests of the poor whites, though they attack in trigger words and suffocate in myths, were essentially the same as the interests of the poor blacks. The Southern liberal understood coalition and how race itself could be turned into support for better schools and streets and medical care for Negroes, though facilities would be separate for a while until the courts could act. He was a negotiator, whose terms were defined often by other forces—the courts, the streets, the newspapers. The Southern liberal of the fifties knew the jungle, because if he didn't he couldn't survive.

When my father retired, the Chamber of Commerce honored him with their Man-of-the-Year award at a banquet at which 1,200 people gave him a standing ovation. Mrs. Biddle's daughter, Mary Duke Biddle Semans (who could have spent her life snubbing Durham and eating caviar, but who loved politics and never ran from a fight when racial injustice was involved), volunteered to pay him tribute because she had been elected to the city council with him in the good government sweep in 1950 and had served as the first woman mayor pro-tem in the city's history: "With his magic of persuasion, a spirit of adventure, and a 'fresh air' quality, he awakened confidence and regenerated Durham's sense of frontier. In days when human relations committees were eyed with suspicion, he appointed one of the first human relations committees

12

in the South, and official communications between groups that had never exchanged ideas were open at last. He cut a clearing in the woods for a race relations breakthrough."

On the way home after the dinner, he sat quietly in the back seat lost in thought for a while. He wasn't a sentimental man, at least not outwardly, but when I asked, he confessed, "I guess I was just wishing that Papa and Mama could have been here tonight."

Every Southerner absorbs the legends of his town, for the South is a storytelling place, rooted in imagery and fables. The legends of the Duke family and their tobacco exploits filtered into the heads of everyone who grew up in Durham. The signs of their dominion were everywhere.

Duke University sprawled in gray Gothic splendor on one side of the town. Duke Street ran straight from the university to form one of the spokes in Five Points, where it joined up with Main Street to create the major commercial artery; the best hotel was the Washington Duke; and the grammar schools and the junior highs were all named for tobacco company executives of various rank in the empire.

Portions of the Duke family still motored about Durham, feeding the legend with fresh tales. It was said that Mary Duke Biddle kept a painter busy twelve months a year changing the colors in the rooms of her pink stucco mansion. It was a huge estate, including a second home for her daughter, surrounded by fences, because, so the story went, of a kidnapping threat after the Lindbergh case. People said that "anybody would have been proud to live in the servants' quarters," which sat close to the road. Passers-by would try to peer through the manicured woods to make out parts of the big house on the hill.

The Jewish merchants in town, as well as the Jewish Yankees who came to Duke to teach, were linked to tobacco as surely as the first Jews who were lured to work in Mr. Duke's factory in the 1880's. Around the synagogue, children could hear the old men tell visitors the story of the Jews and the Dukes, the true white Anglo-Saxons, the only aristocracy Durham had. The story appealed to the Jewish immigrants—how the sons of old Washington Duke brought the Jews down to roll cigarettes and conquer America right from the streets of our home town.

The rest of North Carolina always had considered Durham an

unsavory borough—its air faulted and its life seedy, a brawling two-fisted factory town, without culture or class, bone-dry for legal liquor but flourishing with bootleggers, the kind of place to stay out of on a Saturday night. It had no real traditions—no colonial past and no plantation memories. Some said its name was short for "Dirty Hamlet," nothing but a crossing on the railroad from Raleigh west, with alleys and lanes called Hen Peck Row, Shake Rag, and Dog Trot. Yet fate destined it the site for a historic meeting—between General William T. Sherman of the United States Army, on the tail end of his infamous March to the Sea, and General Joseph E. Johnston of the Army of the Confederate States of America, both of whom had received word of Lee's surrender at Appomattox. They met in a farmhouse called Bennett Place four miles from Durham station in a stunning anticlimax to end in official surrender a war that had in fact been ended two weeks before.

Sherman's army, dismissed from combat, had plundered everything in sight a few days earlier, and now flooded into Durham to talk and gamble and parade with the Confederate soldiers. They broke into John Ruffin Green's tobacco factory and stole all his "Spanish-flavored Durham Tobacco," leaving him a ruined man. But the soldiers had never tasted anything like it, and in just a few months Mr. Green began to receive orders in the mail for more, so he opened again, this time with a picture of a friend's new bull on the pouch, and "Bull Durham" tobacco was born.

From a Yankee prison in eastern North Carolina, Washington Duke began his 137-mile walk home to a burned-out, devastated farm where, miraculously, the plundering soldiers had overlooked a barn full of tobacco. It was enough for a start, and he and his three sons—James Buchanan ("Buck"), Benjamin, and Brodie—cut it up by hand and bagged it and traded it for bacon, flour, and whatever else substituted for money in the broken economy. They built a small factory to work in—if you can call a twenty-by-thirty-foot building a factory—and they called it W. Duke Sons and Company.

Other factories in Durham were making "Ladies Scotch snuff" and cigars, cheroots, and chewing tobacco—especially Bull Durham, promoted so skillfully that people said you could find the sign of the bull on the pyramids of Egypt. Bull Durham even crowed about its profits daily with a steam whistle that sounded like a bellowing bull; the steam cost six dollars a blow and could be heard for thirteen miles around. James Russell Lowell introduced Bull Durham to Alfred Lord Tennyson, and the company began pushing Durham itself as the "Town Renowned the World Around." Nobody could compete with the array of tobacco products offered by "The Bull," and in 1880 Buck Duke turned to his brother Ben and said, "We're up against a stone wall. We're going to make cigarettes."

Cigarettes. Nothing but tobacco rolled in paper, a fad that began in Turkey in the 1830's, and spread to Europe after the Crimean War, when English officers picked it up and "roll your own" began to crop up in the fancy salons of London. Russian royalty employed peasants to roll cigarettes for them and immigrants brought the skill to America. The light and flavorful Bright Leaf from Virginia and the Carolinas, which burned smoothly and smelled almost sweet compared to exotic Arab leaves, already was gaining a foothold for "tailor-mades" in the Northern cities. So how do you start if you are Buck Duke? You search out the people who can roll the best cigarettes in the world and you bring them to Durham. From New York City Buck Duke imported 125 Russian and Polish Jews to roll and pack his cigarettes.

Mike Gladstein in Durham is a descendant of that early group; his father, Moses Gladstein, then nineteen and less than a year in America from Russia, where he had learned to roll gold-tipped cigarettes for a count and countess, became Duke's chief organizer for the trip. "Buck Duke approached my father," Mike recalled, "because he had led a strike at the Goodwin Tobacco Company in New York and had lost his job. My father got all the strikers to come to Durham, right off the picket line."

Most of them were young men, under twenty-five, many with young families, and Duke paid their train fare from New York. What a trip it must have been! They came as a group, all their belongings in bundles, to a place they knew nothing of—trusting and hopeful, surely uneasy and frightened, but together. For days they gazed out the windows at mile upon uninhabited mile as the train clattered through the meadowlands of Maryland and Virginia into the red clay country of North Carolina, finally to stop in the desperate little town of Durham, a new home in the belly of America, and a better life.

The Jews lived mostly in shacks in Hayti, on a street dubbed

Yiddisha Streetal. They spoke little English and gawked at the Durham people when they wandered around town, while the Durham people gawked back at the first foreigners many of them had ever seen. They started a synagogue over Madry's Drug Store and were startled one day when an itinerant Negro preacher turned up who could read the Torah in the original Hebrew for a small fee, having learned it from "a visitation." But there was little time for friends or religion because the factory hours were so long. Early each day, several Jews would gather around dozens of square, marble-topped tables and deftly twist the "long-cut" strips of tobacco into slivers of paper, then paste them with a mixture of flour and water, all the while rolling with just the right touch to form a tight little cylinder. A good man could roll three or four a minute, 2,500 in a twelve-hour day, and the Duke Company paid them seventy cents a thousand, which meant an income of two dollars a day. And with house rent of three dollars a week. . . .

When the Dukes hired J. M. Seigel, a prominent Jewish cigarettemaker in London, Bull Durham hired Seigel's brother David, and from across the world, two brothers sailed to Durham to compete with one another. But with "The Bull," cigarettes were just a sideline; with the Dukes, they were everything.

Buck saw what machines were doing for other industries—Elias Howe's sewing machine, for instance, perfected by Singer—and he kept his ears and eyes open, and even tried to build one in the plant. Within a year, he trotted off to Virginia where he heard that a twenty-two-year-old named James Bonsack had invented a cigarettemaking machine which jammed the tobacco through an endless tube of paper into a circular knife which cut it cleanly. Buck tied up the patents, and brought Bonsack to Durham to install the machine.

The Jews took it calmly at first, while for fourteen months Bonsack and his mechanics tried to perfect the screeching gearbox and the spidery arms on the cutter. And then it happened: the machine began to work for several hours at a time without breaking down, and Buck reduced the work requirement of the hand rollers to a thousand cigarettes a day, and cut their wages to $2.90 a week. It was an untenable position, and the Jews were driven out, the losing side in an early drama of the industrial revolution. They threatened the lives of the mechanics; they threatened to destroy the machines. When they went out on strike, Duke moved in locals

16

to roll the slack that the machines didn't produce. Washington Duke, a decade later, wrote of it with the magnate's perspective: "We have never had any trouble in the help except when 125 Polish Jews were hired to come down to Durham to work in the factory. They gave us no end of trouble. We worked out of that, and now we employ our own people. . . . If good citizens come, well and good, but there are plenty of North Carolinians here who are glad to work."

Once perfected, the Bonsack machine could produce a quarter of a million cigarettes a day, reducing the cost to thirty cents a thousand, and the cost of a pack from ten cents to a nickel. With the end of the hand-rolled cigarette, the Jews who had come to Durham on a magic carpet soon scattered, some to stay in the South as peddlers but most to return to the ghettos in the North. "They were not carpenters or brick masons; they were cigarette-makers," said Mike Gladstein, "and most went back up there to practice their trade." Buck gave Moses Gladstein "a thousand dollars for his services," which he used to open a clothing store in Durham. Few of the others could stay.

The old Jewish men in Durham were fascinated with the story of Buck Duke, and I grew up with the legends of his exploits. The basic reason was surely that the roots of the Durham Jewish community reached directly into Mr. Duke's cigarette-rolling rooms. But also, the Dukes were an aristocracy the immigrants could identify with—not plantation-bound and honey-dipped like the landed aristocracy in the Deep South, but builders of a manufacturing empire, working their way from poverty to riches in one generation.

To begin with, Buck was a public relations genius. He conceived the sliding box to protect the unsmoked sticks in a gentleman's pocket, and never held back on business-boosting advertising schemes, no matter how wild. He called his cigarette "Duke of Durham" and enclosed pictures of luscious actresses in each pack; he hired women to sell it on the road, breaking down the resistance of the stores and females. He gave free packs to the immigrants on Ellis Island because he knew they'd carry the word throughout the nation. He sent his salesmen to plaster billboards and fences from London to Shanghai, transporting cigarettes by medieval oxcart and camel caravan to little villages all over the world.

Buck didn't mind the barroom tactics of the clashing market-

17

place, and he paid off the shippers, hired a private police squad to enforce agreements, slashed prices to drive out a competitor, paid off suppliers to bury a rival, anything he had to do in order to push Duke of Durham out front. He schemed and slashed his way until he was ready in 1890 for the boldest move of all—to follow in the footsteps of his hero, John D. Rockefeller, and organize a trust in tobacco just as Rockefeller had done with Standard Oil.

He called it the American Tobacco Company, the tobacco trust that grew to dominate tobacco—all of it—smoking, snuff, plug, fine cut, cigars, cheroots, and cigarettes, gobbling up even Bull Durham itself as one of the 250 companies and plants that were either absorbed or driven out of business by the giant combine. Buck was thirty-five years old and a multimillionaire.

Then the troubles started.

The churches, the women's bazaars, the boys' clubs and the physicians attacked the morality and health aspects of smoking cigarettes; and trust-busting populist editors like Josephus Daniels in Raleigh called him "Buccaneer Duke" for driving down the price of tobacco to the farmer, for fixing prices and roughhousing competitors.

Back in Durham, old Washington Duke confessed, "I wish Buck hadn't gotten us into this combination. We were doing nicely running our old business on our own and there wasn't all this fuss." He also made an observation that people in Durham quote to this day: "You know, there are three things I just can't seem to understand: ee-lec-tricity, the Holy Ghost, and my son Buck." Washington Duke turned to charity—some said to win back the favor of his home town, others thought it altruism, but most agreed he was concerned with the Duke name and how it would be remembered.

In picking Durham as the subject of his charity, Washington Duke selected a dirty-faced child. When Durham offered twice the money of any other town in the state for the Baptist Female University, the trustees rejected the offer and selected Raleigh because Durham was "lacking in culture, possessed of sordid ideals, and was therefore no fit place for innocent girls to abide in, even though surrounded by college walls."

The loss of the Baptist Female University stung the town, and angered Washington Duke and his son Ben; when they heard the Methodists were thinking of moving Trinity College from the

18

isolation of western North Carolina, Ben convinced his father to donate $85,000 if it would come to Durham. It did, in 1893. "Some say I ought to give my money to feed poor folks," Wash Duke said, "but if I give money to them, they will soon eat it up. I'd rather give my money to make some people who will feed themselves."

But if the old patriarch's hidden purpose was to veneer Buck's swashbuckling reputation from the twin attacks on cigarettes as "coffin nails" and "the devil's weed," Buck would have his own opportunity later in life, after Theodore Roosevelt's trust-busting lawyers broke up the tobacco trust.

Age was creeping up on the tough old tobacco trader, and he began to muse about his money. He read Andrew Carnegie's *Gospel of Wealth*, which said, "He who dies rich, dies disgraced." Once again, he turned to the example of his idol, John D. Rockefeller. "I was born in North Carolina and I am sixty-four years old," he told a reporter. "It's time to begin to think about a monument. I want to leave something in the state that five hundred years from now people can look and say, Duke did that. Every man owes something to the state he was born in."

President William Few, the mild-mannered president at Trinity College, went to see Ben Duke, who personally had supported Trinity with gifts for twenty years. Ben called on Buck and urged him to listen to Few's ideas about a vast university, equal to the best in America.

Ultimately, the Duke family gave $40 million, and Trinity College changed its name and buried Buck, Ben, and old Wash in princely crypts in the Duke Chapel, giving birth to the quip that it ought to have been called the "Father, Son and J. B. Duke University." (Brodie Duke, the fast-living black sheep of the Duke brothers, was buried in Maplewood Cemetery in less auspicious surroundings.) In the center of the campus, they put a statue of Buck, who while he posed (according to Durham legend) ordered the sculptor to put a cigar in his hand. When a few trustees complained it wasn't dignified, Buck replied, "I made my money in tobacco and I don't want anybody out here to forget it." A member of the last class to graduate from Trinity remembered the valedictory address, when a student raised his arms to the assembled faculty and spoke out in dramatic clarity, "And so, my friends, Inhale and Farewell."

19

Ironically, Buck Duke, who once drove the Jews away from Durham, built a university that brought them back—this time as doctors and interns at Duke Hospital and as professors and graduate students on the campus. The growing clusters of families attracted storeowners like my grandparents, who longed to leave the isolated little towns way out in the farming counties and move to a larger Jewish community close by.

TWO

Growing Up in the Family Store

S U M M E R was the special time, the countless days melting together into a silken rush of yellow and pine, the warm, moist earth bursting forth with wildflowers and berries growing free. Summer meant sucking out honeysuckle nectar until I got a stomach ache; chasing lightning bugs at dusk and flicking dozens of them into an old mayonnaise jar with holes in the top we hammered with an ice pick; blowing dandelion puffs in a meadow and pretending they were parachutists floating on the breeze behind the German lines; making slingshots out of the elbow of two branches, using cut-up slivers of rubber from an old inner tube. And it was a time when I slept with my dog, though my mother didn't let me, and sneaked him out at daybreak so she wouldn't ever know; and a time for touching the magnolia flowers just to make them turn brown, or scrubbing at the stain of blackberries that colored my hands for days after picking them wild.

And I was Tarzan wrestling a giant garden-hose snake squeezing the life out of me after it dropped from an overhanging branch; or Flash Gordon on another planet tracking the insect-headed inhabitants through Mrs. Wanamaker's bamboo. But mostly it was cowboys with hats and guns and holsters from my daddy's store. Our wagon trail wound its way from the Fowlers' garage to John Stone's chicken coop, and we would "dum-de-dum" the Indian music that always preceded the thud of the hissing arrow in the back of the lead scout that signaled the attack of the Comanches.

Saturdays meant all day in the movies. I'd watch the feature

21

twice and the cartoons and serials three times, all for nine cents admission—and five cents for popcorn popping fresh right there so you could smell it all over the Rialto Theater. Sunset Carson, Lash Larue, Johnny Mack Brown, and Wild Bill Elliott filled my childhood with fast-draw shootouts, Main Street facedowns, and countless bottle-crashing, chair-busting saloon fights and jailbreaks to clear their name.

Each Saturday, late in the afternoon, I'd wander bleary-eyed out of the movie to start my weekly ritual. First, I'd drop by the shoeshine parlor to listen to the shoeshine boys pop their rags . . . a-shoom ba doo, a-shoom ba-doo POP . . . a shoom ka-boom ba-doo POP . . . to the rhythm of the jukebox jumping in the corner; then a quick pass through the Kress store to smell the cashews roasting and play with the forts and the wind-up toys; over to Woodall's and Durham Sporting Goods to smack a fist into baseball gloves and pick out the right weight in bats.

Walking down Main Street I would always drop in on a few of the Jewish merchants who would give me a big hello and let me roam around their stores. Gladstein's ("We Fit the Big Man") had size fifty pants two of us could stand in; Harry Bergman's Record Bar had a few sexy girls on album covers we could take a long look at when we pretended to play the record; Sonny Kaplan's shoe shop smelled of old leather and had all sizes and shapes of taps we could put on our shoes to sound like marines; and Ray's Jewelry (that was Sam Fink) and Martin Jewelry (that was Harry Rosenthal) carried Mickey Mouse watches as well as sterling silver. "Yankee" Zuckerman (his name was Jacob, which in Yiddish was Yankel, but everybody called him "Yankee") owned a fur shop with a dusty fox fur in the window that had real teeth and beady eyes scowling from a fuzzy head, and felt alive when I petted it.

But most of all I liked to visit Sam's Pawn Shop (Sam Margolis) and Five Points Loan (Leon Dworsky). Old Mr. Dworsky, who blew the shofar in his eighties and was the most pious man in town, used to let me plunk at the guitars and the banjos knowing I wouldn't buy; and I would look longingly at the Boy Scout knives, penknives, hunting knives with belt sheaths, and the two-edged Bowie knives. My mother had forbidden me to have a gun, but in the Dworskys' pawnshop, I could aim a twenty-two rifle, break open a shotgun, and select a nine-inch switchblade to handle. He taught me a lot about field glasses, cameras, toy telescopes, and chromatic harmonicas.

Finally I would end up at our store to get a ride home with my mother and father. Evans United Dollar was just about the biggest store on Main Street and it had my daddy's picture over the elevator. If I got there early, I had the run of the place as long as my parents weren't around. I could try on big old straw hats we sold to colored people to wear in the fields, or whip upstairs to watch one of the girls in a tight hairnet cry away while she chopped up onions in a big washtub for the hotdog stand, or steal a forbidden look at the brassieres and the other pink intimates on the ladies' counter. But the most fun was the stockroom on the third floor—big as half the store—where all the merchandise came in and was opened and kept on shelves to be moved downstairs when we ran short on the counters. If one of my friends was with me, we'd play hide-and-go-seek in the big cartons, or build tunnels out of smaller boxes. Evans United Dollar didn't have a toy department all year long but we did before Christmas, and that meant overflowing aisles of doctor's and nurse's sets you could sneak a few candy pills out of, and Christmas-tree tinsel you could string in your hair, stacks of un-put-together wagons and scooters and trikes with bright bells, and toy trumpets you could pretend to help out with a little by making sure they worked. My dream was to go with my parents to the annual New York Toy Show for buyers (Mother always returned home with a sample of some intricate new toy), which I visualized as a vast display covering Manhattan, with toys popping out of windows in the Empire State Building, the Statue of Liberty crammed full of Lionel trains, erector sets, cowboy hats, and pearl-handled Colt pistols.

When I got to be old enough I helped out in the store during tobacco market time and at Christmas, not because they needed me but because my father wanted me to learn about and come to love the rhythm and the action of the retail business.

Evans United Dollar Store's cycle of profit followed the growing season, as dependent on the Lord's good weather as the farmer was. You could see the town stirring every September at tobacco market time, when the burly chest of Durham opened up, its heart beating in full daylight—the bustle of wagons and trucks laden with huge baskets, the hoarse sounds of the farmers barking orders to the

23

blacks unloading tons and tons of the toast-colored leaves of tobacco. The whir of the cigarette machines in the adjacent factories announced the central action in the process—shredding the tobacco, then blending it and stuffing it into a mile-long cigarette which a blade, quick as a hummingbird's wings, cut to any length from regular to king-size. To most of my friends and to me, however, the gritty nature of the tobacco industry rarely intruded in our lives. As children, we were curious onlookers; the tobacco factories stood as mighty symbols of our town, to glory in and be proud of. An ad for Chesterfields in *Life* magazine: "Why, that's made in Durham"; a pack of cigarettes in a drugstore in Atlanta: "Just look on the back, right there, and you can see 'Made in Durham, N.C.'" Somehow, cigarettes gave us an identity in a teeming, impersonal universe, a way to grab hold of the big world and matter in it.

In the stifling August heat, when my father escaped with the family to the beach to rest up for the gala tobacco market opening in September, the leaves of tobacco plants reached a deep verdant green. Then they slowly mellowed to yellow, turning ripe and ready for the white farmer's family, all seven or eight children helping alongside their Negro sharecroppers, together to pick the crop. They "primed" the stalks, bottom leaves first, until the fields looked like rows of ladies with their skirts up; then up to the tips, gathering and tying the leaves on seven-foot sticks so each cluster of leaves would hang separately, to catch the full impact of the heat from the oil burners in the curing barns. The heat dried it and turned it the golden color that won the nickname "Bright Leaf," the same leaves on the golden keys to the city my father gave to visiting celebrities. The Bright Leaf was also gold to the farmer who poured his soul into the roots and wrapped his muscles around the stalks, for he had pulled the suckers and battled the blue mold and the black shank, the bud worms and the root knot nematodes, the flea beatles and the brown spot, in a death struggle for his crop.

After four days of "yellowing," the farmer stacked the tobacco sticks in squares as high as he could reach, and stored the bulk in pack houses (and, during the Depression, in his bedroom, the old-timers would tell you) to await market time. Then he would grade it carefully, sometimes cheating just a little by mixing a few lesser quality leaves in with the good ones ("nesting," they called it), arranging the leaves in shallow baskets five feet across, each basket piled four feet high with clumps of hand-tied tobacco; then he hoisted it onto trucks to haul it into the towns where the markets were.

My father would take me down to the huge, creaky-floored warehouses, with names like Liberty and Star Brick and Planters, some of them covering an entire city block, to watch the farmers bringing their loads in a mule-drawn wagon or a beat-up pickup. The black warehousemen took over the brawny part, sliding the baskets off the trucks, dragging them over to the weighing station, and then pulling them with long hooks on small-wheeled dollies onto the warehouse floor to line up with a battalion of other baskets. There they stood, a solid half block, row upon row of color from lemon to mahogany, from prime to "trash tobacco," some "fluffy matured" and others dark and "slick as a woman's thigh," a rolling sea of neatly stacked piles awaiting the company buyers to judge finally, in a brief moment, the result of a year of labor. The walls of the warehouse were plastered with signs testifying to the primal nature of the goings-on: "KOOL is buying HERE"; "Depositors National Bank—We Invite Your Account"; "Sir Walter Raleigh—smells grand, packs right, smokes sweet, can't bite."

It was man's work, this process, muscular, action-packed, and earthy. The buyers paraded among the rows of baskets like the general staff reviewing a new regiment, rustling past bundles and reaching deep into piles to pull out the innards, then slapping the extracted leaves on top and winking, nodding, holding up their fingers to the auctioneer. Ah, the auctioneer—superstar of the sale, singing his chant in an incomprehensible nasal twang; finally he would "knock it down" with a sweeping "Sold Ah-mur-ee-kun" just as the radio had it, and you could tell whose basket was blessed with "top dollah" by watching the faces for the big, happy, gold-toothed grin.

The farmer took his tobacco sale bill over to the cashier to pick up his money, the "long green," which he'd wad up and stuff in his overalls. Once when I laughed at a farmer in our store, squatting on the floor and taking off one shoe to pull out a few smelly dollar bills, my father cautioned me: "Never laugh at the farm people. If it wasn't for them, we couldn't even afford to see a movie."

The womenfolk, often with a nugget of snuff tucked inside their lower lip, waited in trucks outside the warehouse, with all the children piled in back, for their man to come out and show his winnings. Then it was time to look over the shopping list—porcelain washbasins, sheets, and clothes to outfit the whole family for winter. Some of them, old friends in a way, came back to Evans United year after year, and learned to trust us to give them "top dollah," too.

It was nothing for a little kid like me, just tall enough to see over the counters myself, to spend an hour or two with a family with a string of "young'uns." We'd fix them up with a half dozen pair of jeans, shoes, a couple of warm coats, shirts, underwear, socks, and sweaters and one nice pair of pants for church. Sometimes the farmer came in alone and he'd fish deep in his overalls for a few lengths of string, saying, "Their feet's this big," and we'd go to pick out some hightops for them.

The first Christmastime I ever worked, at the age of nine, my father and I bargained that I was certainly worth ten cents an hour. I learned to wrap packages, wait on people, and make change for the friends from my mother's sisterhood bridge club who came in to help out with the cash registers. I learned how to punch the clock; I learned how to watch it, too. At the end of the first hour, I went up to Grace, the cashier, who was busy at the safe counting out advances for the cash registers and I said politely, "Excuse me, ma'am, I've worked an hour. Could I have my dime?"

As the years passed, I graduated into putting together the bicycles and the red wagons upstairs in the stockroom, and receiving and signing for the goods from the parcel post, and then punching the cash registers and helping with inventory. And I got curious about the buying trips to New York and the accounting in the office, and began talking to the salesmen dropping in with their samples and would ask my Dad the reasons we bought what we did or why Mother thought one item would be big that fall. They encouraged me, nurtured my interest, and brought me along because the business would be "needing me someday."

They divided the tasks of buying the goods and keeping track of sales, though Mother always seemed more indecisive about such things than Dad did. He bought wagons, bicycles, shoes, men's work clothes, and towels; she bought ladies' ready-to-wear, notions, pots and pans, and lingerie. Mother considered dolls her specialty, an interest she no doubt inherited from her own mother, who discovered thirty years before that a wallful of dolls attracted a storeful of parents and grandparents herding their little girls (and

26

brothers). Relatives and friends kept her busy, too, buying silverware, furniture, and toasters for them wholesale—so many that Dad would say, "She bought something retail once and didn't like it, so she hasn't bought retail since."

I never sat around my father's office but always used my mother's for headquarters. It was usually half full of Israel fundraising materials—stacks of pamphlets with pictures of little waifs drinking milk from a carton handed to them by a Hadassah nurse. Sometimes I would help the Hadassah women stuff envelopes there while Mother went over the community mailing lists, talked to salesmen, signed letters, and generally juggled her life skillfully, somehow managing to keep it all organized.

When I dropped by the store after the movies on Saturday, I loved to sit and watch her type. She had never taken lessons and yet she punched out sixty words a minute with two fingers, a perfected hunt-and-peck that fascinated the seven secretaries in the office so much that they often gathered secretly to watch her poke out a letter.

She had worked in the store since she was eighteen, when her father first became ill and the responsibility for the business fell on her. It forced her to grow up in a hurry, to pretend she knew all about merchandising, to learn to order around men three times her age, even hire and fire managers and muscular stockroom clerks. A crisp business personality masked a painful shyness she had to overcome every day. She maintained a deep intimacy with the older employees, whose children she would buy prom dresses for or send to Duke Hospital for expensive operations. The older women who ran ladies' ready-to-wear and the lingerie departments respected her judgment for the decades they worked with her and loved her for the respect they got back.

But the temporary teen-age girls who worked during the busy seasons saw her only as the "boss lady." "Uh, oh . . . here comes your mother," they whispered when they saw her; just her presence was enough to break up the chitchat and the giggles. If there was a logjam of customers at a cash register, she might charge behind the counter, take one end of some string in her teeth and whip the other end around a package, wrapping four wagons in the time it took me to wrap one. Though petite, she would walk into the stockroom, unconscious of the ordinary limitations of Southern femininity, ordering around the brawny whites, the ones with

27

tattoos on their arms who frightened me but snapped into action whenever she caught them loafing.

While she kept ladies' lingerie and Hadassah moving, my father remained in his office talking with the other stores, looking over balance sheets, calling a supplier in New York, or giving a political interview to the paper. Both of them rarely waited on customers, except for the week before Christmas when all of us went at it together, including my brother home from college for the holidays—a time I always liked because we were so thoroughly a family then, joking, dashing about, congratulating each other on sales, and generally coping with the pressures of the Christmas week.

Dad always said we had a depression-proof business. That meant that if anything happened, it would be the classy stores that would go out of business because people would come to where it was cheapest. I remember how shocked I was when one Jewish man in town said we sold "*shmata* to the yokels and the *shvahtsas*," because it always seemed to me the grandest business in the world and I intended to make it my life. None of the Hope Valley crowd ever came into Evans United, for they preferred Ellis-Stone's, which opened in the high days of the tobacco trust to serve the nouveau tastes of the wives of the overnight tycoons. Ellis-Stone's was still the best store in town; you could tell right away because it had rugs on the floor.

Ours was a poor people's store and we catered to the Negro trade. In the strange contorted world of what passed for Southern liberalism just after the war, Evans United was the first store on Main Street to have restrooms for blacks; we were the only Main Street store with an integrated lunch counter, though it hadn't been easy. When Bus Borland, the county judge, sent word that North Carolina law prohibited feeding blacks and whites together unless a wall separated them, my father told him, "Bus, you'll have to close the store if you want me to do that." Gene Brooks, our lawyer, called a meeting at the courthouse to point out, after exhaustive research, that the legal precedents all involved seated counters, and Bus agreed that it was so, not wanting to make a whole lot of trouble. So my father agreed to remove all the stools at the counter and instructed the carpenters to raise the counter top to elbow-leaning height so that United could proudly retain the only integrated lunch counter in downtown Durham.

28

But "integrated" meant mostly black, especially on paydays at Liggett & Myers, when the Negroes would be standing three deep at the counter, the store filled with the rich pungent mixture of tobacco dust and onions and frying meat. We were the only large store that would cash a Negro's paycheck from the American Tobacco Company even if he didn't buy anything; the first store in town to carry black bride dolls; the first to do away with "white" and "colored" signs on the water fountains (I had been sneaking tastes out of the black side anyway, so I knew it didn't taste different); the only store to devote an entire department to the official new blue uniforms of Liggett & Myers Tobacco Co., caps at half price even if you didn't buy anything else.

And for years, Joe Allen, the elevator boy, played the black Santa Claus because he was one of the best HO, HO, HO'ers anybody had ever heard. He would sit on a chair in the toy department beside the white Santa, greeting a long line of black kids and mothers, while white Santa served a long line of whites.

The day before Christmas, the black welfare program would come by and we'd clean out the toy department at just over cost. (Belk's handled the whites.) My mother loved this part of it—she had taken all the markdowns by then ("Follow that lady with the black crayon, Effie," I once heard an excited customer say to his wife), and since we didn't carry toys during the year, it was a relief for her to move them out, to think about the poor children at the orphanage with puzzles and coloring books and a wetty doll to love. As a family ritual, we would drive through the Hayti section on Christmas morning to see the little black boys in our cowboy hats and holsters, or hell-bent for glory on our skates, zipping over iced-butter sidewalks, and hurtling gutters and curbs as if they were soaring over canyons. One time, when we got stuck with several hundred hula hoops, we just gave them to the welfare. And Fayetteville Street that Christmas morning looked like a vast hula hoop festival, with little black kids wiggling all over the streets, their hips haloed in whirling colors of luminous green and orange.

My ambition was to marry a cheerleader and go into my father's business. I really knew no other Southern Jewish boys who didn't have the same ambition. Yet the story of Jews in the South is the story of fathers who built businesses to give to their sons who didn't want them. It is a drama played over and over again thou-

29

sands of times across the South. My father was typical—he had wanted to go to law school but his generation was caught by the Depression and trapped into a business the immigrant generation started, a business that he merchandised into a success during the war and the years that followed.

I don't remember exactly when the doubt began. Maybe it was when my mother's aphorisms started to sink in and grow, the little sayings that echo through a child's consciousness and mature mysteriously into motivations: "You can be anything you want to work hard enough to be"; or "You can never get too much education." Or maybe it was the dinner-table conversations with my father—Durham politics and what should be done and who would be running. Perhaps I caught the zest of his own real interest.

The truth was that they never thought the business was good enough for them. When the Jewish doctors at Duke and dozens of others in the Jewish community would come to my father for business advice, Mother sometimes would tell him what a great lawyer he would have been, feeling, I think, a sense of guilt at thrusting the responsibility for her family and the business on him, and perhaps even anger at the Depression for robbing them of the chance to consider any other options. "The lawyers have it easier in politics," he would say, "because it's part of the profession to know how government works"; and he spoke in hushed adulation of the great Jewish jurists—Justices Brandeis, Frankfurter, and Cardozo —men to emulate, the greatest of men.

Neither my brother Bob nor I found it easy to break away, because we suffered under the tensions of a beckoning family business while perceiving widening opportunities in the North. My parents were one generation away from the immigrant experience but the values of the immigrant generation were forged deep within them. Bob was the first born—six years older than I—and thus carried the special half of the burden of doing better than his father had done. Fathers inevitably pass that ambition on, and it is no different in the Jewish South, for every immigrant wanted his son to live a better life than he had lived. In the North, however, Jewish tailors sweated over the steam presses to get their sons out; in the South, the small store owners worked to build a place to keep their sons home.

For my brother as well as for me, success as a public speaker substituted for lack of success as an athlete, a special Southern affliction because of the fanfare surrounding football in the South, and more intense in our case because our father had been a three-letter man in high school and a track star at Chapel Hill. Both of us had tried and failed at varsity football and basketball, so that public speaking had to serve as a lame substitute. Our imaginations added the athletic trappings. It was competitive; we practiced every afternoon in front of the mirror at home, and met the opposition in front of an audience (albeit a forced audience required to attend junior high assembly), and the judges announced the decision to the sleepy applause of our classmates (which time could transform into a deafening roar). We excelled at "declamation" (giving a famous speech we memorized), but Bob turned out to be a brilliant, extemporaneous orator and debater, even a national winner, and we framed his certificates and displayed his medals. "The boy shows talent," they said, and it seemed a shame to waste those talents in the retail business.

An infant experiment, television—that tiny box in our living room that so many of my parents' friends crowded around to share with us—had tiggered unsettling fantasies in both of us. We were not raised on television—all of my boyhood memories are of the high-strutting days of radio, of "the thundering hoofbeats of the great horse Silver," and "the Shadow knows, heh, heh, heh." We were, however, the first generation of teen-agers influenced by television and therefore not yet numb to its message; rather, we were mesmerized by the images and activated in our depths in ways we could not fathom. We were speakers in our family; both Bob and I daydreamed of imaginary moments before giant phantom rallies, with a television audience of millions looking in. It was natural to admire the voices the screen gave faces to—to want to climb inside the set and look out instead of always looking in. Edward R. Murrow was my brother's idol, and he decided first to wrench away from Evans United and be a foreign correspondent. He perceived it as a rebellion, but his rejection of the business pleased the part of his parents that looked backward at their roots and were gratified at how far they had come.

But for the second son, the expectation was different. I was channeled into the store to live a life of compromise more in touch with reality. If Bob was to make his way in Washington and New York in broadcasting, I was to carry the family banner in Durham in the retail business and the Jaycees.

During the war the business had grown from one store into six, in little towns like Martinsville, Virginia, and Reidsville, North Carolina. We had changed the name from United *Dollar* Store (invented originally in the Depression when nothing sold for over a dollar) to Evans United *Department* Store so we could carry $14.95 jackets and attract a better clientele. My father spoke to me of expanding into every city in the state once I finished school, and we could work side by side. "Don't worry," he would say, "you can stock sport jackets and button-down shirts like the College Shop," to reassure me the business could be changed to adjust to the tastes of the mid-fifties.

But I worshiped Bob as any boy would, growing up with an older brother who could run faster, throw farther, and dribble with his left hand. I wanted to do all the things he did—to walk to school with him, to cruise the drive-ins after he got his driving license, to put on a string tie for dances. I relished the times he let me center the ball in the neighborhood football games, a harmless way for a smaller boy to start the action, and I practiced for hours. His friends even insisted once that I tag along at Halloween because a little kid always took in more candy during trick or treat. I was waterboy to the slapdash team of friends he put together to enter the county basketball tournament (and got trounced 81 to 38—*my brother?*) and once, when I was seven, I crawled around the dining-room table one hundred times because he told me it would make me "as strong as Captain Marvel." If the business was not good enough for him, perhaps it shouldn't be good enough for me either. At least, his ambition cut me loose from accepting the store as an inevitable goal of my life.

I hadn't mentioned my doubts to my parents, for I think I was suffering from the conflicts inside me, a decision at first hesitant, but growing into a painful certainty—a decision that to my mind would render their life meaningless, judging what they had done as not good enough for the sons they had done it for.

But new values were taking hold. We were the postwar adolescents who learned to doubt the idea that making money was the poetry of life—uncertain because our parents gave us the luxury of uncertainty; groping because "I-don't-know-what-I-am-going-to-do" was a successful stance for us. Cast free of the drive to help only ourselves, we could consider how to help others, except that many of us seemed to care about neither ourselves nor others. For us, the university loomed large as the place for answers—until then, any question would do.

My first two years at the university in Chapel Hill, I pushed doggedly through accounting and marketing, trying to make friends with the straight-arrow, crew-cut crowd of Alpha Tau Omegas and Zeta Beta Taus who were also in the business school. But I discovered the joy of self-expression under the madcap guidance of a bespectacled female English teacher named Jesse Rehder, who wore floppy sweaters and no-nonsense shoes and short-cropped hair. Everybody said she wrote pornography under a pen name. Jesse came breezing into the freshman theme course the first day and plopped herself up onto her desk and looked out over her glasses at our expectant faces, and then declared, "This is the ugliest goddamned class I ever laid eyes on, but I'll read your stuff." And I sat at the feet of Jimmy Wallace, the seer of Chapel Hill, who had wandered around the campus since 1939, with advanced degrees in physics, law, and history, changing young lives in a single soaring conversational evening. His sarcasm and wit swept everything before him as he guided a few of us through Copernicus, ecology, Sir Isaac Newton, the hydrogen bomb, and a round-house denunciation of the spreading honky-tonk blight of gas stations and hamburger stands intruding on the beautiful wooded Chapel Hill scene.

Finally, a summer in Israel and Europe triggered the decision. It would be reading books and writing for me in college; and as a temporary stance to soften the blow, and so my father would not think me irresponsible, I would maybe pretend to think about law school, which I knew he always secretly wanted for himself.

He had to know already. The signs were unmistakable all around town; few of the sons were staying. Gene Brooks had warned him that he was educating his boys right out of Durham by sending them on trips and my brother off to an Ivy League college for graduate school.

And maybe it was so.

School, my junior year of it, was starting in two weeks; I would be dropping out of the business school and I had to explain. It was one of those in-between nights in September with just the hint of fall in the air. We didn't talk much at dinner and it was still light out, a good time to walk. We often walked together, my father and I, especially when there were serious matters to talk about, like

33

would he be disappointed if I didn't go out for football again or did he think my allowance was sufficient now that the price of movies was rising.

I finally got to the point just as we passed Editor Rollins' house and made our customary turn to head back toward home. "I've decided to aim for law school," I said.

His reaction surprised me, as it did on so many things. He said he thought that it was a fine ambition, and that it was what he had always wanted to do; that he would help me all he could to make it through and get set up in practice in Durham if that was what I wanted. The implications for the family were clear enough. It had taken forty years to build the business; it would take just a little while to sell.

They kept the stores for a year or so looking for the right price and the right buyer, maybe keeping them a little while longer hoping I might change my mind. But in the little towns where our other five stores were located, the downtown areas were beginning to shatter under the pressure of shopping centers and sprawling suburbs and discount-house competition. It took formidable energy to fight and grow, and where would it lead anyway?

I came home from school to meet the president of the national chain that bought us out. He had come down from New York, a heavy, red-faced, gray-haired man who wore a diamond ring and drank his Scotch straight by the tumblerful. And while they sat together in the living room talking quietly, I heard him say, "That's too fine a boy for the dog-eat-dog part of the retail business. Maybe he'll come up and work for us."

I drove over as often as I could to help with the going-out-of-business sale. "Mr. Mayor, where is we going to shop?" the Negro women would ask, and my father would say, "Well, the two boys didn't want it and it was time." Slowly, the painful process of selling out began to eat away at their pride—bare places on the counters, unthinkable just a few months earlier; then consolidating departments with the hand-lettered markdowns, the crowds of bargain hunters flocking in to pick over the bones. Dad insisted on and won a concession from the new owners—that they would keep everyone who wanted to stay. But the remodeling would take time and the business was moving into chain-store procedures, and there would be new bosses to please, so sadness pervaded the store like a cloud of defeat.

34

I had classes the last day and got to the store late, about five-thirty, when we were down to just a few bins. Old Miss Cash had been with us for thirty years, and Mother and she were tearfully hugging each other good-bye in what used to be ladies' ready-to-wear. "It's as much your store as ours," Mom was saying and they held each other.

They had already taken Dad's picture from over the elevator, and I saw him across the street watching the workmen take down the Evans United sign. I walked over to stand with him and put my arm around him; he held me, too, as the tears trickled down his cheeks and mine as well.

It hit me hard—what I'd done to him. No longer would he be making big decisions about the stores; no longer would he be the largest independent store owner in town, having lost the visible symbol of his solid citizen-ness; and if he stayed on as Mayor, people would think he needed to (it only paid $2,000 a year, but everybody thought otherwise) and maybe even question his motives for his votes at a city council meeting.

He went home that night and suffered a skipping heartbeat brought on by the weeks of strain and overwork. That demanded ten days of rest in the hospital; I visited him to make sure he was doing all right. He pulled through it fine. Then because it was springtime and exams were closing in, I went back to Chapel Hill to catch up on my work.

Hal Crain, the contractor, kept that Evans United sign in his timber yard for two years in case we'd have to reopen and start again.

35

II

The Immigrants

THREE

To Be an American

. . . ours was a town founded by Aryan Baptists and Methodists, for Aryan Baptists and Methodists. We had . . . two Jews . . . members of the Methodist church and so they didn't count either, being in our eyes and decreed by people neither Catholics nor Protestants nor even atheists but incorrigible nonconformists, nonconformists not just to everybody else but to each other in mutual accord; a nonconformism defended and preserved by descendants whose ancestors hadn't quitted home and security for a wilderness in which to find freedom of thought as they claimed and oh yes believed, but to find freedom in which to be incorrigible and unreconstructible Baptists and Methodists; not to escape from tyranny as they claimed and believed, but to establish one.

The Town,
William Faulkner

"T o be an American." That cry spilled from the heart of the immigrant the moment he arrived in the new land, a country of ideals and promise, holding out untold rewards to any who would work hard at the unromantic tasks of building a nation. First, learn the language, and then speak it cleanly so the children would not be ashamed (it would be easier for the little ones). Then dress and chatter and act as the Americans act. Inevitably the traditions would begin to lose their hold. The daughters would fall in love with the man of their own choosing. The sons would have an education beyond the Talmud, the chance to break out of a cycle that for centuries had locked sons in the ghetto with fathers; now

39

they could become doctors and lawyers, and not worry about the thundering hooves of hostile soldiers and seasons punctuated by violence. They were free, free to choose and not be afraid—even free to challenge traditions, and to consider unthinkable thoughts of worshiping differently, of discarding outdated rituals, of replacing the disorderly service with sermons and English prayers that the Americans would understand and respect.

But in the South the Jews faced a special breed of American. There, to be an American was to be a Southerner. Who can even imagine the strange and twisted soul of the Civil War Southerner, the fantasies that haunted his dreams and his history; the man at war with the values of the nation and yet its most ardent defender; the Southerner, rhapsodic in defense of his institutions, homogeneous and uniform in origins, intolerant of dissent because of a deep commitment to the absolute superiority of his way of life; the Southerner, the believer in caste, caught up with the guilt of slavery and the mystery of the black stirring around him. The Jews were, first of all, white, or at least men who could pass for white. But they would always be outsiders, for somewhere in the roots of populism and fundamentalism lurked a foreboding distrust of the foreigner, anyone who was not a Southerner and not Christian and therefore alien to the sameness all around.

These Jewish foreigners—and there were never thousands of them in one place, only clusters—could sense the violence simmering just below the surface . . . the same fear of violence that kept the slaves in bondage to the whites. The Southerners were not men to be challenged but men to avoid; only to sell to, never to confront. They planted themselves with feet apart, ready to scrap and gouge, not just to curse the Yankees but to tussle with them. They were men enraptured of legends and bondaged to a vaulting rhetoric, who would break out the dueling pistols when honor was pricked, and who on moonless nights in the slave quarters would give full sway to the brute in their loins and then return to the white house with a smoldering guilt over passions unleashed.

The aristocrats lived in big white houses on the plantations, but back on the sorry, exhausted lands in the backwoods lived the "white trash," the nonslaveholding majority of the South—the "crackers" and the "dirt eaters," brawling, lanky, raw-boned clod busters out of the red clay and the smelly swamps, all hog meat and cornpone, the wild hoop-and-a-holler possum eaters, guzzling

40

corn "likker" and hunting coons and skinning rabbits, marrying kin until their genes were as played out as the land. They were coarse and primitive men who envisioned God as the fierce Father of His Savior Son speaking directly to them each vengeful Sunday from the gut-bucket lungs of the soul-saving preacher man. They would be the backbone of the Confederate army, howling rebel yells to curdle the Yankees while riding hell-bent into battle behind the officer-gentlemen from the plantations.

The immigrant Jews saw the gap, not because anybody told them but because it was there—no merchants or tailors or cobblers between the genteel aristocrats and the groveling poor whites, and surely no one to sell or trade to the few freemen and the slaves whatever little things they could afford. First the immigrant must go and seek them, stuffing the trinkets and calico into bulging canvas packs and hoping that all the stories of hospitality and courtesy would be true. The immigrant watched and listened—to imitate, to gossip and glean, learning every day, learning how to be an American.

Think of the first meeting of the peddler and the Southerner: The Jew, back-bent and bone-weary, trudging the dusty back roads, stumbling past the yelping hound dogs and the chickens, to be met at the porch of the patched-up shack by the blue-eyed Aryan with a rifle across his chest and his wife behind him with the children peering around her skirt. The Jew, hesitating momentarily and then motioning to his pack and stammering, "It goot; you buy?"— bowing and obsequious, only to serve and sell. What must these two men have thought of each other!

"Oh, to be an American." What a strange and painful time—to conform to the South that viewed any variation as the curse of the devil. But the peddler would return again and again, with a heavy-laden wagon the next time, and soon the Southerners would await him eagerly, for news and tales and jokes, too, as the immigrant's English improved.

The peddler traveled and absorbed their ways, slowly drifting into his place as another white man. There was no other choice. His special position gave him insights into black and white not only as customers but as men, interrelated but apart. As messenger, he passed along to black and white the tales of the runaway slaves, of the fate of those who aided them, of the violence to the sympathetic voices daring to criticize the slave system, of the talk of war gather-

41

ing like the early stones of an avalanche everywhere he went. The country was dividing and the South was closing ranks. To the Southerners, all the players were rooted in one place, black and white, status sure and unalterable. No one, least of all the foreigners, uttered a word out of line with prevailing opinion. The harmony of views was disturbed only by the news of the stinging indictments of the abolitionists in the North, lashing out at slavery as immoral and lecherous. For anyone in the South who would dare even murmur agreement with those moralizing Northern preacher-jackasses, why they'd just get a few of the boys together to boil up a little tar for the sympathizers, maybe even the lynching tree for the leaders of the runaways, if the night was right for it.

The fear of them, then—no one crossed the Southerner in his native land. The Jew was conditioned to fear authority from the boot of the tsar and the emperor; he knew his place—the perpetual visitor, tentative and unaccepted, his primary concern to remain and survive. Subconsciously, the region would stake a claim to a corner of his soul, too; for he was white and he would acquiesce and become like them in many ways. Yet he was conscious of the differences, of the permissible boundaries of attitude and act, of just how far was too far, and protective enough of his own body and time to take on whatever colors were necessary to get through the day.

Oscar Straus, who eventually led his family to fortune as the owner of R. H. Macy's in New York City, wrote that his father, Lazarus, who peddled near Talbottom, Georgia, "was treated by the owners of the plantations with a spirit of equality that is hard to appreciate today. Then, too, the existence of slavery drew a distinct line of demarcation between white and black races. This gave the [white] peddler a status of equality, probably otherwise he would not have enjoyed to such a degree."

The German Jew soon would grasp the Southerner's penchant for genealogy, and fancifully falsify his roots and his pedigree just as the aristocrats had done. The accents and the easy, gracious, almost high-European lifestyle would be easy enough virtues for the merchant to imitate. He would come to show them what a middle class was like—one or two servant-slaves, not hundreds—though some would emulate the aristocrats completely, and purchase plantations and carriages and slaves.

That surely was the other option: to disappear, be swallowed up in the terrain of the Southern mind and soul, to change names and identities, marry their women, and become Southern white men, so the next generation would be indistinguishable from the Southerners and no child would suffer the shame of his grandfathers.

Between the two choices, time would take its toll. For little children have to play, and go to school, and sort out the influences and pressures around them. They suffered no memories of the ghetto and knew only the South they grew up in. They too would learn as boys to loll in the beauty of the South, to soak up the mists of the marshes and languish in the scents of the pine forests in the spring. They too would be white boys to the Negro and at some point they would know deference and come to expect it of the blacks. Never schooled in the intimacies of Jewish law, they would find it easier to let loose of the minutiae, and circumstance would tear their fathers from the orthodox dictates concerning food and daily living. Growing up Southerners, they would absorb the regional defiance and unrestrained pride, the memories of rising to sing "Dixie" in grammar school assembly and, in history class, the surging poignance on reading Lee's farewell to his troops.

Joseph Proskauer wrote of the ambiguity of patriotism for Southern Jews after the Civil War in his autobiography, *Boyhood in Mobile*, describing his hero worship of his Uncle Adolph, who was wounded at Gettysburg:

> With such a background it was quite natural that I should be a patriotic boy. But, until 1898, patriotism in Alabama was not a simple concept. My grandmother's attic was a storehouse of worthless Confederate bills . . . my uncle's partner, Leopold Strauss, was known only as "Johnny" because he had been a fighting Johnny Reb. . . . I had not seen a Fourth of July celebration. We shot our fireworks at Christmas, not on Independence Day. . . . Until my entrance into college in 1892, I was never quite sure that a "Yankee" could be anything but damned.
>
> Thus my Americanism did not come full panoplied. It was born of conflict. It became whole and complete only in 1898, when we were at war with Spain. General Joseph Wheeler, CSA [Confederate States of America], of Alabama was then made General Joseph Wheeler, USA. A wave of emotion brought Alabama back into the Union. I was home for summer vacation and July the Fourth, there was a celebration

43

in Bienville Square. The Declaration of Independence was once more proclaimed in Mobile; and though the band played "Dixie," it added "The Star Spangled Banner."

There is only scant record of the first Jews with a pioneering spirit who drifted away from the trading centers in Charleston and Savannah into the frontier looking for land and adventure. Abraham Mordecai was one of them. The first white settler to live near Montgomery, Alabama, he married an Indian (permissible, he thought, because he believed that the Indians descended from one of the Ten Lost Tribes of Israel). He would constantly pepper the puzzled Coosawda Indians with questions in Hebrew, hoping for an answer, which would have proved his theory. Mordecai was a colorful character, who lost an ear in a fight with sixteen Indians over his attentions to a squaw. He traded all across Alabama, boiling hickory nuts into oil and trading it in Pensacola and Mobile. Together with two Jews from Savannah, he built the first cotton gin in the state. When a visitor saw him at the age of one hundred in Dudleyville, Alabama, he was eating from a beautiful carved coffin of his own design, which would serve very well as an elegant table until his time came.

The Spanish Inquisition scattered Jews all over the world; and when Colonel James Oglethorpe conceived a plan for a colony in Georgia for the English poor, wealthy English Jews agreed, half selfishly, to finance the trip out of London of their own Jewish poor who were recent immigrants from Spain. In 1733 a boatload set sail for Savannah, the first and only Jews to come to the South as a group. Governor Oglethorpe's patrons were annoyed when the Jews arrived, for they feared that Christians would boycott the colony, but Oglethorpe allowed the boat to land because there was a doctor on board who could treat a current outbreak of the deadly malaria.

From the beginning, it seemed, there would be conflicts among the Jews themselves, even though all together they were just a handful of forty-one souls. As each wave of immigration relaxed its commitments to Jewish traditions in the face of demands and temptations in the new country, each successive wave viewed its forerunners as lesser men, traitors to their pact with God. As early as 1735, a minister wrote the Church of England mission headquarters in London to report on the status of the Jews of Savannah: "We have here two sorts of Jews, Portuguese and Germans. The first having professed Christianity in Portugal or the Brazils are more lax in their ways, and dispense with a great many of their Jewish rites . . . their education in these Countries where they were obliged to appear Christians makes them less rigid and stiff in their way. . . . The German Jews, who are thought the better sort of them (i.e., the better Jews), are a great deal more strict in their way and rigid observers of the law."

The antagonisms between the two groups were also observable by outsiders who puzzled over the conflicts between brothers in the same faith. Of the same colony, another minister wrote in 1738, "Some Jews in Savannah complained . . . that the Spanish and Portuguese Jews persecute the German Jews in a way no Christian would persecute another Christian. . . . The Spanish and Portuguese Jews are not so strict insofar as eating is concerned as the others are. They eat for instance the beef that comes from the warehouse or that is sold anywhere else. The German Jews, on the other hand, would rather starve than eat meat they do not slaughter themselves."

The tensions between the Sephardic Jews from Spain and the German Jews gave way to the next wave of German immigration, as the Spanish Jews all but disappeared into the American melting pot. The German wave, just a trickle since the eighteenth century, gradually swelled into what at that time was the largest wave of Jewish immigration in American history.

The German Jews flooded into America in the mid-nineteenth century when the aftermath of Napoleon's defeat in 1815 produced a succession of laws removing Jewish civil liberties in the German states—in Bavaria, laws limiting the number of Jews in the professions and even the number of marriages; in Württemberg, laws restricting the ownership and sale of land to Jews. Unemployment and overpopulation cast an economic pall over Europe, and not only the Jews but the Italians, Irish, English, and Dutch were emigrating as well; when anti-Jewish riots occurred across Bohemia, and republican uprisings against Prussian draft policies failed in 1848, the Jews saw little choice and whole towns of them fled to America.

These Jews (who were called "the forty-eighters") were small-town Germans, some of them horse traders and cattle dealers, most of them shopkeepers and salesmen, attracted to America by the promise of opportunity and attracted to the South because it seemed provincial, much like the places they had left—farm country and simple, where a man with little capital could work hard and find a place. And they came in such numbers that, as Nathan Glazer points out in *American Judaism,* "Before the Civil War there was also very likely a higher proportion of Jews among the white population of the South than in the Northeast."

These rural Germans formed the bedrock support for the Reform Jewish movement in America. Its center would be Charleston, South Carolina, where spontaneously, in 1824, occurred the first stirrings in the New World against ancient rituals. Forty-seven members of the Beth Elohim congregation, led by the journalist Isaac Harby, petitioned their trustees to shorten the service, to pray in English rather than just Hebrew and Spanish, and to require a sermon or an "English discourse" at each service. Some of the reformers were influenced by rumors of reforms among Jews in Germany, but most of them were not intellectuals, just shopkeepers and merchants who knew little Hebrew and cared less for the theological debates abroad. While Jews in Germany were debating the validity of the concept of the coming of the Messiah, and striking out all prayers treating Jews as exiles from Zion, one historian suggests that the Charleston Jews were more influenced by the debates in American Protestantism over pluralism. Right in Charleston, the internal dissension in the First Independent Church of Charleston had led to the creation of a splinter Unitarian congregation just seven years earlier.

At Beth Elohim, the trustees rejected any changes in the traditional ceremony, and in reaction, twelve of the dissenters committed the "atrocious offence" of organizing "The Reformed Society of Israelites," no longer to worship, they asserted, as "slaves of bigotry and priestcraft" but as part of an "enlightened world." They broadened their demands to include more far-reaching changes—preferring to call the synagogue a "temple," editing their own prayerbook to include contemporary prayers in the service, and worshiping with heads uncovered. The Reform Jewish movement ultimately came to America after the wave of German immigration twenty-five years later, led by a group of foreign-born rabbis who were worldly, self-assured radical theologians; however, this first effort was native and local in leadership, and sprang,

46

out of deep instincts to be more "American," from a group of Jews who openly confessed to wanting a Judaism without European influences, more compatible with the Protestant services of their neighbors. For the ruling "Adjunta" of Beth Elohim, however, any change was a corruption of the faith of their fathers, of a ceremony unchanged since the destruction of the second Temple in Jerusalem. Having survived centuries of persecution, the Jewish elders were under pressure to change just at the moment when at last Jews had attained the highest measure of religious freedom in history.

The Reform group floundered and disbanded after a few years until an accidental fire destroyed Beth Elohim in 1838. Moses Levy yanked the holy scrolls out of the fire just in time. Even before the cornerstone was laid for the new building, thirty-eight members petitioned the trustees that "an organ be erected in the synagogue to assist in the vocal part of the service." For the traditionalists, this would be the last straw. A storm broke over the congregation that resembled, in the words of one historian, a "minor civil war." Families divided over the "great organ controversy," an issue that challenged the sanctity of the Sabbath itself, for playing an instrument on the Sabbath was a labor forbidden by law.

When the Adjunta again turned down the request, the dissenters summoned the entire congregation to a general meeting and reversed the decision on a close vote. Beth Elohim became the first synagogue in America to provide organ music at services, but not without a bitter reaction from the defeated wing of the trustees, who promptly split away to start a new Orthodox congregation they called bitterly Shearith Israel, "the Remnant of Israel." But their departure opened the way for other changes in the ritual— confirmation classes for boys and girls, abandoning the second days of festivals and, much later, establishing family pews. The reforms were of such moment that a thirty-year-old rabbi, Isaac M. Wise, who would ultimately organize and head the Hebrew Union College and pioneer other institutions of the Reform Jewish movement in America, considered leaving his congregation in Albany, New York, where traditionalists considered him a firebrand, to take a position in Charleston. In his *Reminiscences*, Wise, then only four years in this country, spoke of being for the first time in his life the "guest of American aristocrats," in a "city so refined and cultured";

but he rejected the call because friends told his wife that "the yellow fever raged in Charleston very frequently and that the city was very unhealthy."

In 1854 Wise finally settled in Cincinnati, a gateway city to the frontier Jews to the south and the west of him. Wise was possessed of an abiding faith in the curative and transcending powers of a pioneer people on a new continent; and he was immersed in the philosophical challenge of a new Judaism, an American Judaism, which he felt would shuck off the heavy rigidities of Europe, and grow and change and nurture itself in the soil and passion of America.

Wise's great competitor in the Reform movement was Rabbi David Einhorn of Baltimore, already in his forties when he arrived in America in 1855, after the Austrian government had ordered his Reform temple closed. Together at times, Wise and Einhorn battled the traditionalists—men like Isaac Leeser in Philadelphia and Samuel M. Isaacs in New York. Leeser had come to the United States earlier than any of the others and, though a traditionalist, had begun preaching in English, writing for his own Jewish journal, and organizing the first American Jewish Publication Society. All of these men, vigorous and determined, articulate and brilliant, arresting personalities with wide followings, fought each other in sermons, articles, in their own publications, and on public platforms all over the country. For the most part, the traditionalists Leeser and Isaacs clashed with the reformers Wise and Einhorn; but together, all of these men were fighting Jewish apathy and ignorance among the immigrants. They were also changing the image and the expectations of the rabbinate itself, from the learned and pious European judge on all matters domestic and religious, to the stalwart, vigorous, up-front, outspoken, and undaunted religious leader, raising a fist and reaching for the heavens to summon the Jews of America to a new devotion for an evolving Judaism. By subscribing to Leeser's *Occident*, Wise's *Israelite*, Einhorn's *Sinai*, and Isaacs' *Messenger*, Jews in the South and in the West could write letters to be reprinted, and read the sermons and participate in the great debate on the nature of American Judaism.

On one level, the debate was simple: Change one law or alter one ritual, said the traditionalists, and you erode the authority of the Judaic structure and all of Judaism will crumble away. To demand such changes after thousands of years was heretical, opportunistic, atheistic, placing man's convenience above God's laws.

48

Not so, argued the reformers. Did we not abandon ritualistic sacrifice? Judaism must be fluid, flexible, and adaptive to survive. We are not a static people, and here in America we will forge a uniquely American Judaism, and cast off the fanatic and the outmoded traditions, let go the unenlightened customs, and strike out the curious rituals that separate us from other Americans.

But Wise and Einhorn were by no means united. Einhorn was much more radical than Wise, and faced toward the Northeast to the large majority of new German Jews in the big cities; Wise was a moderate who faced West and South to the scattered clusters of Jews in the small towns and in the old cities of the region, like Charleston and New Orleans. While Wise was suspicious of Einhorn's radical views and feared domination of the Reform movement by the Northeast, he saw unity growing out of a new generation of American-born Jews who would demand American-trained rabbis. Thus in 1873 Wise organized the Union of American Hebrew Congregations to found his school, the Hebrew Union College, and train rabbis for the movement.

Dr. Lou Silberman, for eighteen years the Hillel Professor of Jewish Literature and Thought at Vanderbilt University (the only chair of Jewish studies in the South), agreed with the Jewish historian who told him privately that the clash between Einhorn and Wise was a clash between "intellectual reform and yokel reform." Wise's movement was nonintellectual, non-European, and above all, non-German. "Yankee reform," he asserted in an interview, "fit the frontier attitudes of the South—independence, private judgment, suspicion of fancy ideas."

Silberman believes that the study of Jewish history, particularly in the South, is too insular, and not conscious enough of the history and influences of America itself. He wrote in 1957 that the Reform movement in the South "must be understood against the entire background of Southern culture and particularly of Southern Protestantism . . . responding to the expanding frontier . . . the break with the established 'intellectual' churches of the Eastern seaboard; the fierce independence and individualism that found expression in the Baptist churches; all these must be taken into account, for I suspect they were far more influential in determining the particularly independent 'low-church Protestant' configuration of Southern reform than was the German development."

49

FOUR

Tobias–Nine Generations in Charleston

I K N E W I had to talk to Tom Tobias when I first heard about him, for he was a link with Southern Jewish history a century and a half older than my grandparents. For nine generations, his family had lived in Charleston, South Carolina, and I had stumbled on some of his writing on American Jewish history. He fancied himself an amateur historian, and wrote esoteric articles contributing a new shred of evidence on this or a new interpretation on that.

Now I was driving down the marshy coastal lowlands to Charleston to see him—back into time, it seemed—through the ghostly gray moss hanging low from the water oaks, protecting the highway like giant sentinels. Even his name was tantalizing— Thomas Jefferson Tobias—not your normal name for nice Jewish boys in my day. But this was a man whose lineage burrowed deeply into American history, almost the only survivor of the first wave of Southern Jews.

For most people, conditioned to look to New York City as the center of Jewish life in America, it will come as a shock to find that in 1800, Charleston, South Carolina, had the largest Jewish community in America. There were only 2,500 Jews in the United States at that time: four hundred in New York and somewhat fewer in Philadelphia; but Charleston had five hundred, and the State of South Carolina more than a thousand.

50

Charleston early earned a reputation among Jews as a tolerant place where they could be free to worship, trade, own land, leave property by will, and appear as witnesses. Historians think that the major reason lay in the character of Lord Ashley, one of the eight noblemen to whom Charles II gave the Carolinas in 1663. Ashley asked his close friend and adviser John Locke to draft a constitution for the colony. Although the constitution recognized the Church of England as the official faith of the colony, Locke also inserted that "Jews, Heathens," and others should have a chance to acquaint themselves with "the purity of the Christian religion" and "by good usage and persuasion . . . be won over to embrace . . . the truth." In the final version, Jews were not mentioned, but they were allowed to vote from the beginning, making Charleston, according to Charles Reznikoff's *The Jews of Charleston*, the first community in the modern world to grant Jews that right.

The earliest Jew recorded in the Carolinas was a Spanish-speaking Marrano, one of the secret Jews forced to convert to Christianity in Spain and Portugal, who showed up in military records in 1695 as translator for the governor of the colony in questioning four captive Indians from the Spanish colony of Florida.

Located in the inland swamps, Charles Town developed in the beginning as a center for deerskins, rice exports, and, later, indigo, used as a dye for the blue uniforms of the British merchant fleet. By 1775, Charles Town was the largest seaport in the colonies for exports of domestic products—larger than New York or Boston, and even greater in trade with the West Indies than Newport.

Charles Town was a colony founded on slavery, for the slaves were said to have an "extraordinary tolerance" for malaria in the swampy rice fields and the indigo plantations. When the trustees of Georgia refused to permit slave labor or strong liquor in Savannah, thereby smothering future development, a small group of Jews moved up the coast to Charles Town. Some had fled earlier, fearing an attack from nearby Florida, then under the rule of Spain, whose Inquisition they had so recently escaped. So Charles Town grew, instead of Savannah, as a center for Jews in the New World. Later, the parents of Judah P. Benjamin, the future Confederate statesman, sold fruit out of a little shop on King Street, keeping the store open on the Sabbath to the consternation of the Jewish community;

51

and slave trader Abraham Seixas put a rhymed advertisement in the Charleston *Gazette:*

> Abraham Seixas, all so gracious . . .
> He has for sale
> Some Negroes, male . . .
> They are so brisk and free;
> What e'er you say,
> They will obey
> If you buy them from me.

Joseph Tobias arrived about 1729 as a shopkeeper and served also as a Spanish interpreter for the British in their scuffles with the Spanish in Florida. He prospered, bought several ships, and advanced to the high social status of "merchant shipper." In 1749 he became thee first president of Congregation Beth Elohim Unveh Shallom (House of God and Mansion of Peace), the fifth or sixth Jewish congregation in the United States; it was a congregation that would play a historic role in the development of Reform Judaism in America. Two hundred years later, in what must have been a remarkable event for the few who realized its uniqueness, Thomas Jefferson Tobias was elected president of the same congregation, he being the only remaining survivor of the early Jewish settlers of the city.

Thomas Jefferson Tobias greeted me eagerly on the front veranda of his fine three-story townhouse on Charleston's historic old South Battery. The house was completely restored, with narrow halls and steep staircases winding up to the living quarters. The porches on each floor of the house caught the breeze from the sea just as they had done in colonial days. Polite, and precisely the gentleman, he showed me into the library, a wonderland of musty books, tarnished antique silver, and colonial portraits, and beckoned me to sit in a carefully arranged talking corner on a straight-backed cane chair, appropriate for listening, while he sank into a huge stuffed armchair that exhaled air as it nestled him the perfect distance away for an interview.

"Conversation is the greatest fun in the world," he said, settling back in his chair. "What with television today, the art of conversation is dead. Most people think that when you discuss an idea vigorously, you are attacking them."

He was quite undistinguished-looking for one of such lineage—short, and slightly built, with twinkling owl-eyes that shone through rimless spectacles.

But his manner was courtly and graceful, almost classic, contrasted with his clothes—baggy pants and a slightly wrinkled shirt, ill-fitting and disarranged. He was not the kind of man given to impressing others with outward attire but confident enough of inward elegance to project the élan of the upper classes.

He was a man clearly addicted to daydreams; perhaps his purest joy, as a friend described it, "was to unfold a brittle deed from the courthouse vaults and feel the same sand that dried the original ink trickle through his fingers." When he warmed up to an anecdote, he would move to the edge of his chair and wave his arms excitedly, and then relax again deep in the cushions until the next question set him galloping off in new directions.

"The name, yes, everyone wants to know about that. My great-grandfather was such an admirer of Jefferson that the year Jefferson died, he rode all the way to Monticello just to shake his hand. Up until then, our family names had been Jewish—Jacob and Joseph—but the next three generations were named Thomas Jefferson Tobias. But I vowed not to burden my son. He is David so that he can be himself."

His enthusiastic descriptions of Joseph Tobias' early days in Charles Town, of his role as "linguister" during England's war against Spain in 1739, of the social and economic forces molding the growth of the Jewish community, transformed the room into a time machine, and I could hear the clatter of colonial Charles Town and sense the smells of a lively seaport. In 1800 Charleston was the cultural center of America, with two theaters and an opera, frequent concerts by foreign artists, and lectures by the leading literary and scientific scholars of the day. Thomas Tobias loved to talk of old Charleston, liberated and free and open, the city of flirtations and fluttery women and whirling holiday balls, where the Jews shared in the liveliness and excitement of a bustling, frisky time, fighting duels and sailing from the Yacht Club. To listen to Thomas J. Tobias was to tread the brick walkways and dodge the carriages, to speak with planters and slaves, for he was no longer simply the latest Tobias; he became all of them in one, a transfigured Tobias two hundred and forty years old, the blood and

53

flesh come to life as the spirit of a time recaptured and an era dramatized.

He seemed to delight in citing the names of the top social families in Charleston with Tobias blood in them. "I'm the only line of my family that hasn't assimilated or moved away. Why, right here in Charleston, we've got Catholic Tobiases and Presbyterian Tobiases and Episcopalian Tobiases." And then with a grin, he added, "The family always married *up;* I know of no Southern Baptist Tobiases."

I asked if he relished taking aside the haughty daughters of the Confederacy and pointing out to them their Jewish kinship. He didn't understand the question, because it was the question of a new arrival, conditioned to think of Jewish blood as inferior in the noble line of the first families of Charleston, a Jewish relative as a skeleton in their closet. To Thomas Jefferson Tobias any blueblood would be just that much more sanctified with Tobias aristocracy on the family tree. So we sat in a brief silence, he puzzled and confused, looking at me across the centuries, pitying, I began to feel, my lack of self-esteem.

He urged me to spend time wandering through the historic old Coming Street Cemetery, the oldest surviving Jewish cemetery in the South, with grave markers back to 1764, which had recently been restored due to the work of a committee that he headed. The Tobias family buried their dead on their family plantation until 1856, when Abraham Tobias (1796–1856) broke with tradition and was buried in Coming Street. And he wanted me to know that Bernard Baruch from Camden, South Carolina, had come to the rededication in 1964 to place a wreath on the tomb of his great-grandfather, Hartwig Cohen, who had served as cantor to Beth Elohim from 1818 to 1823.

"We've always belonged to Beth Elohim. In 1949, when I became president, I told the Rotary Club that it was the custom and tradition in my family to be president of Beth Elohim once every two hundred years. And do you know," he said laughing, "a friend from one of Charleston's first families came up to me afterwards and told me seriously how impressed he was that two hundred years from now my family would once again have a president of the synagogue."

After 1820 Charleston began to dissolve as a trade center, its growth faltering, as the sun set on its best times. Thermal navigation, by which a navigator dipped a thermometer in the water to tell the distance from the Gulf Stream, released shipping from dependence on the trade winds and made the shorter routes from Europe to New York and Boston more profitable. The Erie Canal boosted the Northeast as a trade route from the American West, and discriminatory tariffs reduced the ability of the South to sell abroad and even raised the price on finished cotton goods returned to the South for sale to the people who grew it. The migration westward began, to new lands unexhausted from the yearly cotton crop, where a small farmer didn't face the impossible competition from the plantation economy and where new immigrants would not have to compete as artisans with the growing numbers of skilled slaves. Frequent epidemics of yellow fever and malaria gave Charleston a bad reputation, especially to the new immigrants from Ireland and Germany, who were inclined to avoid the marshes, preferring to live in a climate similar to that of their home countries.

Why, then, this quirk of history, that the Tobias family alone stayed and struggled in Charleston for another one hundred and fifty years?

"We were a family that lacked adventure," he admitted, unwilling like others in Charleston to treat his presence as any grand achievement. "We came during the Golden Age of Charleston when it was a wealthy and growing city. Despite the fact that from 1820 until the Depression Charleston was on the skids economically and in a frenzy from the disintegrating trade base, despite the fact that the Delta in Alabama and Mississippi was opening to cotton and the land was worn out here, we were so comfortable that we stayed. Charleston bet on the wrong horse—agriculture and slavery—and the North bet on manufacturing. We bet with Charleston."

He had written in special publications about the personalities of some of the early settlers, but most of his energy now was absorbed in a biography of Francis Salvador. "I have my own little fight with the Jews in the North. They like to brag about Haym Salomon as a patriot of the American Revolution. But all he did was give money. Francis Salvador of South Carolina gave his life. He was the first Jew to hold important elective office in America, and the first Jew to die in the American Revolution. That's a real patriot."

Francis Salvador was the son of a merchant in Amsterdam, a distinguished member of a Sephardic congregation in London, whose grandfather helped raise money to send the first boatload of Jews to Savannah against the wishes of the trustees of Georgia. After reverses in London, he migrated to America to reestablish his fortune, and was drawn to South Carolina because his uncle, who was also his father-in-law, owned 6,000 acres of land suitable for an indigo plantation. A man of impressive intellect, well-educated and articulate, he was elected to the First and Second Provincial Congresses of South Carolina slightly more than a year after his arrival, the first Jew in the modern world, according to one commentator, to be elected to office by Christians.

To elect him, his fellow South Carolinians winked at the election law of 1721, which rescinded the earlier right of Jews to vote and hold office by requiring each candidate to be sworn "on the holy evangelists." "Selected" to office would be a more accurate term. The grievances against the Crown were seeding rebellion across the colonies, and only those favorable to the cause were selected for service from the writs of election sent to the "influential gentlemen" in the district. Thus he favored independence, even if it meant war; he voted with the revolutionaries to establish the independent colony and served in the first General Assembly in the independent State of South Carolina.

Less than a month after the adoption of the Declaration of Independence, he was ambushed with a band of the patriot militia by a group of British-armed Indians and Tories, and scalped before help could reach him. Francis Salvador died at the age of twenty-nine, the first Jew to give his life for the American Revolution.

"The Jews of New York will stick with Haym Salomon," Tobias said plaintively. "They think that giving money is more important than deeds anyway."

He criticized the arrogance of the Sephardic Jews in New York who looked down on him for staying in the South, and talked of his own simple happiness, living in the footsteps of the previous generations. "I know where my great-grandfather lived; I own Joseph Tobias' family Bible, inherited with the family papers; I eat with the family silver and have fond memories of the city itself growing up. You see, I experienced no personal anti-Semitism, because I was raised as a member of one of the best families in Charleston. Now I grant you we were never religiously Jewish, but we were always openly and loyally Jewish."

56

He stood up and walked over to a silver cylinder filled with walking canes, family canes of teak and mahogany, some topped by ivory knobs with nineteenth-century dates and initials on them, some with lion-head handles carved in gold. He proudly pulled out an Old South sword cane and unsheathed it dramatically as if he were a dashing musketeer who had surprised the king's guard with a secret weapon.

We walked through a doorway into a long living room, furnished in tasteful antiques, the walls filled with portraits—all relatives. "I love to have my ancestors around me," he declared expansively.

Some of the portraits showed velvet-coated and wigged gentlemen with ruffled shirts, their names on brass plates tacked to the frames which gave the room the spirit of an intimate museum: his great-grandmother, whose husband was a state senator; his father, like his own father before him, a rice broker for fifty years.

A Civil War portrait triggered memories of the destruction in Charleston after the first shots were fired on Fort Sumter in the harbor, and Tobias' brow gnarled as he recalled the struggles of his ancestors to sustain themselves and hold Congregation Beth Elohim together after the Yankee shells battered the synagogue.

"During Reconstruction," he explained, "the best families in Charleston were impoverished. Yet our status went on uninterrupted after the War. It was considered bad manners to bring up money matters in social situations in the South. You might say we were too poor to paint and too proud to whitewash. I guess that's why we talk politics down here. Up North, they talk money."

We climbed a staircase so narrow that the walls brushed both shoulders, the steps at such an incline that it was almost like scaling a ladder. He pushed against a weighty oaken door into his study, a small spartan room with books and papers overflowing from a rolltop desk, the major piece of furniture. He lovingly opened the family Bible, leather-bound with a gold latch, and read off a few entries of eighteenth-century births, and of deaths from knife fights, disease, and old age. One document, dated 1741, reprinted the oath that Joseph Tobias took to become a citizen of South Carolina.

"Notice this," and he pointed to a postscript near the signature which read, "omitted oath of a true Christian." He held it gingerly, as if it would crumble in his hands, and said, "This is a landmark document. They allowed him to take the oath of citizenship to the colony without professing a belief in Christianity, thus opening Charleston up as a good place for Jewish settlement."

He urged me to stop by the Temple Beth Elohim and visit the small museum where a few other of his family relics were on display, along with prayerbooks, early deeds, and drawings of great events in the history of the congregation. He especially thought I would enjoy the tiny bell and the charred scroll from the Civil War synagogue, the only mementos salvaged from General Sherman's march through South Carolina.

The early Jews of Charleston never lived in a ghetto, but were absorbed easily into a growing seaport town. Thomas J. Tobias complained about the Jews of today in Charleston who could do the same thing but chose to live in a development of expensive homes around Confederate Circle that is "eighty percent Jewish." His home is in historic old Charleston in an area surrounded by black slums, though city planners are working to restore the old buildings in hopes it will become a tourist center.

"It is nothing but a golden ghetto over there. I don't approve of it, but I understand. The Nazi experience did that to us. It destroyed our sense of security."

He had talked for almost three hours about all the Tobiases except himself, and it seemed appropriate to ask some personal questions. He confessed to having left Charleston for a time after he was graduated from the College of Charleston in 1928 ("a liberal school but a fine traditional education"), when he had struck out for New York and worked as a reporter for the New York *World.*

"They almost fired me because of my Charleston accent, so every night I read the paper to my roommate, a Yale man, until I got my accent under control."

He missed the South, however, and moved to Atlanta to work on another paper. It was during the Depression, and he seemed to miss the life he had been conditioned to expect. So in his spare time, he joined the cavalry to serve in the Governor's Honor Guard unit so that he could ride horses and play polo on weekends. He met his wife, Rowena, in Atlanta: "She wasn't Jewish. I told her I was in love, but that I was concerned with breaking the family line and the Jewish character of my family. When she offered to become a Jewess, although I knew that Jewish law required that I discourage her, I was secretly delighted. It was a decidely snobbish sort of thing: that my children would remain Jewish and a part of our family history. Being a Southerner, she appreciated my feeling for the family and passed her tests with flying colors."

What most aggravated him about the attitude of Northern Jews?

"They think the Jews of the South are nothing, and automatically assume you are George Wallace and worse. The truth is that the Jews of Charleston, in their hearts, are on the liberal side of things. But most won't say anything because it's bad business."

He understood and appreciated the historic character of the establishment of the State of Israel, but felt that most Southern Jews, especially those who had been in the South for several generations, had come to respect Israel more after its military successes.

"The Southern military tradition is very strong. You know, the slaves were a tremendous threat, and in every community there was a guard who protected the community. Next to the planters, the military was always the most admired. General Westmoreland comes from Columbia, and Congressman Mendel Rivers here has taught us how important military bases can be to the economy of this city. Subconsciously, the Southern Jews respect Israel's military daring and its military success."

We sat down to lunch with one-hundred-and-fifty-year-old family silverware—heavy-handled, irregular, and burnished. For his grandchildren, I asked, whom today would he consider such a giant presence as to warrant a long horseback ride to shake hands? A sustained, uncomfortable silence followed while I pitchforked the salad with a giant weapon his forebears must have used for wild venison. Finally, he smiled like a Cheshire cat and announced, "Old Tom Watson at IBM." He leaned back and roared and I thought of him, so committed to the past as the best of times, riding into the IBM executive offices in velvet knickers and white stockings to punch out a "thanks for everything" on a computer.

Would his only son continue the unbroken line of Tobiases in Charleston? His voice dropped sadly and he slumped in his chair.

"God knows what will happen to all this when I die. He is typical of sons today and isn't interested in any of these things. He was one of the earliest hippies . . . doesn't like to assume responsibility and can't seem to finish anything. I tried to make him care, but he has completely broken the rhythm of the generations. However, my wife says there is a chance. Perhaps so. He is such a marvelous conversationalist."

He stood on the front veranda of his house, rumpled and alone, waving as I drove away, the wind from the Charleston waterfront blowing slightly to ripple the air on a desperately hot August day.

Two weeks later he was dead.

Thomas Jefferson Tobias was buried in the Coming Street Cemetery in the Tobias family plot. The place fascinated him all his life, and he had spoken passionately about it at the rededication ceremony in 1964. "I liked to come in the late afternoons around dusk," he had said, "when my imagination would sometimes picture men and women of the past, dressed in costumes of their times—men in colonial stocks and powdered wigs, and Revolutionary and Civil War uniforms, and women in antebellum crinolines and hooped skirts."

He rests just where he wanted to.

FIVE

The Jewish Confederates Face Reconstruction

Every American community has its leaven of Jews. Ours arrived shortly after the Civil War with packs on their backs, peddlers from Russia, Poland, Germany, a few from Alsace. They sold trinkets to the Negroes and saved. Today they are plantation-owners, bankers, lawyers, doctors, merchants. . . . I was talking to one, an old-timer, not too successful, in front of his small store a short time ago. He suddenly asked in his thick Russian accent: "Do you know Pushkin? Ah, beautiful, better than Shelley or Byron!" Why shouldn't such a people inherit the earth, not, surely, because of their meekness, but because of a steadier fire, a tension and tenacity that make all other whites seem stodgy and unintellectual.

Lanterns on the Levee,
William Alexander Percy

''T H E Jews didn't fight, they just made money off the War," is a canard of every American war, and the Civil War was no exception. When the presence of Jews in the South during the Civil War was even acknowledged, the image was often of the cunning merchant-cheat and the speculator, unpatriotic and therefore un-Southern, an outsider safely behind the lines, a moneylender or a scavenger, feeding off the troubles of the South in its most desolate time.

Yet, according to a list prepared by Simon Wolf in 1895, and

61

published in his book *The American Jew as Patriot, Soldier and Citizen* (which contains three hundred pages of lists and biographical data taken from family recollections and other inexact sources), approximately twelve hundred Jews served in the Confederacy, including twenty-four army officers and eleven navy officers. Other accounts, claiming Wolf is incomplete, have placed the number as high as ten thousand. There were so many that General Robert E. Lee could not afford an exception to allow high holy days furloughs to "soldiers of the Jewish persuasion in the Confederate States army." He wrote in 1861 to Rabbi M. J. Michelbacher, "Preacher Hebrew Congregation, House of Love, Richmond, Virginia," that "I feel assured that neither you or any other member of the Jewish Congregation would wish to jeopardize a cause you have so much at heart by the withdrawal even for a season of a portion of its defenders."

For the Union, almost six thousand Jews served, according to Wolf's account, but only sixteen officers. (Eight hundred more names were listed but not classified.) In the South, Jews even organized two Jewish companies—at West Point, Georgia, in the first month of the War, and at Macon, Georgia, in 1862, for the stated purpose of the defense of Savannah. Jewish companies were also organized for the North—in Chicago and Syracuse. However, most Jews, North and South, were reluctant to separate themselves as Jews and chose to enlist in the regular army units.

All over the South, Jews rallied to the Confederacy as ardent Southerners; for now that fate had cast the gauntlet, they would fight for the glory of the Southern flag, as steeped in the honor and insult as the other white men they fought with.

In Charleston, one hundred and eighty Jews joined the Confederate army; M. C. Mordecai's steamer *Isabel* was outfitted into a blockade runner; Benjamin Mordecai organized the "Free Market of Charleston," which was supporting more than six hundred families at a cost of eight thousand dollars a month by late 1862; and David Lopez, a talented builder and architect, constructed one of the torpedo boats, the *David*, which in 1863, in Charleston harbor, seriously damaged the federal warship *New Ironsides* in the first successful torpedo attack in naval history.

In Montgomery, Alabama, Mayer Lehman was cut off from his brother Emanuel in New York City, but because the Lehman family was so trusted by the governor of Alabama, Emanuel was sent to England to raise funds for the Confederacy. (Little wonder then that Mayer named his eighth child after his friend Hillary Herbert, Confederate colonel and congressman from Alabama. Herbert Lehman would become governor and United States senator from the State of New York.)

In Chattanooga, Tennessee, the War split the Ochs family. Julius Ochs (the father of Adolph Ochs, who would ultimately buy and build the *New York Times*) joined the Union army, but his wife Bertha remained loyal to the Confederacy and was once arrested for trying to smuggle quinine in a baby carriage to wounded Confederate soldiers. Bertha was a charter member of the Chattanooga chapter of the United Daughters of the Confederacy, and when she died she requested that a Confederate flag be placed on her coffin. Julius was buried next to her in a coffin draped with the stars and stripes.

Down in the ranks, the stories of bravery would be passed from generation to generation as Southern Jewish families swelled proudly at the portraits of Confederate infantrymen over their mantels.

Max Frauenthal, from Port Gibson and Summit, Mississippi, served as a member of the 16th Mississippi Infantry and distinguished himself at Bloody Acute Angle during the battle of Spottsylvania Court House in Virginia, where General Grant said, during the bitterest part of this battle, "We will fight it out on this line if it takes all summer." Later, a Judge A. T. Watts of Dallas, Texas, who was a member of the company, remembered Frauenthal as "a little Jew, who, though insignificant, had the heart of a lion in battle. For several hours, he stood at the immediate point of contact amid the most terrific hail of lead, and coolly and deliberately loaded and fired without cringing. . . . I now understand how it was that a handful of Jews could drive before them a hundred kings—they were all Fronthals." It would not be the last time that a Jewish name was mispronounced; for years in Mississippi, Confederate veterans referred to any brave man as "a regular Fronthal."

Private Isaac Gleitzman of Arkansas fought under the daring command of Nathan Bedford Forrest. While the Confederacy awarded him its Cross of Honor for "conspicuous gallantry in the field," he was proudest that he had never eaten any *trefa* or nonkosher food during his entire four years of military service. His

63

family retains to this day the two mess kits he carried with him during the war, one for meat and one for milk.

But the South would reward with its highest honors the generation of Sephardic Jews, by 1860 almost totally assimilated, made up of men who had married outside their faith and drifted away from Judaism until they blended smoothly into the slaveholding plantation life of the aristocracy—men like Judah P. Benjamin (known as "the brains of the Confederacy") who served as United States senator from Louisiana before becoming attorney general, secretary of war, and secretary of state to the Confederacy; Henry Hyams, the lieutenant governor of Louisiana; and Dr. Edwin Moise, the speaker of the Louisiana legislature. Even though they were indistinguishable from other Southerners in style and language, they could retain a cultural curiosity about their Jewishness, both an awareness and a respect, that would astound a visitor who had assumed they had long since abandoned any consciousness of their roots.

Just before the War, Salomon de Rothschild of the Parisian branch of the noted banking family traveled to New Orleans, where he met with Benjamin, Hyams, and Moise. "What is astonishing here," he wrote home, "or rather what is not astonishing, is the high position occupied by our coreligionists, or rather by those who were born into the faith and who, having married Christian women, and without converting, have forgotten the practices of their fathers . . . and what is odd, all these men have a Jewish heart and take an interest in me, because I represent the greatest Jewish house in the world."

Judah Benjamin would abandon formal Judaism, but neither the South nor the North would allow Judaism to abandon him. Cruelly, anti-Semitism stalked him throughout his career, as if to mock his success with ancient hatreds. When the South began to sink in despair, Benjamin, as secretary of war, emerged as a convenient target of attack for the military failures, the lack of supplies, and the gathering disillusionment with the cause. Thomas R. R. Cobb, a brigadier general and member of the Provisional Congress of the Confederacy, said "a grander rascal than this Jew Benjamin does not exist in the Confederacy, and I am not particular in concealing my opinion of him." In the Confederate House of Representatives, Congressman Henry S. Foote of Tennessee affirmed that he "would never consent to the establishment of a supreme court of the Confederate States as long as Judah P.

Benjamin shall continue to pollute the ears of majesty Davis with his insidious counsels." Foote argued that Jews were engaged in illegal trade with the enemy "under official protection" and were "undermining our currency." A writer to the Richmond *Enquirer* believed it "blasphemous" for a Jew to hold such high office and suggested that the prayers of the Confederacy would have more effect if Benjamin were dismissed from the cabinet.

Blamed by the South for its miseries, Benjamin also was rarely mentioned in the Northern press without some reference to his being a Jew. Other senators bitterly attacked both him and another Jew, Florida Senator David (Levy) Yulee, known as the "Florida fire-eater" because of the passion of his proslavery views. Levy had helped draft Florida's first constitution, and led the effort to gain admittance of Florida to the Union. However, he urged secession as early as 1849, and was the first senator to announce secession of a state when the break finally came. After the War, he spent five years in a federal prison; he and Jefferson Davis were the last two leaders to be pardoned. Levy not only renounced Judaism and changed his name to "Yulee," but also promoted the legend that he was not Jewish at all but descended from a Moroccan prince by that name. Andrew Johnson, as a senator, later to succeed Lincoln as the seventeenth President, told Charles Francis Adams of Boston, "There's that Yulee; miserable little cuss! I remember him in the House—the contemptible little Jew—standing there and begging us to let Florida in as a state. Well, we let her in, and took care of her and fought her Indians, and now that despicable little beggar stands up in the Senate and talks about her rights." The future President also had choice words for Judah Benjamin: "There's another Jew—that miserable Benjamin."

As the War dragged on and the structure of the South began to unravel, the romantic dreams of easy victory turned to blood, death, starvation, and destruction; and the nation, at its most desperate moment, erupted with the most virulent explosion of anti-Semitism that America had yet experienced. In the North the Jews were the secessionists, the "rebel spies," the "speculators," the "counterfeiters driving Anglo-Saxon firms out of business," the "cause of the inflation," the dark and shadowy presence behind all the troubles. An Associated Press writer in New Orleans wrote an article stating that "the Jews of New Orleans and all the South ought to be exterminated. They run the blockade and are always to be found at the bottom of every new villainy."

The South lay in ruins, decimated by fire and plunder, its ports isolated for years by blockade so that the shelves were barren in the shops, its factories turned to charred rubble by a deliberate scorched-earth policy, its money worthless, and its economy in turmoil. Without foodstuffs or farmers to raise food in the midst of battle, the scarcity sent prices soaring in a runaway inflation to make a broken people more miserable. In Memphis, on the Mississippi River, at the line of battle, thousands of bales of cotton sat in the warehouses, half hostage and half gold, the target for speculators and adventurers and Yankee soldiers who saw a way to steal whatever the South had left of any worth and turn it to huge profit by selling it in the North to the reopening textile factories so long deprived of Southern cotton. President Lincoln told a friend, "The army itself is diverted from fighting the rebels to speculating in cotton." Charles A. Dana wrote the Secretary of War, "Every colonel, captain, or quartermaster is in secret partnership with some operator in cotton; every soldier dreams of adding a bale of cotton to his monthly pay."

Generals Ulysses S. Grant and William Sherman considered all the speculators as leeches on the system, bringing in gold for cotton which would be convertible into arms. Sherman had earlier complained of "swarms of Jews and speculators" who were flocking into Memphis. For Sherman, the terms were synonymous.

On December 17, 1862, Grant issued what Rabbi Bertram Korn called in his volume *American Jewry and the Civil War* "the most sweeping anti-Jewish regulation in all American history," General Order No. 11 providing that "the Jews, as a class violating every regulation of trade established by the Treasury Department and also department orders, are hereby expelled from the department [of Tennessee] within twenty-four hours from the receipt of this order."

Southern Jews who had lived in Tennessee for decades, even former Union soldiers, were forced to pack up their families hurriedly and leave. When one man and his wife questioned a soldier, they were told, "It's because you are Jews, and neither a benefit to the Union nor the Confederacy." But the political struggle to rescind the order would not be argued in behalf of the Jews in the South; instead it would be based on the more blatant injustices to Jewish loyalists to the Union cause.

Cesar Kaskel of Paducah, Kentucky, had seen thirty men, some with Union military service, and their families deported without trial or hearing, and he hastened to Washington to see President Lincoln. He stopped in Cincinnati to ask the assistance of Rabbi Isaac Wise and together they began to stimulate petitions, letters of protest from Jewish leaders to Washington, and resolutions demanding revocation of the order. Congressman Gurley of Ohio, a friend of Rabbi Wise, arranged an appointment with the President, and Kaskel brought affidavits from leading Republican party members and military authorities. Korn's book reported the following quiet conversation with the President—almost charming in view of the intensity of his visitor.

Lincoln: "And so the Children of Israel were driven from the happy land of Canaan?"

Kaskel: "Yes, and that is why we have come unto Father Abraham's bosom, asking protection."

Lincoln: "And this protection they shall have at once."

Lincoln walked over to a big table and wrote a note to the general-in-chief of the army, Henry W. Halleck, directing him to telegraph instructions canceling the order. He wished Kaskel well and told him that he was free to return home. When a delegation of rabbis and other Jewish leaders called on the President to thank him, Lincoln told them that he could not understand what compelled the general to issue it. "To condemn a class is, to say the least, to wrong the good with the bad. I do not like to hear a class or nationality condemned on account of a few sinners." In Allan Nevins' words, "All honor to Lincoln!"

The *New York Times* referred to the order as "one of the deepest sensations of the war" and criticized Grant, saying that "men cannot be condemned and punished as a class without gross violence to our free institutions." Most newspapers gave the popular general every shadow of doubt; some, like the Washington *Chronicle*, called the Jews "the scavengers . . . of commerce," and others criticized the general as "thoughtless" while praising his military record. The order followed Grant into politics and became one of the major issues in his election of 1868. He never apologized or explained, though he wrote a congressman during the campaign, "I have no prejudice against sect or race, but want each individual to be judged by his own merit. Order No. 11 does not sustain this statement, I admit, but I do not sustain the order. It would never have been issued if it had not been telegraphed the moment it was penned and without reflection."

In analyzing why Grant issued the order, Korn points out that he had a month to revoke it and that it would never have been revoked had it not been for pressure from Kaskel, Wise, and the Northern Jewish community. Over a month before, he had written General Webster in Jackson, Tennessee, to "give orders to all conductors on the road that no Jews are to be permitted to travel on the railroad southward from any point. They may go North and be encouraged in it; but they are such an intolerable nuisance that the department must be purged of them." Korn concludes that Grant had been thinking about the problem for some time and that "he was willing to believe that all the thievery was due to the presence of Jews—the 'bogey man' of social mythology." Korn also points out that "only Jews, and not all traders, were banished; cotton traders as a group were never expelled."

The Cincinnati *Enquirer* suggested that Grant and Sherman had been influenced by influential cotton buyers and their officer cohorts in the army to make way for larger profits. The price of cotton was lowered from forty cents a pound to twenty-five cents a pound the day after the order was issued; thus the speculators who remained profited from the order. Isaac Wise charged in his journal a few months after the order, "The Jews bought cotton from planters at forty cents a pound; the military authorities with their business partners, agents, clerks, portiers, etc., intended to buy that staple at twenty-five cents a pound . . . they could sell it in Eastern cities just as high as the next man—and the Jews must leave, because they interfere with a branch of military business."

Lincoln's cancellation of the order diminished greatly the rising fear of Jews in the South that the Union victory would thrust them again into the kind of anti-Semitism they had fled in Europe. The Northern Jewish community had stood beside the Jews in the South, demonstrating a sense of community that transcended sectional bitterness. Northern Jews had publicly petitioned their government to revoke an order by its most popular general in the midst of a war, and the head of the nation had agreed. For Northern and Southern Jews who had escaped from countries where such unfairness would have been shrugged off, the decision by Lincoln made them know that they had found a home in the new land, and that its paper promises as the protector of minorities were real and concrete. The War itself had given Jews on both sides the opportunity to stand and fight with their neighbors, and when it was over, for most of them, they were much more "American" than when it began. For this War, like all wars, had accelerated the process of acculturation for the participants. It had been a totally American battle without foreign troops or clash of foreign ideology—only brothers could fight. Bitter as that experience was for the nation, for Jews in the North and the South to taste the fire of American dissension was to be welcomed by other Americans into the bosom of the nation.

It is difficult to measure the contribution of the Jews to the recovery of the South, because most Southern historians have neglected them as a factor, more from oversight than from careful research. It is fair to say that they played an important role, and in some cities, a crucial role, in reorganizing the marketplace after the War.

The War had destroyed everything. The plantation economy was wrecked, though cotton was still king. Half the men returning home were crippled, all of them destitute, without capital, seed, fertilizer, or even an organized market in which to sell anything. Merchants swept out their dusty stores, but they had no credit with which to assemble any saleable goods. The dilapidated plantation houses were peeling whitewash, their finery plundered, the era of elegance but ghostly memory. Nothing of the old way remained, especially not the old system of factorage, the economic foundation of the system, whereby plantation owners and farmers would agree to meet their obligations in a year. Factorage had been an idea based on trust and optimism, and the broken South could afford neither.

The wholesale merchants and the railroad magnates in the North sensed a new market in the recovering South, but they knew they would have to devise a whole new system of distribution to sell their goods. They decided on the new institution used so success-fully on the frontier—the general store—and they would build it around a simple credit idea grounded solidly in the rich soil of the rural South. The store would accept from the farmer a mortgage on his crop, backed up by the land, in exchange for implements, seed, fertilizer, and other supplies for the coming season. The stores popped up at every crossroads, and the wholesalers selected promising young Southerners to run them. (When a young Confederate veteran hesitated to open a general store because he might go broke, the railroad man asked him, "How can you go broke when you ain't got nothin'?") The storeowner served as postmaster, undertaker, referee in local spats, news carrier, political leader, and supplier of everything from corsets to cornmeal.

But the system also could sustain the house-to-house peddler to track the miles between small farmers and the millions of emancipated slaves, buying needles and thread for their wives and trinkets for the children. Some of the blacks called him the "rolling store man," and white and black accorded him a place of honor when he arrived to spread out his pack on the floor, opening the spices and the nutmeg to fill the room with wondrous smells, arranging the ribbons and the bits of colorful cloth on the floor to reveal the only prettiness the womenfolk had seen in years. The Jews longed to settle down, and looked for places to open small stands, and then later, little stores, which they would merchandise into prosperous businesses.

By the 1880's, when the largest wave of Jews from Eastern Europe began to flood America with millions of new immigrants, the merchants in the farm supply stores held the South in an iron grip of dependency—they would usually demand a mortgage on the property in case of crop failure to cover the lien contract, and many of them were becoming land rich in the process.

The Jews opened cash stores and brought competition to every little town; their presence began to break the hold of the farm supply system on the farmer. They carried clothing, mostly, and when they stocked other items, they kept the general store owner honest in his prices. They set up simple credit systems to allow buying on time, and they slowly brought back a sense of style to the South. Since the Jewish storeowner traveled to the North to buy his goods, he served as adviser to the Southern ladies on the latest fashion, and would bring her special cloth and new patterns to make the most fashionable dresses. Members of the Rich family in Atlanta, the Thalheimers in Richmond, the Godschaux family in New Orleans and the founders of Neiman-Marcus in Dallas were early Jews who built department-store empires out of the thirst in the South for quality and style. At least twenty-three towns were named for Jews who owned the plot where the post office was built or used the crossroads as a center for their peddling: places like Manassas, Virginia; Marks, Mississippi; Kaplan, Louisiana.

In the trading centers, like Mobile and Charleston, New Orleans and Memphis, now building again, Jewish merchants set up wholesale warehouses to be closer to their markets and buy in

70

larger quantities to channel more goods directly into the region. In an 1865 woodcut of Main Street in Little Rock, Arkansas, four out of six stores were owned by Jews. In 1866 in Galveston, Texas, twenty-one out of twenty-six merchants were Jewish; two years later, five out of seven retailers listed in the directory in Galveston were Jews and three out of five wholesalers in dry goods, including the Lasker family, which became wealthy in Galveston before migrating to greater fortunes in New York City.

A recovering South suggested opportunity to the new Jews streaming from Russia and Poland to the "Promised Land"— 2,800,000 from 1881 to 1924—crowding into the pushcart pandemonium of the Lower East Side of New York City, packing the tenement houses and scrambling for wages in the sweatshops or the streets.

The South was only fifteen years away from the end of the Great War when almost four million slaves were newly freed, Atlanta was just beginning to rebuild from the devastation of Sherman's march, the South was still smoldering in the lawlessness and racial violence of Reconstruction. Only the most foolhardy or the most desperate immigrants would take the chance. But why not try? First, to stock a peddler's pack at the Baltimore Bargain House— little risk in that—then look for a place to settle and send for the family. Surely then, his relatives would come. . . .

Another generation of Jews was poised to play out the drama again.

SIX

The Lonely Days Were Sundays

I n the midst of the Colonial Dames and the Daughters of the Confederacy, who traced their immediate ancestors back to Gettysburg or to the early settlements of Jamestown and Edenton, the soul of a Jewish Southern boy stirred with confusion as he struggled to understand. He felt none of the stain of Southern history, none of the dishonor at the defeat, none of the guilt over the inhumanity of slavery, none of the fascination with the intricacies of the battles. All of that saturated the air, and he lived in it and wrestled with it and tried to unravel its secrets, but his roots had hold of him in another way, perhaps because he was a Southerner, and a Southerner's roots matter to him even if the soil is in Eastern Europe. He fixed on the mysteries of Poland, Lithuania, and Rumania, wondering what would have happened if his grandparents had not been courageous or maybe afraid enough to leave their friends and their neighborhoods and the familiar fields around the villages to strike out across the broad expanse of Europe, out into the forbidding sea to the new land of America. Had they not come, he would have been trapped in the cruel battlegrounds of Europe, herded into death camps to face the horrors of the gas chambers, and he knew deep inside him that he could not have summoned the inner force to survive.

No, the ghosts of the Confederacy did not haunt him. He grew up not with the stories of the exploits of his great-granddaddy at Vicksburg but with the adventures of his grandfather in Lithuania. He remembered not the humiliation of Reconstruction when they

72

said the Negroes ruled the whites from Northern edict, but the quiet, incessant struggle for survival in the nineteenth-century South when his grandparents spoke broken English, and neither heard the faint tunes of Dixie nor stirred at the sight of the tattered flag. His grandfather told him how he just tried to sell a few things each day so that at the end of the week his grandmother might set a lovely Sabbath table.

On my father's side, I have only the young boy's memory of old people: My grandfather Isaac Evans peddled in North Carolina for a time before opening a small store in Fayetteville; he always wanted one of the grandchildren to write his life story and he talked a great deal to us when we would listen. My grandmother Sara Newmark Evans, whom we called "Sadie," was a dutiful but outgoing woman not given to reminiscence; she said the times were too hard to merit remembering and better to forget. She worked in the store when my father was growing up, and everyone said her judgment was better than Isaac's. ("Ask Sadie," he would tell the salesmen.) Though their lives were sparse, she always reminded her son to drop a few coins in the little blue box in the kitchen "to build a homeland for the Jews." She radiated sweetness and relished the household virtues—she taught me how to peel an orange with one curl of the knife and how to knit once when she stayed with me for several weeks while my parents were traveling.

My grandfather on my mother's side, Eli Nachamson, died a few years before I was born, and I carry his name; Jennie Bloom Nachamson, my grandmother, died when I was six, but I feel I know more of her, because she had eight daughters and finally a son who filled the first nephews with stories, and she left a written record. The last year of her life she dictated her life story to one of the daughters, and when I stumbled on it three years ago, I asked each of the nine children—my mother, who is the oldest, and my seven aunts and my uncle—to write remembrances of growing up so that we could have a family history for the twenty-three first cousins, living in split-level homes in suburbs from North Carolina to California and Florida. Jennie's recall was phenomenal, and her warmth and wisdom shine through every word of the story.

My great-grandmother brought Jennie, age six, and the older teen-age children to Baltimore when the Jews left the village of Linkerva in Lithuania. Tsar Alexander's dread May Laws of 1882

73

authorized the Russian peasants to expel "vicious" inhabitants by special "verdict," thus opening to confiscation any Jewish shop in competition with the peasants, forcing the Jews to bribe permission to stay in their misery. The laws also set drastically low quotas for the universities, for the licensing of Jewish doctors and lawyers, and new limitations on ownership of property, the right to domicile, the right to travel, or even the right to be a watchmaker or a baker. The tsar's bureaucracy did not stop at oppression through the laws: The authorities plotted and sanctioned by lax law enforcement a wave of anti-Jewish riots—pogroms—in which hundreds of Jewish shops were looted and burned and any Jews on the street hacked to death or castrated or torn apart, leaving the smell of terror in the air.

The word "America," an idea more than a place, they whispered it all along the alleys and the lanes, and hundreds were going and sending back letters glowing with news and hope.

But "Mama" could not risk such a journey, not with Jennie limping badly from an early bout with infantile paralysis. Then, one Passover evening, her husband died from so simple an affliction as appendicitis, for there was no doctor in the village.

Now her attention turned to her only son, a frail and sensitive boy, artistic and serious, who studied so much that everyone said he would be a rabbi. Mayer was approaching the age when he would be drafted into the tsar's army. In the early nineteenth century, Tsar Nicholas decreed the drafting of Jewish children at the age of twelve; the predatory recruiting agents broke into houses to drag the screaming youths away, off to the brutal barracks masters in the training camps to be beaten and starved into conversion, then to serve twenty-five years in the army, another name for forced labor. Tsar Alexander II, the "liberator tsar," sensing a dangerously disaffected minority of millions of people, abolished the edict in the 1860's, moving the draft age to eighteen and the term of service to six years. But the Jews never lost their suspicion of army service, a time of back-breaking hardship and danger, perhaps to serve in Siberia and never to return.

None of that for her son. One Friday night, she arose from the table and announced abruptly to the family, "We will go to America."

"We landed in America on Ellis Island," my grandmother wrote, seeing the city through the eyes of a six-year-old girl, "and as we waited for examinations for admittance, I saw a man give his children a queer-looking thing which they ate. He looked at me and gave me half of one. I had never seen nor heard of a banana before, and I shall never forget the taste. I have all my life searched for a banana with this flavor."

She marveled at the clothes and shoes and toys piled in the store windows, not realizing they had glass in them. "This is America," she thought. "How wonderful that anyone can take whatever they want."

Their name was Hyatt, acceptable enough; but everyone else was getting a new name to be more American, and they wanted one too. They chose Bloom. They joined relatives in Baltimore, where the older children immediately enrolled in night school to learn English and worked in shops during the day to help with the family income.

For a time, my great-grandmother did housework for other immigrants, but the pay was so bad that she became a peddler. Even for a one-dollar item, she would have to return ten times for the installments. She scrimped to get young Mayer out of the tailor shop he worked in, because she feared what the heat might do to his health, and somehow she saved fifty dollars to pay a man to teach him the pants cutter's trade. Because she did not want to leave Jennie alone, she opened a grocery store in the front room of her apartment; she would bring as many as ten live geese home at a time, fatten them up with dumplings for a week, kill them, and stay up all night picking the feathers and saving the down, saying, "For pillows, Jennie, for your dowry."

Jennie discovered books through the Sabbath school library, and read *Alice in Wonderland* over and over, and *David Copperfield* so many times "I felt like he was a member of my family."

For her brother's wedding, her beautiful new sister-in-law made Jennie a long dress of flowing white organdy with a pink slip, her first flowery dress, and she remembered that several young men asked her to dance. "They did not know I was lame; with my long skirts while dancing, it was not noticeable. I grew up that night. I determined I would always look pretty and wear nice clothes."

In 1904, when Jennie was eighteen, her mother decided it was time for marriage, and she invited potential suitors over to meet her. Jennie was nervous, and one by one she rejected them. One night she met a young cigarmaker named Eli Nachamson, "a fine

75

Hebrew scholar with a studious face" whom she liked because he was "gentle and refined." But he was so shy on their first meeting that he had very little to say. On their second meeting, they went with her brother to see the famed Yiddish actor Jacob Adler in *The Merchant of Venice*, and since they had little opportunity to talk, she invited him over the following night. The next Sunday, Eli arrived with his father, "a learned man with a long, red beard," who surveyed the family and talked with Jennie. They announced their engagement that very evening. At the engagement party a few days later, Eli "quietly took my hand under the table and put the engagement ring on my finger, closing his hand over it." It was the first time they had touched.

Jennie made everything she could for her trousseau—underwear, dresses, linen, and pillowcases for the pillows her mother had stuffed with goose down years before.

After several false starts trying to be a tailor, Eli managed a small living making cigars and selling them on the street. They opened a cigar store, and kept it open every day in the week, from seven in the morning until ten at night and on Saturdays until midnight.

When Sara, her first child, was born, the family did not have enough money to pay the doctor bill, and the debt preyed on Jennie's conscience for months. Finally, with great reluctance, she secretly pawned her engagement ring for twenty-five dollars to pay the bill. Eli was heartbroken but vowed to work harder.

As spare as life was, she always found the money for white diapers for the baby and a white tablecloth for the table, even though her in-laws thought such taste extravagant. "I just could not bear to eat on a newspaper-covered table."

Once, during a holiday, Jennie boarded a streetcar and went to a factory where she bought twenty-five dollars' worth of toys which she and Eli sold on the street for seventy-five. "I think we were prouder of that fifty dollars than anything we have ever done since." Eli raced down the street immediately to redeem the ring.

But Jennie was growing more and more unhappy with the Baltimore ghetto. It was a rough neighborhood, with shootings and stabbings in the street on Saturday night, and brawls near the store. After three years and two more daughters, and with life more and more disheartening, they bought a store from Eli's brother-in-law in Dover, North Carolina. The in-laws had gone to Dover originally out of desperation, and with some hope of opportunity, since it was a town of fewer than a thousand people, most of whom worked in the lumber mill. With the only dry-goods store in town, they were assured of a small living. It seemed too far away to Eli, but Jennie jumped at the chance.

"Sara is getting older and understands more. Here, we don't know who our neighbors are, or what she is going to hear and see in the streets. It will be better there for the children. We can always get plenty of milk and eggs from the farmers."

Eli left several months early to learn the business and prepare the apartment over the store, and when he sent for her, Jennie bid her mother a tearful farewell and hobbled onto the train with an armload of chicken and cakes and a handful of daughters for the fifteen-hour trip to Dover.

"It was a very poor-looking place with muddy, unpaved streets and wooden boards for sidewalks." Once the children were settled, they decided to have a grand opening the next Saturday.

"Everybody in town came over during the day to look at the store and to look me over. Some sat around the store for hours, watching me, as I waited on customers. I got the greatest thrill of my life when I looked in the register at two o'clock in the afternoon and found that we had already taken in fifty dollars. In Baltimore, in our cigar store, our biggest day had been thirty-five dollars."

When the next daughter was born, "all of our country friends came to town just to see what a 'Jew-baby' looked like."

They prospered in Dover: They brought in new kinds of merchandise that the townspeople had never seen before—pretty patterned materials and lace. They allowed Negroes to try on clothes before buying, a breakthrough for the town that caused a lot of talk. Theirs was the first store in town to run a sale with give-aways—successful too, Jennie remembered, because they gave away a washtub to anybody who filled it full of merchandise; and Jennie gambled on an entire window display of dolls, so many that Eli gasped when the cartons arrived, but they sold every one.

Almost everyone in Dover kept a pigsty just outside the kitchen window so they could toss slops into the yard. Jennie could not bear the smell, especially in the summer, and she convinced the town council to pass an ordinance prohibiting it as a health hazard. This caused an uproar in the town. One man, who kept sixteen hogs behind his store, went around saying, "The Jews and the hogs don't agree."

Still the store was doing well and she was happy in Dover. But "the lonely days were Sundays—Sundays when I watched the town people going to church, while we stayed upstairs in our apartment. Then I would feel like an outsider in this little community. I would have hunger in my heart for my own people. I would visualize a Utopia—a village like this of all Jews—going to temple on the Sabbath."

She organized a Ladies Betterment Society and taught the women in town what first-aid knowledge she had learned from all the girls' bouts with the mumps, measles, and chicken pox. She took her turn at the local church with visits to the sick. But at meetings, "I imagined myself conducting a meeting of all Jewish women."

Once, when she was invited to a real country wedding, she noticed that afterwards all the guests gathered around with the family, the women to gossip and dip snuff and the men to share a chew of tobacco off the father's prize plug. "The hostess came in with a big can. I thought perhaps she was going to ask for contributions for the newlyweds, but as the can went around, each of the guests spit into it. It was the funniest thing I ever saw."

Eli opened a "moving picture parlor" in a vacant building next to the store—"two nights a week for colored people and the rest for whites." Even though the films kept breaking, everybody in town lined up to see them, heralding the parlor as the biggest event in town since the great fire burned the lumber mill down. But they had to close after a few weeks because "every time we turned the movie machine on, all the lights in town would blow out." Always ready to try whatever was newest, Eli also bought the first automobile in Dover, and Jennie remembers her neighbors scampering over to the store on Sundays, lined up with their children freshly scrubbed from the night before, as she and Eli piled all the daughters into the back of the Maxwell for a drive in the country.

Many of the farmers would beg Eli to speak Yiddish for them, just to hear the sounds, and some would bring their families in for a blessing in Hebrew, the tongue of the Israelites. Eli would receive them all piously, as the direct descendant of Isaiah and Moses, the same blood as Jesus, and raise his hands solemnly while they all squeezed their eyes tightly shut. He would sing out a beautiful *bruchah* in his best tenor, just like on the Caruso records he owned, while glancing out of the corner of his eyes at Jennie, hiding her face in embarrassment in some crinoline. To entertain

78

his daughters, he would stand on his head and allow them to keep all the change that jangled out of his pockets.

Once when Jennie caught three of the girls dipping snuff with Venus the maid, instead of yelling and fracturing the relationship, she taught them how to mix cinnamon and sugar so they could all have a snuff-dipping party on the back porch together.

Finally, after the fifth girl was born, they decided to move to Kinston, ten miles away, where they bought a house with a large yard for the girls to romp in, and gloried in their first indoor plumbing. For Jennie, Kinston meant breaking out of her island of loneliness into a real Jewish community of nineteen families! She was so excited that she founded the Daughters of Zion, to pursue the work she knew that Henrietta Szold was doing in Baltimore. They immediately affiliated with a national Zionist organization called Hadassah to "help keep us in touch with what went on in the world"—the first such chapter in North Carolina, and perhaps in the South.

Jennie and Eli would make lots of new friends at the Jewish weekends in the spring and summer, when small-town Jews from all over eastern North Carolina would gather at Holt's Lake. The Kinston Hadassah chapter hosted a statewide meeting of over 150 Jews, and when the famed Zionist, president of the American Jewish Congress, Rabbi Stephen S. Wise agreed to come, she hosted a dinner in her home for him that even the most prominent non-Jews in town attended. She remembered it as her "proudest moment," but she also trembled when she spoke to the crowd, which at the last minute had summoned her for an impromptu speech. "Though I have no idea what I said, when I finished everyone cheered."

When the sixth girl was born, the other daughters sat on the front porch listening to "Mama scream out with pain," clinging to each other in fear; no one ever entered the hospital for anything as common as a birth, not with so many excellent "colored midwives" in town.

With so many children, Eli bought a cow, and took one of the girls out milking with him each morning so he could squirt warm milk in her mouth; on Passover especially, the Jewish people in town would come over to his barn to fill their kosher containers with milk from the "Jewish cow." He joined the Shriners, and Jennie became active in the Eastern Star, the PTA, and the Red

Cross. She was an American and no one could say that she was neglecting community obligations for Hadassah; to make sure, she tramped through Kinston selling Liberty Bonds and received an award for selling more than any other woman in town.

In the fall, during tobacco market time, Eli loved to go down to the warehouses and pick out the best leaves, then roll a few cigars for the farmers. His "masterpieces," he called them. The circles would form around him when he arrived, and people would call out, "Hey, Big Eli, roll me a see-gar." He deftly twisted the leaves and presented his prize with the flair of a magician, while he sang out to the crowd, "Be sure to shop at Nachamson's." He became so well-known that they even used "Big Eli says" in their newspaper ads. Jennie went all out on dolls again at Nachamson's and ordered ten thousand one Christmas—a cheap line from ten cents to a dollar and a better group at five dollars—more dolls than people in Kinston! Eli begged her to send some of the boxes back while there was still time, but she stubbornly held out. ("She knew little girls," he admitted.) They had their biggest doll sales ever and became known as The Doll House. Though Jennie refused to have a Christmas tree, and once scolded the children for hanging stockings on Christmas morning, Eli took the daughters to the store to let them pick out any doll they wanted. After that, the girls "looked forward to Christmas as much as the Christian children."

At Passover, the girls drew lots to select the sister to steal the matzo in behalf of all of them and Eli made certain it would be a different child each year. Jennie went to special pains to keep a kosher table all week. On Succoth, Eli herded all the family out to the back of the house to help build the arbor out of branches and hang fruit from the roof.

After the seventh and eighth daughters were born, Eli and Jennie talked a great deal about a problem just over the horizon. The conversations were triggered by the growing attractiveness of the older girls and the gentile boys in Kinston who kept pursuing them for dates. Jennie hit on the idea of moving to Durham, near two universities, where the girls would surely meet lots of nice Jewish boys; a manufacturing town where a business might do well; and a tobacco town where "Big Eli" could present his cigar act, now perfected, in the big time.

Eli took the train to investigate and make arrangements for a second store just before Jennie's ninth child was due. He had not spoken with Jennie about his dismay that there was no son to carry on his name; he did not want her to feel guilty, or the little ones to sense his disappointment. Jennie was tired and they would not try again; surely God would not blame him for stopping after nine tries! He did well in Durham that day and was anxious to tell Jennie about it. As the train pulled into the Kinston station that night, he looked out the window to see a huge crowd, over a hundred people holding torches, and he thought to himself that Sergeant York or Babe Ruth must be on board. He made his way to the door and when his face appeared, they shouted to him in a torrent of voices he could barely comprehend—but he understood enough. "It's a boy, Eli! Eli, it's a boy!" He froze, and tears welled up in his eyes as his best friend, Sam Hirshfield, helped the hulking baker, Lonnie Crabtree, hoist Eli to their shoulders for the torchlight parade to his house. Jennie was propped up and waiting with the baby in her arms when he arrived, the most serene smile ever on her face, and she murmured faintly when he kissed her, "Say hello to your son, Eli." She would always remember that he reached over to unpin the diaper just to see for himself.

The house in Durham provided a "setting" for her girls, and Jennie was pleased. On Sunday nights, she always prepared an open house, and as many as fifty boys would show up from the universities, and girls too who were in Chapel Hill for the weekend or who just wanted to be where the boys were. The Nachamson girls would skim the fashion magazines for the latest styles in long gowns and even flapper dresses, and Jennie could copy them down to the last piece of shimmy fringe. The girls formed their own band, too, called the "Harmony Sisters," with Grace on drums, Sara on the flute and saxophone, Naomi on the violin, and Irene on piano. The younger ones—Eve, Doris, and Mary—worked up a snappy dance routine which they called "The Nash Sisters" and performed at Jewish functions all over the state. Once when both sets of sisters performed to promote a sale in the store, during tobacco market time, they drew the biggest crowd since *The Jazz Singer*—so big that Eli had to move the show to the theater down the street.

A young man from Fayetteville named Emanuel J. "Mutt" Evans began to pursue Sara seriously, bringing his jalopy "Josephine" over every Sunday for an outing, which she looked forward to as a relief from the pressures of the store she was managing while her father was ill. Mutt's competition was Caesar Cone from Greensboro, the wealthy heir to the Cone Mills, whose family had made a fortune from new materials they called "denim" and "flannel," and whose sleek Bearcat-like convertible made Josephine seem like the rattletrap she was. Mutt always said that half of chasing a Nachamson girl was winning over her mother, and Jennie encouraged Sara to marry him in the long talks at night on her bed, when Sara came in from a date.

He was a lanky, handsome small-town boy with string-bean legs who played basketball and set the Southern Conference record for the half mile on the Carolina track team. Even then, people were drawn to him. Sara told Jennie he had a gentleness to him and a lot of common sense, the kind of person others liked to sit and talk to because he knew how to listen. He had enough self-confidence to win a scholarship selling more subscriptions one summer to *Pictorial Review* than anyone else in the South. He crossed up once when he wrote Sara a thank-you note for a weekend and another girlfriend an affectionate love note, putting each of them in the wrong envelope. When he called Sara to apologize and ask for the note back, she said, "If you want it, come over here and get it," knowing that otherwise he would be too embarrassed to call again. Though he lacked sophistication, she saw qualities in him she wanted in her man; besides, it was fitting for the oldest sister to marry first.

Ask anyone who lived in North Carolina in 1928 about the Mutt Evans–Sara Nachamson wedding in Durham, and they will tell you that there has never been anything like it. With a wedding to plan, Jennie decided on "store-bought" clothes for the girls. All the sisters were attendants, and ten of Mutt's fraternity brothers served as groomsmen. Little Bill came down the aisle last as ring bearer, all dressed up in a black and white satin suit, carrying a velvet pillow. When the rabbi asked the best man for the ring, he turned to Billy, who looked up matter-of-factly and announced, "I dropped it." They were married with the best man's college ring.

The Nachamsons delighted Emanuel's father (he never called his son "Mutt"), Isaac Evans from Fayetteville—such a lively, closely knit family, such lovely girls, and a large business that Emanuel might go into. He couldn't have been happier.

My grandfather Isaac left no written record of his life, but he sensed the drama in it—the early years in Lithuania when he slept

82

on a stove to keep warm; the memories of hunger and deprivation when he was thirteen, which he always said was the reason he was so short. He shuddered when he told us of the death of his father one week after Isaac joined him off the boat in Plainfield, New Jersey, ecstatic to see him again after two years apart while his father had worked to bring him over. Isaac remembered the day the old man stepped outside on the porch, and a group of careless boys accidentally shot him in the temple with a rifle. His mother— "Bubba," we called her—lived to be 104 years old, and I remember once as a small child climbing on her lap and feeling her wrinkled, trembling hand brush my cheek.

He had tried everything in New Jersey—had driven a bakery wagon, had become a cutter in a clothing firm, a job he quit because they made him work on Washington's birthday and from what he knew from his citizenship lessons, that was unconstitutional. He had even opened a three-and-nine-cents store (to undercut the five-and-tens) but nothing seemed to work for him.

For seven years he had courted my grandmother, Sadie Newmark, but her family didn't think he was learned enough. In spite of this (and the fact that she towered over his five-foot frame by seven inches!), his persistence won her over. The Newmarks claimed a close kinship with Elijah of Vilna, known as the Vilna Gaon, the Talmudic genius in Lithuania who spoke ten languages and brought mathematics, science, and geometry into the academies; he had been called by one historian "the most massive intellect since Spinoza." Magnificent misfits in the new country, the Newmarks would not deign to work. They were scholars in long coats, who argued and debated philosophy and religious minutiae all the day, and settled an argument or two in Plainfield for the new immigrants, earning a few dollars as relics from the old country.

Isaac loved to travel, and the combination of curiosity and the hard times in New Jersey, coupled with the rumors that peddlers were doing all right in the South, lured him to North Carolina. He left Sadie and Emanuel, his new son, and told her he would send for them when he could.

He told me that when the train stopped in Fayetteville, he got off and said to himself, "This looks like as good a place as any." And it was close, but not too close, to his brother-in-law in Rocky Mount, who had come South a year earlier.

His first pack cost him **forty dollars**, a sum he won in a lottery, and he ordered his assortment from the Baltimore Bargain House like all the peddlers. Off he went into the countryside, armed with a few boiled eggs, not because he kept such strict kosher now that he was so far from other Jews, but he just couldn't bring himself to eat the "*hazer* flesh" (pig meat) staples in the countryside. The farmers put him up for the night, and seemed eager to see him when he came—to hear the news and look over the merchandise. He sold shoelaces, buttons, needles, pins, a few bolts of cloth, stockings, ribbon. He would never forget his first sale: an alarm clock that he couldn't collect on after the down payment.

As soon as he could, he bought a horse and wagon, and carried a larger assortment of goods—perfumes, shoes, eyeglasses, aprons, and housedresses. The Baltimore Bargain House paid the railroad fare of the peddlers to come up and restock, so annually he planned eagerly for the trip, looking forward to seeing other friends from across the South. The farmers, looking on him as an authority, questioned him constantly on biblical problems—the begats, how big was Noah's ark, the amount of alcohol in the wine at the Last Supper (about 18 percent). He always had a ready answer so as not to disappoint them.

One night, the Jenkins' stable caught on fire and he helped the brigade put it out. For that favor, Mr. Jenkins rented him a store with a room over it for the family for ten dollars a month. The next day, as he was sweeping it out, someone asked him what he was selling. He didn't know, but the farmers were coming into town more now that the roads were getting better, and he felt he would do all right. Since there were already two or three Jewish clothing stores in Fayetteville, he opened a furniture store.

He sold wooden cupboards on tall legs which the customer set into four pails of water in order to keep the mice out of the grits, flour, and sugar. He stocked Washington stoves, cribs, churns, and kerosene lamps, but his biggest sellers were the "cornshuck and cotton" mattresses with striped ticking that crinkled when you moved around on them.

Isaac dreamt of all the places he might go someday—adventurous dreams, like standing on the Great Wall of China or riding a camel to the Sphinx. More than anything, though, he wanted to see America, and he told his grandchildren constantly about the trip he made in 1932 with his teen-aged son, Monroe, out to California to the Olympics, trading razor blades, laxatives, and aspirin for gas and food.

Later in his life, I found him in his living room reading a book about the first submarine under the polar ice cap. "Now that is a trip I would love to make," he told me, "only I'm too old to travel any more. But you can travel with books, did you know that? When I finish this," and he held it up above his head like bounty, "I will have been under the North Pole."

Isaac worried that the grandchildren understood no Yiddish, and he strove mightily to teach us, especially when our parents went on a trip and left us with him and Sadie for a week or so. From him I learned that *fashimult* was how you felt when you saw your worst enemy driving your new Cadillac off a cliff; that the *alta kockas* were my grandfather's friends; that *kook-off-der-kinder* meant that I should show off; *a bissel* is what you answered whenever an older person unleashed an excited string of Yiddish with the word *fashtay?* in it somewhere, thinking that you spoke it fluently after you used a phrsase like *Leba-dicka-velt* when a friend brought you a cool lemonade on a hot day. I especially enjoyed the commercial phrases that he used around the store: *chak-kees* (what Woolworth's sold); *ganuff* (a shoplifter); *yiddisha kop* (when you added a sale of several items in your head); and *tray-gezunt-a-hait* (after you sold a garment to a Jewish customer).

Sadie wanted the children to learn music, but Emanuel was just too interested in baseball to practice. She insisted, he balked; she bought a violin, he wanted a new glove; she sent him off to lessons when the other boys wanted him to be lead-off hitter. One day he pedaled angrily to his violin lesson with the case strapped onto the rear of the bike, when suddenly the wheels skidded out from under him, sprawling him into the street. Dazed, his knees skinned and his wind knocked out, he saw a wagon rattling toward him less than a block away. He reached over his shoulder, unfastened the violin, and slid it gently under the wheels of the passing wagon, smiling at the delicious crunching sound and the resonant "boing" as the strings snapped. From that week on, he spent his afternoons playing baseball.

Since he was over six feet in height, classmates started calling him "Mutt" because of a five-foot friend whom they nicknamed "Jeff," the two of them the only Jews in his class. He fought it for years until a baseball game at Fayetteville High when, in a

85

memorable inning, he put out all three batters with sparkling glovework at third base, and the team called him "Heinie" after a famed New York Giants infielder, Heinie Manush. Faced with that kind of choice, he settled on "Mutt."

He decided on Chapel Hill for college because Isaac could not afford to send him out of the state, and most of the North Carolina Jewish boys were going to Chapel Hill anyway. Once they arrived, they found themselves excluded from the fraternities there, so a group of twelve boys decided to form their own fraternity. He remembered a rule they voted in the second year—no more than five brothers could walk across campus at any one time, so that other students would not think that the Jews traveled in a pack. When his group picked Tau Epsilon Phi to affiliate with nationally, the few German Jews like Caesar Cone selected Zeta Beta Tau, in order to remain aloof from the sons of the newer immigrants.

He hoped to go to law school, and Professor Frank Graham helped him get into Harvard. But he had met the oldest Nachamson girl by then, the one with the big green eyes; her father was very sick and there were no men to help in the business. They would marry and he would think about it for a year. The next year was 1929 and the entire family needed all the help it could muster.

The Depression tore into the South with special fury, wrecking the small-farm economy and driving the already poor into destitution. Tobacco prices tumbled to ten cents a pound. My father remembered the enormous burden that dropped on him as a young college graduate when his father-in-law died, that feeling of responsibility for the entire Nachamson family—Mrs. Nachamson, my mother's seven sisters and her brother. Little Bill was seven years old and my father virtually raised him as his own; mostly, though, he worried about marrying off the seven girls.

My mother would remember harrowing scenes from those days: a sign in a shop calling for "One man wanted" and fifty or sixty men lining up early in the morning, jostling each other furiously to get in first. On some days, no one would come into the store at all, and the salesgirls just stood around whispering to each other. When events pressed in darkly on the store, they agreed among themselves to come in every other day, so everybody would have part of a job. To attract customers, the store sold eggs at twenty

86

cents a dozen or gave away free hotdogs at tobacco market time. When the hard candy and the small chocolate began to soften in the summer heat, Mother came up with the idea of putting them together in cellophane bags and calling the new package "Flaming Mamies." To her astonishment, and for reasons she never fathomed, the candy sold out in three days.

To keep the synagogue going, everyone prevailed on my father to assume the awkward task of raising money on the eve of Yom Kippur, the holiest day of the Jewish year when every family in town was sure to be present. They raised half the budget between the sacred opening prayer, Kol Nidre, and the evening service because it was the only way to pay the rabbi and meet expenses.

One day in 1933, a friend called Dad to report that the lobby of the bank was filled with people, and that if he was smart he too would rush down and withdraw all his money. The panic inside the bank shocked him, the long lines waiting for the cashiers, who deliberately slowed down the process, stalling until closing time. He told me he could sense the desperation trembling in the voices, and he wedged his way through the crowd into the president's office. "They're cutting their own throats, Mutt," Mr. Mewborne said helplessly.

Back in the lobby, Dad was seized with a deep frustration and suddenly, on impulse, he leaped up on the check counter and shouted the crowd to silence. "I came up here to get my money out just like you did. But no bank can stand up to a crowd like this. I own United Dollar Store and I've got a lot more in here than anybody in this room. I'm leaving it in. Join me. If we all stand together, we can get through this time together."

The crowd hesitated, and then they started to break up and turn away from the tellers and file out quietly into the street, and he walked slowly back to the store wondering if he had done the right thing. The bank stayed open for another year and managed an "orderly dissolution," financial terminology meaning that nobody lost everything.

The specter of those years haunted my parents all their lives, for the Depression had severely shaken the faith of the immigrants in America. It gnawed on my mother until the day we sold the business twenty-five years later and she exclaimed, "Thank God we won't have to worry about a depression anymore."

III

The Struggle Against Conformity

SEVEN

Kosher Grits

I N the South today there are only traces of the early conflicts between the German Jews and the East Europeans. German arrogance and East European jealousies fed on each other, but many of the differences vanished with the financial success of the second generation of East Europeans, coupled with the growing homogeneity of American life. The Reform temples in the South simply could not have survived had they maintained their German exclusivity; so they took in the new Jews with money, so many that by sheer numbers the new Jews were able to edge the old families out of positions of influence. They were not ready to break so completely with their roots, and once in control of the temples, they introduced more Hebrew into the service, in some cases brought back the bar mitzvah, and generally reined in the radicalism of the early reformers.

Still, one can pick up the echoes of the old conflicts and, by rustling among the memories of old Jews, some of the flavor of the earlier times. It wasn't only the subconscious pressures to assimilate into a region where differences were penalized, but the years were eroding the distinctions as the generations dissolved into the Southern soil.

An old German woman in Atlanta remembered her girlhood, when her parents discussed the nature of the Friday night service: "The *sounds* were crucial. We wanted it to sound less Jewish—an organ, no Hebrew, rewritten music to sound like hymns, and an orderly service. And the *sights*—stained glass windows, no skull caps or prayer shawls, families sitting together."

91

In Charleston, a younger German man (German only in origin, everything else pure South) who had married a Methodist girl felt comfortable in the temple of his grandfather: "Why don't they show the Reform Jews on television?," he asked. "If people could see our services, they'd think they were in church again. We ain't *that* different."

Home life among the children of the early German immigrants had a distinctly Southern flair. This was Friday night in Anniston, Alabama, at the turn of the century: "First, Mama blessed the lights. And then, we always had our favorite Sabbath meal—oyster stew; steak, ham, or fried chicken; Mama's homemade biscuits and corn bread, too; hoppin' john [a mixture of black-eyed peas and rice]; and sweet potato pie for dessert."

And the stories that they heard in southern Georgia were not the Yiddish folk stories so rich a part of Jewish lore, nor the tales of the early days in Lithuania that animated my father's boyhood. Instead: "Mama read me Uncle Remus, propping me on her knee and acting out Br'er Rabbit and the Tar Baby."

At dinner one night in Montgomery, a young man answered, "Do we keep kosher? Sure, I eat kosher grits."

Life could have its poignant turns for the small-town Jews, isolated and alone in the rural South, watching the children drift away. Mayor Harry Applebaum of Yazoo City, Mississippi, now over eighty, helped his father load "everything we had" onto a barge in Vicksburg the day after the news reached them that a great fire had burned Yazoo City to the ground. They came up the Yazoo River "because Papa said they'd be needin' shoes," and opened a successful dry-goods store there. "He was right. Why, they didn't even wait for us to get 'em on the shelves."

He was proudest of the bill he introduced in the legislature to legalize liquor, and though it failed ("They come in with a pint on their hip and vote dry"), he shook the state enough, he reported proudly, to be invited to New York to appear on the Herb Shriner Show.

Applebaum joined the temple in nearby Lexington, Mississippi, because "they got a lot of Jewish people over there—must have eight or ten families." The rabbi from Jackson would come up once a month for services. It was Reform because "that's the only kind of Jewish religion you can have down here and stick to it."

It saddened him that all six of his children converted to various churches, but "the young generation has gotten away from us.

Used to be, if I went out after dark, I got a whipping. Now, they don't start going out till dark." He felt that he had done all he could to raise his children as Jews but that "the Jewish religion is about played out down here in Yazoo City. You can't tell the young generation they can't ride around on Friday nights or eat popcorn or go to the picture show on Saturday."

They buried Harry Applebaum's father in the Catholic cemetery because he had told the local priest, "That'll be the last place the devil will look for a Jew."

The German Jews with ties to the Civil War, like most Southerners with relatives who fought in it, celebrate the event with photographs and paintings in their homes, and framed Confederate money and discharge papers on the walls. Sipping tea in rural Virginia, an old dowager smiled at the mention of General Robert E. Lee. "You could look into General Lee's face and it was like a benediction. Why, to me, he ranked with Moses. We knew that in him there was something to emulate."

In Montgomery, Alabama, an old family patriarch pulled out a letter which purported to be written the day after Jefferson Davis' inauguration, which spoke of "my thrill today . . . at standing five feet from Jefferson Davis" when he took the "oath of the Presidency." (The old man's son doubted its authenticity and attributed it to a social-climbing aunt.) The letter expressed concern whether "President Davis has the understanding to lead us through the coming travail. . . ." When the old man saw me taking notes feverishly, he leaned over close to me and said, "I wish you wouldn't publish this." Why not, I asked. "Well," he answered, "Jefferson Davis is mighty popular down here and we don't like to go counter to the stream." (Today, on the capitol steps in Montgomery, a six-pointed Star of David marks the spot where President Davis was sworn in. No one knows how it got there—some just call it the mark Judah Benjamin left on the Confederacy.)

Gertrude Weil, ninety-one, led the state suffragette movement in North Carolina and served as the first president of the statewide League of Women Voters. Miss Gertrude, as everyone in North Carolina always called her, scandalized the state by openly professing to be a socialist in the forties and campaigned furiously ("tart-tongued," one author wrote) in Frank Graham's 1950 Senate campaign.

I talked with her a few months before she died, in the house she grew up in, her father's home—once a stately mansion on the edge of town, now surrounded by a filling station and the farmers' market, an anachronism amidst the rushing cars and the noisy streets of downtown. To pass through the front door is to enter an old world of faded tintype photographs and velvety antiques. Though she lived in another age, she was still brisk and witty, and penetrating in her insights into Jews in the South.

"Where were you born, Miss Gertrude?" She narrowed the question with a flash of humor.

"Right here in this room," she answered, pointing to the bed in the corner, and indicating by the force of her gesture that she had every intention of dying in the very same bed.

She was alert and lucid, with a commanding vocabulary—a brilliant woman still.

She had not joined the United Daughters of the Confederacy, though eligible, because she felt it an "unnatural patriotism" and the War an event "that should be forgotten." For that reason, she criticized the German Jews who seem to enjoy "looking back," romanticizing their forebears and exaggerating the elegance of their lineage. Miss Gertrude, it seems, was old enough to remember the warts on certain personalities, the hardship of Reconstruction, and she therefore saw the humor in how time distorts those years and the people. The Southern German Jews, especially in Richmond (whom she called the "Jewish F.F.V.'s," the initials for "First Families of Virginia"), had carried "this aristocracy to ludicrous extremes," for there was only a "superficial difference" between the early Germans and the new immigrants. By "superficial" she meant religious customs, for "I had never seen a *yarmulka* [skullcap] until the Eastern Europeans arrived." But the new immigrants "worked just as hard as we did and made successes," and it seemed foolish to her to see any status in arriving "just a few years earlier."

She observed that, in one important way, it was easier to be Jewish in the South because "the gentile community expects the Jews to have their own community and be loyal to it." Because fundamentalists respect religion in the South, she felt that Jews who are "civically useful" and "declare themselves as Jews" will be the most respected by the gentile community.

Her face was covered in shadows and her voice would sink to barely audible levels, as if speaking from another time, giving the ideas she expressed a surreal quality of absolute truths. "It's the Jewish men who intermarry, not the women," she stated, because women are raised more in "the beauty of Judaism." Though she felt social assimilation was inevitable as the economic and social barriers against Jews crumbled, she considered it "the greatest threat to Jewish survival because religious education is lax . . . theology is nonexistent, and differences are disappearing." Surprisingly, for I had heard no other German Jew express it with such fervor, her solution was to develop closer ties with Israel and to place more emphasis on Jewish education.

Her interest in Israel went back to the turn of the century; she explained that her parents had visited Palestine in 1909 and had written a series of articles about it for the Goldsboro *News Argus*. Miss Gertrude criticized those Jews who are indifferent to Israel, "the most exciting and thrilling thing happening in Jewry, each person there a story of heroism." She said, "I hold no license for the Jews of the American Council for Judaism who seem to want a Judaism without Israel. I don't know what they have unless it is a theology and who can believe in theology these days?"

She talked intimately of the stories her parents told her of the Civil War and the early struggles of her family; then she paused suddenly and looked out the window. "Of course, this all sounds very old to you, but it's just one lifetime, you know."

Jews in an isolated circumstance have always worried about the attitude of the gentile community toward them; but in the South, the spirit of "what will the *goyim* think" can assume strange shapes and cause unexpected turns in attitude and act.

In Arkansas, a small congregation of fewer than fifteen families went deeply into debt to build a tasteful, small temple because, as the chairman of the building fund confessed, the fundamentalists in town expected everyone to have a church to belong to, and "by having a building they didn't think we were so odd."

Jews lived in Galveston for twenty-seven years without a temple, but then built one in reaction to critical editorials in the local press chiding them for being the only religious group in the city without a house of worship when only "a few thousand dollars would be sufficient." (The editorials suggested that building a temple might be a way to dispel prejudice against Jews as too tight-fisted with money, and welcomed them "as evidence of prosperity" since "they never settle in any place where money cannot be made.")

A Mississippi rabbi complained about the lax attendance at his Friday night services, but admitted, "I never have any trouble with Sunday school attendance. It's the thing to do here on Sunday mornings."

The chairman of the search committee in another Southern temple told of the qualities that the committee looked for in a rabbi today. "We're looking for a 'pulpit rabbi'—a good speaker, one who makes a good appearance, that the women like, you know, a good dresser, not too much scholarship, someone the gentiles can respect. His wife must be a sweet girl who will mind her manners. And we always ask, 'What is your view on civil rights?' and he is supposed to say, 'I will not do anything to endanger the Jewish community.'"

A Reform rabbi in another city remembered that after his interview for a job, he knew he had an assured offer: "I had blond hair and blue eyes and it was all they needed."

The Southern atmosphere is pleasant for a rabbi; they are respected, are called "doctor," and many of them stay for long periods of time. "Professionally," said a Conservative rabbi, "it's a nicer life here. It's the Bible belt, and the clergy has a higher standing. People in the South are less urbane and sophisticated, it's true, but they take religion a lot more seriously."

Most congregations in the South expect their rabbis to spend large portions of their time relating to the gentile community, and because of the curiosity about Judaism, almost all of them do rather well at it. "I have preached from most of the pulpits, have my own radio program, and frequent television exposure—sign-off prayers and Sunday morning guest spots," said a Virginia rabbi, "and frankly, I have a much more loyal following in the fundamentalist community than in the Jewish community." Like most rabbis, he runs a model seder every year, with enthusiastic attendance from the fundamentalist churches. "They love it as the Lord's supper."

When the American immigration laws tightened in the twenties, there were no new Jews to gamble on the South; and in New York among the recently arrived, the reputation of the South turned sour. The lynching of Leo Frank in Atlanta hovered like a black cloud over the region, churning up insecurities and fear, at the

96

same time that the South was on the skids economically. All in all the South became a poor risk for the Jews. The Jewish communities slowly stagnated and most of them began to see their numbers dwindle and their freshness fade.

The rabbis in the Reform temples across the South settled into their communities comfortably, enjoying the easy pace and the intimacy, spending virtually their entire careers with a single congregation: David Marx at Temple Sinai in Atlanta from 1895 to 1949; Edward N. Calisch at Beth Ahabah in Richmond from 1891 to 1946; Morris Newfield at Temple Emanuel in Birmingham from 1895 to 1940; Ira Sanders at B'nai Israel in Little Rock from 1926 to 1963; Eugene Blachschleger at Temple Beth-Or in Montgomery from 1934 to 1961; Julius Mark at the Vine Street Temple in Nashville from 1926 to 1948; Meyer Lovitt at Temple Beth Israel in Jackson, Mississippi, from 1929 to 1954; Julian Feibelman at Temple Sinai in New Orleans from 1935 to 1967; Abraham Feinstein at Congregation Mizpah in Chattanooga from 1929 to 1969; and Harry W. Ettelson at Temple Israel in Memphis from 1925 to 1954.

All of these men were powerful personalities, many of them the first rabbis in the South who spoke English without an accent. Deep-voiced, dramatic men, they deeply impressed the fundamentalist community with their appearance and bearing. To rock-ribbed Baptists they seemed the very embodiment of the prophets themselves. Every sermon was a soaring, learned, carefully honed presentation of the roots of Christian thought in Jewish law, and the little country churches showered them with adulation as bearers of the "word" from the chosen people.

"You can't help yourself," a small-town rabbi confessed. "You become what the *goyim* expect you to be. If they treat you like some kind of Old Testament prophet, you start acting that way."

EIGHT

Zionism in the South

> *"Have you heard of [Dr. Herzl's] plan? He wishes to gather the Jews of the world together in Palestine, with a government of their own. . . . I am not objecting; but if that concentration of the cunningest brains in the world was going to be made a free country . . . , I think it would be politic to stop it. It will not be well to let that race find out its strength. If the horses knew theirs, we should not ride anymore."*
>
> Concerning the Jews,
> *Mark Twain*

F R O M the beginning, the issue of Zionism plagued the Reform movement, trying earnestly to forge a new Judaism in America that would shun such self-conscious ideas as the Diaspora (Jews scattered across the earth longing for a return to Zion). In 1890 Isaac Wise led the effort to place the Central Conference of American Rabbis (the Reform organization) on record against "any attempt toward the establishment of a Jewish state," and at one time, in a frequently quoted statement, characterized Zionism as "a momentary inebriation of morbid minds and a prostitution of Israel's holy cause to a madman's dance of unsound politicians."

Jews in the South were not strangers to the idea and the dream of a homeland for the Jews. In fact, at one time, the South itself was considered as a possible site for the Jewish state. The silk-hat banker Jacob Schiff, concerned about the conditions on the East Side of New York (and embarrassed by the image it created for New York's German Jews), pledged half a million dollars in 1906

98

to the "Galveston Project," which helped direct more than ten thousand East European immigrants through Galveston into the South and Southeast.

Schiff selected Galveston over New Orleans as a port of entry because he wanted a less glamorous city which would not tempt the Jews to stay. (Many drifted through east Texas and into Louisiana anyway.) In Rabbi Henry Cohen he obtained an energetic, humane, and dependable director, who set up an organization that met every boatload, to teach the immigrants English and to assure —in sending a butcher to Kansas City, a locksmith to Omaha, a shoemaker to Shreveport—that there was an opening in each town to fit the skill of the immigrant.

In addition, Schiff persuaded Israel Zangwill to abandon for a time his plan to build a Jewish state in Uganda, East Africa, and cooperate in directing Russian Jews to Southern ports instead of to Ellis Island. Zangwill went along in order to win Schiff's favor for his dream of an autonomous Jewish state in Africa, Brazil, Australia, or Mesopotamia; he even considered Nevada or a state in the South and promised Schiff the cooperation of his Jewish Territorial Organization if Schiff would agree. Schiff felt that Jewish immigration in the Deep South would place Jews in competition with Negro labor and urged the Southwest as a better site. He wanted to restrict the choice of immigrants only to those who did not keep the Sabbath. Zangwill insisted that such a restriction would lead to "euthanasia of the race and religion," and Schiff backed down.

But Schiff's goal of sending hundreds of thousands of Jews into the heartland never materialized because of the united opposition of the Jewish press (Schiff accused them of worrying about the loss of circulation and influence), the preoccupation of Zangwill's organization with his own project in Angola, and the lack of cooperation of the immigration inspectors in Texas. In addition, Russian immigrants considered New York as synonymous with America, and the steamship companies found it more profitable to aim their advertising literature at New York City than at Galveston.

Earlier, in 1881, there even had been an abortive effort to set up a Jewish colony in Louisiana, which the sponsors hoped would blossom into a Jewish homeland in the South. Sicily Island, Louisiana, was the first colony established in America by the Am Olam movement, a "back to the soil" movement in Russia that advocated immigration to America, not as "nonproductive" commercial

99

middlemen, which the movement believed to be one of the causes of anti-Semitism, but as productive farmers. With farming as a base, the movement planned to establish in the United States a Jewish state based on socialist and collective ideals. Sicily Island was the first of twenty-five such efforts, most of them failures, in such far-flung places as Cremieux, South Dakota; Cotopaxi, Colorado; New Odessa, Oregon; and Alliance, New Jersey. There was also a short-lived effort in Newport, Arkansas, but the whole group soon migrated to St. Louis.

All together, 173 men came, financed in part by their own money and by funds from the New Orleans Jewish community and from the Hebrew Immigrant Aid Society in New York. Leaving their wives and children at the Continental Hotel in New Orleans, they embarked by steamer for the colony 350 miles away. The night before, they celebrated with a Hanukkah feast and a ceremony inducting several of them as naturalized citizens. Then "a procession with flags and lanterns proceeded through the streets," serenading the homes of the rabbi and of Isidore Newman, the New Orleans philanthropist who helped raise the money.

They cleared about 450 acres, planted grain, corn, and vegetables, dug wells, and built cottages. But the high hopes turned to despair as the Mississippi River rose in April to flood their lands and infest the colony with the dread malaria. A settler wrote his family that "even emancipated slaves steered clear . . . a climate so hot that eight months out of the year . . . the thermometer rises above blood heat during which time there is the stench of the swamps and of the bodies of animals and birds dead from the bites of snakes and scorpions that abound there." They abandoned the island, saying " . . . in the paradise promised, [we] found only serpents."

Theodor Herzl's efforts to declare and rally a world Zionist movement at the turn of the century confronted Reform Judaism with a full-blown movement to counter. At Hebrew Union College, teachers with Zionist sympathies were ousted, and the Central Conference responded with a steady barrage of anti-Zionist resolutions as the East European immigrants, for whom Zionism was a fiber of their beings, bitterly assailed the Reform Jews for their assimilationist views. After the British mandate of Palestine in 1922 (and partially responding to leadership within the Reform movement from such eloquent Zionist Reform rabbis as Stephen S.

Wise and Abba Hillel Silver), Reform leaders agreed to mute their criticism and work for an internationally sanctioned homeland, while condemning the Zionist idea of statehood and political independence. For twenty years, the truce in the Reform movement, with some exceptions, seemed to work. The Central Conference remained neutral and treated Palestine as a beneficent religious-cultural project.

But in 1942, with America mobilizing for a world war, a group of thirty-three Reform rabbis with Zionist sympathies introduced a resolution at the annual meeting of the Central Conference to promote an American Jewish military force (to defend Palestine after the Allied defeats in Libya), an idea smacking of the kind of separatism that was so repugnant to traditional Reform thought. The debate over the resolution raged for hours before passing 64 to 38, with twenty-seven rabbis requesting that their negative votes be specifically recorded. Rabbi Edward N. Calisch of Richmond, a former president of the Central Conference, was a leader in the opposition.

Within a few months, a group of ninety-two rabbis, including seventeen from the South, met in Atlantic City to adopt "A Statement of Principles by Non-Zionist Rabbis"; a smaller group proposed a lay organization "for a righteous onslaught on Jewish nationalism." They called it the American Council for Judaism, a name chosen because they felt that an anti-Zionist group would succeed only if it adopted a "positive view," with Americanism as its central focus. In a few more months, Lessing Rosenwald was elected its first president and Rabbi Elmer Berger of Flint, Michigan, its executive director. (The Rosenwald family split on the Zionist question. Lessing was one of the major financial backers of the American Council and William served as national chairman of the United Jewish Appeal.) Their central statement of purpose in 1943 was to become an issue in every Reform temple in the South: "We oppose the effort to establish a National Jewish State in Palestine or anywhere else, as a philosophy of defeatism and one which does not offer a practical solution to the Jewish problem. We dissent from all those related doctrines that stress the racialism, the nationalism, and theoretical homelessness of Jews. We oppose such doctrines as inimical to the welfare of the Jews in Palestine, in America, and wherever Jews may dwell." The language was couched in religious and philosophical terms, quiet and restrained.

They called themselves "non-Zionists" instead of "anti-Zionists," and based their differences on historic biblical issues.

But out in the hinterlands, the ideological fires flared fiercely. In Houston, Congregation Beth-Israel, one of the oldest and wealthiest Reform temples in the South, and dominated by members of the American Council, adopted a set of "Basic Principles" that laid out the issues in bold-faced, ten-gallon terms "to safeguard at least a segment of the Jewish people of this nation against indictment before the Lord for worshiping a false god, ZIONISM." They adopted bylaws conferring a second-class, nonvoting membership on any members of the congregation who advocated Zionism, kept kosher, or desired the extensive use of Hebrew in the service. The resolution was so stark in its bluntness that it became the focal point of a national debate: "We are Jews by virtue of our acceptance of Judaism. We consider ourselves no longer a nation. We are a religious community, and neither pray for nor anticipate a return to Palestine nor a restoration of any of the laws concerning the Jewish state. We stand unequivocally for the separation of the Church and the State. Our religion is Judaism. Our nation is the United States of America. Our nationality is American. Our flag is the 'Stars and Stripes.' Our race is Caucasian. With regard to the Jewish settlement in Palestine we consider it our sacred privilege to promote the spiritual, cultural, and social welfare of our coreligionists there."

The resolution passed in the congregation 632 to 138, but 142 members and the assistant rabbi resigned to form a new, rival temple.

In Houston, as in Reform temples all over the country, an influx of East European membership from second-generation immigrants rising on the economic and social ladder had increased tensions over the Zionist question. By 1930 a survey by the Union of American Hebrew Congregations of forty-three Reform congregations in eleven major cities revealed that temple memberships were composed of equal proportions of Jews from East European and German backgrounds; of those who were foreign born, fifty-seven percent were from Eastern Europe and only thirty-three percent from Germany. In the rabbinate as well, German predominance was vanishing and rabbis of East European origin, with sympathetic views on the idea of a Jewish homeland, were assuming pulpits everywhere except in the major cities of the South, which

102

would attract more moderate rabbis after World War II. Moreover, the Conservative movement in America, more liberal than Orthodox but more traditional than Reform, was beginning its period of greatest growth, providing for the second generation of East Europeans a middle way as a new alternative. It had started in anger in 1883, after the notorious "*trefa* [nonkosher] banquet" celebrating the first graduation of Reform rabbis from Hebrew Union College. By 1940 Conservative congregations had proliferated into 190 communities from the original twenty-two in 1913; they would spread to 350 by 1950 and to 668 by 1959, into every major Southern city, ready to challenge the older Reform temples for leadership.

In the South, always lagging behind national trends, still struggling to recover from the Depression, shunned by Jews in the North because of the lack of opportunity, the old German Reform rabbis were entering the last era of their rabbinate, and the anti-Zionist rhetoric of the American Council occupied a high place in their pulpits.

The centers were Richmond, where Rabbi Edward Calisch gave the Council organizational impetus and leadership, and Houston, where Rabbi Hyman Judah Schachtel gave it outspoken support. The Council also had a following in New Orleans, but would never be large elsewhere, even in Atlanta. Nevertheless, the Council was always more vocal than its numbers would indicate and more influential because some of the wealthiest and most respected old families belonged.

During the late thirties and forties my mother traveled all over the South for Hadassah, making her speeches at meetings and banquets, raising money for Hadassah causes and pitching strenuously for support for Israel. She remembered a frightening time in Jackson, Mississippi. She rose to speak at a crowded Hadassah meeting, when suddenly the president of the temple burst through the door at the back of the room and huffed his way to the dais where she stood, grabbed the Israeli flag that stood alongside the stars and stripes behind the lectern, flung it across the floor, and stalked out. A woman who was there that night called it a "turning point" for the Jewish community.

"Most of the women thought they were coming to a meeting to help the little children who had survived Hitler, but some of us had planned a major meeting for Hadassah," she recalled. "After Al Rosenfield tore down the flag and your mother made her speech, half of them resigned and pulled out of Hadassah until just a few years ago. It was a real ruckus."

Al Rosenfield, now in his seventies, runs a small ladies' dress shop named Field's on Capitol Street in Jackson. I dropped by to see him and talk about that night.

"Mr. Rosenfield?" I introduced myself to a bone-thin man with cold eyes and leathery skin, standing in front of a rack packed full of coordinated pants suits and summer blouses. "Twenty years ago when my mother came to Jackson to speak, you walked up to tear down the Israeli flag." His jaw dropped in shock and his face drained of color. I was using my most innocent tone of voice, so he wouldn't think I was some ghost of Israel returning to render retribution. "I'd like to know how you feel about it today."

He looked around the store to make sure no customers had heard and then grabbed my arm and pulled me toward a door at the rear. I followed him into a small, cluttered office, and he sat on a desk chair, swiveled around to face me, leaned in close, and then said with a deep Delta accent, "Now, son, run that by me again, real slow."

Before I finished repeating the story, he leaned back wistfully in his chair, his hands clasped behind his neck, gazing at the ceiling as if to recast the scene. "I sho' did stir 'em up, didn't I?" he drawled proudly, like a former all-American remembering the night he won the game with a field goal in the last second. Then he bolted forward in the chair and, as if to assure me that he harbored no regrets, added, "Shoot, I'd have tossed that flag out the window if there'd been one open."

He said that everybody in Jackson knew how he felt, even today. "Those people over there in Israel think of me as part of them and I plain resent it. Here, they always bother me for money: I just cain't seem to shake 'em." He had been seized with fury that night and had torn down the flag because "I just don't believe that the church and politics mix."

Surely, he must be curious about Israel, having heard so much about it. Would he like to visit and see for himself? "I have no more desire to go over there than I have to paddle up the Amazon River in a canoe sweating bullets."

He complained bitterly about the Northern Jews doing things

104

that embarrassed him, jeopardizing his business and the lives of all the Jews in Mississippi, people "like the Rosenberg traitors and those civil rights workers" who made his friends "suspicious." "They all ought to stay up there and leave us alone, because they all hate Mississippi. It's my home." And then, as if to stake a firm claim on his Mississippi credentials, "I didn't come here yesterday, you know."

The war changed everything, leaving its raw impressions even on the distant world of children in the South. He was just another flickering figure on the movie screen for me, but the audience always hissed when they saw him—funny black mustache, a tongue of hair plastered down the side of his forehead, strutting in his shiny boots. We imitated him, we wartime children, with a plastic comb pursed between our upper lips and our noses. Then we would screech out an exaggerated "Sieg Heil," shoot our hand in the air in mock salute, and fall down laughing at him, as if he were some Chaplinesque clown. We told boyhood jokes about him during the war.

"You'll die on a Jewish holiday," the seer told him. "Are you sure?" said the little German mustache, shocked at the prediction. "Of course. Any day you die will be a Jewish holiday."

But when my mother told me that he meant to "kill all the Jews," and I overheard two men at the synagogue say that if they won, he would "set up gas chambers right here in the *shul*," the newsreel villain, distant and unreal, suddenly was transformed into an intimate personal demon. And when the movies showed him haranguing some incredible ocean of people packed into an ornate city square in Munich, his fist raised to challenge God, his voice rising and falling in soaring emotional rhythms, inspiring the mob into primal fury, arousing the superrace, I would think that he was screaming, "I will kill all the Jews." And the crowd would respond by saluting the air in agreement, shouting, "Sieg Heil, mein Fuehrer."

The news trickling out of Nazi Germany subdued the enthusiasm of the rabbis for the idea of the Council, and convinced the mass of American Jews that some homeland was necessary. Any Jews on the fence, and there were many before the war, swung strongly to support the Zionist cause, though they avoided the

105

label. The stark truth of the war bit deeply at American Jews—no country would take the Jews of Europe. There would have to be a homeland they could always go to from now on.

The establishment of the State of Israel in 1948 briefly irritated the old German families in the South, but the opposition gave way eventually to a pride in the achievements of Israel, respect for its military daring and success as a nation.

The president of a now-moribund American Council chapter in a major Southern city confessed that the success of Israel had undermined most of the enthusiasm for his organization. "We haven't had a meeting in four years," he admitted, "but we keep it going informally to act as an anchor to the Zionist extremists—you know, just to keep them honest."

He was a fourth-generation German Jew, for whom the establishment of the State of Israel was a profoundly disturbing event, and he was repeating by rote paragraphs of rhetoric from years ago. "Sure, it was okay for the refugees, you know, the poor Jews and anyone else who wanted to go there, but not for me. We were Americans by citizenship and Jews by religion. I mean, did the Baptists have a country?"

His deepest worry at the time was the implication that loyalty to Israel might call into question his loyalty to America. "I was afraid that Judaism would become a political issue here because Israel would change us from a religion into a race; that Jews would be persecuted more because people would think that they were more loyal to a country across the sea. And we were at home here, and not about to leave for someplace else."

For him, the issues were local, now, like the East Europeans who spend too much time raising money for Israel and not enough on the local community. "The United Jewish Appeal just drains off money we could use here." He felt then as he does today, that "Jews are scattered all over the world and that's the way it ought to stay." The reason why the East Europeans set up organizations like the Jewish War Veterans ("It was typical. They should have joined the American Legion") is that they "ghettoize themselves because they aren't as comfortable as we are in the gentile community." He admitted that the phrase "Jewish state" upset him even today, but that "I'm not as gung-ho anymore. To tell you the truth, it's been pretty lonely down here the last few years."

He felt that Elmer Berger, the director of the Council for twenty years, had intruded the Council too intimately into the intricacies of

Middle East politics, and was glad to see him resign after the 1967 Six-Day War. "Berger was damn near pro-Arab he was so anti-Zionist and he just about ruined us." (Berger, in an interview with the *New York Times*, characterized the massive Jewish support of Israel as "hysteria," and charged that Israel had embarked "on aggression" in the Middle East. Promptly, five distinguished members of the board disavowed those views, including Stanley Marcus, the owner of Neiman-Marcus in Dallas. Sometime later Berger quietly resigned.)

My mother's commitment to the idea of the State of Israel was closely bound up in the shock and dismay over the sweeping slaughter of Hitler's "final solution." The children of the immigrant generation could surely see the photographs of the ovens in Auschwitz and say, "There, but for the grace of God, go I," for the only difference between the victims and the survivors was the decision to emigrate to America a few decades earlier. But what of Southern German Jews, now several generations into the American experience? What was their reaction to it?

"If it could happen to the Jews of Germany who were bankers and composers and doctors, it could happen anywhere," said a man in Atlanta whose family had come to America five generations earlier. "It filled me with self-doubt. And the Russian Jews here put it to us. I remember one old woman wagging her finger at me and cackling, 'So you think you are safe here, don't you? Well, so did the Jews of Germany!'"

Some of the descendants of the early Germans just didn't identify with the victims of the concentration camps. "We didn't have any relatives in the camps," said a man in Chattanooga. "Well," another woman remarked, "how did you feel about the little starving children in Biafra? Sure, it was a tragedy, but it didn't touch me." In New Orleans, a wealthy German woman described her feelings as "about like the flood in Florence—isn't it a shame about all that art."

The Jewish philosophers call it the sense of "Am"—peoplehood—the degree to which any Jew feels a part of all Jews everywhere. The closer the Jew was to the immigrant experience, the greater the identity with the victims of Hitler's inferno. It would be a gross injustice to paint a picture of all Reform Jews in the South as blissfully unmoved about Germany, but in the words of one rabbi, "The Reform Jews cared; they did not grieve."

The trauma of the German death camps sombered most of the

107

German Jews and softened the attitudes of the East Europeans toward them. "Zionist or not, Reform or Orthodox, shoemaker or lawyer," said a Zionist leader in Atlanta, "there was no difference to Hitler. After the war all Jews were alike, and deep down we all knew it."

The State of Israel profoundly changed the image of the Jew in the South. The underdog region, celebrated for the fierceness of the boys in gray against the overwhelming odds of Yankee cannons and superior numbers, deeply admired the Israeli courage when outmanned and, above all, respected a winner. "Them's damn fightin' Jews," a filling-station attendant in South Georgia said to me. "I always thought Jews were yaller, but those Palestinian Jews, man, they're tough."

Senator Hyman Rubin of Columbia, South Carolina, attributes Israel's popularity in the South partially to its reputation as a "scrapper." He referred to a recent Republican poll in South Carolina which showed that the most admired profession was the military and the most admired trait was not honesty or religion, as one might expect, but "toughness." So Israeli toughness rubbed off on Southern Jews, so much so that a legislator in a Southern state reported that an admitted Klansman saw a newspaper picture of Moshe Dayan on his desk and blurted out, "I admire that man more than anyone else in the world today except for George Wallace." A rabbi summed up, "If the gentiles appreciate something, it's always O.K."

Southern support for Israel is closely bound up in the tenets of the fundamentalist church, related to the belief in the return of the Jews to Israel as a precondition to the Second Coming. Thus, Israel is not an aberration of history but a fulfillment of a portion of the New Testament prophecy. Flonnie Maddox, the mother of former Governor Lester Maddox, has built a reputation in Georgia as a Bible-thumping speaker on the Sunday night evangelical circuit. Bruce Galphin wrote of her in his book, *The Riddle of Lester Maddox:*

> In early 1968 she traveled to the Holy Land with a group called the Intercession for Israel, whose mission is to convert Jews to Christianity. She is all on the side of the Israelis in their war with the Arabs. When an Israeli remarked to her, "We'll have Jordan," she replied, "You'll have every inch of it. God said you could."

The Moslem Mosque of Omar in Jerusalem, she is convinced, "is going to be removed. That's scriptural. Solomon's Temple is going to be rebuilt for Jesus. They're building a throne for him to sit on. . . . I'm going to sit with him on his throne. . . . [Jerusalem] is going to be my home for a thousand years."

There is also a sense in which the Israelis represent a white enclave encircled by dark and heathen peoples; so that a member of a Baptist church which had integrated in Birmingham could write a letter of protest to the local paper, pointing out that "the good Jews of Israel have maintained their purity as a people" by refusing to be overrun by the Arab nations surrounding them.

In the tense period just before the Six-Day War in 1967, as part of a national effort by national Jewish organizations, a group of the most prominent Jews in Georgia visited Governor Maddox to urge him to issue a statement supporting Israel, hoping that statements from American politicians across the country might forestall the outbreak of war in the Middle East. Maddox, according to one man who was there, readily agreed to the statement, and then surprised the group by volunteering that "everybody ought to be for Israel." They were all relieved but curious as to why Lester Maddox, at such a moment of peril in Jewish history, would offer such a sweeping opinion. Maddox winked. " 'Cause I ain't never seen a camel yet that can outrun a Cadillac."

"Israel has brought Jews up off their knees onto two feet," said a pawnshop owner in downstate Virginia. "For the first time, I feel more like a tank commander than a suffering old Jew. We'll whip the Russians and the Egyptians, too, if we have to."

He was reflecting on what he felt was the dramatic change in Southern political support for Israel once the Russians began to pour arms and missiles into Egypt. Senators like Harry Byrd, Herman Talmadge, and Strom Thurmond, always supporters of Israel in the Senate ("It's easy for them," a Jewish leader said. "They ain't no Ay-rab votes down here"), began to find new allies on the right and became outspoken partisans for American aid and arms. Eldon James, former national president of the American Legion from Hampton, Virginia, and Ed Fike, associate editor of the Richmond *Times Dispatch*, traveled the speaker's circuit for the United Jewish Appeal. Southerners also appreciated Israel's "eye for an eye" military style: The conservative Richmond *News Leader* complimented Israel when it bombed the Lebanon airport in retaliation for Lebanese support for Arab guerrillas who were shelling the Israeli settlements on the usually quiet Lebanese border; it suggested that "this country could well imitate Israel" when responding to incidents like the capture of the *Pueblo* by North Korea.

Old Reform families in Atlanta suddenly were pledging substantial sums to the emergency appeals of the UJA; Ben Cone, Jr., in Greensboro, converted from the Episcopal Church back to Judaism and headed the Israeli Bond campaign; enthusiasm mushroomed in other Reform temples where, a rabbi reported, "it used to be that the mere mention of the word 'Palestine' on Yom Kippur was enough to ruin the sacredness of the occasion." What had happened, almost imperceptibly, was that Jews who were not enthusiastic supporters of Israel were put on the defensive by the respect for Israel and its popularity in the gentile community. In short, the very fears that had caused the Reform community to recoil from the support of a Jewish state in 1948 ("What will the gentiles think?") turned them pro-Israel in 1967. A Reform Jew recalled as his own turning point a call from a retired admiral who said, "Ed, I'm glad you Jews kicked the shit out of 'em."

And the new breed of Reform rabbis, the men who had served in World War II and replaced the generation of rabbis who had been at their temples for four or five decades—Rothschild in Atlanta, Grafman in Birmingham, Wax in Memphis—all came to realize that identification with Israel was the only hope for the American Jewish community. With the support (and pressure) of the rising number of members in their congregations from East European backgrounds, all the Reform congregations in the South would pull back from the so-called classical Reform to a more moderate position on most of the ritual changes that had marked their temples in earlier days.

NINE

"Miz Evans" and Mister Mayor

I'Ve never quite understood why both my parents immersed themselves so thoroughly in the organizational aggravations of the Durham Jewish community. They were not religious people, but their work in Zionist organizations and the local synagogue drew them as religious rituals—a way to act out their Jewishness, to relate to the world as Jews, to express emotional ties with Jews everywhere, but most important, to relate to each other. They communicated as equal partners, just as they did in the business downtown. My father acted more out of instinct and habit—city, church, and university were the natural burdens of the civilized man of his community. But for my mother, nothing carried a higher priority than her work for Israel; even his election as mayor took second place. One thing was clear—in the Durham Jewish community, I was Mutt *and* Sara's boy.

The walls of the playroom downstairs reflected decades of activities—plaques and awards from civic organizations, the university, and Jewish organizations: my mother's lifetime membership on the National Board of Hadassah; my father's "outstanding young man of the year" award from the Chamber of Commerce; certificates for planting trees in Israel; appreciation plaques from the Tau Epsilon Phi fraternity at Chapel Hill; an award from the University of North Carolina Alumni Association when he served as president; a parchment from the seven consecutive statewide United Jewish Appeal campaigns he led, and another from the ten statewide Bonds for Israel campaigns he was chairman of. Yet Mother

111

frequently complained, "If we had only lived in a bigger city, we could have done so much more in Jewish life," to which Dad would invariably reply, "No, Sara, we would have been lost in the shuffle."

We never kept kosher, but we didn't serve ham or bacon in the house; neither of them read Hebrew even fairly; we didn't go to Friday night services all that often, and they kept the business open on Saturdays and worked then, too. But Mother always insisted I be present for the major Jewish holidays, and for Friday night meals, the special time for friends, guests, and family.

My father presided with great style then. He would stumble through the first part of the blessing before the meal, then hand the "holy wine" to me for the second part, all the family and guests joining in at the end to sing the tune I had learned at camp. On Passover, when no less than twenty-five people attended, including Jewish girls from Duke that Mother was anxious to fix up with boys from Chapel Hill, he transformed the table into a jovial city council meeting, calling on each guest to read sections of the Haggadah so that everyone would stay involved. He tried to update the symbols, like comparing the four cups of wine to Roosevelt's four freedoms—which would cause my grandfather Isaac to complain vigorously, but he would plod on, calling on Grandpa to "give the next reading in the original Hebrew."

Both my parents were accomplished public speakers. From him, the words spilled out, smooth and liquid, flowing as from any politician who had welcomed as many American Legion conventions, cut ribbons on as many stores, and greeted as many evangelists as he had. She on the other hand dreaded every appearance, the process supercharged by the burden she felt of raising money for Israel. I never heard her make a light speech. It was always tortured and emotional. She would agonize over her Hadassah speeches for days, mumbling in the bedroom while practicing before the mirror, honing her phrases and inflections. On a tour of Southern cities like Memphis and Montgomery, where she traveled as Hadassah's Southern accent, she could bring an audience to tears and then cry along with them as she talked about the plight of the Jews and the need for support. She could spellbind a crowd. Once during a speech when some vandals tossed a rock through the window of the *shul*, she kept right on talking to a crowd so thoroughly engrossed that no one even flinched.

Everyone always told her she had "the mind of a man"—by that they meant that she understood the intricacies of finance, the

112

vagaries of the business world, the sensitivities to the politics of Jewish organizational work. Being the oldest daughter in a family of nine, she had learned to manage people, a skill that saved her when her father became ill, forcing her to drop out of college to manage the store in Durham. Her mother, Jennie, had worried about her as a little girl, watching her personality change with the family financial responsibilities weighing on her. Sara was the serious one, the responsible one, the child Jennie counted on to take care of things at home while her mother worked at the store, the one the other girls rebelled against and even enjoyed disobeying, who couldn't play with the others because she couldn't seem to integrate her position of disciplinarian with being a playmate. As adults, they would all affectionately call her "Miz Evans," to acknowledge her special place as head of the family.

Hadassah had been her life from her early twenties. My grandmother Jennie wanted to see Palestine before she died, so in 1933, Dad scraped together the money for Jennie, her limp from childhood polio growing worse with age, to see the promised land with her daughter. The experience fired my mother's idealism and her sense of mission, and from then on she devoted all of her emotional and physical energy to Israel through Hadassah. For years she was president of the Durham chapter as well as of the seaboard region, and she represented the South on the National Board. Year in and year out, she would argue the gritty details for the annual donor affair; battle with the Federation when the men wanted to cut down on the percentage contribution to Israel because of local needs; and sit on the telephone for hours and hours squeezing ads out of local gentile businesses for the Hadassah yearbook, complaining of their reluctance to my father, who would make it a point at the next Kiwanis Club luncheon to tell the president of Montgomery-Aldridge Tire Company that he really ought to buy a larger ad because "those women treat that yearbook like their shopping Bible."

"Hello, Mr. Aldridge, this is Mrs. E. J. Evans. We're trying to save the children again this year . . ." I honestly felt that she built the Hadassah hospital, brick by brick, right at that phone on the breakfast table.

I had seen it happen again and again—a half dozen young wives of Duke professors and interns, newly elected board members, uncertain and apprehensive, traipsing to our house night after night in the summer and fall to plan the annual Youth Aliyah fund-raising affair or to plot out that year's Hadassah program. Most of them were not informed, and Mom would have to fire them up again about Israel, unrolling several posters from El Al Airlines she had picked up on her last trip to New York, to decorate the community room at the synagogue the night of the affair.

Then a shy, hesitant voice might complain, "But this is my first year, Miz Evans, and I've never spoken before a crowd that big before . . ."

"Don't worry, Ruthie, we'll write it all out for you and you'll stand up there straight and it'll be terrific."

Jewish pygmalions, all of them, and thus did Hadassah in Durham go on and on.

"You see," she would point out as the eager neophytes took notes furiously, "the character of Youth Aliyah has changed . . . not just saving the children from the Nazi holocaust anymore [she was starting from point zero that night] but immigration from Arab lands and South America . . . God, what a shock Argentina was . . . and then from Rumania and Russia, but we're not supposed to say much about that or they might stop it"—bringing confidential news from national conventions or straight from a private letter to American leaders from David Ben Gurion.

"Now, remember, it takes six hundred dollars to save a child—to buy milk, clothes, blankets . . . and our campaign is not just for members of Hadassah, but for everybody in Durham and Chapel Hill." Then, she would unveil the national kits, which over the years she had streamlined for local use.

The women would leave and she'd smile and touch them farewell, ever charming and correct, and then she'd collapse in a chair. Exhaustion! "I just can't do it another year, I just can't." We heard it exactly that way for twenty years. Durham was her battlefield, no one to be left out or let up on, as if God himself would judge her by the money Hadassah raised in our home town.

She rarely took time for community work. "Who'll take care of the Jews if we don't do it ourselves?" she would ask. But once, when she agreed to be chairman of the women's division of the Community Fund, they broke all records. "These Durham women just never had worked with some good old Hadassah techniques," she explained. She indulged in no other outside activities, even though she was a good enough musician to have once played the saxophone in the Nachamson family band and the flute in the Duke orchestra (the only girl in a black-tie orchestra wearing a red dress to concerts so that she stood out like a "rose in a coalbin").

Neither of my parents was ever active in the B'nai B'rith organization. Located up dingy stairs above an old store downtown, the B'nai B'rith "lodge" mostly drew the poker players who kept the card room stale with cigar smoke, and bridge club ladies who didn't care so much about Hadassah and preferred meeting there rather than at someone's house. I asked my mother why she never participated and she stated, "They said they cared about fighting anti-Semitism but I felt the best way to do that was by working for Israel."

She read constantly about Israel, and worried so much about its future that often she couldn't sleep. Whenever I crept in as a small boy to kiss her goodnight, she, with cold cream on her face, would be reading the Hadassah newsletter, or the Joint Distribution Committee reports, or a Zionist Organization of America emergency flash to special leaders. When Hadassah rummage sales occurred, she would always march me up to my closet to defend every stitch of clothes, hanger by hanger, as crucial to my wardrobe.

She served on panels discussing the Middle East at Chapel Hill and Duke, and would fire off letters to the editor to correct a visiting Arab lecturer who had distorted a piece of history about the Arab refugees or the U.N. partitioning in 1948. Once, when a Duke professor we invited over to dinner expressed some doubt about the wisdom of establishing the State of Israel, she said to him, "People like you used to worry me. But now we have the state and I can't be bothered with your complexes any more."

During World War II, when newspaper columnists scorned reports of extermination camps as typical Jewish exaggeration "too vast for credulity," my parents signed more than fifty affidavits for refugees who had to have assurance of a job from an American citizen in order to receive a visa. A few worked in the stockroom of the store until they could learn English and find more permanent work, but most of them remained strangers whom my parents never heard from. Mother recalled the Rose family reunion in Durham when Fanny Rose introduced her to a roomful of people— little children and young couples—saying, "None of these people would be here today had it not been for the Evanses."

After the war, my father even arranged for two former fighter pilots from Reidsville, both gentiles, to fly for the newly declared State of Israel when the Israelis put together their slap-dash air force of cast-off planes and soldiers of fortune.

The first time we included the memorial prayer for the six million in the Passover seder ("suffering under a modern Pharaoh"), I piped up and asked, "Who decided that everybody was supposed to say the new prayer?" She answered quickly, "The Jews did."

She was a sucker for any painting that had a scene of Jerusalem, olive trees, or flowing white-bearded Jewish prophets. She conceived the idea of mounting postcards of the Chagall stained-glass windows on black velvet and giving them as gifts to all her friends and sisters. Every sister was active in Hadassah, making inevitable a triumphant trip to Israel they took together a few years ago, just the eight of them, leaving the men at home. To celebrate the event, the Jerusalem *Post* carried their picture with an appropriately intimate caption, "Sara and her seven sisters."

A couch separated two bookcases in the den: Mother kept one side and Dad the other. Her side consisted, among other things, of seven or eight picture books on Israel, *Marjorie Morningstar*, *The Living Talmud*, *The Eddie Cantor Story*, *A Bird's Eye View of Jewish History*, *Only in America*, *The Life of Theodor Herzl*, a biography of Henrietta Szold, and a home guide to the Jewish holidays. His side featured *The Last Hurrah*, *The Age of Moguls*, *Tobacco Tycoon*, *The Story of Durham*, *The Speaker's Encyclopedia of Stories and Quotations*, *All the King's Men*, *How I Made Two Million Dollars in the Stock Market*, *2,500 Jokes for All Occasions*, and popular books on Israel, like *Cast a Giant Shadow* and *Exodus*. The den was for the new books; the old books we kept in the playroom downstairs. Though they both read books mostly of professional interest—either Jewish, political, or business—she loved the permanent quality of the written word: "Nothing lasts that isn't written down," she always said.

She and Jennie influenced my father enormously. They applauded his leadership in Zionist causes and he began to catch the spirit of the ideology and revel in the meetings with the giant Zionist personalities of the thirties and forties—unbelievable, my parents thought, that Mutt and Sara Evans from North Carolina would be going to Washington to hear speakers like Chaim Weizmann and Stephen S. Wise. Zionists were rare in the South in those days—Zionism was considered radical politically, a cause for dreamers, a waste of time and money, even in the Jewish community where the Evanses were known as the *"fabrenta"* Zionists (translated literally as "red hot"). They were young people, attractive, very Southern in personality, in a movement dominated by an older generation of European-born leaders from New York who cast across the South and considered them "gems in the desert."

In the Beth El Synagogue at home, where he served as president for ten years, my father tried to play peacemaker in a congregation that spanned the generations and the extremes in religious conviction. The spiritual titan, old man Solomon Dworsky, kept a skullcap on his head down in his pawnshop—a small, feisty personality with fierce blue eyes and a faint Yiddish voice that camouflaged his iron will. He would sit on the front row at services wrapped in a huge bedsheet-sized *tallis* and tap his fingers while muttering "hun-uh" if the cantor tried to skip anything. Mr. Dworsky was the scholar of the dominant Orthodox wing of the *shul* board of trustees—unyielding watchdogs, though some of them like Nathan Lieberman would often try to mediate. (Nathan's credentials as a purist were somewhat damaged the night his beautiful daughter Annette won the Miss Durham contest, with the Orthodox community cheering her on from the audience with an occasional "C'mon Hannah-la.")

On the other side was the next generation of men, who could have been their sons—men in whose lives religion played a smaller part. They were more concerned with attracting new membership, building a new building, driving to services in a new car, and streamlining the service. The targets for the debate were the potential new members on the Duke faculty, men like Donald Kaufman in urology, who rarely came to services but just might if he understood more and felt that there was a happy atmosphere in Sunday school for his children. My father once described the situation to a gentile friend as "trying to run a church made up of Baptists, Methodists, and Catholics, and conducting a service to please everyone."

The battles raged over resolutions to expel from membership those who intermarried or did not keep kosher or did not close their businesses on Yom Kippur. Even if a gentile wife converted, the old men insisted that she be refused membership, arguing that membership entitled her to burial in the Jewish cemetery, and the idea of spending eternity lying next to a converted *shiksa* would send the Orthodox men into convulsions that my father feared might hasten the event. The arguments over firing the rabbi or shortening the service or sending more money to the yeshivas could easily turn into shouting matches and spasms of God-summoning righteousness—old men stalking out of meetings as they sought to talk across the chasm to another generation already lost to Orthodoxy.

The clashes were not always between the generations. Sometimes jealousy and prestige motivated the debates among the middle-aged men who ran small loan companies or were accountants, those for whom the synagogue was the only power arena, the only activity outside the home to acquire whatever recognition life held in store for them. They liked to argue over money matters, proposing to remove memberships from families that could afford to give more but didn't, or trying to cut back the allocation of funds to Israel, which would bring my mother to her feet for an all-out plea for Durham's role in the future of the Jewish people. Some just felt a surge of importance if they could argue with my father, sarcastically calling him "Mister Mayor" while accusing him of lacking principles over religious issues he somehow had to find a compromise for. Like Jews everywhere, every man had strong views, passionately held, and the discussion on religious questions could be ugly, rude, and personal. My father once told a city council meeting that "being president of a congregation with Orthodox, Conservative and Reform members makes handling a group of twelve city councilmen a cinch."

Inevitably, the older generation passed from control, a sad event symbolized by the decision to build a new combined synagogue–community center on a better side of town near Duke University. Beth El received a good start on a building fund during the war, but the local banks discouraged churches from seeking building loans, because in a small town the banks found it difficult to foreclose in case of default. My father and five others personally endorsed a note with the Negro life insurance company for the remaining money. Max Lieberman and my mother served as co-chairmen of the building fund, making it clear to all contributors that pledges for the new building would not allow them to decrease their contributions to Youth Aliyah or the United Jewish Appeal.

118

I once asked my father why he put up with the irritations of long meetings and bitter debates, especially with his other community work drawing him to meetings two and three times a week. "Well," he said, "I just felt I could keep the congregation from breaking up."

TEN

"Jesus Loves Me"

The South is . . . Christ-haunted.
Mystery and Manners,
Flannery O'Connor

I O N C E went to a summer night revival on the side of town
where the mill hands and the poor whites lived. Three of us had ventured over for some free fried chicken and barbecue, since there was
nothing else to do. The tent flaps were up so there would be some
breath of air passing through; inside the tent, I sat toward the rear
on a straight-back folding chair and pulled off the sneakers my
mother made me wear, so I could join my friends who were drawing aimlessly in the sawdust and wood shavings below with their
bare toes.

Sunday night revivals, summer entertainment in many a Southern town, provided an excuse for people who belonged to different
churches to come together and visit with each other, drawing all
ages and all sects into a community-wide event preceded by several
weeks of ballyhoo. They usually started before dark with a church
supper and lasted several hours, ending maybe at ten. If it was
done professionally, you could just sit there and take in the Ozark
College choir singing "He Walks Me," or the Todd Twins—one
playing the banjo and the other the guitar—little shavers who
could pick a five-string claw-hammer style and startle the audience
to cheers with their toe-patting, upbeat rhythms for the Lord;
always an accordion solo by a young stud with his hair slicked
back, who would flutter up the girls the way he could sail into a
song; a twelve-year-old bow-tied preacher boy who would bob and

120

weave for Jesus in a high squeaky voice ("That little feller'll sure be bringing in the flock some day"); and then the Elmer family with Ma on the piano and Pa leading the two girls and little Bo harmonizing their favorite hymns like "Washed in the Blood of the Lamb," with the audience finally clapping and singing along. All this led up to the moment they had all been waiting for.

The evangelist seemed to appear suddenly at the microphone and patiently waited for the crowd to simmer down to receive him. He opened his Bible dramatically, holding it so the pages spilled over his hand, leaving his other hand free to pound the podium, poke an accusing finger at a sinner, or raise a palm to heaven when he needed to. The church ladies sat prissily correct, poised and ready, fanning themselves with Jesus-in-the-Garden-of-Gethsemane fans from the local funeral parlor. The little children climbed in their fathers' laps for cuddling in an uneasy moment. The teenage boys in church pants too short for them sat in one row together, where they could glance across the aisle from time to time at the clump of blushing girls in long-sleeved blouses (it wasn't nice to show bare arms).

The preacher always started up slowly, probing and testing his audience, watching the amen corner carefully, gauging his speed and his intensity, easing stealthily into the sermon like a hunter quietly loading his shotgun so as not to flush the covey of quail too early. But you could sense him catch his stride and quicken the pace; once in full gallop, for the next hour visions would fly all around the tent and surge into the audience, and he would stop from time to time and say, "Let us pray," and everybody would close their eyes clam-tight while he'd keep on driving, threatening a terrifying apocalypse if you didn't repent and personally pledge yourself to Jesus.

"The Lord wants us to pick up His cross. The devil is a deceiver, a liar . . . he won't let you sleep. He'll trick you into gambling and drinking and smoking . . . the wages of sin is death; but salvation is in Jesus Christ. Do you curse, swear, or talk ugly?"

Well, I had pretty much done some of those things, especially cussing, and I had sneaked a taste of something awful from the bottom of a glass at my mother's bridge party, and a bunch of us had smoked rabbit-weed on a Boy Scout camp-out, so I would start to squirm like a sinner in my folding chair, which I hated sitting in to begin with because it was rented from the funeral home.

"You can't steal salvation. It was blood bought and He shed it

121

for you. You have to earn salvation on your own. The blood of Jesus Christ cleanses you and can be that salvation. It took the blood of Calvary to save mankind—the blood of Jesus was pure as a lamb and you can be born again."

That blood stuff always made me a little squeamish—free flowing, stomach-turning, terrifying. They loved it, even seemed to want to wash in it or pretend to taste it when they sipped the juice at church—ghostly, magical blood smeared all over them, purifying and redemptive.

"He took your place on the Calvary Cross; and His bones were twisted for you. For God so loveth the world that He gave His only begotten Son."

The people just sat there dead-still, not flicking an eyelash, hypnotized almost, while the preacher plowed on with a pounding, rhythmic, physical sermon, screaming purple patches of arm-waving and sweat-pouring salvation, with an all-out, both-barrels presentation of a muscular, hard-hitting Christ whose beckoning arms and encompassing spirit would bring eternal joy and everlasting love if only that very night in that very place you would open your hardened heart and accept Him. "And He washed the feet and gave wine to the weary traveler . . . not the fermented devil's brew you drink today. . . . I hate people who twist the Bible for their own purposes."

The microphone would be turned on full tilt, engulfing us in tremors of sound until the message plunged into our soul, and released a deep gushing liberation. "The only way a sinner can stand forgiven before God is to stand in Jesus Christ."

And he wasn't satisfied just to get the people there to accept Jesus . . . he wanted *everybody*. Somehow, I hadn't counted on that.

"The Bible tells us that if a fruit tree doesn't bear fruit, you cut it down and plant a new one. Well, God does that. And Grade-A fruit, my friends, is a new convert. There are people here tonight who have been in the church all their lives and never led anyone else to church. My friends, if we have a hundred people here tonight, we ought to have a hundred soul winners. One soul each . . ."

And I wasn't sure, but it looked like he was pointing right at *me!* Suddenly, instead of just watching him pray and whoop it up for Jesus, they were summoning Jesus to come snatch me away—*I* was the target for the sermon, the reason for the meeting, the errant soul brought to this mystic site for cleansing and capture.

The people were moving with him now, enraptured by his swaying, finger-jabbing savior sounds—honey-voiced love-begging one moment and sizzle-tongued hellfire the next. He had worked them up far as they would go and it was time to slap them with the message.

"Are you saved?" he cried out, both arms spread open to the congregation like the very gates of heaven. "When you die will you go to heaven? Oh, say it, say it, 'I am saved,'" and the crowd murmured, "I am saved," and he had them now and knew it. "Say it again." And they did, everybody around me and my friends too, cutting a glance at me out of the corner of their eyes.

"Now, raise one hand, friends," and he showed them how. "Lift it high as you can. Lift it and say 'I am saved.' Higher. You can do it. Let Him in your heart. If you can't lift it, something's wrong."

My chair turned to ice steel, shooting cold terror up my spine. As every other hand in the tent reached for the heavens, I sat there paralyzed, alone, all alone, frozen into motionless fear, sensing that every eye had turned to the nonbeliever to see what I was going to do. I was awash in cold sweat on a death-hot night, not belonging there, and praying my own prayer to whisk me home where I could scrunch under the covers in my bed. Suddenly someone grabbed my wrist and pulled my arm up high above my head, and my lungs stretched and the blood stirred and the liquid rushed to my pounding heart. "My God, it feels *good!*" I blurted, shocked at the sound of those words. Wild-eyed and afraid, I jerked my hand away and bolted out of the tent as fast as I could, heading for home.

And while I pumped for all I was worth, I could hear the microphone in the distance still blaring the Lord's word: "Come down front here and kneel . . . will you come, my friends? . . . that's it, just line up right here. . . ." My head was racing my heart for home—suppose I had stayed and been left alone on my row, the only person sitting while the whole tent filed down front to kneel and pray. And then a shattering thought—maybe I had converted right there and then by that shot of energy rushing through my raised arm. I didn't know what you had to do to convert anyway. So I ran home to my mother thinking Jesus had gotten me at last and vowing never to go to one of those things again.

123

Southern Jews encounter a special kind of Jesus—a constant presence, a real, honest-to-goodness anthropomorphic personification of the Son of God Himself perched on the shoulder of every believer as friend and comforter, punisher and all-powerful. The Southern Jesus still walks among us, capable of miracles: curing the sick and making the lame to walk and the blind to see; a haunting righteous figure, stern and straight-backed, ever present and vigilant, able to mete out instant justice for bad acts and keep accurate count of the good for the moment. He would come again to measure us all on a thundering judgment day.

For Jews who live outside the major Southern cities and grow up swimming in a sea of Bible-belt fundamentalism, the confrontation is inescapable; it can be piercing, humorous, pathetic, and unnerving. The mystery of Jesus terrified and captivated me, like a wisp calling from a marsh to lure me to some misty, shrouded consecration. His life, the miracles He performed, His death and resurrection all enticed me, not out of beauty or passion but out of a morbid fascination . . . a combination of irresistible rapture and mortal fear. Was there a life after death, a heaven to frolic in and a hell to burn in? And was I excluded by some ancient sin, so fundamental a crime that God was eternally angry at me? Judaism never spoke of the life after death as the reason for life itself; and thus there were no answers for Jews, only questions. And as a Jew, I was always an outsider though there was a role for me in their scheme—to return to the fold and atone for rejecting Him. That was the shame, the oppressive burden of Christian history. Some Jews in the South crumble under it and others try to ignore it; some slink and hide, others despair, but most absorb it and block it out, and survive. All of us in the South had to face it in one way or another.

"Be especially careful of the *goyim*," I heard from the old men around the synagogue. "Converting a Jew is a special blessing for them."

And so it was that Christianity wanted me—yea, needed me to feed its ultimate prophecy and hasten His return to earth. And there wasn't much time, for the mass conversion to bring on the Second Coming, closer each day than the day before, to redeem a world caught up in torment and sin, a world on the brink of the fiery retribution that the Lord would summon when He decided to return—fire and ice in a cataclysmic, brutal, cosmic catastrophe—

a final clap of thunder and then the explosive rapture of a soaring, blinding reappearance.

Children translate the phenomenon of deity into a strange and wonderous banter, out of innocence in playmate interactions, mixing friendship with unintentional cruelty and misdirected love.

"Why don't you believe in Jesus?" I was asked again and again in my childhood, at playgrounds and parties, by strangers and friends, by the more probing sons of ministers who wanted to discuss it further, and by the good old boys who would be happy with almost any answer.

Usually, I would compliment Jesus and try to leave it at that if I could get away with it. "I believe Jesus was the greatest man who ever lived," was my standard reply, hoping that would end it in blurred agreement. As I grew older and more confident, I graduated to an ecumenical, "Well, he was sure a great prophet, just like Moses, Isaiah, and Paul." (I abandoned that one when someone asked me if I would therefore "accept Moses as my personal savior.") But if the question was asked by the starched, clean, fuzzy-cheeked type who went to Fellowship meetings on Sunday night and wore white sweat socks with a blue suit and squinted at me suspiciously like I was some incarnate evil, then I knew I was in for some sharp probing and I'd have to be more specific. "I sure do agree with you that he was the most perfect man that ever lived and the best teacher, but we just believe in the Father alone."

Not belligerent, but it might have sounded so; invariably, the persistent ones would come back with: "If you think He was the greatest man that ever lived, then you must also think He was the greatest liar that ever lived, for He Himself said that He was the Son of God and the Savior of Mankind." Of course, they hadn't counted on my ace in the hole, the stopper that usually ended argument and left them crumpled and confused: "Jesus was a Jew, you know." Their chins would drop, they would stutter and try to escape, but not before I finished them off—"and so was Mary and all the disciples too."

Of course, the ones steeped in Bible debate would admit that Jesus was Jewish because the Jews were "the chosen people," chosen, that is, not like we considered ourselves chosen to bring the law to mankind, but chosen to be the instrument by which Jesus came into the world. But then, they maintained, the Jews rejected Him, and if we don't repent and convert, we will nosedive directly

125

into the waiting jaws of hell. But I learned to hold my own in one of these rare toe-to-toe battles, because He said right on the cross, I'd always point out, that He died for all man's sins, and therefore the Jews didn't reject Him, mankind did.

Still, why the Jews? I would think. Maybe we *were* kind of special. I remember a girl, the kind who always smiled when she argued, her hair pulled back severely, pasty-faced and anemic, with that syrupy missionary ring in her voice, the kind who played the piano, wore hose with her sandals, and viewed the Jews as "early Christians," offering this opinion: "I don't know why Christ chose the Jews; He could just as well have chosen the Orientals or the Negroids. Perhaps He chose the Jews because they were receptive to Him, the same way a teacher chooses her pets."

Grammar school especially was heavily oriented to good Christian upbringing, so we started off assembly each morning with the Lord's Prayer, but I would never close my eyes, for fear that would be real praying. Mostly I would just look down with my head bowed enough so people couldn't see my eyes were open, and make hissing sounds during the part that went "and forgive u*s* our trespa*sses* a*s* we forgive tho*se* who tre*s*pa*ss* against u*s*." Singing hymns was trickier, because everybody's eyes were open and people next to you could tell right away you weren't singing, so it demanded a lot more ingenuity. One maneuver I used often was to sing all the words except "Christian" or "Jesus," stopping or humming the notes when the forbidden words came up, or substituting "Moses" for "Jesus" whenever it occurred. Thus, when I led my class in for sixth-grade graduation, I marched shoulders back and head erect singing out proudly to all the parents at the ceremony, "Onward hum-hum soldiers, marching as to war, with the cross of Moses, standing at the fore."

Easter was the scariest holiday and no amount of talk about bunny rabbits, baskets filled with paper grass, purple baby chicks, and colored eggs could muffle the horror of the nails being driven into His palms, the thorns digging into His brow, the blood trickling down His forehead, the utter power of the stone rolling back from the tomb so they could intone mournfully, "He has risen."

Easter was a time for singing "Gladly, the Cross-Eyed Bear," and it was a time for your best friends to worry about the Second

126

Coming for they "knew not when or where" Doomsday would arrive but were made so aware of its imminence at Easter that they were afraid it might happen while they were sitting on the toilet.

Easter touched everything. It even ruined the beautiful white and pink dogwood trees with the legend that after the tall stately tree was used for the cross, God gnarled its limbs and stole the aroma and left the blossoms touched with blood where the spikes were driven in. Easter was a time to brag about how the Last Supper was a Passover meal, and get your answers ready to "why the Jews killed Christ." "We didn't do it; the Romans did" was best because it was confirmed in all the gladiator movies; but a Jewish friend once stumbled apologetically into "We didn't know he was the Son of God; we thought he was just a prophet." (The Jews were always rough on their prophets.)

Easter was also a time when the half-mad Bible-toting mendicants of both races would walk the streets downtown screaming again and again with unsurpassed lung power, "The Lord told me to tell the world that Jesus was sure to come." Once, when I was over in back of the grammar school shooting marbles in the dust with a friend, a huge, fat black woman, wearing white robes and a white habit, with a red cross on her mountainous breasts, was trudging toward town yelling that message every few minutes. She veered off her route toward us and asked in a booming voice, "You believe that Jesus is soon to come, son?"

"No, ma'am," I answered meekly, still on my knees looking up. "I believe he was a great teacher."

"A what?" she sputtered.

"Well, ma'am, I think he was the greatest teacher that ever lived," and I scooped up my prize shooters and headed for home.

My best friends worried about the disposition of my soul, friends like the twins Buck and Billy Farrell, the three of us inseparable until I moved out of the neighborhood in the eighth grade. They were not identical twins. Billy had the delicate hands of an artist and startled blue eyes; he painted, but wasn't the fierce type, thirsty for life. He groped, this somber and detached boy, wandering through the day like a sleepwalker from a distant place, often lapsing into inexplicable pauses in conversation, not pensive pauses but vacant gaps of silence. He had no friends that I ever knew about. Buck, too, stood alone but he was a hulking brute of a boy

127

who could smash a snowball into another guy's face and then glare him into meekness. In neighborhood football games, all of us were afraid to tackle him, knowing he would club us with those powerful forearms, developed as a child hatcheting the small branches off young trees in the wooded lot behind his house.

Billy was childlike into his teens and sensitive to slights; because some of the boys on our block teased him about his paintings, he seemed to overcompensate to prove his manhood, jumping from absurd heights and daring us to follow, or climbing higher into trees than anyone else would risk. Billy painted in rich oils, religious canvases like the Bible scene his mother hung in the living room—a colorful judgment day depicting Christ rising out of the orange and blue holocaust, soaring into the heavens with the faces of Mary and the key apostles folded cleverly into the whiteness of His robes and the billows of the clouds. Everyone avoided Buck, fearing his explosive temper. He had dark forbidding eyes set deep in their sockets, and his moods swung wildly from smoky melancholy to unbridled silliness, animated by a hoarse, uncontrolled laugh, toothy and excessive, always roaring too heartily at small jokes. When they fought, and that was often, the cruelty erupted with a primeval fury reserved for two beings struggling for air in the same womb. The violence mesmerized us, the resounding pop on the jaw invariably followed by a fleet-footed Billy barely escaping a lumbering Buck, and hiding out for hours while Buck stalked the neighborhood with his hands balled into tight fists.

I experienced Christianity through the Farrell boys, for they believed, or said they did, because they were too afraid not to. I'm sure my differences were as unsettling to them as their beliefs were to me. Sometimes a chilling confrontation would poke through the boyhood calm and shatter my equilibrium.

Once, when I spent the night at their house, Billy shook me awake with a shocking intensity to tell me about a fiery dream. "I don't want you to go to Hell. I want you to be in Heaven with us. So be saved, Sonny, please be saved, so your soul won't burn up."

Once the orbits of our lives changed, I saw little of them, though we all ended up at the university, and I knew they were living together in a rooming house just off campus. I remember seeing Billy at the beginning of our sophomore year, after he had spent the summer in Indiana trying to sell Bibles. Huddled in failure, he moaned over the humiliation with mournful words that wilted as

128

the sounds slipped over the edge of sanity. "I didn't sell a one . . . not a single one," and he looked beyond the trees into himself to fix the blame. A few months later, Buck found him dangling from a steam pipe in their living room, with a hi-fi almost burned out from playing over and over again the religious music he hanged himself by.

Southern Jewish parents have to face a literal Jesus, and they do the best they can. "Is He true?" you ask, and they answer, "Well, they sure do believe it, and you have to respect their beliefs if you want them to respect yours. . . ." But in the early years, I wanted to believe, too, especially when Billy and Buck skipped off to vacation Bible school each June and left me sitting on the curb waiting for them to come home each day with the little copper ash trays they made, and the birdhouses and the jewelry boxes fashioned out of cigar boxes, chattering about the missionaries in South America or the character stories about Peter and Paul. I did believe, too, in miracles through prayer. When my dog was run over and I faced the idea of death for the first time, I was deeply consoled that we would be reunited when the dead were roused on judgment day.

Southerners bathe in hero worship and Jesus was a folk hero to my friends and to me. He could feed the multitudes and star in the Christmas story, heal the lepers and preach the Sermon on the Mount. "Do y'all have somebody like we got Jesus?" I was once asked. Thus, I summoned Moses to replace Jesus on my religious pedestal, mainly because he came along as a respectable substitute at Passover, usually near Easter when the Jesus legend became unbearable. Moses was more than that, of course. He could talk to God, get Him to open up the Red Sea, tap water out of a rock, and turn a rod into a snake. Moses was a tough-ass leader, too, who could lick the Egyptians, free his people, and climb up on Mt. Sinai all alone to receive the Ten Commandments. Perhaps I was reaching the age of awareness, but living in the Bible-drenched atmosphere of a stifling New Testament drove me to Old Testament stories out of self-defense. After all, the Christians acknowledged the primacy of the Old Testament, and its very age made it closer to the roots of faith and truth than any later document.

I would imagine Goliath as big as our three-story house and would aim rocks at my roof to see if I could hit him right between the eyes. And when my mother showed me a picture that revealed that David's slingshot wasn't Y-shaped like mine, but just a long, leather strap he wore at his side and then flung around his head like a cowboy slinging a lariat, it just didn't seem a very good way to aim a rock. I confirmed its inferiority when I almost broke a window in the house; I tried it again, and hit the garage directly behind me. But then, just because *I* couldn't didn't mean that David couldn't, and certainly a little kid going out to face Goliath would take the best slingshot he could find.

The emotional reality of religious isolation came crashing grimly into my life in the Christmas season, that six-week countdown that left me a solitary speck of gloom in a madcap world of ecstatic celebration.

It started just after Thanksgiving in grammar school, when the class decorated the room with cutouts of jagged Christmas trees covered in sparkle dust, gingerbread men with red-candy buttons, and red paper Santas smiling through cotton beards. The project that received the most attention was the large papier-mâché replica of the Nativity in the front of the classroom. The most artistic students molded figures out of chicken wire and the rest of us dipped strips of newspaper in flour and water and helped pat them into shape. I'd always try to shift around and work on the animals or the stable walls so I wouldn't have to get involved with any of the real holy stuff. The eyes of the donkeys and the sheep were painted to make them look as if they were peering curiously into the wooden manger, that dark place of innocence and mysticism; and the scene would stay there for weeks haunting our arithmetic class and the spelling bees, the smell of real straw from Gorman Reagan's farm wafting through the room, even Frances Page's baby doll looking frighteningly authentic once they wrapped the rags around it. I remember wondering if Baby Jesus ever wet His swaddling clothes, a thought so irreverent it got me through a lot of Christmases, and started me on a course toward the development of a Christmas survival kit consisting of various sacrilegious insights: What must the stable have smelled like with all those cowpies around? Did Baby Jesus' halo stick around when He messed up His pants? What did He think when He was my age and discovered, like Superboy, that He could walk on the water and make it thunder? The real religious ones in class called it "Jesus' Birthday," but they never blew out candles for Him and what would a cake look like anyway with almost two thousand candles?

130

The most dismal moment came during the sixth-grade assembly at the annual presentation of the Christmas pageant, when the choir would recite all the verses of Matthew while the rest of us acted out the drama. The teacher assigned me, the only Jewish boy in the class, the honor of playing Joseph, the number one boy's role, but I knew right away that I couldn't go through with something that close-in to the manger. I worried for days what to do, not telling my parents because they might pull me out of the play altogether, and call too much attention to me. Finally, I dredged up the courage to talk to the teacher, and carefully explained that I didn't think this was such a good role for me and, though I was honored to have been chosen, I would be just as happy as a shepherd boy or as the Star in the East. No, she thought, they were somewhat religious roles too, and she would try to think of something more secular and less objectionable. I ended up, typecast no doubt, as the tax collector, the heartless representative of King Herod, pounding the table, demanding oppressive taxes from poor pregnant Mary and dutiful Joseph, thus forcing them to leave town for that historic rendezvous.

I played the role with verve, in Arab headdress made from a bath towel. At the performance, under brilliant direction, I was so excessive that I got the biggest laughs of the day. Joseph plunked down a few coins but that was not enough for me; then he pulled out his pockets and shrugged in pantomime poverty, but that didn't cut any ice; he even gestured toward his doe-eyed wife in her delicate state of pillow-pregnancy, but my heart was stone to the holy couple. Finally in disgust I ordered them away with a sweep of my arm and he took gentle Mary off the stage to flee to Bethlehem.

I could always happily sing "Jingle Bells" and "Rudolph," but the Christmas carols often required chin waggling for an entire chorus, moving my jaw and head in rhythm without making a sound. Sometimes, when the whole song was bad, like "O Holy Night," I would tuck my chin in and hunch down behind Bobby Northcutt so nobody would see me not singing at all. Once, when I asked my teacher if I could be excused from making a scrapbook of the Christmas story, she refused, "because it is important to learn about other religions" (as if we weren't drowning in Baby Jesus talk already).

Hanukkah, the Jewish festival of lights, offered pale competition

131

for Christmas—puny candles against a dazzling tree, "Rock of Ages" against the tyranny of carols and decorations that took over the stores, the radio, the schools, and the imagination of all my friends. Parents billed Hanukkah as "better than Christmas," an unintentional error that placed a minor Jewish celebration beside Christianity on parade, like comparing sandlot baseball to the World Series. Hanukkah simply could never substitute—for one thing, it lasted eight days, and was almost always out of sync with Christmas, so you had to explain to your friends that you didn't sneak and open your Christmas presents early, but that your holiday was different; and that could lead to a "You mean you don't celebrate Christmas? Why not?" So I usually played with my toys in secret until Christmas day. I would always save the gifts from my friends until Christmas morning because it didn't seem right to open gentile gifts on a Jewish holiday and, besides, if I waited I'd have a real surprise to talk about in the afternoon when they came over to show off their stuff, rather than pretending that I had ripped open eight-day-old toys that very morning. (My father violated the rule only once with a beautiful bicycle waiting in the living room on Christmas morning, and I rushed out in ecstasy to race my friends all over the neighborhood.) It didn't make up for much when little Billy White said, "Gee, eight days of presents . . . I wish I was Jewish."

Mr. Farrell made a ritual out of going to the woods to select a Christmas tree; he would take me with the twins to search for one with just the right height and plenty of branches, and haul it home in a half-open car trunk. I would even help decorate it if they asked, and I remember thinking that Christmas trees were all right until Buck told me that the star on the top stood for the Star in the East. Seems as though the Christians had a way of taking the fun out of everything. Some of the Jewish families in town had a "Hanukkah Bush," but you never found a star on the top, though one time I saw a six-pointed Star of David up there. (One couple from Duke crowned their tree with a glazed bagel.)

"Will Santa visit our house?" I asked my mother.

"No."

"Why not?"

"Because we're Jewish," followed by a long explanation of the beauties of Judaism and the story of Hanukkah.

Now I knew that Santa didn't like bad children—all my friends

132

in the neighborhood talked about that for weeks ahead of time—
how if you were bad, he would leave switches and pieces of coal in
your stocking. So everybody was extra careful because—*he's
makin' a list, checkin' it twice, gonna find out who's naughty and
nice*. . . .

Archie Braswell told me that Santa wouldn't come to my house
because we were Jewish, and sinners because of what we did to
Christ. It wasn't bad logic and it tied Santa and Jesus together in
my mind. Santa punished for being bad and rewarded for being
good, just like Jesus; Santa was a folk hero with hosts of followers
and, just like Jesus, we Jews weren't supposed to believe in him; he
was a miracle worker who could fly through the air and heed all
your prayers, just like Jesus; and Santa was omniscient just like
Jesus, an ever watchful, inescapable disciplinarian when you were
sinning: *He knows when you've been sleeping, he knows when
you're awake; he knows when you've been bad or good, so be good
for goodness' sake.* And everybody really believed in him, just like
they believed in Jesus, because they put out carrots for the rein-
deer, and milk and cookies for Santa.

To me, then, Santa was not a harmless old legend but a semireli-
gious, forbidden symbol of Christianity's temptation of the Jews—
a red-suited, jolly-fat Jesus in disguise that they dressed up gaily so
as to hook us on the whole package.

And Christmas Eve when we Jews were out of line with the
planets, there was an entire universe of expectant little moppets in
perfect harmony scrambling around in pajamas, listening for the
"noise on the roof" and jolly Saint Nick, while I lay in my bed
knowing he would pass over our house, his ho, ho, ho a sinister
reminder that the bad Jews down there didn't deserve a visit. Even
more fearsome, with all the houses to visit, maybe he wouldn't
notice that we were Jewish, and sail on down our chimney and
come in the living room, get furious when he didn't see any stockings, and leave coal all around and maybe tear up the couch in
anger. (One Jewish friend solved this one cleverly. On Christmas
Eve his parents lit all the candles on the Hanukkah menorah so
when Santa Claus came down the chimney, he would know they
were Jewish.)

In my father's store a huge red-ribboned Santa's mailbox stood
in the corner, with a stool in front so the children could climb up
and reach the slot to drop their dreams off to the North Pole. I once

133

wrote a letter to Santa and crept over to the box to send it off without anybody spotting me:

Dear Santa,

I don't know whether you know me or not but I was hoping that you could come by this year. I'd like a cowboy hat and two guns like Red Ryder. I'll put out some milk.

Your friend,
Sonny Evans

Finding out the truth about Santa was one of the biggest reliefs in my life, and didn't shake me up at all as it did Buck and Billy. It had bothered me anyway how somebody that fat could get down the chimneys, and how he could soar around in a single night to all those houses, and whether his bag could hold all the toys for every child in the world. Billy worried though that if Santa weren't real, Jesus might not be real, either.

Mr. Hardison, the pot-bellied stockroom clerk who ate moon pies and guzzled eight-ounce R C Colas (he'd wipe his mouth on his wrist and then his wrist on his dirty T-shirt and say after a huge gulp, "You wanna belly-washer, kid?"), transformed himself into a beautiful Santa for our store, and one November, when I confronted him with the truth, he led me into the darkest corner far from the naked lightbulbs that lit the aisle, and reached way up on the highest shelf to slide down the box with the Santa suit in it. The bigger stores downtown with the best toy departments hired Santas to wander around and accost little children to find out their secrets. In the years just beyond the fantasy time (and because of Mr. Hardison), I could tell right away they weren't real because they had vinyl leggings over their shoes instead of big black boots, and the beards were cotton and slightly yellowed from last year's coffee breaks.

Any part of Christmas was for them, not us; though in later years I always felt mistletoe was all right for kissing gentile girls (in *their* homes). And we always mailed "Season's Greetings" cards instead of "Unto you a child is born. . . ." And the gifts at Christmas were never wrapped in Christmasy paper with angels or holly but in white paper with ribbons for a little holiday disguise, so they wouldn't be able to spot it right away as a nonbeliever's gift under the tree.

Because my dad was mayor, it was customary for the neighborhood churches to come by when they were caroling. Zola would have coffee ready for them, and my brother and I would go out on the front porch and stand arm in arm with Mom and Dad and smile graciously and nod approvingly while we listened to "O Little Town of Bethlehem" and "Joy to the World." The girls would always ask me to join them and come singing for the rest of the night, but I was suspicious that they were a good deal more intent on soul winning than street singing. Once, when I was home alone and heard them coming up the street, I quickly turned off all the lights and sat quietly in the darkness while they passed our house to serenade the Loves next door.

Age brought the insight that all Christian churches were not alike. There were some forty Baptist churches in the county announcing services in the local paper each Sunday, and I despaired at trying to figure out the distinctions between such deliciously fascinating labels as the free-will Baptists, the foot-washing Baptists, the hard-shell Baptists, and the total immersion Baptists (the "sprinklers" and the "dunkers" some people called them). I didn't even understand the fine line between Presbyterians, Methodists, Episcopalians, and Church of Christ. The confusion was intensified by the full-page ads for the healers coming to town and the articles about the snake handlers who worshiped by the injunction in Mark 16 that the followers of Jesus "shall take up serpents; and if they shall drink any deadly thing, it shall not hurt them." They kept screen-covered boxes filled with rattlesnakes and copperheads near the altar, and when the prayer meeting reached a frenzied, swooning moment, the preacher would plunge his hand into the box and pull out the writhing snakes and hand them all around for the congregation to fondle and kiss; then they would drape the snakes around their necks and arms and if the rattler didn't bite they were not sinners; if he did bite and they died, then they probably were. And one time, on the front page of the Durham paper, there was a picture of a small blond girl, eyes tightly shut as she stuck her tongue out to touch the slithering tongue tip of a meaty diamondback her preacher clutched by the head just inches away.

The Methodists and the Presbyterians in school ridiculed the Southern Baptists for their primitive, unquestioning acceptance of the faith and for their soul-saving rituals. They would sing to the tune of the Pepsi-Cola commercial:

Christianity hits the spot
Twelve apostles, that's a lot.
Immaculate conception and virginity too
[three quick claps]
Christianity's the one for you.

Turning the radio dial on Sunday mornings swept me up in the rich sounds of the Protestant clergy, laying it on the flock with all the varieties of elegance and earthiness that form the spectrum of Protestantism in the South: the giant sonorous organ at Duke Chapel and the sophisticated theological vocabulary and splendid Scottish brogue of Dr. James Cleland; the respectable, sleepy sermons of the Methodists, the congregation politely singing the hymns, dutifully plodding through all four verses; the let-it-all-hang-out, foot-stomping, soul-rousing black churches, the ministers always flat-out for Jesus, straining for breath, their sermons punctuated by the "amens" and the blues-beat gospel songs of pain and deliverance.

The roadside reminders summoning the whizzing motorists back to the faith always delighted me as a boy, so incongruous among the Burma Shave and praline picket signs. The most common put forth a simple "Jesus Saves" (and Jewish friends would always say "but Moses invests"); or "Repent, sinners, Jesus is coming"; but I liked the imaginative ones shaped like a cross with "Get Right" on the vertical slat, and "With God" on the horizontal.

Invariably at parties in high school, meeting someone for the first time they'd want to know what school you went to, what grade you were in, and finally, "And what church do you go to?" I would often answer "Beth-El Church," not wanting to come on so Jewish and thereby trigger a question like, "Is it true y'all only got half the Bible?" And when cheerleaders and majorettes broke out their crosses at Eastertime to sing in the all-city choir, displaying Christianness on their sweaters to advertise the purity in their hearts, normal Southern girls were transformed into plain-clothes Magdalenes, beguiled, protected, untouchable.

Any deviation could make a boy feel ineptly Jewish. John Stone was a tall, tow-headed country boy who lived down the street, the oldest boy on the block, and respected because he raised chickens in his back yard and used to take us down to his father's feed store, where he lured wolf rats out of the bags of feed in the storeroom with slivers of greasy bacon so he could blast them with his twenty-two rifle. John kept two hound dogs in the backyard too, and often went hunting with his father for squirrels and doves. He invited me to go once but I couldn't because my mother pointed out that "Jews aren't allowed to hunt living things for sport, only for food." So I never could own a rifle, but John never did understand. He thought Jews just couldn't shoot.

I was elected president of the student council in junior high school, which brought with it the uncomfortable honor of opening the first assembly in the school year with a prayer, usually leading into the Lord's Prayer. As that was unsafe for me, I panicked and talked with my father about it. It was a common problem with him, he said, because he was often called upon to offer a prayer at civic luncheons, since that was such a good way to get the mayor on the program without listening to a long-winded speech. While he sometimes gave a translation of the Jewish blessing over the bread, he explained, when it was an occasion that called for more he had an old reliable prayer he would share. I copied the prayer, a Jesus-less prayer, which we called the "Mayor Evans Old Reliable Prayer," and I've kept it for almost twenty years under the glass on my dresser at home:

> Heavenly Father, may thy blessings rest upon us as we meet in friendship and fellowship this morning. Bless, O Father, our comradeship and make of it an instrument to further thy will. Keep us loyal to our aims and teach us the ways of brotherhood and understanding of one another. Blessed and praised be thou, O Lord, eternal source of sustenance and happiness. Amen.

My father once took me down to the big tent to welcome an evangelist to town, and we both stood in the front row while the preacher opened the meeting with a prayer. It was the first time we had been together in that kind of situation. Both of us bowed our heads, and as the preacher started in, I glanced up at my father out of the corner of my eyes, and lo and behold, his eyes were open too! I blushed because it was the first time anyone had ever observed my praying trick, but before I could turn away embarrassed at being caught, he winked—not a quick wink, but a big, knowing, friendly cheek-wink, as if we both knew each other's secret now.

After a few preliminary announcements, the evangelist said, "Mayor Evans is here to greet us. Now, y'all listen to the Mayor 'cause he's the same religion as our Savior."

Once he was elected, I became the target of a number of conversion efforts by several oddballs in town who firmly believed that I was the key to the Second Coming; converting the son of a prominent Jew, I suppose, might pull out the linch pin of the Jewish community and cause all the Jews to tumble into the caldron of Christianity. One old Southern lady in chalk-faced makeup, who wore a lopsided, wide-brimmed black hat to cover her bluish-gray hair, traipsed around town with her sickening-sweet smile to give out Salvation Army magazines and other tracts, leaving them in barber shops, doctors' offices, and beauty parlors. I started getting notes in the mail from her with wild scribbling about "He's Coming Soon," and special conversion pamphlets designed for Jews, with Hebrew letters in them and selected passages from the Old Testament prophesying the coming of the Messiah. She hung around downtown, especially on Saturdays when the pamphleteering business was best. On several Saturdays in succession she followed me around, waiting until I was in a situation where she could corner me, and then slapped the pamphlets on me with a few cackling warnings about unconfessed sins and no mercy for my soul. One day, she stalked me to the barber shop, and when I had climbed in the chair and was absolutely defenseless under a striped barber's cloth, she made a beeline straight for me to hit me with another tract. No way out, now, but I envisioned a lifetime of these confrontations and I couldn't take it any longer: "Please lady, take your Jesus books and cram 'em." She never tried to convert me again.

Through it all, a fierce inconsistency began to gnaw its way into my subconscious, plaguing me until it erupted in a profound moment of unsettling confusion, a rare time in adolescence when a boy challenges his basics. One would hope that such thoughts would come at quiet, dramatic times—in a moment by the sea or while walking in the woods. Mine happened in the Carolina Theater during the last few minutes of *The Robe*, after watching several hours of brave Christians, whipped into the arena to face the hungry lions, singing all the while in protest to a cackling Peter Ustinov as Nero. It hit me with incredible force that someone must be lying. Either Jesus was true or He wasn't. If He wasn't, then a lot of people were wrong. If He was, then why fight it?

138

If all your friends believe that Jesus came and was crucified; if you respect some of them as intelligent and informed human beings; if churches, music, paintings, movies, and sculpture of great passion and genius have been created; then all of them—da Vinci, Michelangelo, the Popes, MGM, and all my friends—had either been victims of the most massive farce in human history or else subject to a mass hypnosis over time and on a scale never before attempted. I was shaken.

The rabbi and my parents helped me though the crisis. Surely, they said, there have been Christians in the world for two thousand years. But Judaism had existed for five thousand years as an inspiration to thinkers, artists, and musicians too. It was just that I didn't know about them and would have to learn.

You're concerned about Jesus, they argued, because you've seen the picture and he's easy to visualize (true enough; he was also in *Quo Vadis*). But, they pointed out, if you took a vote, there would be more Moslems and Hindus in the world than all the Christians put together. (And if you allowed the Buddhists, Shintos, and Confucians to vote, the non-Christians would win in a landslide.) I didn't have to spend the rest of my life in a search for the one true faith, they assured me, for men worship God in many ways. To be Jewish was to belong to the people who brought the law and the Book; and my most important job was to learn and ponder, to listen and do.

The rabbi put me through a solemn bout of his own special brand of soul saving, and since I had raised enough hell for one week, I let it go at that. Besides, my parents loaded more Jewish books on me than the number of sex guides they left conspicuously in my room the night I accidentally said at the dinner table that something was "screwed up."

Deep down, though, Jesus still worried me.

ELEVEN

Mister Speaker

ASSIMILATION can be a glacial process psychologically, slow and steady through the generations, masquerading in all manner of shapes. In the small towns, the loneliness of Jews was overwhelming at first, the immigrants having come from all-Jewish ghettos in the old country. However, they were not ostracized, as one might expect; instead they experienced the Southern ambivalence of religious respect and personal curiosity, and below the surface a degree of animosity that friendship would overcome.

The acts or nonacts of Jews are outward manifestations of inner conflicts. The overcompensations in personality derive from an urge to be more Southern than other Southerners—to laugh harder, to know more jokes, to be a more chivalrous, hell-raising, accommodating good old boy; to be more accomplished, popular, intelligent (but never to show ambition too plainly). In a small town, without a wider Jewish community to buttress a sense of religious independence, it is a great deal to ask a family to be the only house on the block with a somber mood at Christmastime, the only house without lights in the front yard or decorations in the window . . . at least it is a great deal to ask without passing resentments and longings on to small children.

Some Jews gave in slowly, others acquiesced totally, a few watched their children convert and blend in completely. The Jews on the edge are part of this story, for conversion represents one extreme on a continuum of responses to being Jewish in the Bible belt. There are no statistics on conversion that I know of, but I was

140

curious to learn about it. I soon realized, however, that in interviewing converted Jews, it was impossible for me to fathom the stories of revelations filled with hallucinations. So I searched for a family going through the process of total assimilation, with some ties to Judaism still evident.

I suspected that if I found the family I was looking for, I would discover conservative racial attitudes as well. With regard to religion, the non-Jewish community looked on Jews as the chosen people, a special link to their biblical roots. But on racial attitudes, the Southern small town never compromised. There was a special fury toward the sympathetic white, the "nigger lover," in the civil rights drama. In that atmosphere most Jews learned to keep their attitudes to themselves, but over time, especially as the South grew more insecure and whites sought out confirmation for their views in the unanimity of the other whites around them, the protective coloration of a few Jews turned stark white, with the slogans, phrases, and idioms of the white majority.

I had hoped I could find a family headed by a man in politics, so that in dealing with racial and religious assimilation I would be on familiar terrain. I like politicians, for they embody society's tensions and yet must function in a very real world.

But Jews are not active as office seekers in the South, though a significant number have held office in the last twenty-five years (see Appendix B). Most Southern Jews are apolitical, more worried about their mortgage payments and the crab grass than elections; they are hesitant to step out into the controversial arena of political campaigns because, like everybody else, they want to avoid unpleasantness and risk. In addition, Jews in the South still have a lingering insecurity about the reaction of the gentile community to any Jew with authority, and thus are doubly careful.

The reason is the race issue. Race permeates Southern politics like the twilight mist hanging in the marshlands that slither with the sounds of night creatures. It is always just below the surface of every public utterance, a chorus of whispers in the clatter of elective politics.

Almost all the Jewish officeholders in the South have been moderate figures, have received the black vote, see themselves as examples for the Jewish community and as symbols for the gentile community. That doesn't mean they are outspoken proponents of civil rights. Until recently, any white who would even meet with

141

black leaders was a "liberal" in the Southern political spectrum, and no black expected a white candidate to pledge publicly anything more than "to be fair to all people." However, when the opposition was railing against the Supreme Court, blasting integration, miscegenation, and demonstrations, then soft talk and reason was a reassuring enough sign for blacks and for white moderates.

Few Jews have run for statewide office because, as a young legislator put it, "the yokels downstate just aren't ready for it." When I asked one Jew who did run statewide what the experience had been like, he drew deeply on his corn-cob pipe and said, "It's the closest thing to Little Theater."

The Southern Jewish politicians defy most generalizations. They are as skillful as other Southern politicians and, in terms of personality, run the gamut of Southern types—the friendly country boy, the stemwinder, the sincere young man, the earnest statesman. In the small towns, they can be the leading citizen running for mayor; in the cities, they are often the vigorous young lawyers in the state legislature. Only a few are conservative defenders of the old order.

The immense black voter registration in the South since 1965 is sweeping away the old-style segregationists and modifying the behavior of those few who have made the transition. The last institution to change has been the state legislature—even after reapportionment, the last bastion of rural dominion.

To master a legislature in any Southern state takes a man of extraordinary ability; in South Carolina, he would have to be rural in his politics and small-town in his demeanor, a plain-talking man farmers could respect and governors would fear. Only incidentally would the script cast Mr. Speaker as Jewish.

For three years, the members of the South Carolina legislature faced four portraits—two of them were of Jews. The four were Stonewall Jackson and Robert E. Lee, Bernard Baruch of Camden and Solomon Blatt of Barnwell.

Solomon Blatt (pronounced Blot) has been speaker of the House of Representatives in South Carolina for thirty-three years, longer than any other man in its history and possibly longer than any other man in the history of any state in America. He has served continuously, except for a four-year stint from 1947 to 1951, when, after he opposed Strom Thurmond for governor, Thurmond ousted him from the speakership for someone more favorable to his administration.

The portrait that looks down on the state legislature features Blatt in a stern pose—sitting in the purple robes of his office in a high-backed speaker's chair, holding his gavel in his hand, his bald head starkly white against the dark brown background. The Anderson, South Carolina, newspaper once described him as the "Barnwell Jew," but his fellow state legislators refer to him as "King Sol." Governor Thurmond branded him one half of the "Barnwell Ring," the other half being state Senator Edgar Brown, who is also from Barnwell and for twenty-nine years has held the Senate's two most powerful jobs: chairman of the Senate Finance Committee and president pro-tem.

At the height of the legend of the Barnwell Ring in the forties, the governor, the chairman of the Ways and Means Committee, and the state chairman of the Democratic Party all lived in Barnwell County along with Blatt and Brown.

Brown is now eighty-three, Blatt seventy-five, and the Barnwell Ring still encircles and dominates South Carolina legislative politics, though not with the zest of its heyday. As protector of the textile, banking, and utility interests in the state (Thurmond attacked them in his populist cycle as "the interests"), the Ring has come together at the end of every session of the state legislature for three decades to compromise issues between the House and the Senate and to hammer out the state budget. Brown's definition of the Ring as "two old men who sometimes agree and sometimes disagree" is not as true today as it once was. Reapportionment is draining their control over the legislative process, and the new voting blocs represented there must be bargained with, not run over.

Moreover, Brown and Blatt have not been on close personal terms since Brown supported an opponent against Blatt in 1960; and patronage questions in Barnwell, personal and law-firm rivalries, advancing age, and outsized egos have aggravated their confrontations and made compromise more difficult for two men who must know that each session of the legislature may be their last. After all these years, they are like two old men sitting across from each other, each waiting for the other to keel over.

Blatt rarely speaks on the floor of the legislature, but when he does it's an all-out, tear-jerking, emotion-ridden performance, regardless of subject. Crying real tears in 1966, he made a bitter speech attacking the reenactment of the South Carolina compulsory school law, which had been repealed a few years earlier to allow whites not to send their children to integrated schools. It was the first time in eight years he had taken the floor to speak on a pending issue, but he gave his most memorable speech: "You may want a sixteen-year-old so-and-so to sit by your granddaughter," he shouted, "but Sol Blatt will fight and die to prevent it from happening to his granddaughter." When he was asked whether he would rather have sixteen-year-old illiterates walking the streets than in school trying to get an education, Blatt answered, "I'd rather have them in the streets. They can be avoided there. I don't want them sitting in class with my granddaughter, holding hands during May Day activities, playing with her, and going places where they go." And then he cried out, "Let's don't try to teach them free French and Latin. Let's teach those unfortunates brick masonry and English. But let's don't force 'you know who' with little children who don't want them."

In 1966, voices like that were seldom heard even in the halls of Deep South legislatures; a stunned House heard Blatt in silence and then voted down their speaker's position 73–32.

After the speech the Charlotte *Observer* blistered him: "His attack took on race baiting typical of a Vardaman, Cotton Ed or Pitchfork Ben. . . . Back in the 1900's Mississippi's James Vardaman warned that educating the Negro would spoil a good field hand and make an insolent cook. Blatt departed only slightly from this reasoning."

Blatt was offended by that editorial. "For some reason," he told me in an interview, "the Charlotte *Observer* has never cared for me. I wonder if it isn't because I am Jewish."

He denied that he was referring to Negroes when he used the word "so-and-so" in the speech, and claimed that the newspapers had misconstrued his meaning. "It's a common expression with me—I see an old friend and I say, 'Why, you old so-and-so.' Well, I didn't particularly refer to a Negro. I wouldn't want a sixteen-year-old white boy sitting next to my six-year-old granddaughter. I don't think that's the place for an older boy to be, and you start compulsory school attendance and that's what you have. They all construed it as an attack by me upon the Negroes; while I intended it to include Negroes I did not mean to exclude whites."

144

I asked several legislators who heard the speech whether they agreed with the Speaker's interpretation. "No one who was there that day had any doubt what Sol meant," one of them said.

For five months every year, Sol stands at stage center—guiding, blocking, begging, pontificating, recognizing, ratifying—traffic cop and stern school marm, a personal favor for potential friends, a swift ax for old enemies. King Sol keeps it moving all session long, lunching with lobbyists, granting an interview, adjusting the language of bills, ramroding an amendment, standing aside, compromising with the Senate, and making the law. Sol Blatt commutes to Columbia for five months every year, and the rest of the time, in his Barnwell office, he builds for the moments when he works his will. He shuffles through his mail; receives callers from industry, governments, and the press; places call after call after call to line it up for the next time; takes care of constituents and travels the circuit to visit the Rotary clubs, the Jaycees, the American Legion posts, and the county Democratic meetings.

Sol doesn't just guide the House, he drives it. During sessions, he is a mixture of stuffy formality and statehouse "good old boy." He always keeps the two top buttons fastened on his three-button suit. In the midst of a long debate, he may leave the podium for a time to confer with members or straighten out a legislative snag. At that point, he transforms himself from Imperial Uncontested Leader to back-slapping Salt of the People. Sol recasts himself into a hands-on politician—squeezing, rubbing, touching, whispering to a colleague, their arms flung about each other like two little boys telling secrets.

Solomon Blatt's whole life is the South Carolina state legislature—a world of great issues like liquor-by-the-drink, a soft-drink tax and small-loan regulations, a world he moves in with the sureness of the man with the green stamps to trade. Sol is strong because other men are weak, easily turned by the greed for smaller favors: the paved road, an appointment to a state commission, a nephew admitted to college. And for an entire session some scrap with each other for zoning powers and more pay; and state agencies claw at each other for more funds; and the governor marshals his friends for the program he hopes to go to the United States Senate on.

But in the end, it'll be Sol and Edgar again—as it has been for thirty-three years, "giving it prayerful consideration" (Edgar's favorite phrase, which earned him the nickname "The Bishop"). They'll lop off millions here and there, let a favorite bill through, and kill others. They'll reach the compromises with the governor's men, with the textile interests, and the liquor lobbyists; they'll take the brunt of the attack from the press as they always do because they have Barnwell County locked up anyway.

Barnwell is an attractive little town of six thousand people sixty miles south of Columbia, not unlike hundreds of other small towns in the South. The square has its Confederate monument and the stores encircle a square dominated by the old brick courthouse. The football sticker on the back of a car full of high school students could describe the two most prominent citizens—"The Barnwell Warhorses," it says. Speaker Blatt and Senator Brown have law offices across the square from each other, the better to spy on one another when the legislature is not in session. ("Bishop Brown has to have his own Jew," people in Barnwell used to say, referring to Brown's law partner, Herman Mazursky, who served as mayor of Barnwell for thirty-two years until he died a few years ago.)

The Speaker is working this Sunday in his law offices, which are in a small building to themselves, modern and impressive—wall-to-wall carpets, piped-in music, paneled walls, and in the back, a new addition for an expanded library. The office is decorated with the memories of his speakership—plaques, photographs, flags, and other mementos. Tintype photos of his mother and father in East European dress occupy an honored place, alongside pictures of his two political heroes, James Byrnes and Bernard Baruch.

"They used to call us the three B's," he said seriously, "Baruch, Byrnes, and Blatt."

Blatt is a chunky man, and his handshake conveys the toughness of an experienced dusty-shoe politician used to reaching out and grabbing the sweaty hand of a sharecropper. His eyes seem enormous, magnified by glasses so thick that for years he has never driven any farther than the few blocks from his home to the office without a chauffeur.

Sol wants to impress. All politicians want to be loved, but Blatt's transparent vanity is a renowned weakness. He smothers a visitor in a fawning sheet of graciousness. While he speaks the slow drawl of the Southerner when he needs time to think, mostly his pace is quick and natural. He never plays dumb, is wily on politically sensitive matters, and can't be cornered. Like all politicians, he can wind-bag on an issue he has handled often. There is much of the introvert in Sol Blatt, but today he is trying hard to be the big, open, magnanimous man of public affairs.

Blatt uses being Jewish the way most politicians use the "little log cabin"—the young boy of immigrant stock, risen from humble origins to the position of great power in the politics of his state. He calls himself a "segregationist in moderation" and feels that other Jews would be wise if they followed his example or stayed quiet on racial matters.

But he is a surprisingly blunt and candid man on what are essentially very personal questions: his own lack of religious practice; the conversion of his wife and children to the Episcopal church; his personal position as an example for other Jews. For most Jews whose families have drifted so far from Judaism, and whose formal ties to Judaism are so tenuous, it would be easier to cut the thread than to hang on the way he does.

How would he compare himself to his father? He turned to the picture on the wall. "Well, he was a better Jew than I am." For Solomon Blatt, more the Southerner than the Jew, it still seems necessary to keep the faith as a pledge to the memory of his father and mother.

He talks with obvious relish about his parents. "My father used to get all of his meat from Augusta and he went down to Charleston and learned how to butcher a chicken for the holidays in Blackville. He did keep his store open on Saturdays to keep going, because a merchant couldn't take in enough during the week. Saturday was a big day. My mother would help my father in the store some, but she wouldn't tear up a piece of paper on Saturday—she would make the customer tear the paper for her. And my father smoked, but he would not smoke on Saturday."

In his early days in Barnwell, Blatt said he tried to help start a congregation in the area with several other Jews. "We tried one time to bring the rabbi over here from Sumter on Sunday afternoon, and he had services at the picture show in Blackville, but it narrowed itself down to just three or four of us going, and he quit coming."

He keeps few Jewish traditions today. "My trouble is that you can always find some reason why you can't go to church and the

147

result of it is that I don't go anywhere. To be perfectly frank with you, the only thing I really keep is the Yom Kippur fast. I stay away from business and read some prayers and start of course the night before."

He sometimes reflects on the isolation he has experienced, revealing attitudes of a man who has spent his life in the Bible belt. "I've always regretted that I didn't have a rabbi that I could go to occasionally, because I often feel the need for one. I'd love to go. But I've reached seventy-five years of age now, and I have to do a lot of riding on weekends—to Columbia or Charleston or Augusta. The speaker's job requires me to."

I asked him whether he had ever had any brushes with the Ku Klux Klan. He said that he had lost votes because of the Klan, and trials because Klansmen were on the jury. Then he added, "Some years ago there was a bit of activity on the part of the Klan, and some of my best friends joined it. I always said that a man has a right to join whatever he wants to join. I happen to belong to a Masonic lodge. I joined it; I was invited to join; I wanted to join and I did. So I would not say to any fellow that he shouldn't join the Klan or anything else he wants to join."

Blatt says that he feels a special burden to conduct himself in a manner which would reflect well on the Jewish people. "Any Jew," he asserted, "has got to be a step higher than the ordinary fellow."

He then pulled out a copy of his speech to the Hebrew Benevolent Society in Charleston in 1959, in which he warned the Jewish people about involving themselves in the integration fight. In that speech he declared, "There are dangerous inclinations among some of the Jewish people in America, out of the goodness of their hearts, to establish themselves as a minority force in the tragically exaggerated storm of political propaganda which surrounds and confuses the Negro question in the South." Blatt said that he made that speech because it was a "mistake for the Jewish people to become very active in this thing, because I knew in my heart of hearts that when the time came, those who would be punished as a result of it would be the Jewish people."

He felt the prophecy had come true. "And if you observe what's happened, where the burnings took place, it's been Jewish merchants to a large extent who lost their place of business as a result of the break-ins and the fires. Just exactly what I predicted came true."

148

It seemed to disturb him that no one heeded his advice. "We're paying the penalty for what's happening—the Negroes turning against the Jews themselves."

Basically he felt the Jews ought to be quiet on the race issue. "The less said by us about this thing the better off we are all going to be, and the better off the people who are connected with us and the blacks will be too."

All Jews in high positions had to be especially careful. "If I make a statement, the Jews get condemned for it. This is a fight we shouldn't participate in because we're going to get destroyed as a result of it."

Blatt is satisfied that his time in the speakership "has reflected with credit on the Jewish people . . . I think that . . . the honors that have come my way . . . clearly indicate that what I have done is in the best interests of all the people, including the Negroes and the Jewish people."

He bristled at any suggestion that he has ever hidden his Jewishness, or that he ever would. "In every speech I ever made of any importance, I have referred to my Jewishness, and how proud I am of being a Jew. Because I couldn't have loved my mother and daddy as I did love them, and now love their memory, without being proud that I was their son and proud that I was a Jew. I have said it from the banquet table, I've said it a thousand times in South Carolina, and I don't hesitate to say it. I am just as proud of being a Jew as anybody in the world can be proud of any religious affiliation that they might have."

He also feels that it is impossible for a Jew to deny it, even when he joins a church. "Once you are a Jew, you are a Jew as long as you live. Even if you go to the Baptist church or the Methodist church . . . you're a Jew . . . that's what you are, you never get away from it."

Blatt said that he was asked several times to run for governor, once very seriously by a group of businessmen who "offered to put up all the money I needed for the campaign if I would just agree to run. I told them that they had paid me the greatest compliment I ever had and how grateful I was; but I wouldn't even consider it, and there were two reasons for that. First is, I couldn't be elected, and second is, I don't want it."

He thought that being Jewish would have stopped him. "They would have used it against me."

149

Yet he recalled the day his portrait was dedicated in the House, when former governor James Byrnes had stated, "The political career of Speaker Blatt in his county and this House is a refutation of the misrepresentation frequently made in some Northern states that the people of South Carolina are anti-Semitic."

In his own view, his clean record, confirmed by the honors heaped upon him, has helped open the way for others. "I believe by my conduct the Jewish people have become more acceptable in South Carolina, and it is much easier for a Jewish fellow to be elected for public office now than it would have been some years ago."

"He never overlooks support in any camp, racially or politically. Not only blacks like us, but Republicans. He'll invite us all down to Barnwell quick-as-you-please." Jim Felder is one of the black legislators elected in 1970, the first since Reconstruction. He led the Voter Education Project in South Carolina from 1967 to 1970, organizing a campaign that increased the registration statewide from an unsure 140,000 to a hard-count 180,000. The newspapers like to point out that he was also the noncommissioned officer in charge of the casket team during the John F. Kennedy funeral.

"I respect his shrewdness and his ability to grasp any situation and squeeze it politically," Felder added. He pointed out that Blatt has thirty years of IOU's with small county legislators. "You just can't beat him on something he is against without working hard and long and steaming up a whole statewide campaign."

Blatt's interest in University of South Carolina athletics is legendary. Last year, over three hundred colleges pursued a black quarterback from Sumter named Freddy Solomon. "It all started in the Peach Bowl two years ago," Felder asserted, "when West Virginia, with two black halfbacks running that ball, ran all over South Carolina. It dawned on Sol and a lot of others that a lot of talent in the state was going to waste."

Blatt remembered that Jim Felder was born and raised in Sumter and called the new legislator to ask him if he would talk with the boy's mother. "I knew the family, and went to see her," said Felder. Freddy Solomon wanted to sign with the University of South Carolina but couldn't pass the admission requirements. Still Jim Felder knows that Solomon Blatt will remember the favor. "I chalk it up as an IOU. I haven't hit him yet . . . but I will."

150

With contacts all over the state from his voter registration days, Felder isn't just another legislator but a young black leader deserving the Speaker's personal attention. He recalled another example of Blatt's shrewdness: "He gave me my first choice in the committee assignments, which was education. And I was one of five he put on the very important reapportionment committee and that was his own personal move." Then Felder smiled. "Not only can he say he appointed a black, but I represented the big cities, too. He hit two birds with one stone," and, of course, kept the rural legislators in control of the committee.

Blatt knows that the key to statewide power for him is keeping his constituents in Barnwell happy so that they will return him to the legislature again and again. Felder has talked with black leaders in Barnwell County who have supported Blatt for years. "He gets the black vote in almost every election," Felder said. "He paves your road, gets rural water, and brings electricity for the blacks. They'll tell you that you just can't bite the hand that feeds you."

Arnold Goodstein is an intense young lawyer elected to the legislature in 1969 from Charleston as a third-year law student. He's a twenty-eight-year-old new breed politician, who fashioned the labor-black-liberal coalition in Charleston into a winning issues-oriented campaign.

Goodstein has led the battle in the legislature to allow Sabbatarians (Jews and Seventh-Day Adventists) to keep their businesses open on Sunday when they close on Saturday. Even though he considers himself an open and positive Jew, he finds Sol's clumsy efforts to be Jewish from the podium embarrassing. "Sol will go out of his way to tell jokes and kid us in public. He'll say something during a debate on the floor like, 'That's a good point but you go to the wrong synagogue.' "

Blatt feels his podium humor is just good fun, "just having a grand old time when we kid each other in the House. I don't attempt to hide it. A man ought to be proud he's a Jew, or quit."

Ethel Blatt (the daughter of Moses Green of Sumter) greets strangers enthusiastically, a warm simple-seeming woman with a permanent smile so large her eyes crinkle in a constant squint. Vivacious even in her seventies, she must have been an enormous asset to Solomon Blatt in the early years. She is spry, insistent,

151

eager to please; she grabbed me by the arm and dragged me into the den where once again the walls were plastered with platoons of pictures of Sol at parades, dedications, dinners, and graduations.

"I don't have many honors," she declared, eager to have me read her prized award, "but I am proud as I can be of this." It was a plaque engraved, "To Mrs. Solomon Blatt by the vestry congregation of the Church of the Holy Apostles, Barnwell, South Carolina, in grateful appreciation of her devotion and loyalty as church organist for the past 20 years, May 27, 1962."

She chattered on, "And for the twenty-fifth anniversary, they gave me a silver cross to wear with my vestments. I declare I was so surprised and proud . . . I want to be buried in it." I nodded and she didn't pause. "You see, I was Episcopalian in every way except for taking communion. I had studied it for fifteen years and thought it was silly not to convert. But I waited five years to tell Sol. I was scared to tell him, but he said that if I wanted it bad enough to go right on. So I waited until my youngest grandchild was confirmed and I was confirmed too. All the children have been baptized, and of course Sol Junior has converted too." She punctuated her soliloquy with a simple statement of resolution: "We're all Episcopalians now."

Sol spoke of Ethel's conversion in private. "When she came to me about this, she said she had been seriously thinking about this thing, and she was concerned about it and didn't want to do anything I didn't want her to do. She wanted to know how I felt about it. I said, 'Now honey, this is a matter for you to decide. If this is going to make you lead a life that you are going to get more out of, if it means more to you spiritually and otherwise and this is what you want to do, you do it. I am not going to say yes or no. It isn't my problem; it's yours.' "

The phenomenon of religious conversion mystifies most Jews, who prefer to explain it away on other grounds than pure revelation or change of faith. They can understand conversion because of love, conversion to resolve problems for children, conversion for social reasons, or almost any reason other than a religious reason. Without knowing, I would guess that most conversions in the South involve the Episcopal church. Despite its formal orthodoxy, it is still in some peculiar way least demanding in terms of personal commitment and the most desirable in terms of social standing. However, in Ethel Blatt's case, the motive is elusive. She played the organ on Sundays for twenty years, placing herself in the sanctum of the church where surely she must have sensed the cultural and emotional moods of the church seeping into her. Ethel Blatt's conversion, then, was not a sudden one filled with a dazzling vision of the Savior in her room. William James wrote of such conversions in *Varieties of Religious Experience* in 1901. He drew the distinction between "volitional" conversions and "conversions by self-surrender," the latter being those of "striking instantaneous instances . . . often amid tremendous emotional excitement." He explained that "in the volitional type, the regenerative change is usually gradual and consists of building up, piece by piece, a new set of moral and spiritual habits" characterized by two aspects: "the present incompleteness which he is eager to escape from and . . . the positive ideal he longs to encompass."

Ethel and Sol Blatt have lived their lives as prisoners of the approval of others—she, out of total harmony with her community for fifty years, no doubt the object of clucking gossip of the Southern biddies who must have prattled endlessly about her in church on Sundays, seeing her there at the organ as the Jewish outsider. She must have been drawn psychologically to them by the sense of belonging she found from a life revolving around the church, rehearsing the scheduled hymns Sunday after Sunday and at Easter and Christmas. In that milieu, conversion must have brought Ethel Blatt some peace; no more apologies and explanations of why she didn't believe, and no more guilt for harboring secret feelings. Now she was a celebrated member of the finest church in Barnwell.

We sat on the couch in the den where a crumpled Sunday *Times* lay mixed together with a number of South Carolina papers. Blatt said that he reads seven newspapers a day and, "when I have finished those seven papers I don't feel like reading anything else. I don't read many books. People send them to me but I just don't have time to read them."

He leaned back, ready to brag a bit. "The people of Barnwell have been good to us and I will always be grateful—why, they just bring us all kinds of food. Some hunters brought so much deer meat, my freezer has been full for a year; four and five hams at a time; one man brought twenty-five pounds of fish—you know, I just love catfish stew; bushels of peaches, corn—our cook makes squash that tastes like cake—and since they know I love tomatoes I

153

get them by the peck, enough to fill this room. We feed the whole neighborhood in the summertime."

Ethel interrupted, "Stop talking about your food, Sol." She beckoned. "Come over here. I want you to see a picture of my granddaughter." It was a photo of a pretty blond girl in a white picture hat and a large hoop skirt. "This was taken at the Old South Ball," she said.

The Speaker is a prodigious worker with no hobbies except the House of Representatives. He likes to come home late and eat dinner at a card table in the den while watching the evening news on television. On the other hand, Ethel likes to eat in the dining room like a lady, so they each do their thing alone. "Funniest eating couple you ever saw," Ethel said.

Blatt told how he went to see his father, then an old man, to tell him that Sol, Jr., was going to marry a non-Jewish girl. "I said, 'Now Papa, I want to tell you and Mama something—you may not like this—she's not a Jew. She's a Christian, but Ethel and I have talked it over and we want Sol, Jr., to be happy.' When she finally went over to see my father and mother, they were just taken away with her. If I could have picked the whole United States over to find a girl that I wanted to marry my son, I would have picked her."

How did he feel about intermarriage now, having experienced it in his own family? "I would hate to see eliminated from the face of the earth the people who established the first real religion in the world and who believed in God and had God believe in them. But at the same time I just don't believe that you can tell a Baptist you can't marry a Methodist or a Christian you can't marry a Jew. I think that the happiness of the people involved ought to be taken into consideration. But I do not want to see wiped off the face of the earth everything that God himself put there, upon which is founded the greatest religion of the world."

One of the key places of decision making in the city of Columbia while the legislature is in session is the Palmetto Club, which, until a year or so ago, excluded Jews. Senator Hy Rubin, the only Jewish member of the State Senate, once refused to go even when invited. By virtue of his office as Speaker of the House, Blatt belongs.

"I get terribly disturbed when I see a place like the Palmetto Club in Columbia," he complained. "Jewish people have a terrible time getting in there. I happen to be in there because I was one of the first ones invited; when I joined I never knew this was going to be a problem."

He resented the delays that went on when Sol, Jr., applied, and peppered the membership committee with letters until they finally took him into the club a year and a half later. "I wrote some damn strong letters about it and I got right in the midst of the damn fight myself." At his request, Blatt's annual birthday party, which has grown into a big event in Columbia, was moved from the Palmetto Club.

On the other hand, his solution to an invitation to the annual meeting of the Textile Association at Sea Island, Georgia, was to object to the fact that Jews were excluded from the resort and then arrange to stay at the beautiful home of the executive vice-president of the Textile Association rather than in the hotel. "It's much nicer in the first place, but we do have to go to the hotel to eat. I resent it, of course, but there are some things that I feel I should do as Speaker."

One Jewish businessman in the state said, "On being Jewish you've got to give the old bastard credit. Whenever there's a fight on the country clubs he's usually there trying to help out. But none of his family is Jewish and when he dies it will all go with him."

Blatt admits that he voted for Nixon and Agnew in 1968. "I happen to be one of those who under no circumstances would vote for Hubert Humphrey, and he was the nominee of the Democratic Party. I just couldn't swallow him."

Why did he not vote for Wallace then? "I didn't because I didn't figure that Wallace had a chance, and frankly I don't think that on all the issues that confront the world he's a big enough man to handle them. We have more issues beside the issue of integration and segregation, and this is where his strength is."

Would he agree with Wallace on segregation? "No, I won't. I don't know how far I would go with Wallace." Then he told how a Negro had taught his father to sign his name and how he "had always had great admiration for anyone who was capable of pulling himself up by his own bootstraps. I am not concerned about his religion or the color of his skin." He then denounced "wholesale integration" and busing.

Did he think Wallace stirred up a lot of unnecessary feelings? "I think it's unfortunate that we have groups in both camps that have

155

done this. There are blacks who stirred it up, and a lot of it is done by those blacks who are not intelligent and never intended for their children to obtain all this education they talk about."

(Frank Best, Sr., head of the Wallace Forum Association, which organized for Wallace in '68, said that the American Party would never organize in the legislature against Blatt. "We don't have to. There's no conflict between us and him. This is a matter of political philosophy and Sol Blatt believes in what we believe in.")

Blatt rarely travels outside the state, and has flown only once, so it is unlikely he will ever respond to the efforts of a few prominent South Carolinians to arrange a trip to Israel for him. The Speaker admires the Israelis; one legislator remembers "he couldn't sit still during the Six-Day War."

"I am very proud of the progress they have made over there in Israel," he said. "I am mad at my government because they don't give them help at this time. These people took a piece of earth that nobody else in the world wanted and made it into one of the finest and most beautiful spots in the world. I just wish now that there were some way the people over there could push a button and blow up every damned Arab in the whole damn country that the Jewish people didn't want."

He told a story about going with Governor "Jimmy" Byrnes to Williamsburg, Virginia, for a speech and sitting in the front row with a congressman who had once visited the South Carolina legislature and made a speech Blatt objected to. The congressman from Virginia happened to be sitting next to Blatt and turned to him to ask, "Say, whatever happened to that little Jew who was Speaker of the House down there?" Sol says he looked him straight in the eye as he said, "I'm that little Jew and I'm still Speaker."

Charlotte *Observer*, June 13, 1971 (column by Jack Bass):

In a bombshell announcement that opened a political battle of historic proportions, Rep. Rex L. Carter Thursday launched a campaign to oust veteran House Speaker Sol Blatt from his powerful post. . . .

A growing band of restless "young Turks" put the pressure on Carter, who as speaker pro tem since 1957 has been Blatt's protégé. In effect, Carter was given a decision to either challenge Blatt next time or watch someone else do it. . . .

Carter moved two days after Blatt told a small group of newsmen, "Old man Blatt is not going to retire until God retires him or the people retire him."

Blatt has another year to serve on his present term. A new speaker will be elected by the 124-member House after next year's election. . . . Carter indicated he will encourage progressive-minded candidates statewide.

The storm clouds gathered through the summer until Governor John West, concerned about the implications for his program, met with Little Sol (now Judge Sol, Jr.), who was worried about his father's health. They worked out a compromise giving Sol one more term. Everyone agreed, thus assuring Sol of an exit filled with accolade rather than acrimony.

Thus will end the legend of the "Barnwell Jew," who will serve again as he did in the beginning, simply as the representative from Barnwell County, only now with the designation "Speaker emeritus." They will name a building after him and he will settle into the memories and the friends of thirty-three years of power to comfort him in his old age. I asked him if he was afraid to die. "I know as God is my judge," he said, "that I have done a lot more good than I have done bad. I begged my God to let me be a good Speaker and a good representative and of service to my state. They are the very words in my prayers and I thank God every day for the long life he has given me. I've been Speaker longer than any man in the history of the world. Some people you hear say they are ready to go. Well, I am not ready to go. I've still got some fence mending to do."

Shortly thereafter, Senator Edgar Brown, the other half of the Ring, announced his retirement as well. The legislature appropriately recognized the end of an era: across the street from the Blatt Building stands the identical twin—the Brown Building. The two old men from Barnwell will finish their careers in a draw.

157

IV

Coming of Age

TWELVE

Mister Jew

T H E warehouses of the Liggett & Myers Tobacco Company stretched four city blocks from the factory to Durham High School, the all-white school in town where daughters of Duke University professors met the sons of tobacco factory workers, a public school unusual for North Carolina because such a high percentage—fifty percent—went on to college. Boys named Buddy, Bubba, Bucky and Bugs strode the great stage at the Durham Athletic Park, a crumbling midtown baseball stadium that was converted every September, sloshy pitcher's mound and all, into a football place for the maroon-and-white Bulldogs to pile drive to victory.

It was the fifties, the era of "White only," moon pies, and "For the prevention of disease only. . . ." "Ah don't care if it rains or freezes, as long as ah got mah plastic Jesus." Being gross, poon-tang, and "no shit, sherlock." "You look sharp as a Jew salesman at a nigger picnic." It was 3-D glasses, knock-knock jokes, and "shee-ee-it." Esther Williams and "Lawdy, Miss Clawdy." "Colored people please step to the rear," and "Why don't Jews eat pig meat?"

Girls had pajama parties and wore ponytails, Peter Pan collars, short shorts, saddle oxfords, and pennies in their loafers. "Your Daddy's a nigger lover." Boys sported pegged pants, Bermudas, belts-in-the-back, Windsor knots. "I tried to Jew him down." Cool was a butch, crew cut, a flat top, or a D.A. He was cute, neat, out-to-lunch, or a weenie . . . a creep, a dream, a brain, a stud, or a grind. "Niggers love to ride around like a Jew in a Cadillac." There was the Royal Shaft, raising a hickey, French kissing, and getting a bad reputation.

161

"A Jew is just a nigger turned inside out." "What d'ya mean, jelly bean?" Wearing shades. "That's the way the cookie crumbles." "Don't nigger-lip it, just smoke it." Rocky Marciano and " 'bout time we had a champyun." "Bee Boppa loo la, she's mah baby," and "Move with me, Annie." Low-slung Chevies, scratch off, neckers' knobs, and flaps. "You ain't a man 'til you split the black oak." Breathing in her ear, everything but, stacked, bedroom eyes.

We worshiped the goddess of popularity, who compressed individuality into a tight mold of conformity, manipulated our language and our personalities and our dress, all in the name of respectability and approval.

The cheerleaders were the girls who didn't try too hard to keep their skirts down when they whirled—Betty Lou and Mary Miles and Annie Best—the strutting majorette twins Ellie and Mellie Adcock, all of them flirtatious and nimble with boys and with cheers.

My name was "Sonny" then; and there were other Jewish guys I knew named Snooky Rose and Chubby Strauss, Spider Schwartz and Spuds Rabinowitz; Jewish girls named Daisy Belle Seligman, Luci Lee Abramson, Bootsie Goodman, and Bunny Leibowitz.

It started early, the teachers' exhortations to better behavior because "you are one of the chosen people"; my presentation of the "meaning of Yom Kippur" after I was absent on a Jewish holiday; the spillover of questions at lunchtime and on the playgrounds and the reaction from friends who never thought about it before. The burden of being Mister Jew envelops you in a cocoon of self-consciousness, an extra dimension to whatever you say or do—the small voice always whispering, "What impression are you making?"

Mister Jew has to know his religion, not in the deep and penetrating way a philosopher would learn it, or in the searching way a seeker of solace would pursue it, but in a defensive, facile, articulate way, geared more to answers than questions. Mister Jew wants to be respected, not just liked, because his mother tells him that others will judge all the Jewish people by his actions. Mister Jew wants to make good grades, not the best grades because that will be resented, but good enough grades, and make them effortlessly so that he will not let down the expectations of parents and friends and girls who expect him to be smarter. Mister Jew means that he

162

mustn't dress flashily, because everybody expects Jews to do that. Mister Jew is never loud, and if he lets himself go at all, he worries if he has gone too far, or at least far enough to confirm a stereotype. Mister Jew means that he gives a little more to the March of Dimes and the Community Chest during classroom collections but never so much that people would say that he is being showy. Above all, Mister Jew never offends, never disagrees fiercely, never looks for a fist fight or an argument; he blends in well after he is accepted because he works at friendships consciously, constantly, and sometimes deviously.

To excel, to do better, to make it big and strive for the very top, had always been a part of our family chemistry. My father stressed leadership by example, that Jews had to be twice as good to achieve half as much. Dinnertime was a time for discussion of whatever was on anyone's mind, and I learned to try to hold my own early with my brother and my father, who was always careful to listen to my opinion and give it respect, equal validity and weight, though I was six years younger than my brother. For us, how you spoke mattered, and public speaking was an art to be cultivated and a skill to be honed, a projection of person and personality to others who would judge you superficially. Language is part of politics in the South; surely, the silver-tongued heroes out of Southern history—Calhoun, Jackson, Jefferson—could summon the language. And if leadership was a part of our mission in life, then the sons must learn to speak. There was something else to it as well. My grandparents had emphasized public speaking to my father because they both spoke with accents and nothing gave them more *nachas* than to hear the grandchildren speak beautifully. As early as I can remember, I was reciting when my grandparents came for Passover, at Friday night services, and in school.

"Look up Edna Constable," my father advised when I arrived at Carr Junior High. I did, and began a six-year relationship that continued long after I took the one course she taught. Miss Constable was a compact, five-foot dynamo, the civics teacher who loved to teach government and felt that students had to participate to learn—so she pushed debate and oratory, which to her provided insights into how the Constitution was drafted and the laws were made. She dragged us to City Council meetings and the state legislature; she invited local officials to class to speak; she was adviser to the school newspaper, the student council, a civics club,

163

and the speech club, and mixed all of her bulldog ambition for her students with an outpouring of love, the secret ingredient that made a young boy strive for her in ways he would never strive for himself.

She would haul her favorites inexorably into the annual declamation contest, requiring a memorized speech and a presentation before the whole student body. "No excuses. You'll enter and you'll win," she asserted. First, we had to select a speech, and Miss Constable would pull out her secret envelope with dozens of sure-fire presentations to pick from. We decided on Franklin Delano Roosevelt's Declaration of War, because, as she said, "Roosevelt saved us from the Depression and won the war"; she had not let anyone use it since my brother had won with it in 1942, when he was in the seventh grade.

We practiced every day, and she suggested I try all the gestures that win the judges' fancy—the arms spread wide, the clenched fists, a step forward. She taught me not to be so sing-songy and to pace my voice for dramatic effect. I was too short to stand behind the podium, so I tried standing on a soft-drink crate, but that made my head look like a peanut on a tobacco stick. She decided on a bold gamble: I would walk out to the side and stand alone, facing the audience bravely without props. We rehearsed it for hours.

A week before the contest, on a Boy Scout overnight camping trip, I waded through some weeds and became infested with a terrible case of poison ivy. The juicy bumps spread like lava up my leg and arms. Two days before the contest, it spread to my crotch and at the final rehearsal Miss Constable even commented that I looked "restless" on the stage and that I seemed in a big hurry to run through it and get it over with.

The public speaker's greatest fear clutched me—suppose, in the middle of the most dramatic part, standing alone beside the podium, suppose when I was demanding that the Congress declare war on the Imperial Nation of Japan, suppose just then I was seized with an excruciating itch and had to scratch myself furiously in front of everybody. . . .

On the day of the competition, I emptied out a small bottle of aspirin and filled it full of calomine lotion, the pink, gobby medicine that everyone dabbed their poison ivy with, and tucked the bottle and a wad of cotton away in my book bag. Ten minutes before the competition, I crept into the boys' room, saturated a piece of cotton, and wrapped it neatly around my afflicted organ.

164

The stage had three seats on either side, for the boy and girl finalists, and I saw my parents slip into the rear of the auditorium. I had to sit through all the girls' selections—a recitation from *Gone With the Wind* by Carole Herndon; an original nature poem by Dorothy Battle Rankin; and Joanna Holloway's children's story with a growling bear. The cotton was drying and I began to squirm halfway through Gordon "Brain" Rosser's "Catiline's Defiance," when, mercifully, my turn arrived.

I strode to the spot Miss Constable had marked with blue chalk, and began "Mr. Speaker, Mr. Vice President, members of the Congress, the Supreme Court . . ." and I felt the cotton slide slightly forward. "Yesterday, December 7th, 1941," and I tried desperately to hold onto it with an intricate hip movement, "a day that will live in infamy . . ." but I could feel it slip off and depart; then the internal horror as I sensed it inching down my pants leg, and as I reached ". . . bombed Pearl Harbor," the piece of cotton, tubular-shaped and pink, dribbled from under my cuff to roll gently into place beside me on the stage. Gamely, I finished, but as I sat through Hank Bissette's "I Speak for Democracy," I stared transfixed at the vagrant puff looking like a giant pink boulder resting heavily on the stage and prayed it would disintegrate.

As we left the stage, I tried to be casual when I snatched it up and stuffed it in my pocket. If Miss Constable noticed, she never said anything. She hugged Mister Jew tightly when we won.

Hebrew school on Tuesday and Thursday afternoons required a long walk through town past Durham Sporting Goods (to bounce a basketball) and past the Criterion Theater (to look at photographs of scenes from the current movies).

"Hey, where ya goin'?" my friends would ask.

"Just downtown to look around," I would answer. No one ever knew I was headed for the synagogue.

When I was six, I learned to read Hebrew, but I never really progressed much further, because no one ever tried to make the breakthrough to speaking it. I was so slow that sometimes when we read the silent prayer at services and the old men would *daven* away (rocking back and forth as they raced through the prayer), I would read the same prayer in English twice as fast just so I could sit down when they did.

The rabbi tried gamely to give some Jewish content to our lives, but with so few of us, he had to lump everyone from the junior and senior high schools in the same class so we would have enough students, and it was just too demanding for the older kids, after a day in the iron-disciplined world of the Misses Maude Heflin and Inez Page, to hold it in much longer. Besides, no one had any stake in making good grades in Hebrew school, and we calculated how to drive poor Cantor Kaminetsky to exasperation. His daughter Aviva was the smartest girl in the class, and better known to us as the "holy terror" because she was just the opposite—perfect in Hebrew school and something less at high school. The rabbi and Cantor Kaminetsky drew the line at throwing things, but Lubah Freedman and Carol Bloomfield giggled incessantly as we passed each other notes; and Carol Fink colored Adam green in the kindergarten coloring books. And Harvey Peck wore his skullcap at a jaunty angle over his forehead and made faces that had us collapsing in hysterics when the cantor turned to the blackboard.

The training for my bar mitzvah required individual sessions with the rabbi, and extra time preparing for it to learn the *haftorah* section I would sing and the other prayers to go with it. Now the incentive changed—I didn't want to make a fool of myself in front of all the relatives, and that meant hard work and long hours of learning melodies, stretching for a reading proficiency in Hebrew and memorizing a speech the rabbi wrote about manhood and milestone ("I want to thank my beloved rabbi for his spiritual guidance . . ."). I didn't feel like a man, really, or know how I was supposed to feel, but it was nice for a thirteen-year-old boy to hear others say that I was a man now.

Relatives and friends of the family flooded me with presents, special gifts so it was easy to understand that this was not just another birthday. I went to synagogue on Friday nights and Saturday mornings for a few months to case the action so I would know what to expect.

The relatives starting flocking in for the weekend on Wednesday, since my mother's family—eight sisters and one brother with some two dozen first cousins—turned every bar mitzvah into a family reunion. They stayed up late on Friday night, and the whole family piled into a single hotel room, children and aunts, sitting all over the beds, listening to memories of the big seven-passenger Nash their "Papa" used to pour the children into on Sundays for a drive, the sisters singing the songs he used to lead them in during the ride.

166

The service on Saturday morning went off with minor hitches, like my leaving out a whole sentence, but my father offered his usual advice that "a hundred years from now, we'll never know the difference."

I sank in relief at the end, feeling an enormous sense of satisfaction that I could handle such an assignment: memorize a speech and make people cry, and sing a whole twenty minutes without stopping. And at the end, my mother choked up presenting me with a white Bible from Hadassah with my name on it.

I stood at the door with the rabbi; everyone hugged me and kissed me and pinched and gouged my cheeks and told me I was wonderful. Zola squeezed me especially and said, "You is my boy, too."

The highlight for the guests and relatives was the dinner dance that night at the Carolina Inn in Chapel Hill. To add novelty, my mother rented a Greyhound bus with a bar in it to take all the family and guests over.

The presence of my mother's sisters always transformed her in some magical way from the mother I trusted to the sister they knew. They shared so many secrets, had so much to chatter about, as they gossiped about former beaus and old friends they had seen recently. They were teen-agers again, giggly and tittering; they simply abandoned the men they married to face each other, and the uncles survived in the sure acceptance that this was just one of the costs of marrying into the family.

Madcap Aunt Irene, who at the age of five painted blond-headed Sonny-Boy Wilson with black paint, became the family clown when she loosened up; Mary, who gave show business a try in New York and ended up singing with a band on a Caribbean cruise before Grandma Jennie dragged her back to North Carolina where she eventually married Uncle Harold and settled down in Miami, would sing "My Yiddisha Mama" while all the sisters grew misty.

When the band took a rest and put their instruments down, it was time for Aunt Eve and Aunt Dodi to play the piano and sing together, dusting off the old Nash Sisters routine for a run-through of "Off the Water Wagon, One, Two, Three," and "Melinda, the Mousey," while the old boyfriends, who used to gather at the Nachamson home in Durham and had now come from Greensboro, Charlotte, and Wilmington for my bar mitzvah, all sighed and remembered.

167

Meanwhile, over the little meat biscuits, gefilte fish balls, fried chicken, and Zola's chopped liver, Uncle Tommy and my father discussed the shelving business with Uncle Paul, who was in five-and-tens, and they pulled my other Uncle Harold into it because he ran a Polynesian restaurant in West Virginia (and was the only Jewish sheriff in all of Appalachia).

Aunt Grace put her arms around my neck and with her nose a few inches away whispered sincerely, "Remember, you can fall in love with a rich one as easily as a poor one." Irene proposed a classic toast "to life" (in Yiddish, *l'chayim*). She rose dramatically to speak in her most drippy Southern accent. "I'd like to propose a toast to Look Hiyum," and Naomi screeched, "Who's he?" and everybody roared. Aunt Ethel, who married a rabbi, waited patiently until there was a lull, and then presented every sister with a handmade purse she had spent several months crocheting. Uncle Bill, the ninth child and the only boy, just sat there in his customary bewilderment at his sisters' antics.

We cousins crowded around our own table, sneaking glasses of champagne behind the drapery and pretending we were really drunk, reeling around out of control until my mother pulled us to a stop. "Oh, Sara," Aunt Grace advised, "let him do what he wants. He's a man now." My mother asked me if I had danced with all the aunts since I was the guest of honor, but she was the only one who believed that anybody remembered me. To escape more cheek pinching, I ducked out the side door and headed for the big bus waiting outside.

I peered through the window on the door of the bus, and could make out the driver, named Bobby, short sleeves of his dark gray uniform rolled up even shorter, a lanky kid in his early twenties, cigarette dangling and portable radio blaring country music, his bus driver's hat pushed way back on his head.

"What's this 'bar mister' they keep talkin' about?" he wanted to know. We talked for a while and he told me how bored he was waiting for everybody to come back, but the company broke in new drivers on short-haul charters with a lot of waiting and that's the way it was.

"Y' know what I'd like more than anything?" I asked, not waiting for a reply. "A big, juicy hamburger with lettuce, tomato, and lots of ketchup."

168

"Me, too," he answered wistfully, and suddenly he lit up like a pinball machine that's just coughed up two free games. "Let's go and get one."

Bobby started up the big Greyhound. It heaved into gear and he wheeled it out of the driveway, roaring off through the campus.

"Hey, where you going?" I asked, stunned.

"The Blue Light Drive-In, man," Bobby answered, bearing down the twisting hill out onto the highway to Durham, twelve miles away.

I perched in the lead seat to look at the bugs dancing in the headlights, ripping through the darkness in my shiny, blue bar mitzvah suit, sopping up my Southern-boy fantasy of directing my own personal Greyhound.

We pulled into the Blue Light and groaned to a stop amidst all the jalopies and the startled teen-agers sipping milkshakes and rubbing up against each other. Bobby beeped for a waitress, and I leaned over and whispered to him, "Make mine all the way."

The crowd was waiting at the entrance of the Carolina Inn when we returned, and when the door opened I jumped down nonchalantly.

"Where the devil have you been?" my father demanded.

"To get a hamburger," I said sheepishly, and Uncle Leon started laughing.

"What else would you expect a bar mitzvah boy in a Greyhound to be doing at midnight?" he said.

In the summers my parents made certain that I received the maximum Jewish exposure by sending me to the several Jewish camps that dotted the state. As many as a thousand Southern Jewish kids went to Camp Blue Star and Camp Osceola in the North Carolina mountains, but there were also camps with a more Zionist orientation if parents preferred that. Young Judea, a youth organization with the strongest commitment to Israel, ran a series of camps under its own name; and Brandeis Camp Institute, for the few years it was open in North Carolina, modeled its camp after an Israeli kibbutz, complete with a daily routine of work in the cornfields, an Israeli staff, the daily study of Hebrew, and discussion groups on various Jewish subjects. (The German Jews from New Orleans and Atlanta sent their kids away from the South—to Jewish camps in Wisconsin and Maine with Indian names like

Nebagamon and Chicagami or postcard names like Walden or Trip Lake.)

I went to all of these camps at various stages of growing up, and while they offered the usual activities—swimming, horseback riding, canoe classes, overnight hikes—all of them tried to create, some more intensely than others, a positive and open Jewish environment—they kept kosher, taught Israeli folk dancing and folk songs, classes in arts and crafts, painted and sculpted biblical subjects, and presented plays with Jewish themes in the drama and music workshops.

Herman and Harry Popkin at Camp Blue Star near Hendersonville, North Carolina, built a veritable camping empire in the postwar era, based on a light mixture of Judaism with camping fun for boys and girls of all ages. Herman served for many years as director of the Southern Zionist Youth Commission in Atlanta and Harry was B'nai B'rith Youth Director for District 7, which extended from Alabama, Mississippi, and New Orleans to Tennessee and Texas. Together, they traveled the South in jobs that gave them credibility with parents and put them in constant touch with young people. With contacts in every city, they began to drum up interest in a small camp—starting with sixty boys in 1947—that today can look back on more than 10,000 alumni and every year draws more than 1,500 campers and 300 staff back to six camps on a 600-acre site.

There were always more girls than boys at the camps because mothers were more anxious for their daughters to spend summers in a supervised setting than at home running around with older boys. The small-town girls arrived with trunks full of jeans and workshirts, while the Atlanta girls sported coordinated outfits and silk scarves. The thirteen-year-old girls chased the senior boy counselors constantly—tugging, hitting, and snatching their hats and dashing off, pushing them into the lake and hoping for attention. Some girls were miserable in the competition, but others took it stoically and learned perhaps that it was possible to have fun without a boy around, especially if there were plenty of other girls in the same situation.

The Southern Jewish camp was close to nirvana for small-town boys confronting, for an entire summer, acres and acres of Jewish girls in tight shorts and delicious T-shirts, and sharing with them softball games, chilly nights snuggling by a campfire, and long discussions about God and life. The adolescent sex-play was harm-

170

less, stirring and limited for campers (because we were required to be in our bunks after taps), but the adventures after lights out for counselors drew some boys I knew back to camp for thirteen summers straight, working up the entire ladder of responsibility, from counselor-in-training to junior counselor to full-fledged senior counselor with all the rights and privileges thereof.

On Fridays, we spent the entire afternoon cleaning the camp thoroughly—airing bedding and swabbing out the cabins—all in readiness for the Sabbath. At sundown, we fifteen-year-olds climbed out of our University of North Carolina sweatshirts and into our whites, the Sabbath uniform complete with a white silk skullcap, and strolled up to the dining hall where we sang Sabbath songs during the best meal of the week, followed by a melodic *birkat*, the grace-after-meal, that the Israelis taught us. As campers, we planned our own Friday night services, a special experience in the mountains. Sometimes we held them in a wooded glade transformed into an outdoor synagogue, where we sat tingling in the night air, bathed in the glory of a tinted sky, watching stars pop out during the service as the mountains turned into a massive black rolling background, sanctified by the sounds of worship. We called on all the talent in camp, making use of the music study group as a choir, selecting all the readings from favorite novels or poetry, allowing guitar solos and wood flutes. At the end of the service, all of us gathered round in concentric circles and sang "Shabbat Shalom," the song of Sabbath peace, while swaying slowly to the music with arms about each other, candlelight flickering off our faces. Finally there were warm kisses and squeezes and a quiet wish to everyone for a "good *shabbos*," with a slightly softer kiss and tighter squeeze for the girls you really liked.

The camp strained itself to maintain Jewish content in its program, and imported rabbis and writers for discussions of issues like intermarriage, keeping Jewish holidays, and the differences between Orthodox, Conservative, and Reform Judaism. I became an expert in the ritualized discussion of "What is a Jew?" (not a race or a religion, not a culture or a people), because I had sat through it so many times. I would hold myself back until just the right moment to make the point that it was all of these and none of these alone; and I would make sure that I beat my cousin David to that marvelous insight, since he wanted us to think he too was brilliant.

Still, I had never really thought about the relationship of Israel

171

to American Jews or considered the "God-idea" or the "God-process," as one speaker put it, and for the first time we discussed such things with other kids, instead of having adults tell us what to believe. Friendships and romances blossomed that were deeper than anything we had experienced before; this was linked closely to the sensuality of the Judaism we were experiencing in that setting, coupled with the mutual self-discovery coming out of an experience calculated to create and resolve an identity crisis at the same time.

The Israelis who helped staff the camps were always extraordinary people—artists mostly, who were studying in the United States. They were vital personalities, relaxed in an open-faced natural Jewishness, easy and unforced, jabbering away in Hebrew, homesick and eager to return and serve—the first real foreigners that most of us had ever met. They came in couples usually, the wife a dancer or a singer and the husband studying engineering but for the summer fixing cabin rooftops and tending the camp garden—two or three acres of corn and vegetables that we weeded and watered to simulate the kibbutz experience, picking basketfuls all summer so we could experience the joy of eating food we had grown ourselves. The Israeli wives were different sorts of girls from what I had ever encountered before—self-sufficient and independent, with a disarming directness and not a whit of false charm. They had strong, lovely legs that could outrun and outjump most of the boys. They wore no makeup but were more beautiful than girls who did, simple in dress and serious in manner, both cool and poetic. They spoke matter-of-factly of living so close to danger in Israel; of how death intensified their lives. Once, when early in the summer several boys held back from folk dancing because it was "sissy," one of the Israelis summoned her husband—a broad-shouldered and mustached man whom we respected as tough and heroic—and he swept her up in a whooping, exuberant *hora*, so infectious that soon we were all dancing with them, leaping as high as we could to keep up, finally dropping out exhausted while they danced on.

When the summer ended and the parents arrived to pick up their children, they were startled at the wrenching, emotional farewells, and the vows of loyalty and affection and determination to come back again next summer. For the rest of our days, it seemed, one sure way that Jewish kids all over the South could

172

start a long conversation was by asking, "What years were you at Blue Star?"

In the seventh grade, I had wanted to play drums or the trumpet, but my mother eased me cleverly over to the clarinet, quieter and more tolerable. By the time I reached high school, I played in the band under the baton of Mr. Enloe, who somehow heard sweet sounds when he knew we were flat but realized that was the best we could do. I marched in all the parades, and in the back of the bus on band trips after the team took on the Rocky Mount Blackbirds, I cuddled with the girls who played chimes or the flute, but stood back in awe from the majorettes, who aimed for bigger game. It slowly dawned on me that the band was only a backdrop for the real action. I made my decision after a night game, when defensive lineman Bugs Compton stopped to talk for a few minutes to some of the lowly band members, blood on his uniform, a gaping hole in his smile, football helmet in hand while a cheerleader with her blond hair stood gently resting her head on his grass-stained pads. At that moment, I decided to hang up my clarinet case and buy some cleats. I was going out for football.

"What do you need it for?" my mother asked. "Certainly not to get into college; it will hurt your grades, you could even be crippled. . . ."

But my father had been a three-sport letterman at Fayetteville High School and he knew he was talking to one of Durham High's greatest future halfbacks. Hadn't I starred in neighborhood games, diving for passes, swivel-hipping past Buck Farrell, kicking the ball out of bounds on the two-yard line? We took a long walk and he confessed that once, when he had been knocked out in a game, his mother came out of the stands and right down on the field to see if h' was all right. "Promise me one thing," he warned, "if you start, don't quit." There was another thing I didn't tell him: someone at Hi-Y meeting had asked me if it was true that "Jews aren't athletic"; I just couldn't sit on the sidelines tooting my horn for another year—that was no place for Mister Jew!

Elmer Barbour, the coach who greeted the seventy-five potential heroes in the god-awful August heat, smiled sadistically as we grunted through the sit-ups and the push-ups, and the head rolls to strengthen our necks, and the wind sprints to make certain that only sixty boys showed up the next day. A summer of standing in

173

front of the mirror doing "Charles Atlas dynamic tension" exercises hardened me to a lean 137 pounds for the early ordeal, and I made it through the first cut.

Coach Barbour used ridicule as his major weapon of incentive, tobacco juice oozing from the side of his mouth, a spit in disgust and a grumbling "she-ee-it" his most excessive form of compliment. He squinted fiercely at the talent, wobbled on knees that were puffy from old college injuries, and cussed with the verve of a chronic crapshooter.

When Barbour issued uniforms, most of the team received new pants, made of stretch material so the potential tacklers would slide off their sleek bodies; I got a worn-out, faded pair of pants with shredded knee pads so baggy that I had to use a belt from home to hold them up. While most of the team received new, smooth, white plastic helmets with white chin straps, Barbour handed me a cracked, twisted, misshapen old leather helmet from the war years. Mister Jew looked like a prune in a sea of glossy eggshells.

When I threw up after practice one day, Barbour started calling me "ole eel-eye" (having seen my real name, Eli, on a medical certificate we had to fill out). When my mother made me miss two days of practice because of Rosh Hashanah, he said, "That's the goddamnedest excuse I ever heard"; when I tried to be a punter, he advised me, "You're too valuable at fullback to waste your energy kicking"; and when I missed a signal and ran into our halfback, he accused me of being a "snot-nosed camel turd." Everybody caught it from Barbour, not out of his desire to humiliate, though he certainly never restrained his creative impulse, but he knew no other way to express any affection. I cringed then, but to be swept up in Elmer Barbour's profanity branded me a true member of the team—a player in bad standing like all the rest.

One day, just before the first game, Barbour gave me his old number—number 23—out of a twinkle-eyed fondness for his incompetent runt fullback: "Here ya go, eel-eye, wear it with pride." And I accepted it with all the drama of the old gunfighter passing his notched pistols to a boy. He teased me differently after that, more personal and less the butt of his old classics. When Coy Olive suggested that "with your Jew brain, you oughta switch to quarterback," I went to see Coach Barbour, who reacted with "You're smart enough but you ain't got the hands"; once in sweeping theatrics before a full-dress scrimmage, he pepped us on with

174

"We want a will to win on this team . . . from the top, Bass, to the bottom, Evans."

Buddy Bass co-captained the team as our bruising all-state half-back, sawing linebackers in half on the straight ahead handoff, the Bulldog bread-and-butter play. He was such a vicious tackler that he rumbled on defense too, from defensive left halfback where opposing ends paid the price for looking back over their shoulders for a pass. During practice, when a few of us would go out for passes against the defensive backs, the scrubs would fall over each other in line to avoid Buddy, who played hard-nosed full-steam football all the time. Once, when it looked like "Freshman Charlie" Rogers had drawn Buddy, Charlie bent down to pretend to tie his shoe and politely said, "You go ahead," and Mister Jew crouched in his three-point stance and looked up . . . into the glaring fierce-ness of Captain Bass. I sprinted out five steps and gave Bass a terrific head fake to my right . . . but he didn't go for it; then I threw him my own Evans special spin-fake-button-hook-stop-and-go . . . but Bass didn't bite; I then cut away into the right flank and Willie Jack "Red" Holt lobbed the ball and I looked back over my right shoulder and saw it coming, slow and spirally, when KERBLAM—Bass hit me like a falling safe, my helmet went flying and we skidded on my nose almost ten feet toward the side-lines with Bass riding on top. The next day in English, when Mattie Holloway asked me about the scar on my nose, I told her with casualness covering pride, "Oh, it's nothing. Buddy hit me in practice yesterday."

Harry Galifianakis anchored the line, a 220-pound guard whose parents were Greek immigrants who spoke poor English and ran a little restaurant for blacks downtown with which they put four sons through college. Everybody called Harry "the Greasy Greek," but I just couldn't; luckily I managed to quash "the Hustling Hebrew" when the nicknames were being passed around.

Sometimes, one of the stars from Duke would come over to work out with us, and if he could coherently put some sentences to-gether, he would deliver one of those muscular Christian athletic speeches: "In football, we got the first, second and third teams. But on the God Squad, everybody's first team. So get in the game of life and star!"

Friday night was game night, and that meant skipping the Sabbath meal with my parents and asking Zola to fix a steak at

175

four o'clock in the afternoon, just as the coach directed, early enough to be digested. Fighting a bad case of the butterflies, I set out for the school dressing room at six o'clock so that the manager could tape my ankles; and then I began the slow ritual of silently climbing into the warrior's gear, all of us together, close and fearless.

At seven-fifteen, Coach Barbour took the first team aside for a private last-minute prayer while the assistant coach pumped us up with a "Stomp those mothahs" that ended with all of us roaring a mighty whoop of determination. Then we'd start to run clickety-clack in our cleats across the concrete floor, out the door for the short trot to Durham Athletic Park and the dash full-steam into the bright lights, while the crowd went berserk and the cheerleaders showed their pants in a whirling greeting. Warm-ups were important to me since I knew that I would never play in a game, and I gave it all I had, particularly certain to dive into the grass to mess up my uniform a little so the hero-worshipping kids after the game wouldn't know I didn't play. During passing drills, I summoned all my skill because every time number 23 caught a pass, a cheer would burst forth from my old friends in the band, complete with a blast from Carmen Huckabee's trombone. In the shower room with seven of the grimy heroes afterwards, I once secretly noticed that I was the only circumcised gladiator soaping down. I turned to face the wall.

Mister Jew didn't play in any games that fall, but I stayed for the whole season, as I had promised my father, long enough for Buddy Bass to write in my yearbook under the team picture, "You'll play a lot of ball for us next year."

Her name was Natalie, and together we were alone, she the only Jewish girl and I the only Jewish boy in our class. For years, we smiled at each other in the halls, cautious but affectionate, and slightly resentful that parents and the Jewish community expected us to be romantically entangled. We were friends, intimate and understanding, both of us rebellious against the biblical force of history and calling on each other for reassurance. When she went to the junior-senior prom with Sykes Carter, my mother blamed me; if I had not fallen from my duty, such a tragedy would not have occurred. It was almost as embarrassing when we did end up going to something with each other—usually an important event

176

like the senior class play, when mothers really made an issue of it. Then, walking arm-in-arm, we were both mortified because everybody knew we didn't date ordinarily and that I was with her only because we were Jewish. Sometimes, gentile girls would say, "You'll marry Natalie, won't you?" or make a point of reminding me that while they liked me a lot, if I didn't take Natalie to a dance, she probably wouldn't be able to go at all. Years later, when both of us gained perspective, she told me that her mother expected her to be attractive enough for me to take her out, and that she judged herself some sort of failure if she didn't succeed. As we imagined it, our mothers talked and plotted at Hadassah meetings, and complained to each other of their miserable fate in such a small town and hoped for the best.

But for two years my heart belonged at first secretly and then openly to Liz Jordan, homecoming queen and acknowledged beauty of the class. She projected that graceful kind of beauty that Southern girls have perfected through history, long brown hair framing big fluttering brown eyes, trusting and dreaming, with an easy smile that stirred the boys she graced with it—and she graced us all. We thought of her as aristocratic and "ree-fined," a proper girl to whom we attached all the essential Southern virtues— sweetness, softness, thoughtfulness, elegance, and modesty. Her mother was active in the Methodist church women's group, and she in the youth fellowship.

Liz was the classic Southern beauty; she walked with a long, confident gait, perhaps "flowed" is a better word, but didn't try athletics at lunch period, preferring to languish like a vision on the sidelines. She was serious in her studies but never openly smart, thus never a threat. She was popular even with girls because she never spoke a harsh word of others and worked hard at avoiding the terrible high-school charge of being "stuck-up." No one ever caught her primping; if there was any sexiness to her, it smoldered in her innocence, her lack of awareness of her power and unconcern for its impact; her most potent weapon was her unattainability, for few boys had the self-assurance to try.

Liz had what we called a "good reputation," and it was natural that everyone should vote her honors like homecoming queen and secretary of the student council, for she exemplified our aspirations for womankind. We had served as class officers together, and if I was selected president of the student council, not only would I have

177

a good excuse for not going out for football the next year but Liz and I could work with each other over the summer, and I would probably be able to crown her homecoming queen at the game that fall. With lumbering Tom Lee, the big, bad defensive lineman and co-captain of the football team making the nomination speech for me at assembly, and a brisk campaign consisting of posters that said "Even Bugs Bunny Says Vote for Sonny" and "Your vote is a must for a guy you can trust," I won the right to kiss her cheek on that warm homecoming night, and exult in pictures of us together in the morning newspaper.

I walked her home from school each day and we would usually stop at the West Side Pharmacy for a Coke. After, at the corner a block from her house (and safely out of view of her mother), we would hesitantly brush good-bye. Finally, she invited me to be one of her escorts for the statewide debutante ball in Raleigh.

"You're not going and that's it. It's final. *Final!* Do you hear me?"

"But, Mom, it's only a dance."

"We're doing it for your sake. Of course she's a nice girl—but that's just the point."

It was the first of several furious confrontations with my mother over not dating Jewish girls, which I usually resolved simply by not telling her. But this date required the rental of a white tie and tails, money for flowers, and the car for the weekend, and Mother won easily. Sadly I told Liz I had other plans. (It never helped to sneak out; at every movie I imagined there was somebody from the Jewish community to spy on me and report back.)

From the time I was old enough to drive, or climb in a car with someone who could, my parents had packed me off to B'nai B'rith conventions to be with other Jewish kids—statewide meetings in Raleigh and Charlotte, regional get-togethers in Columbia and Charleston, and South-wide weekend conclaves in Atlanta and occasionally Birmingham and even New Orleans.

In any North Carolina city the entire Jewish community rallied to host the convention, opening their homes to the children of their friends from across the state. A light cloud of parental approval lent an atmosphere of happy permissiveness, and the kids thronged to these conventions with titillating expectations of romantic entanglements. Girls, as many as ten, would pack into a house, and it was not unusual for the "lovers," like Bobby Kadis from Goldsboro, to date five different girls in a single weekend. Carloads of boys would drive around until early morning visiting the clusters of girls in each home, chattering about sex constantly but too shy to do more than keep moving to the next house. It was so much fun that a Greek boy named Pete from Raleigh came to every convention because he looked Greek enough to pass for Jewish.

The convention began with a Friday night "mixer" and then Sabbath services, a religious concession that B'nai B'rith insisted on as justification for the event. When a mother asked what happened at convention, you could start with, "Well, after services on Friday night. . . ." On Saturdays there would be a picnic and interclub softball or basketball games. And there was always fierce face-to-face politicking over the election of statewide president (called Aleph Godol—the "Big A") and the selection of statewide sweetheart.

The conventions included kids from seventh grade to twelfth, and the pathetic differences in development came clashing together at the big Saturday night formal, usually held at the Jewish Community Center. Kids in various stages of pimples, braces, and slipping falsies would mill around, trying to avoid the concerned mothers serving punch and spongecake on the sidelines. The girls stumbled around in clunky high heels, heavy eye shadow, twisted garter belts, and the general misery brought on by all that newly acquired female paraphernalia. Boys worried about somebody seeing an embarrassing lump in their pants. A few college guys wearing fraternity pins always showed up to big-deal their way around the girls, dangling invitations to weekends at Carolina, though the Yankees who strutted around the place had not yet learned that they had come basically for rush purposes and shouldn't "snake" too severely on a potential pledge.

We also went to rush parties at the Chapel Hill fraternities, a superintensive short course in the more graceful aspects of college life—throwing up at football games, passing out at parties, guzzling beer and Purple Jesus (grape juice and gin), and sitting around trying to blend in by checking out coeds, talking to hometown girls you were grateful to see, and trying to think of something to say to guys from New Jersey and Brooklyn.

High-school girls from all over the state went to college weekends. Mothers couldn't forbid it, since there were so few Jewish boys at home for them to date, so they compromised and risked sending a daughter up to the "sin centers" earlier than they wanted to. After all, how bad could all those nice Jewish boys be? Pretty bad. It wasn't only that a tenth-grade girl from Lumberton couldn't handle the smooth, big-city line of a guy from Passaic, but how was she to get back to the motel at two o'clock in the morning when he had passed out over the beer cooler?

Atlanta dominated the politics and the spirit of the regional conventions because the B'nai B'rith Youth Organization (BBYO) was so popular and all-consuming there. They had dozens of clubs: AZA for boys, with names like SOZ (Sons of Zion), MOT (Men of Torah), LOJ (Lions of Judea). The girls belonged to clubs named DJG (Devoted Jewish Girls), Ahava ("love" in Hebrew), and Anne Frank.

Much of the activity was a rehearsal for later fraternity and sorority life; it was not unusual for the Atlanta kids at the University of Georgia to have been in the same club with each other for over ten years. The chapter sweetheart, a singular honor for an Atlanta girl, led the cheering at chapter games, made up songs to sing at conventions, created a chapter banner, and generally served as confessor and social chairman to fix up the shy boys in the club.

There was no girl like the Atlanta Jewish girl—she reigned over the South with sureness, calculated charm, and a knowledge of men that came from starting early and never having to try hard. She placed unrelenting pressure on an out-of-town blind date to perform, to tell snappy stories, and give her an imaginative good time. The problem started with the fact that Georgia Tech and Emory brought hundreds of Jewish boys to Atlanta, where there were too few college-age Jewish girls; thus the college boys began dating high-school girls, which forced the high-school Jewish boys to drop down into junior high. To small-town boys from North and South Carolina, the Atlanta syndrome produced an accelerated sophistication—eighth-grade girls who knew about mascara and uplift bras and how to order in expensive restaurants. The "T.A.G." (Typical Atlanta Girl), as she was known all over the Jewish South, was fickle, easily bored, overconvinced of her attractiveness, ungrateful for casual evenings, and spoiled by expectations inflated by years and years of fawning college men.

In a small town, the last month of high school becomes a poignant turning point, for many of us had been in the same class

180

for twelve years, grown up with each other through harsh teachers and sandlot football, through happy nights of bicycle tag and Halloween mischief, plotting together adventurous intrigues of stealing scuppernongs or busting one of Mr. Wannamaker's ripening watermelons. We would scatter now, to college or to the army or to jobs in Durham or just off to somewhere, most of us never to see each other again.

We were fitted for graduation robes before exams, sometime in May, a magic time in Durham when the wisteria blooms and the Duke Gardens explode in color and the bumble bees grow fat and pokey from an excess of nectar in the morning glories and honeysuckle. Somehow, we steeled ourselves for the last exams, and managed to study between the rounds of graduation parties, out of habit and pride more than necessity.

When I walked to my locker after the history exam, the hallway had sprung alive with whispering and alarm, an uncustomary excitement all the more upsetting because it was so out of harmony with the otherwise sweet-sad mood of that final week.

"Did y'all hear the news about the Supreme Court?" The words raced each other to get out, full of uncertainty and shock. "They say we're going to have to integrate. Go to school with *them*. Right here!" The story came out in snatches, rushing over me in waves—"the niggers," "next year probably," "they'll mess up everything." Still, none of us realized the implications—by the end of the day the talk was all about putting in extra water fountains and "colored" restrooms.

Several of us headed downtown after school to find out more, silent until Willie Honeycutt broke the somberness. "Do you think they'll come to our junior-senior?"

It was the kind of question that Mister Jew always avoided out of instinct; he wanted to stall for time until he could get home for dinner with the Mayor.

"I guess so," Mister Jew said. "But they'll probably keep to themselves."

"But suppose one of 'em breaks in on you to dance with your date?" one of the football players in the group asked.

"We'll whup ass," someone else answered. And then another voice objected. "I ain't no nigger lover and I ain't going to any dance they're at."

The phone rang most of the evening, and my father finally took it off the hook so that we could finish dinner.

"What's going to happen, Dad?"

"I just don't know." He was tired and drawn from the day. "It was all so sudden. I just hope the whites don't make trouble. It's going to test everybody. At least we have a summer to cool off and work it out."

It wasn't the first we teen-agers had heard about integration. A few years earlier, when the back-of-the-bus rules were changed, we all had to ask ourselves questions like, "When you're sitting beside a Negro man, is it polite to give your seat to a white woman?" The answer was no. Coming home from school, the boys in class used to race each other for the choice seats next to the Negro men so we could keep our seats the entire trip.

Liz and I went to the graduation dance, she in a puff-sleeved, pale green dress, and I held her closer than I ever had before. (Natalie dated Sykes Carter because after three exhausting years, our parents agreed to give in for this all-important last night of high school.) It had never occurred to me so starkly that there were no Negroes in our class, but now I wondered about next year's dance. The Center Theater put on a midnight show, courtesy of the PTA, to keep us all in one place, and I found my mind wandering in the darkness, thinking of the Negroes in next year's class who would be sitting here too (though probably up in the third balcony in the "colored only" section). Every high-school scene began to take on a black dimension—the lunchroom, the classes, the football practice, the games. But they were fleeting thoughts. This was graduation night, a sweet moment to cling to as long as we could.

Liz and I sat on a swing on her front porch, holding hands until sunrise, confessing nervousness about college and telling soul-secrets about ourselves. The streets were deserted until a car full of seniors shattered the quietness with a blast of the horn; they sped by waving, on their way to the beach.

"It's time to go," I said, hoping her mother wouldn't catch me there at daybreak.

"Good luck, Sonny." She smiled. "We'll see each other often; I just know that."

I crept into my bedroom with the sun of the new day in my window, already making plans for camp that summer and college in the fall.

THIRTEEN

Intermarriage Southern Style

> "He's Jewish, isn't he?"
> "Yes, he is."
> "He looks like the better kind, though. He must be or
> that little sweetheart wouldn't have married him. . . ."
> Well, so he was a Jew. Did it matter? No. Yes . . .
> That he should have finally these suspicions about a
> Jew marrying his own daughter . . . Yes, he sup-
> posed that was what worried him the most. The guests.
> Well, if they had thought anything at all they had not
> betrayed it in their looks. They had been ladies and
> gentlemen. They had turned their bright, Protestant
> eyes upon Harry's face, found it warm and gentle, and
> had shaken his hand. Perhaps they had said. "This is
> a special Jew. This is Peyton's boy."
>
> Lie Down in Darkness,
> William Styron

"THERE is a dramatic rise in intermarriage," says Reform
Rabbi Jacob Rothschild of Atlanta, who refuses to perform them.
"When you lived in a ghetto, you didn't meet non-Jews and therefore couldn't marry them. We've worked for an open society, so the
ghetto doesn't do it for the Jew anymore. Jewish parents have to
emphasize positive Jewish values in the home."

It is not just the Reform Jews who account for the rising
number of intermarriages. Rabbi Harry Epstein of the Conservative Ahavath Achim Synagogue in Atlanta expressed his own
frustration in dealing with young people today: "They call me
prejudiced for preaching against intermarriage; they call Judaism

183

a narrow religion. 'Why can't people who are in love marry?' they ask. But youngsters growing up don't see a wholesome Jewish home nowadays and what can parents expect?"

Today, in the South, almost all Jewish students go to college, where they are meeting non-Jews from similar suburban homes who have been nurtured by the same television memories in an era when secular concerns are smothering religious identity. Organized religion is struggling to reach the young, who often share values about society that they feel transcend differences in formal religious affiliation. "At Naomi's confirmation," said a fifteen-year-old girl from Atlanta, "we wrote our own service, had an electric guitar, and sang protest songs to march to the ark; for a change in mood, she played a tape of Barbra Streisand singing 'People Who Need People.' "

The economic gains of Southern Jews since World War II have produced a generation of Jewish kids similar to their gentile schoolmates, and the response of the gentiles has changed as well. "It used to be that any Jewish boy who married a gentile girl married a manicurist," said the president of a congregation in Arkansas. "Not any more. They're moving out with society girls now who used to turn their backs on them."

A wealthy gentile girl who is marrying a Jewish boy and who belonged to an upper-crust sorority at the University of Georgia provided this insight into the late sixties: "It was the society girls' form of protest to go out with Jewish boys; I mean, we couldn't date Negroes, right? And once it started, we just found them more fascinating and flattering to be with. Frankly, until I met my fiancé, I never dated a guy who was so deeply interested in what I had to *say*."

There was nothing like a fascinated gentile girl to raise the self-esteem of an uncertain Jewish boy. With her, he felt more exciting to be with, his Southern manhood confirmed by her interest in him, his sexuality stirred by venturing out of the tribe to the arms of the eager stranger. This response was strongest of all in the small-town South, where the tribal feeling was accentuated by a Jewish community that raised its children almost as brothers and sisters. It was a familiar Southern syndrome, a variation of the "massa" in the sweet arms of his lady in the manor house secretly yearning for the wild taboos in the slave quarters. And if Southern writers are correct in stating that the starched white women fantasied being an

184

uninhibited slave girl on soft Southern nights, then here was her chance with an acceptable surrogate.

More often, though, the Southern woman saw her Jewish mate in more classic terms—as a man who could dominate her intellectually, possessing her mind while worshiping her body. The sexual implications of this role-playing could have its ironic moments, as one gentile wife pointed out: "He lusted after me as forbidden fruit while I thought he was more poetic and gentle as a lover than the Southern fraternity jocks. There were times when things got downright ridiculous—like when he wanted to make love and I said 'talk to me first.' "

The state schools attracted thousands of small-town girls who were confronting the confusing world of clashing ideas and morality for the first time without parental restriction. A University of Alabama coed talked about the attraction to the Southern version of the "Jewish intellectual": "At some point in their freshman year, the fundamentalist girls used to like to date a Jewish guy, because he was sure to ask a lot of questions she couldn't handle. She was usually at the point where she wanted to rebel anyway, and he was her liberator. And since there was a premium on converting a Hebrew, she could rationalize it as a missionary opportunity."

Most studies (though there are none for the South) have shown that the rate of intermarriage between Jewish men and gentile women far exceeds the rate for Jewish women and gentile men. A gentile wife suggested that "perhaps all the girls have bought the line I heard all my life—that Jewish men make better husbands."

Most of it, however, was more circumstance than design. The Jewish girls were sent off to the cities after college while many of the boys went back home to the family business. The boys at home couldn't fall in love with someone who was not around. With the Jewish girls away at college, they naturally turned to the non-Jewish girls next door.

Urban Jewish novelists write books about families of the second generation in Brooklyn, the Bronx, Long Island, and New Jersey, portraying the stereotyped overbearing mother and a noodle-spined father. But Southern Jewish girls in my experience are much more deeply influenced by their fathers. Part of it is the Southern girl's orientation to men—flirtatious and dependent, bringing out the protective, dominant traits in her men, practicing

185

on her father, who conditions her to expect men to idolize her and keep her on the famous Southern pedestal. Because life in the South is less competitive, the Southern Jewish princess is less driven by her mother than is her Northern counterpart, and more the apple of her father's eye. If she is competitive (and she often is concerning Jewish boys), she masks it in a coating of femininity; if she is dominant (a quality not altogether absent in her mother or in Southern women generally), she is more subtly dominant from her household base, twirling her man around her finger with her wiles rather than squashing him under her thumb or waving her rolling pin.

The magic at work between Northern Jewish boys and Southern Jewish girls was always something to behold. The Northern Jewish boy just wasn't prepared to meet a Jewish girl who was carefully schooled in the Southern art of flirtation. She thought he was worldly, with his easy banter of the New York subway system and intimate descriptions of Lindy's and Greenwich Village; she huddled under his sheltering wing while he handled waiters and roadmaps; she was noncombative, with none of the *shrek* he was accustomed to in Northern girls; and with all her Southern softness and innocence, she was acceptable to *his* mother. When Northern Jewish boys met Southern Jewish girls, it was strictly no contest.

"During the war," said one woman who lived in a Southern town near one of the dozens of military bases which sprinkle the South, "we married off every old maid in town to one of the Northern boys who came down. It was a bonanza."

However, the Southern Jewish girl, in dealing with Southern Jewish boys, faced a peculiar quandary. In the South, parents were stricter with daughters than with sons, but they would instinctively loosen up on the rules if a Jewish boy was involved—the girl could stay out later, go to a youth convention in Charleston or to a college weekend while she was still in high school (which made her very adept at long-distance relationships). Conditioned by her mother to respond more strongly to Jewish boys (because there were so few around), she found herself pressing a little harder when Jewish boys were involved. By trying too hard, she caused an adverse reaction in the Southern Jewish boy, for he compared her, to her disadvantage, with the more elusive Southern belles. A Jewish boy in North Carolina who married a gentile girl offered this commentary on the situation: "Jewish girls were always much more

186

verbal and a lot less coy. They were blunt, buddy-buddy, too close in, as if automatically there was supposed to be something between us. They used sex to get invited to weekends to eye my fraternity brothers. And they thought they were my intellectual equal, and I didn't like that. I guess I wanted a girl who was more Southern than Jewish." In a psychological sense then, a Southern Jewish boy could have a much more "Southern" marriage with a gentile girl who looked up to him, than with a Jewish girl who thought herself her daddy's treasure.

If every Jewish boy was a potential marriage partner, the Southern Jewish girl faced a sexual dilemma—to retain her reputation, yet keep his interest. That pressure often caused her to vary her behavior, being a little more careful with Jewish boys than with gentile boys. A Jewish girl from Little Rock put it this way: "I always felt I was safer with Jewish boys because they wouldn't sleep with a girl they were not going to marry, but who wanted to get married in high school? And, there were so few Jewish boys, I worried about reputation a lot. So I guess I was a little faster with gentile guys because I was less concerned about getting involved; unless he made a big thing out of the fact I was Jewish. Then I had to prove to him that Jewish girls were nice girls too." A Jewish college girl said she would never risk a sexual encounter with a non-Jewish boy because "Mother told me I could get cancer of the cervix."

Such were the problems for the Jewish kids growing up in the small and medium-sized towns in the South. In the major cities like Atlanta, Savannah, Birmingham, New Orleans, and Richmond, the possibility of a boy or a girl leaving for college without ever having dated a gentile was much greater, because parents could apply pressure against it without feeling they were robbing their child of a chance to go out at all.

While there are no comprehensive statistics on intermarriage in the South, Erich Rosenthal looked at marriages involving Jews over a four-year period in Iowa and Indiana, two states with population patterns similar to much of the South. Of 676 marriages involving Jews in Iowa between 1953 and 1959, 42.2 percent were with non-Jews; in Indiana, of 785 marriages involving Jews from 1960 through 1963, 48.8 percent were with non-Jews. Startled by these statistics, a rabbi in Iowa polled all his colleagues in the state, and found that of the ceremonies at which they had officiated, 9.3 percent were intermarriages. However, Rosenthal's original survey included civil ceremonies without rabbis.

Although most rabbis in the South are reluctant to perform intermarriages, a friend of mine in the Deep South who wanted to marry a gentile girl recently found seven rabbis who would officiate in Mississippi, Louisiana, and Alabama—two if they made the gesture of taking some instruction before; two if they studied after; and three without studying at all.

In 1959, the American Jewish Committee tried to probe the differences in attitude between members of Reform temples and Orthodox synagogues in a study of 3,000 families. The Southville Survey by Manheim Shapiro stated that, while 75 percent of the young people with two foreign-born parents disapproved of inter-marriage, only 52 percent of those with two American-born parents did so. Eighty-five percent of Orthodox-affiliated Jews disapproved and 55 percent of the Reform-affiliated disapproved; 20 percent of the Reform members, compared to only one percent of the Orthodox, said it would make no difference.

No studies in the South have examined the higher rate of con-version to Judaism by the non-Jewish partner, but most rabbis in the South agree that it is on the rise now that suburban parents, Jewish and gentile, have so much in common. Since converted wives are renowned as sticklers for the laws and the holidays, this could be a growing factor in reducing some of the objection to intermarriage. A rabbi told me the story of the Jewish boy who complained to his mother that his newly converted wife was driving him crazy wanting to keep kosher, celebrate all the holi-days, and drag him to temple every Friday night. "Don't come complaining to me," his mother said. "I told you not to marry a *shiksa.*"

The immigrant generation had scrambled to get the young immigrants of both sexes together, realizing the connection be-tween religious customs and intermarriage. In Memphis in 1880, the Memphis *Avalanche* printed a notice on Rosh Hashanah that "Jewish ladies" like Hattie Schwarzenberg, Birdie Hesse, and Mattie Goldsmith "will tomorrow receive at their home" the coun-try boys who came to the city for the high holy days.

Sometimes the Jews in little towns tenaciously shouldered enor-mous financial burdens and occasionally dreamed up ingenious devices for holding on to the young and give a Jewish substance to their lives in the hopes of keeping them Jewish. The North Carolina Association of Jewish Men in 1955 pledged the money to support a circuit-riding rabbi in a "chapel bus," equipped with a battery-powered Eternal Light (that stayed on when the motor was off), an ark, and shelves of books in a library area for teaching and worship. The bus roamed through eleven towns in the Carolinas and Virginia, holding Sabbath services, bar mitzvahs, confirmations, marriages, seders, adult Bible and Hebrew classes, and religious instruction for several hundred children. When the circuit rider wheeled into Hickory, North Carolina, and parked just off Main Street near the farmer's market, gentiles flocked around the new mobilized messenger from the chosen people. The minister from the Baptist church showed up to peek in, the mayor welcomed them, and everybody who toured the bus got a free *mazuza* to take home as a souvenir.

The bus project was the brainchild of I. D. Blumenthal, a Charlotte millionaire who was president of the association for eight years and had exhibited a long history of concern for the cohesion of the Jewish community in the state. During the Depression, he bought Wildacres, a 1,400-acre estate, from Thomas Dixon, who had written *The Clansmen* and made enough money from D. W. Griffith's movie version of his book, *Birth of a Nation*, to try to develop a writers' and artists' colony in the North Carolina mountains. Ironically, Blumenthal turned Wildacres into a center for B'nai B'rith Youth Organization institutes, rabbinical meetings, human relations conclaves, and annual meetings of the North Carolina Association of Jewish Men. (Jewish kids always joked about what an appropriate name "Wildacres" was for youth conclaves.)

Most of the towns built small temples in the 1950's, and the circuit rider switched to a car to serve the congregations that could not afford a rabbi; today Rabbi Reuben Kessner spends a Friday night a month in Whiteville, Lumberton, and Jacksonville, North Carolina, and in Myrtle Beach, South Carolina, in what he calls "the greatest educational challenge in all of Jewish education." He thinks nothing of driving two hundred miles for a one-hour Hebrew lesson, and he is proudest of the nine bar mitzvahs he has trained children for in the last five years. "They are my children and I love them all."

189

The small-town Jews need only look to the larger cities to see that it takes more than a religious school and a rabbi to keep out the powerful forces of the majority culture. There all of the traditional institutions of Jewish exclusion are wilting under the pressure of the young in the South—the Jewish fraternities on the college campuses, the Jewish community centers in the major cities—mostly because of the mounting pressure on the discriminatory practices of the gentile country clubs and fraternities, and the need in the eyes of Jews who might qualify for admission to get their own houses in order first.

The Jewish community center in the South is a postwar phenomenon which in almost every larger city has taken over from the houses of worship as the new center of Jewish life in the community. Built with funds from the Orthodox, Conservative, and Reform groups (but usually with major contributions from the postwar new-rich), the clubs are spacious, modern structures offering a whole spectrum of activities—swimming pools and gyms, card rooms and steam baths, adult classes in ceramics, water colors, and Jewish history. In Richmond, Charleston, Memphis, and Charlotte, membership in the centers is open to non-Jews. In Memphis 15 percent of the membership is non-Jewish; in Richmond, 30 percent is non-Jewish.

The fight over open membership was bitter in some cities, pitting the generations against each other in still another value clash. A board member who participated in a major Southern city said, "The debate was a classic. Some said that Jews had no other place to go and this was our own. A few worried about gentile girls in bikinis around our boys. Others were afraid that blacks would come and swim once the bars went down. But the most telling argument was the feeling that no decent and self-respecting gentile would want to join our club. It reminded me of Groucho Marx's statement that 'any club that invites me isn't good enough for me to join!' "

Benjamin Kaplan in *The Eternal Stranger* interviewed extensively in three small Louisiana towns to trace the disintegration of small Jewish communities in the South over many decades. He concluded that "assimilation . . . is a gradual process because Judaism is multiple in ingredients, and its elements are dropped singly over a time span ranging from years to generations." He pointed to a process he called "de-Judaization" in the early set-

190

tlers—the "work rhythm" of the American week which caused the storeowners to give up the Sabbath; the impossibility of keeping a strictly kosher home; the social mobility into the high-status class of the community which demanded a high degree of conformity to class standards, which in turn required discarding Judaism. In one community, of the sixteen marriages over a twenty-year period involving a Jewish spouse, fourteen had been to non-Jews; but in another community in which strong leadership made a remarkable difference—a slightly larger community, with a small temple, a sisterhood, a B'nai B'rith organization, and an educational program, all drawing participants from six surrounding towns—of sixteen marriages over a twenty-five-year period, there were but three to non-Jews. However, even there, Kaplan concludes that "the communal structure rests on a thin foundation," for the "creative minority" is getting older, and "there are no longer any [European Jews] available to replace [them]."

The process of assimilation is subtle and goes beyond overlooking religious laws or marrying gentiles. Yet the mothers and fathers of the second generation fear these outward manifestations, especially intermarriage, as the final steps toward disappearance.

Perhaps nothing can really explain the mystery that draws a man to one woman and not another, the complicated forces at work, or the downright mischief of it. At least in the South, the barriers that kept Jews and gentiles apart are crumbling, leaving the choices more open, and the decisions more personal than ever before.

FOURTEEN

Big Wheel on Campus

W H E N the time came to select a college, my mother urged me to consider Brandeis University, or the universities of Alabama, Georgia, or Florida, where a lot of Southern Jews were. But she couldn't overcome a lifetime of conditioning that drew me inexorably to my father's and my brother's alma mater (and all my uncles, too), the University of North Carolina at Chapel Hill, just eight miles away.

Growing up, we rarely missed a home football game when the Carolina Tar Heels were involved (so named because during the Civil War, some Yankee general had said that Carolina boys "retreat as if they have tar on their heels"). On Saturdays Dad would come dashing home from the store, urge the family through a quick lunch of fried chicken, stuff some fruit in our pockets, grab the binoculars and the cushions, and hurry us out the door. I once counted up that I had seen fourteen consecutive Duke-Carolina games from the time I was eight years old until I was graduated from college, and was forced to miss my first one while I was on a Navy ship in the Pacific trying to find out the score.

The day before freshmen were due for orientation week, my parents drove me over to Chapel Hill. We had argued mildly two weeks before when my mother insisted that I write down "Jewish" on the housing application in the space calling for roommate preference. She insisted, "You've had no Jewish friends in high school and we want that to change." I complained, saying I didn't want to end up with a "bunch of loud-mouthed Yankees." But my father had intervened, and I complied. I sighed gratefully that afternoon when I checked and found out the housing office had assigned me with two Southerners (Jewish boys from Virginia).

It wasn't too difficult meeting people that first week, we were all so afraid and innocent of college ways, eager to please and be accepted. I ran into Kelly Maness from Greensboro and Ned Meekins from Raleigh, whom I had met at Boys' State a year before when we were all high school student body presidents, and we hung around together because we thought that maybe we would be running as a team for class office. The Farrell twins and Whit Whitfield from Durham High showed up, and I waved hello to the Jewish boys from all around the state I knew from B'nai B'rith conventions and Camp Blue Star.

With fraternity rush coming up in two weeks, the freshman class was already beginning to split off into cliques, as the prep school boys who already wore Bass weejuns and charcoal gray began to chatter a lot among themselves. Kelly and I picked up our envelopes together. He had more than twenty first-night invitations; I had five—the three Jewish fraternities, one non-Jewish that was in so much financial trouble that everybody was invited over, and Sigma Chi, one of the "class" houses. I had been so conditioned to think in terms of Jewish fraternities that, until titillated by the card in that envelope, I had never considered any alternative. I let my imagination soar and toyed with the possibility of pledging Sigma Chi.

That night, Kelly and I strode manfully over to the Sigma Chi house together, hot-shot freshmen with an ice-pack of surface cool over a caldron of apprehension. Once inside we were immediately split off from each other, Kelly ushered through a living-room door to the inner sanctum of the house while I was maneuvered skillfully to a corner of the living room for a short face-off with another brother.

"You Evans?" queried a crew-cut stud, his beer belly hanging over an alligator belt.

"Yes, Kelly and I are friends. . . ."

"Uh, uh—not here. You'll probably want to go TEP or ZBT or Pi Lam, being Jewish and all." He took my arm and guided me toward the front door. "We've cooperated with them through the years by promising not to go after their best guys. So please forgive the mistake." By then we were on the front porch where he could shake my hand and wish me luck.

The TEP house greeted me enthusiastically. I was a "legacy," because my father had helped found the chapter in 1924, and they were wondering where I had been.

"Hey, man, what you been up to?" a grating Yankee accent insisted on knowing.

"Uh, over at Sigma Chi," I replied sheepishly. I told them the story, and they roared so heartily that I felt I had to squeeze out a laugh too.

"Hey, man, don't you know Sigma Chi means Sign of Christ?" Another Yankee slumped his arm around my shoulder in intimate pretense. "I bet you were the first Yid they ever let in that place." I winced. "Yid" was a word a Jewish Southerner would never use to describe himself.

The Jewish fraternities put out a maximum effort to pledge Southerners, because family relationships were so entwined among the Jews in North Carolina that if a fraternity lost a key boy from Fayetteville, say, it might lose out in that city for a decade. The alumni sensed the critical character of rushing much more acutely than we ever did, and they would scrabble for pledges in their home towns, for if Leon Schneider's son Eliot belonged, a vital continuity would be maintained. For years my father and I, along with a lot of other alumni and their sons, had been stopping by the TEP house after football games, and I had sensed the strength in his friendship with Harry Schwartz from Charlotte and Leonard Eisenberg from Winston-Salem. The Jewish fraternity in the South was its own community within a community—close, loyal, and eternal.

There were only fifty Jewish boys going through rush, and the competition was rugged among the Jewish houses; the strategy consisted of mobilizing a core group to commit early, and plotting with them to organize a "snowball" from inside the class.

They urged me to engineer one but all I could do was talk to two or three boys I liked. I parroted clumsily the arguments that I would perfect and use for the years I would be rushing others: that there was no real social life without fraternity because Jewish girls didn't like to visit guys who were "unaffiliated"; that it was better to be with your own kind; that the Jewish houses had higher academic standards—they organized study halls and even kept files of past quizzes in certain courses and old themes that had received "A's"; that you'd make friends for life, not just for college; that

194

alumni could help with jobs and advice; and that you could stay with brothers when you visited New York.

I met the Yankees—Artie and Ritchie and Ira; Maslow, Kushinsky, and Greenblatt—some of them tough types out of Brooklyn and Jersey City who loved big-stakes card games and a violent drunk; some of them flashy and impressive with Thunderbirds and Corvettes from Great Neck and Scarsdale who took to Southern women like Jesse James to the banking business; others from Far Rockaway and the Bronx, who just wanted to make it—through medical school or the business school to the stock market or a big corporation, away from the shops and groceries of their fathers to something on their own. I didn't appreciate the distinctions between Long Island and Brooklyn Heights—it was all Broadway lights and the Empire State Building to me, and they all came from that vast uncharted non-South known as *The North*, products of paved playgrounds and the Dead End kids, of bums in the Bowery, hot dogs in the street, rattling subways, and Mafia shakedowns.

They came South for all the expected reasons: because they heard the business school was good; because they wanted a new experience and new people and had no idea what was in store for them; because they couldn't get accepted at any other school; or because their parents had stopped by once on the way to Florida and had become captivated with the beauty of the place.

We Southerners were still attached to the world of high school and parental approval; they were cut loose and flying on a four-year lark, and could lose themselves in the sure knowledge that no one would know and care. They camouflaged their Yankee provincialism by calling us "brown-baggers" and "grits," although they had never traveled anywhere outside "The City," but because they knew the difference between the Brooklyn Bridge and the IRT, they thought they knew it all. They pretended cocky knowledge about women and ear blowing and how to unbutton a blouse with your eyes closed, and we just listened in amazement, wide-eyed students at a nightly tutorial taking mental notes on the details for a future exam.

We were idealistic and trusting; we saw them as cynical, fierce survivors, good at cheating when they had to, driving and uptight, more individual on a campus that preached conformity, more selfish and alone. They came from high schools that had no students to teach on Jewish holidays and they peppered their language with

195

words like "tuchas" and "plotz," "Big Macha" and "schlong." School for us Southerners was more of an extension of home; we saw our parents frequently, were polite to visiting alumni and girls, concerned about campus reputation and the "good fraternities" sitting in judgment. The Yankees were unfettered and just didn't seem to give a damn what others thought. They bitterly blasted the South in bull sessions, and we defended it, not knowing enough to counterattack on the North. They were always great at basketball but terrible at football, had an insufferable addiction to nose jokes and giving the finger at football games and outrageous displays of temper and emotion at brothers' meetings. They never asked for butter, but reached for it; they waved off a plate of food they didn't like and stalked off to the peanut butter and jelly table; they belched openly and made off-color remarks in front of Southern girls. They tended to make their best friends inside the fraternity and rarely ventured out to campus activities, unwilling to confront the anti-Yankee bias.

The Yankees could be loud and obnoxious—God, how they were loud—embarrassing us with a big wave across the campus and a friendly yell of "How ya doin,' shmuck." "Shmuck" was a Yankee word, and it could be used both as an endearment and a biting epithet. If a rushee wore his national honor society pin during rush week, he was definitely a "shmuck." But if your roommate introduced you to his date and you said, "I love him even though he wets his bed," then your roommate might reply with, "You're a shmuck, you know that?" and his words would ring with the quintessence of friendship.

The pledge master was always the biggest, toughest, meanest, most engaging mixture of father confessor and slave master that the upperclassmen could find. In Brooklyn's own F. F. Kulinsky ("Fat Fred" we called him), they found the ultimate—stocky like a football guard, bellowing and bull-necked, who wallowed in his role like a hippo in a mud bath—but a sweet guy after you waded past his blustering, volatile personality and got to know him.

When "Kulinsk" barked out "Hey pledge" to summon you to some duty, it was like the piercing command of the drill sergeant; he infused those two words with such scorn that fifteen years later, when he called Artie Sobel in New York and began the conversation with "Hey pledge," Artie confessed he was scared all over again.

196

When the brothers criticized Dickie Shulman for walking too effeminately, Kulinsky gave him swagger drills every day for a month as a corrective. Kulinsk, cigar in his mouth, counting "hut, two, three, four," waddled along the sidewalk beside poor Dickie, his fire-hydrant legs and bulbous rump in perfect rhythm to his personal rhumba-rendition of John Wayne busting into a saloon.

And when Curtis Gans washed a brother's car with steel wool, Kulinsk convened a pledge court at three in the morning, complete with sheets and candles, to pass on the deep and mystical concern for Curtis' fraternal future.

Kulinsk taught us how to drink beer on a memorable night at the annual brother/pledge beerbust. "You gotta learn how to handle beer, and enjoy it. Like there's nothing better than a beer with a steak, or a beer with a pizza. And you gotta know how to sip suds with a friend, or order one for a girl; a beer is elegant, manly, and delicious." He made us all line up straight, and broke open each beer with spurting delight. "Now *guzzle*, you putz-heads." We turned them up and spit up all over the wood paneling and each other and he sat there, a Roman emperor, laughing wildly at his triumph in college indoctrination.

As the years passed, I went home with the Yankees and invited them home with me and we came to know and like each other. Chapel Hill softened them over the years as it sharpened me or maybe I began to see them in less stereotyped terms. They learned how to get along with Southerners and I learned to love the Yankees. Once, on a debate team trip to NYU, I made a special trip out to Coney Island for a Nathan's hot dog they always raved about, and brought back a Care package of two dozen with Nathan's own special mustard for a joyous midnight hot-dog orgy.

I dated their sisters in New York and invited them down to Carolina for weekends. It was the beginning of a serious "Northern girl" phase, a fascination with the sharp-tongued, matter-of-fact, smart-assed Jewish girl who responded so appreciatively to my courtly ways. They delighted in hearing me say "yes ma'am" to our house mother, never failed to be bowled over when I helped them with a sweater or opened doors for them. I wasn't uptight and their brothers were, and it puzzled them—my inflections and colloquialisms, and carefully honed naïveté, flattering them constantly with easy Southern banter. "Did anybody ever tell you," a girl from

197

Brooklyn once said, "that going out with you is like dating a gentile?"

We lived for TEP house-party weekends, when you piled your dirty socks and underwear in the closet because girls might visit the rooms; the place would be transformed from a zoo into a fantasyland of postcard collegiate cleanliness.

Since Orange County was dry, "Penguin" Lieberman and Malcom Coplon made the liquor run to Durham on Thursday night, "Duck" Saunders assembled the gin, grape juice, lemons, and secret herbs to begin brewing the Purple Jesus.

Buddy Schiff and the social committee would start planning nine months in advance, to beat the other fraternities and reserve motel rooms and boardinghouses for the girls, the ballroom at the Carolina Inn for the Friday night formal, the cabin near East Lake for the Saturday night bash, and the extra football tickets for alumni.

The girls started arriving by bus from Women's College in Greensboro at mid-afternoon on Friday. Gentile girls had to be special to get invited—either beautiful to impress the brothers, or wild (to impress the brothers). The North Carolina Jewish girls had been traipsing to house parties since the tenth grade, and we greeted each other warmly, while we looked over their shoulders at the new crop of freshmen girls who had been fixed up with the gamblers and the losers in our house.

The girls held up well under the more primitive pressures of the system. Seventy Jewish girls were isolated at Women's College, no more than twenty at Duke, and less than five on the Chapel Hill campus, which only accepted girls as juniors and seniors. There were fewer than a hundred and fifty Jewish boys at Carolina, so it was essential to make a good impression at one of the fraternities. If she made a wrong move, she could turn off an entire house, so most girls followed the lead of the N.C. local veteran house-party goers and were nice to everyone, even if they were having a rotten time.

"Reputation," that elusive mother-presence that stalked the girls of the fifties, exaggerated the dilemma. If they were too aloof, the brothers called them "frigid." If they were too warm, they risked a "bad reputation," which could result in a girl's leaving school in disgrace; for that reason, they rarely drank more than a few sips of a drink or ever lost their presence.

Lurking behind the fraternity pressures, behind the good times at college, lay the great prize, the *raison d'être*—to get married before graduation. Part of it was Jewish conditioning from mothers who had done just that, but for Southern Jewish girls, there was a special stress, because the alternatives were so frightening: leaving home ties altogether, finding a job, moving away to Atlanta, or even trying New York. The system made it worse—the "freshman fling" gave way to the "sophomore slump," the "junior jumps," and the "senior shakes," as each new group of girls intrigued the boys more than the girls they already knew. In two years, the girls were intimate with Carolina and had cased Duke and the University of Virginia for prospects; if things weren't going well (and they usually weren't), most transferred south to the universities of Georgia or Florida.

The Friday night formal always included dinner and a speaker, with presentations and awards. My father often spoke at these events since he was a founder of the chapter and had stayed involved as a financial adviser for thirty years, watching mortgage payments, raising money for the new building fund, making his annual presentation on the secrets of rushing, and occasionally intervening when a Yankee blackballed a Southern legacy. He drew my mother into it as well, and she would redecorate the house every few years with the most durable furniture she could find in New York. Once, out of gratitude for designing an additional wing of bedrooms and a new dining area, the fraternity invited her to give a few remarks at a banquet. When she lauded the "outstanding Jewish fraternity in the nation, where Jewish boys and girls come together . . . ," I was told that three Yankees, each dating a surprised gentile schoolteacher who thought this was just another fraternity weekend, slid under the table and out of the room.

The Saturday night cabin party after the football game highlighted the weekend. (We had to rent a cabin to avoid the crotchety old hag who lived across the street and rocked on the porch of her crumbling little house and often called the police to complain about the "Jew noise.") Couples necked in cars parked all around like a drive-in movie, or sweated together inside, where slow dances alternated with the Lindy, and where we'd stand in a circle watching a nervy couple, always a Yankee with a "wild" date, do the dirty bop.

By Sunday, we prayed for the girls to leave, but not before our

199

house mother, "Ma" Cohen, unleashed an all-out Jewish brunch of salami and eggs, homemade strudel, pumpernickel toast, and lox, bagels, and cream cheese from the delicatessen in Raleigh.

Student politics drew me, initially out of high-school habit, but I soon learned that student government at Chapel Hill prided itself on a long tradition of concern for campus issues. The student budget of $150,000 was appropriated solely by the student legislature, with no university administration control, since in the 1930's the students had voted on a $20-per-student activity fee, which the trustees empowered them to spend independently. Students at the University of North Carolina, I was told over and over again, were privileged to have this unusual power over their own affairs and were often the envy of students elsewhere.

We were always caught up in battles over priorities for expenditure of money—whether to build a campus radio station; to purchase new television sets for the dormitories; to allocate funds for Negro scholarships. And the *Daily Tar Heel* covered the debates and political maneuver with all the seriousness of the Washington *Post*'s coverage of the United States Senate. Student government and the newspaper created a forum for issues over which we had no real power, though we were a noisy pressure group. If we blasted the governor for refusing to do anything about the integrated group of UNC students who were turned away from a state park, the state papers picked it up. If we shouted through a resolution condemning Orval Faubus in Little Rock, the wire services would send it all over the South. It was a grand and glorious game that attracted all the starry-eyed young men who dreamed of running for governor someday and wanted to begin making friends early and shaping their political style.

In such an atmosphere, the president of the student body loomed over the campus as the biggest deal around—he inspired the entering freshmen with a fighting speech on student freedom; his picture often appeared in the *Daily Tar Heel;* he could announce with flowery statements the appointments of his friends to committees; and he presented his courageous annual State of the Campus address to the student legislature, text reprinted in full in the paper. I resolved early to try for it, probably because there had never been a Jewish student-body president at Chapel Hill, and as Mister Jew in Durham, I had been running for class offices since

200

junior high school. And I am sure that, subconsciously, I wanted to emulate the first Jewish mayor of Durham.

Other influences began to stir inside me, too. Students pointed to the window of Thomas Wolfe's dormitory room and to Betty Smith's house, and looked forward to the annual visit of Carl Sandburg from Flat Rock or the conversations with North Carolina literary legends like Paul Green and Phillips Russell and with the new writers like Max Steele, John Ehle, and Richard McKenna.

These were tumultuous years after the Supreme Court decision, and the South struggled in the backwash of reaction and defiance. Controversies and fears swirled all about us, but North Carolina, the "valley of humility between two mountains of conceit" (South Carolina and Virginia), quietly acquiesced in the wings while Arkansas and Virginia, Mississippi and Alabama played out the tragedy of defiance on center stage.

A handful of us in student government anointed ourselves the "new Southerners." We were deeply perturbed that the South was entering an era profoundly different from anything we had grown up with, but determined to listen to the voices of reason and restraint. After the Supreme Court decision every Negro on the street took on a new dimension—we would all be together now, in the same schools, the same neighborhoods, the same offices. Suddenly we were aware of just how little we really knew about him, the black stranger, who was neither meek nor aggressive, suffering nor lustful, pitiable nor irresponsible, as we had been taught. The adjustments to the new relationship would demand more of him than us, as both white and black struggled to overcome the twisted history distorting the hesitant acceptance of the future. Black and white young people were all part of the New South, groping for a way, yet understanding the violence simmering in the soul of the old South we grew up in.

We projected our concern onto student government, because that was the only outlet for action our generation of students perceived. Demonstrations and overt defiance were out of the question, for an arrest or expulsion would be reported on our college records and surely be judged by future employers, graduate schools, and bar examiners. Such were the restraints at the end of the McCarthy era. We treated the smallest risk-taking as a sign of our courage, especially any signal of sympathy for the cause of Negro advance.

By university policy, the nine black students lived together on the top floor of Steele dormitory, isolated from the rest of the student body—a commentary on the sad impact of tokenism. The first time I visited them and heard stories of the barbershops downtown that wouldn't cut their hair and the restaurants they couldn't eat in, the personal insult rather than the social injustice pained me. It had always been so in the South, but now that they were students, what was tolerable before was suddenly unthinkable. But we were not an outraged generation; we were the first generation of Southerners in the new age, and the style of the decade dictated a cool, detached, play-it-safe response with quiet resolves supplanting personal action.

The two political parties that battled for control of student government represented the classic college constituencies—the University Party, dominated by the fraternities and sororities, versus the Student Party, dominated by groups with nonfraternity interests—graduate students, dorm rats, and returning veterans. Both parties pursued all the votes with programs and candidates, so the membership in neither was pure. On race, especially, the University Party was more conservative, because the membership in fraternities came out of the elitist Southern tradition of gentlemanly segregation, some of them cultivated in all-white Southern prep schools with no populist influences to leaven their views, most from families new to money, products of the postwar economic boom for whom acceptance into the DKE house represented the ultimate status for their sons and recognition for the family. Many of the fraternities had secret clauses in their charters or initiation ceremonies prohibiting minority groups to membership, and the presence of Negroes on the campus coupled with a national campaign against discriminatory clauses made them uneasy with the prospect, already enforced at some colleges, that someday they might have to prove nondiscrimination by actually pledging a black. Beyond that, the University Party existed primarily as a device to parcel out honors to the Greeks, and they really didn't care much about issues at all.

The Student Party shied away from outspoken pronouncements on race because of the gap between the leadership in the party and the voters in the dorm. The leadership considered itself guardian of the soul of the university, protector of its liberal tradition, custodian of its place in history. It therefore attracted to party meetings all the boys who took themselves terribly seriously—earnest

202

do-gooders, the verbose intellectuals, the consumed activists, the small-town high-school class officers hungry for recognition and struggling to articulate issues they had never thought about before.

To outsiders, there was little ideological difference in the two parties; we exaggerated the differences out of self-importance, a need to believe, no matter how fanciful, that the state and nation were listening, thereby adding importance to our great debates and rationalizing the time student politics soaked up. The Student Party alumni, symbols to us that we mattered, straggled back from time to time to an enthusiastic reception—Allard Lowenstein, former president of the National Students Association, for a speech on the oppression in South Africa and Mississippi; Dick Murphy, former student-body president and then assistant to the chairman of the National Democratic Party, with the latest news on Eisenhower's faltering heart; my brother Bob, former student government attorney general, then CBS correspondent in the South and in Moscow.

On campus, Jimmy Wallace served as elder statesman, a rapier wit whose memory for personalities and events reached back into the thirties. Having run and been defeated three times for editor of the *Daily Tar Heel* during the war years, Jimmy had founded Rho Dammit Rho, his fraternity for the "undaunted"; but his greatest moment, and a Student Party legend we told with relish, was a one-vote victory for delegate to the first international student congress in Prague, in which Al Lowenstein (a New Yorker whose mother came from Birmingham, Alabama) was dragged to the meeting to cast the deciding vote for Wallace, the campus radical, enabling him to edge out a blond, brown-and-white-oxford, fraternity-man great-grandson of a former governor named Junius Scales, later convicted for conspiracy to overthrow the government as chairman of the North Carolina Communist Party.

The Jewish fraternities reacted to campus politics in complicated ways. As was the pattern all over the South, ZBT by and large rushed and pledged the Reform Jews and anxiously sought to project the big "frat-man" image—dating campus queens, wearing coats and ties to class. They joined the University Party and served as legislative leaders and party chairmen, supplying much of the brain power in the party platform and party-sponsored legislation. Invariably, however, in the spring when hundreds of fraternity and sorority members flooded the nominating convention to wheel and deal for the high stakes, the big fraternities would shut the ZBT's out of campus-wide nominations.

The wise heads in the TEP house guided me to the Student Party, where a Jewish boy wouldn't have to battle the big fraternities for important nominations. (The annual ZBT–TEP football game was a brutal battle of the Reform Jews against the East Europeans. Of course, we didn't know it was precisely that and it has only struck me in recent years, so naïve was I then, but there was something about being "zeeb'd"—our name for the condescending way the ZBT's treated us.)

Presiding over the S.P. was "Mister Chairman," Joel Fleishman, the latest contribution of the Fleishman clan of eastern North Carolina. The original seven brothers had sired twenty-seven sons, who scattered across the state like locusts, opening, so it seemed, a Fleishman's Clothing Store in every little town in the state. Joel left Fayetteville, N.C., to attend high school at the Yeshiva in Baltimore. His freshman year at the university, he brought his own pots and pans and a hot plate to Chapel Hill so he could cook kosher food in his dorm. He refused out of high principle to join a Jewish fraternity. His laugh—a high-pitched cackle—reflected a hyped-up exuberance that glued the Student Party together in a spirit of joyous warfare. He resolved all disputes by delivering his political judgments with pontifical finality, crisp and unchallengeable.

Joel loved opera and could flip through his mammoth record collection to fill our chasms of cultural ignorance with any aria that crossed his mind. He took voice lessons but none of his friends would let him sing, so he found an outlet acting as cantor in synagogues around the area during the high holy days. To shape up his voice, he would rehearse, mixing Kol Nidre liberally with *La Bohème*, as he dashed around in his convertible, top down and oblivious to the astonished pedestrians recoiling from the warble and blast of his tin-foil tenor.

Joel taught me not to say "sir" to waiters in fancy restaurants ("They like to be treated as waiters; that is why they have chosen a profession of personal service"); he instructed me on the different uses of burgundy and chablis; that lobster bisque was a soup requiring a spot of sherry; that sitting in a steam bath was the most civilized way to lose weight; that if you can't go first class, better to stay at home and wait until you can. He bought his suits at Brooks Brothers and smoked Parliament cigarettes while speaking up for the rights of the common dormitory man.

When detractors charged that he was too aloof to win elective office, he merely ran for the legislature and clobbered his opposition with indefatigable handshaking; he became so involved tutoring, finding extra tickets for games, and driving his constituents to the infirmary and to Durham that he became an unbeatable fixture.

He worked incessantly making friends all over the country and kept a cross-referenced file on everyone he met by birthday, county, political party, and potential. His Christmas card list ran to several thousand names. As chairman of the Carolina Forum, he was responsible for bringing speakers to the campus and arranging their schedules, so we were often willingly roped into a lunch with Wayne Morse, a chat with Eleanor Roosevelt, or a seminar with Edward R. Murrow or Adlai Stevenson.

The University Party leaders despised Joel; he outworked them and out-thought them and they viewed him as some sort of eccentric politico who took the game much more seriously than it deserved to be taken; he in return held their life style in total disdain for its philistine emphasis on beer and ball games, hell raising and the gentleman's "C."

Chairman Fleishman took charge of my political career and guided me carefully through three successful elections, grooming me each time for the next step, making certain I didn't run for offices I couldn't win, and building credentials for the final race for student-body president. By my junior year, the numbers were going against the U.P. Although college enrollment was rising, the number of students joining fraternities and sororities remained the same, and thus the base of U.P. support was shrinking. Now that the Student Party was going to nominate me, a fraternity man, the U.P. leaders decided to counter with an unprecedented step: nominate a popular nonfraternity man. They hoped to hold the traditional University Party vote, counting on the loyalty of the big fraternities faced with a nominee from a Jewish fraternity, and cut into the S.P. dorm vote by charging that their candidate was the "true voice" of the dormitory man. It was a brilliant strategy that did credit to the ZBT brain trust running the U.P. (and motivated in part, I always thought, to stop the TEP's from winning a high-prestige office which might be translated into a rushing advantage).

Bill Baum emerged the perfect choice. He was former state-wide president of the North Carolina Conference of the Methodist Youth Fellowship, planned to study for the ministry, and had worked his way through school. He formerly had been an S.P. member and knew the weaknesses of our precinct organization intimately; he had switched parties for political opportunity in the U.P. and had won a student legislature seat in a hardened S.P. dorm district by personal charm and hard work. Baum was a seasoned campaigner, smooth, appealing, articulate. Above all, he was a gifted public speaker who had lost a leg in a childhood accident, and when he hobbled to a microphone and dramatically propped himself up on his crutches, a hush always came over the crowd as it became more attentive. We were in trouble.

Tom Lambeth, my campaign manager as well as the party statistician and historian, scrambled through the records and concluded that I had to win forty percent of the fraternity vote. "You know what this means," counseled Fleishman. "You've got to go up to fraternity court and get votes from guys who don't think you're good enough to belong to their houses."

Walking over to fraternity court, the old aching sense of inferiority sent shudders of apprehension through me. Now I was forced by my own ambition to return to the scene of that earlier rejection when, as a callow freshman, I swore I would never come back to them again. At the Tri Delt candlelight supper, when a flirtatious girl asked, "And what fraternity are you?" I watched her face sag into indifference, and then imagined her passing it around as I sat there with the eyes of fifty girls fastened on me, taking my measure as I tried to eat spaghetti cleanly. Back at the Sigma Chi house, the president interrupted dinner to introduce me to the impassive brothers hunched over their plates, not even bothering to look up. "Just go on eating your dessert, fellas," he said awkwardly, trying to cover their listless inattention, "I would like to introduce the Student Party [smirk] candidate for president." It all seemed hopeless.

In the fraternities and sororities, Lambeth instructed me to wear an Ivy League suit and a button-down shirt. But in the dorms, I campaigned in shirt sleeves, knocking on doors and brightly drawling to a group of four guys playing poker, "Hey, how're y'all. I'm Sonny Evans, candidate for president of the student body and I'm running on a platform that never interrupts a card game," and they'd invariably chime in, "You've got my vote."

The biggest issues in the campaign broke during a face-to-face debate at the Westminster Fellowship when we were asked our opinions on the university policy of placing all Negro students on the same floor of a selected dorm, regardless of the desires of the students. Baum said he wouldn't "agitate" for change because "the student body is not yet ready to cope with it." I knew my answer would hurt in the fraternities and disenchant part of the Student Party dorm vote, but after visiting the black students isolated up there, I knew the time of reckoning had come. I criticized the university for pursuing a policy of "segregated integration" and said that "the purpose of student government is to see that each student is treated equally. If the dining hall were not open to all students, I would take a stand. I feel the same way about the dorms."

The audience applauded vigorously, but these were the goody-goody religious liberals, and Bill knew it. When the *Tar Heel* bannered the headlines, "Baum, Evans Answer Questions on Racial Issue at Carolina," the Yankees in my fraternity said, "That's telling those rednecks." But two S.P. precinct captains called to tell us, "He blew it."

On election night, I paced the floor upstairs in the student union, fidgety and nervous, glancing from time to time at Lambeth's charts with the bellwether districts marked in red, while the elections' board counted the ballots downstairs. New York pledge Louis Lefkowitz ran back and forth with the results on a slip of paper copied from the huge blackboard below; Tom would post them to his chart and suggested, "Keep a sharp lookout for Town Men's II, Louie. If we do well there . . ." At midnight, Tom looked up with a big smile and said quietly, "Congratulations, Mister President." It was the closest election in his memory.

A few minutes later, Louie burst through the door and yelled out, "Baum's waiting downstairs and the place is packed," and Tom pulled out a short victory statement he had written that afternoon. "I've got the concession statement in the other pocket," he said with a smile, patting his coat. I walked shakily down the stairs to a steamy crowd of buzzing party workers and flickering flashbulbs to shake Baum's hand, my shoulders stinging from the backslaps of the well-wishers, girls squealing and hugging me; over in the corner studying the returns on the blackboard intently, I saw the mayor of Durham and the "mayoress," as he always called her, joy evident through her tears. Mom squeezed me and murmured how proud they were, and Dad shook my hand tightly, reaching all the

207

way in like he taught me when I was small. He spoke in the hard-headed, grudging tones that one political pro reserves for another.

Allard Lowenstein showed up as he usually did for election nights and he offered this crisp appraisal: "Everybody heard they might have a Jewish president so they went out and voted for Sonny Evans to stop Bill Baum." Lambeth pointed out that we had won by carrying the lesser fraternities and sororities, which had members who were once blackballed from the Dekes or the Tri Delts.

The next day I floated to class with a phalanx of the Yankees behind me, all of them for the first time decked out in fraternity pins, like a flying wedge of strutting ducks chasing a canary. Chapel Hill glittered in a shimmering spring day and the apple-blossomed branches covered the walkway to class in a canopy of pink and white fragrance. The coeds from the Tri Delt House now smiled eagerly and I smiled back. A star-struck freshman asked me to autograph a poster and when I stopped to accommodate my new fan, Artie Sobel from Far Rockaway sidled up behind me and leaned in close for a quick word: "You're a shmuck, Evans . . . you know that?"

V

Discrimination

FIFTEEN

Anti-Semitism in the South

Eugene thought of this young Jew years later with the old piercing shame, with the riving pain by which a man recalls the irrevocable moment of some cowardly or dishonorable act. For not only did he join in the persecution of the boy—he was also glad at heart because of the existence of some one weaker than himself, some one at whom the flood of ridicule might be directed. Years later it came to him that on the narrow shoulders of that Jew lay a burden he might otherwise have borne, that that overladen heart was swollen with a misery that might have been his.

Look Homeward Angel,
Thomas Wolfe

W H E N E V E R a Southern Jew tells another Jew from outside the South about his home, invariably he will be asked, "So how is it for Jews down there? Pretty bad, huh?" Most Jews have heard that the South is more anti-Semitic than any other part of the country, a conclusion that squares with the mythology of the Klan and confirms the national view that the South is a violent, savage place for all minorities.

That is simply not the case. Most Jews in the South live in a relaxed atmosphere without fear for their safety or worry over their future. Even though there have been a number of incidents over the last fifteen years, Anti-Defamation League studies have consistently shown that there are far more threats and incidents directed against Jewish institutions in the major cities of the North, where most Jews live, than in the South (see Appendix C).

211

Yet most of the studies and polls on this subject since 1940 have concluded that the South is indeed more anti-Semitic than any other region. Why this disparity? Why do Southern Jews themselves perceive the South so differently from the social scientists who test the attitudes of other Southerners?

One reason, I think, lies in the nature of survey research—in its inability to weigh influences rather than measure them, in values hidden in the questionnaires, and in lack of knowledge about the social and cultural intricacies of the South, which leads to a misunderstanding of Southern answers to questions devised for a national survey. But the basic reason lies in the complexity of the Southern mind. This question is central: How intense are religious anti-Semitic beliefs when racial prejudices are so deeply held? Probably because there are so few Jews around, most Southern Jews admit to very few instances of personal, overt animosity—name calling or school-boy scraps. It is true that incidents and prejudices don't necessarily go hand in hand, but Southern Jews don't explain the calm of their South that way. They attribute the lack of personal anti-Semitic incidents to the presence of the Negro, whom they refer to as "the lightning rod for prejudice" (a phrase I heard many, many times). And while studies show that people with anti-Negro attitudes are more likely to possess other kinds of prejudice, no poll can measure the impact of a fiercely held racial prejudice on the passion with which such a personality holds other kinds of prejudice, or the likelihood that he will act on his other prejudices.

George McMillan has written articles and books on the Ku Klux Klan, and knows more about the Klan mentality than any person I have ever met. He has interviewed dozens of psychiatrists for a psychological biography he is writing of James Earl Ray, the assassin of Martin Luther King. "Prejudice can be focused," he told me. "To hate blacks is not to hate everything else equally as well. If blackness can become symbolic enough in a psychological sense, then hatred of blacks can sufficiently fill your psychological needs to hate."

Not only is the intensity of religious prejudice against Jews probably lessened because of the presence of the Negro as the "lightning rod for prejudice," but the poor white senses an economic competitiveness with the Negro that he does not feel with the Jew. Historically, the freed slaves gaining skills gradually took on white jobs; later, integrated unions put blacks in the textile mills that formerly ran all-white machines. If economic competition with the immigrants was a major cause of anti-Semitism in the North, Southern fears were too focused on the threat from Negro advance to worry about the few Jews there. Whatever else one can say about gentile attitudes toward Jews, Jews are considered white men first and live most of their lives as part of the white majority.

My purpose is to raise questions about the conclusions and the assumptions behind the polls, and to suggest that other evidence—psychological, economic, historical, even impressionistic—deserves to be weighed before making sweeping generalizations about the attitudes of Southerners toward Jews. Moreover, I hope to point out that the South is much more complicated than imagined, and that polling, when done with insight and special attention to Southern idiosyncrasies, might be able to unravel some of the mysteries in the Southern attitude toward Jews, which, like so much of the South, I have found to be ambivalent, variable, and inconsistent. I don't know whether the South is more or less anti-Semitic than the rest of America, and have doubts that such a subjective question can be measured or has any meaning in terms of how life is actually lived. However, perhaps a more comprehensive survey of regional attitudes will someday be taken which will probe the question with greater subtlety.

Some data on Southern attitudes toward Jews was included in a national poll by the Gallup organization in 1959 for the American Jewish Committee and the Anti-Defamation League; the results are reported in an A.D.L. manuscript by Oscar Cohen entitled *Public Opinion and Anti-Jewish Prejudice in the South* (1950). But the most comprehensive national effort, including some Southern statistics, comes from the A.D.L. five-year research project, conducted in association with the Survey Research Center at the University of California at Berkeley. Four volumes of a projected eight have been published, all by Harper and Row: *Christian Beliefs and Anti-Semitism*, by Charles Y. Glock and Rodney Stark (1966); *The Apathetic Majority: A Study Based on Public Responses to the Eichmann Trial*, by Charles Y. Glock, Gertrude J. Selznick, and Joe L. Spaeth (1966); *Protest and Prejudice: A Study of Belief in the Black Community*, by Gary T. Marx (1967); and *The Tenacity of Prejudice: Anti-Semitism in Contemporary America*, by Gertrude J. Selznick and Stephen Steinberg (1969).

In *The Tenacity of Prejudice* the authors conducted more than two thousand interviews, sampling by age, sex, education, income, race, religion, and region, constructing an "Index of Anti-Semitic Belief" based on a number of negative statements about Jews: Are Jews "shrewd and tricky in business?"; "powerful in finance and business?"; "disloyal to America?"; etc. In their conclusion, the authors stated that the greater concentration of anti-Semitism in America is in the South and the Midwest, where the least educated and most fundamentalist populations live.

Lucy Dawidowicz, a professor at Yeshiva University, took the book to task in the July 1970 issue of *Commentary* magazine, in an article which went directly to the question "Can Anti-Semitism Be Measured?" Ms. Dawidowicz complained that she found the authors' reliance on survey data, to the exclusion of literary, historical, and journalistic sources, to be "intellectually constricting." She asked, "How does one measure the extent and intensity of anti-Semitism? Is there a National Bureau of Standards for the study of social phenomena which has specified the standard content, density, or weight of anti-Semitism?"

She objected particularly to the use of the data on intermarriage in their scale, saying, "We see, for instance, that they consider a Christian intolerant if he is against intermarriage with a Jew. . . . By making approval of intermarriage a barometer of tolerance, Selznick and Steinberg must logically regard a commitment to group survival as an obstruction to the creation of a prejudice-free, neutral society. . . . Oddly enough, nowhere is an effort made to deal with the question of legitimacy of group life, religious or ethnic." She summarized by complaining that the authors do not really help us in measuring anti-Semitism with their scale, ". . . for anti-Semitism has no commonly accepted boiling or freezing point; no standard weights or intervals have been assigned to religious anti-Semitism, political anti-Semitism, economic anti-Semitism, or authoritarianism or ethnocentrism. All together, the disparity among the various scales raises serious doubts as to their validity."

The other weights in the scale require examination from a Southern perspective. For example, the authors listed the statement that "Jews always like to be head of things" as a measure of intolerance; yet, in city after city of all sizes across the South, Jews who are leaders in their community confess that they take on extra community burdens because there are so few Jews in the commu-

214

nity that they feel a special responsibility to do so; very frequently the gentile community asks that they do so.

Another measure of individual intolerance in the scale was a positive answer to the question that "Jews still think of themselves as the Chosen People." I can't imagine a fundamentalist Southerner answering that question positively and meaning it as a derogatory statement about Jews, because he himself still views the Jews as the chosen people.

The authors admitted that agreement with the statement "Jews stick together too much" was a weak measure, but treated it as a factor anyway for comparative purposes. However, most gentiles in towns across the South would surely observe that Jews indeed do "stick together," seem to take care of their own, seem much more centered in their social life around the community center or the temple, and radiate a special feeling for each other at social functions or simply in passing on the street.

The authors asked a number of questions about Jews as businessmen: "Do you think of Jews as being more ambitious than other people? Do you think that on the average Jews have more money than most people? Do you think of them as so shrewd and tricky that other people don't have a fair chance in competition?" The book did not compare the Southern answer to this set of questions with that of other regions in the country; but in a region where Jews have risen in such a short time from peddler status to middle class—in small towns where everyone knew by name the storeowners on Main Street and could see with their own eyes the stores being remodeled and the new homes being built, had heard about the son that the clothing store owner was putting through law school and had watched the children of the immigrants studying harder and winning honors in high school—it would not be surprising to find positive answers to these questions without attributing intolerance as the motive for the answer.

In the chapter on racial attitudes of religious groups, Southern white Protestants were asked which group they thought was most in favor of racial integration—Protestants, Catholics, or Jews. Over half (54 percent) had no opinion or said there was no difference, 22 percent said Catholics, 15 percent said Protestants, and just 9 percent named the Jews. Alfred Hero, in his study on *The Southerner and World Affairs*, noted that only 15 percent of white Southerners thought that Jews *favored* integration (10 percent said that Jews opposed integration, and 67 percent did not know). Hero concluded that "most Southern Jews have been so quiet on controversial issues, including race, in the South that Southern Gentiles have greatly underestimated their real divergence from Protestant thinking on public and social questions."

Finally, when the authors asked whether Southern whites would be disturbed if their party nominated a Jew for the Presidency, 41 percent in the South answered "very much," or "somewhat disturbed," 31 percent in the Midwest, 26 percent in the Northwest, and 19 percent in the Northeast. Actually, the proposition they offered was, "Suppose your political party wanted to nominate a Jew for President of the United States—*that is, a religious Jew who would go to synagogue every week the way a Christian goes to church every Sunday?*" (My italics.) It would be interesting to ask a few Southern Baptists what impression they received from the phrase "religious Jew who would go to synagogue" (my guess would be that they would respond with New York City images). A Gallup poll in 1959 asked the question without that phrase nationally: "If your party nominated a generally well-qualified person for President, and he happened to be a Jew, would you vote for him?" The negative answers were 25 percent to 45 percent lower: 33 percent in the South; 25 percent in the Midwest; 22 percent in the West; and 11 percent in the Northeast.

Neither poll looked behind the answers to reasons for the objection to a Jewish candidate for President—whether there was stronger commitment in the South than in other regions to the role of the President as a religious leader for the nation; whether Southerners felt differently about candidates for Vice President, the Senate, Congress, or local office; whether the differences were due to education and income rather than region. Southerners traditionally have harbored a great suspicion of the Northeast, especially of New York City, and Jews have been closely associated with New York in the media. It might be interesting, for example, to ask Southerners, "Would you vote for a Northerner for President?" and compare the results. My guess is that Southern antipathy to outsiders would show up more forcefully than negative attitudes toward Jews, especially Southern Jews. ("You ain't like them New York Jews," I was once told. "You're a white Jew.")

Whatever the objection to voting for a Jew for President, it is a fact that Jews have served in local offices throughout Southern

216

history. Since the end of World War II, Southerners have elected at least twenty-seven mayors (including my father and two uncles), thirty-eight state legislators, and sixty-six other city councilmen and miscellaneous officials (see appendixes A and B).

Why then measure the degree of anti-Semitism only by polls on the Presidency without probing the underlying reasons? Did the voters perceive these local candidates as Jews? (Most of them had Jewish names.) Could it be that Southerners will vote for Jews who are neighbors because they perceive Southern Jews differently from Jews in general? Did being Jewish help these candidates in the black community? Did working-class voters sympathize with the underdog (as seemed to be the case in Atlanta, where Sam Massell's Jewishness became an open issue in his campaign for mayor)? Why not poll and analyze the results in terms of the impact of a Jewish candidate on various constituencies?

In their monumental study of the 1940's, *The Authoritarian Personality*, the authors (Adorno, Frenkel-Brunswick, Sanford) tried to develop an anti-Semitism scale of fifty-two items, to distinguish between opinions and attitudes, and between the different images of Jews as individuals, groups, and culture. They found, among other things, what they called "a syndrome of unenlightenment" that linked intolerance to personality; that personalities manifesting intolerance toward one group had a high degree of intolerance toward all groups because of certain human needs repressed during childhood. Thus if individuals were living a "primitive cognitive style, with an apocalyptic orientation toward reality" which blamed societal pressures for their sorry state, if they possessed an intolerance of cultural diversity and racial prejudice toward Negroes, they were more likely to be caught in the "syndrome" and show intolerance toward Jews and other minority groups as well. *The Tenacity of Prejudice* twenty years later tended to confirm that view, finding that "anti-Semitic prejudice is firmly imbedded in a network of beliefs"; but instead of focusing on personality, the authors tried to prove that anti-Semitism was part of a "culture that embodies anti-Semitism . . . which individuals acquire through the normal processes of socialization." To the later study, the more pertinent question was "why some people *reject* anti-Semitic beliefs," and the authors asserted that they found the reason in the "countervailing forces" of democratic values transmitted through the educational institutions. They felt their survey showed that the better the education, the less likely was an individual to hold anti-Semitic views, though the authors acknowledged but seemed to disregard the presence of anti-Semitism in some highly educated individuals. Since the South held the higher numbers of people with less education, the study concluded it was more likely to be caught up in "common culture" assumptions about minority groups.

The problem with this conclusion lies in the peculiar quality of Southern culture with its all-pervasive racial atmosphere. In the South, the ordinary distinction between culturally acquired prejudice and psychologically motivated prejudice is blurred. The authors of *Tenacity* state that if prejudice is learned, education can help overcome it. But it seems to me that if it flows from psychological needs for objects of derision and from racial fantasies, its mysteries are beyond the capacity of devices as superficial as a questionnaire and a one-hour interview. In short, then, the South is much too complicated to rely on a poll that says that lack of education is the key to anti-Semitism.

In a 1950 study of forty cases of mentally disordered patients by Ackerman and Jahoda, called *Anti-Semitism and Emotional Disorder: A Psychoanalytic Interpretation*, all forty cases displayed common patterns, "strikingly similar" to backgrounds consisting of rejection of the child by one or both parents, marital problems of parents, and intensely confused and unresolved Oedipal situations. Other studies have isolated factors unrelated to the education of the people studied, like numbers of Jews in a region, past contact with Jews, and the nature of the contact. In the South, past studies in educational institutions have linked anti-Semitism with the frequency of contact and amount of direct competition with Jews. In 1942 a study of 502 college-age youths in Southern and Northern institutions found that "Northern students were more prejudiced against Jews than Southern . . . ; children of skilled workers, clerical workers, and farmers were *less* prejudiced than those of business and professional men . . . there was some tendency for anti-Semitism to increase with parents' income . . . subjects who had the greatest opportunity for contact with Jewish persons showed *higher* prejudice than those with less opportunity for contact."

Hero compared surveys in 1945 and 1959 and found that "the proportion of Southerners, as of Northerners, who said that they

218

had heard any 'criticism or talk against Jews in the last six months' declined considerably between 1945 and 1959" (only 8 percent in the South in 1959 as compared to 13 percent in the North). Hero then concluded, "This interregional difference was understandable considering the few Jews that have existed in many Southern locales."

However, regardless of the fact that many Southerners do not know any Jews personally, the South is most vulnerable to religiously based prejudice, for it is the home of the Southern Baptists—more than nine million of them—the bedrock fundamentalists who testify to their passions every Sunday in church. But even here, the attitudes are more complicated than one might think.

In the first book in the A.D.L. series, *Christian Beliefs and Anti-Semitism*, the authors, Glock and Stark, "were entirely unprepared to find these old religious traditions so potent and widespread in modern society." After building a theoretical model and testing it thoroughly on the West Coast with three thousand people, they then compared the data nationwide and found, with regard to the South, that 66 percent of the Southern Baptists believed the Jews "were most responsible for killing Christ" (18 percent believed the Romans responsible, the percentage average for all Protestants on Jewish responsibility was 58 percent); that 80 percent of the Southern Baptists believed, "The Jews can never be forgiven for what they did to Jesus until they accept Him as the True Savior" (33 percent of all Protestants agreed); that 35 percent of the Southern Baptists agreed that "the reason the Jews have so much trouble is because God is punishing them for rejecting Jesus" (as compared to 13 percent of all Protestants; however, 54 percent of the Southern Baptists disagreed); that 90 percent of the Southern Baptists personally approved of "converting Jews to Christianity" (48 percent of all Protestants agreed); that 38 percent of the Southern Baptists were "not presently acquainted with a single Jew" (as compared with 13 percent of all Protestants); and 52 percent of the Southern Baptists "do not know a single Jew well" (as compared with 25 percent of all Protestants).

The disquieting aspect of the poll is that large numbers of Southern Baptists, without personally knowing any Jews, hold the theological view that there is a religious stain on the Jews, and that they can never be forgiven without conversion.

The poll was not without its surprises: 46 percent of the Southern Baptists think of "Moses, David and Solomon as Christians" (43 percent of the Southern Baptists thought of them as Jews); while 84 percent of the Southern Baptists thought of the twelve Apostles as Christians, 43 percent of them thought of "Judas, who betrayed Christ," as a Jew.

The authors tried to correlate religious feeling with secular anti-Semitic attitudes and concluded, "The causal chain that links Christian belief and faith to secular anti-Semitism begins with orthodoxy—the commitment to a literal interpretation of traditional Christian dogma. Orthodoxy, in turn, leads to particularism —a disposition to see a Christian truth as the only religious truth. Particularism produces a two-fold response toward religious outsiders. On the one hand . . . missionary zeal . . . but when others reject the call . . . religious hostility . . . culminating in secular anti-Semitism." Perhaps, but orthodoxy is a private culture implying a denial of the goals of society, and therefore it might indicate a prejudice not just against Jews but against everybody else. If so, then the Jews are not the only targets of the orthodoxy and must be compared with other groups to determine the intensity of the hostility.

Is the link between religious and secular anti-Semitism justified? The authors dismissed the positive attitudes of Southern Baptists as "neutral" factors—that 71 percent believed that "Jews are ambitious and work hard to succeed"; that 32 percent believed that "an unusual number of the world's greatest men have been Jews." The authors' retort was that "Jews are frequently thought to be especially intelligent and talented by persons who nonetheless dislike them. Indeed one theme in anti-Semitism is that the Jew constitutes a grave threat because he is such a worthy opponent."

Religious dogma infects the Southerner's life, casting the Jews as renegades from God's new family, but religious anti-Semitism does not exist in a vacuum. When I finally found a woman in the South who had never known or met any Jews except in her Bible, and told her I was Jewish, she sputtered out the words, "Young man, you're gonna bust hell wide open." Yet this same woman condemned "Hitler's men," thought the Jews deserved "their own home," and respected me as one of the "chosen people"; she admitted that while she worried about my soul, "wild young people are in a whole lot more trouble than you are."

Acknowledging the deep-seated pools of religious anti-Semitism,

220

the factors which erode and balance those beliefs need more careful examination before assuming they automatically lead to secular anti-Semitism: how the Southern tradition of hospitality to visitors influenced the early treatment of Jews; how the humanist tradition of Southern populism undermined anti-Semitism; how the elevation of the little man affects attitudes toward the underdog; how much Southerners respect the work ethic that Jews so represent in the Southern mind; just how Southern politeness and manner toward all whites influence the actual treatment of Jews they know and come into contact with; why Southern women show up in studies as less anti-Semitic than men.

If the Negro is the "lightning rod for prejudice" racially, Catholics in the South seem to serve the same purpose religiously. An old Jewish woman in Virginia warned me, "Remember, the *goyim* hate the Catholics a whole lot more than they hate the Jews." Anti-Catholic bias was a crucial part of the rebirth of the Klan in the 1920's, an important issue in the South in the Presidential elections of 1928 and 1960, and of course a dominant influence on the Catholic Church in the South.

Because of the small numbers of Catholics, the Catholic Church in the South is more defensive in posture, less committed to the search for converts, more worried about survival than expansion. In Mississippi, Bishop Joseph Brunini, the bishop of Natchez-Jackson and the ranking prelate in the state (who, incidentally, grew up in Vicksburg with a Jewish mother), said that 75 percent of the Catholic marriages in Mississippi were intermarriages with Protestants (South-wide, the figure is 60 percent for Catholic intermarriage). Thus do Catholics blend in with the Southern terrain, so much so that with all the ugly atmosphere surrounding Catholic-Protestant relations in Mississippi, very few Catholic buildings were bombed or threatened in the period between 1954 and 1970 (Bishop Brunini could remember only two instances of threats and one act of violence in sixteen years). In addition, though every opinion poll finds severe anti-Catholic bias among Southerners, Catholics are *not* kept out of the country clubs or socially discriminated against in other ways.

Why is it that Christians will vote to keep Jews out of country clubs and not Catholics; that the Klan will plot to bomb synagogues but not cathedrals; that debutante balls will include Catholic girls while excluding Jewish girls from the same social class?

221

The difference, I think, is the passage of time and how time has transformed Catholics in the eyes of other Christians. The earlier prejudice against Catholics pitted militant and narrow Protestantism in an ancient quarrel with the Roman church over the superiority of two absolutist faiths. But in the South, Protestantism was never just a religion; its superiority was tied to race, as W. J. Cash has pointed out, regarding attitudes toward Jews and Catholics in his classic *Mind of the South:*

> The case of the fear and hatred of the alien menace in this country so little used to aliens is even more manifest . . . the presence of the Negro and the long defensive fight against the alien-infested Yankeedom had vastly intensified in Southerners generally a feeling, common in some degree in most peoples, that they represented a uniquely pure and superior race, not only as against the Negro, but as against all other communities of white men as well. . . . The Jew, with his universal refusal to be assimilated, is everywhere the eternal Alien; and in the South, where any difference had always stood out with great vividness, he was especially so . . . [but] for the Protestant all through the centuries, the Catholic even more than the Jew has stood as the intolerable Alien.

The Southerners were terrified by the strange sights and sounds and angered by the imaginary linkages of power come to enslave them: the queer sounding Latin liturgy, the suspected plot among Catholics to subvert the government and set up an ecclesiastical state; the loyalty to the Pope in Rome (could the fierce reaction of the Southerners to the imagined Catholic loyalty to a "foreign power" have been a subconscious influence on German Jews who feared the same reaction to Jews once the State of Israel was proclaimed?); and the differences in church style: the kneeling, the nuns in black garb, statuary in the church (the fundamentalists allow none). To the plain people in the Baptist churches all of it smacked of a devilish black ritual, mysterious and superstitious, obscure and threatening.

As the next generation of Catholics absorbed Southern accents and attitudes, fundamentalists viewed them more as a religion than as a race. Whatever else drove them apart, they stood together at the foot of the Cross.

The racial link between Jews and Negroes in the fundamentalist mind threads through Southern literature. Eudora Welty described an itinerant black piano player in a short story entitled "Powerhouse."

Powerhouse is playing! . . . He's here on tour from the city. . . . There's no one in the world like him. You can't tell what he is. "'Nigger man?" he looks more Asiatic, monkey, Jewish, Babylonian, Peruvian, fanatic, devil. . . .

The Jews, not being Christians, must be something else, and that something else was a "people"—the "chosen people," but with alien blood and Middle Eastern features, a genetic difference, a separate race with swarthy complexions and large noses. The Jewish race proclaimed its separatism when it rejected the Cross, the shadowy symbol of commonality between Catholics and fundamentalists. Whereas time might cure the Catholics by assimilating them as Christian Southerners, only conversion would save the Jew.

However great the antipathy between Southern Protestants and everyone else, the threat from the fundamentalists drove Jews and Catholics together in the small towns of the South, both of them the "put-upon" faiths, targets for Klan literature, suspect, lonely, and surrounded. "Hell, we're the only two people in town who drink in front of our wives," said a Jewish storeowner in a small town. In a community filled with temperance ladies, an Irish-Catholic and a Jew seem to have a lot to talk about.

How much hate does a man require to fill his needs? If anyone could discover that Southern fundamentalists have their racial "hate energies" absorbed by Negroes first, and if whatever is left over religiously is consumed by the Catholics, how much more would remain to be spent on the Jews? How far can survey research be trusted in weighing different kinds and degrees of hate? Survey research, it seems to me, is weakest in the area of prejudice, because it is so dependent on how the interviewee reacts to the stranger asking intimate questions about an unpleasant subject. It would be natural to want to reflect accepted attitudes or to please the interviewer (a particularly Southern trait, wanting to be agreeable to an interviewer posing negatives for a reaction). A 1946 study in New York City experimented on two thousand people by selecting interviewers with stereotyped Jewish appearances and with Jewish names. In general, they found "that *fewer* anti-Semitic responses were given to those of Jewish appearance . . . the lower economic group was markedly more anti-Semitic and more sensitive to the appearance of interviewers . . . Catholics and Protestants showed increasing anti-Semitism with the interviewers they took to be non-Jewish."

While the presence of some anti-Semitism in the South is apparent, it must be balanced against a high degree of pro-Semitism, which is partially responsible for the success of the Jews in the South. One Jewish woman in South Carolina put it, "In small towns, the Christians liked to have their favorite Jew. We weren't really superior. We just did better because of a presumed intelligence on the part of the gentile community and their need to prove that they were good people."

Harry Golden has called this ambivalence a kind of "philo-Semitism" and describes the process this way:

There is a touching naïvety in the small-town Southerner's respect for the Jewishness of the Jew in his community. It springs from the Southern Protestant's own attachment to Biblical Judaism, which is manifested in the basic tenets of the several denominations. . . . As the Jew in a small Southern town goes about his business of selling dry goods or ready-to-wear clothing, he rarely suspects the symbolic role enacted for the Gentile society roundabout him—he represents the unbroken tie with sacred history and the prophets of the Bible, he is the "living witness" to the "Second Coming of Christ," the link between the beginning and the end of things.

A small-town editor tied the treatment of Jews to the Southerner's guilt over race: "Jewish people were white and they were the good and generous people. We felt sufficiently guilty about colored prejudice to make up for it with them."

Southern philo-Semitism is not just a recent phenomenon. The most dramatic example occurred just after the Civil War, through the voice of North Carolina's Confederate hero and former governor, Zebulon Vance.

Zeb Vance had been the wartime governor of North Carolina, was reelected governor in 1876 after Reconstruction, entered the United States Senate in 1879, and stayed there until his death in 1894. Vance was an orator of gigantic talents, with a rich and resonant voice, possessed of the power at a very young age to sweep away a crowd and carry it for his point of view. Even at age thirty-three, he was the kind of man North Carolina would turn to for leadership in its most desperate era. He could be obscene with the troops and flowery with the ladies; his hair was long and swept back ("flowing like the mane of a fine stallion," a historian wrote) and some would say that on the platform he was so impressive in appearance that once he had risen to speak, no eye could be taken from him.

After the war, he supplemented his income throughout the rest of his life as a speaker on the lecture circuit—eulogies, after-dinner speeches, commencement addresses, tributes, and tent speeches and appearances. His most famous speech was entitled "The Scattered Nation," a testament to the Jews in grandiose, expansive language, which he delivered, according to one historian, more than a hundred times from 1874 until he died, in every major city in America.

"The Jew," he proclaimed, "is beyond doubt the most remarkable man of this world—past or present. There is no man who approaches him in the extent and character of the influence he has exercised over the human family. His history is the history of our civilization and progress in this world, and our faith and hope in that which is to come. From him have we derived the form and pattern of all that is excellent on earth or in heaven. . . ."

He spoke of the ability of the Jews to survive, even though "for eighteen hundred years [they] have been scattered far and near over the wide earth . . . and their scattered unity makes them still a wonder and an astonishment." He pleaded for tolerance, beseeching his audience to "let us learn to judge the Jew as we judge other men—by his merits. And above all, let us cease the abominable injustice for holding the class responsible for the sins of the individual. We apply this test to no other people."

None of his biographers has discovered how Vance developed such positive attitudes toward the Jews. He was friendly with Jews in his hometown of Statesville, particularly with a Jewish merchant named Samuel Wittkowsky, who protested when a squad of Union cavalry rode up to take Vance off to prison at the end of the war and insisted on driving the Governor in the dignity of Wittkowsky's own fine buggy.

Vance's mother read from the Bible to her children ("She was the most correct and impressive reader I have ever heard offstage," he once wrote, "and I am satisfied that whatever of elocution I have came from her"), and he developed a feeling for the ancient Hebrews, since she required him to memorize large portions of the Old Testament as a boy.

It is possible that his friendship for Wittkowsky and his memories of his mother's Bible reading combined to make the Jews in human history a natural subject for him, one in which he could demonstrate his knowledge of the Bible and call on passages from the classics. The uniqueness of a former Southern governor and United States senator saying such things must have appealed to fundamentalist audiences; all in all, it was a popular lecture that would take him all over the nation. Yet North Carolina was the last state to remove constitutional restrictions against Jews' holding office, and it took a Reconstruction legislature drafting an all-new constitution in 1868 to do it, after Vance's term. As governor, he had been too preoccupied with the war to take on such an issue, even though a bill had been introduced in the legislature in 1861.

Still, there had been no speech by a public official like "The Scattered Nation," and Jews in the South benefited from such resounding words from so respected a Southern leader. It was reprinted in journals and newspapers all over the region and raised the prestige of Jews wherever he spoke.

Like the rest of the United States, the South has had its anti-Semitic episodes, its share of incidents and ugliness. The question that I have sought to explore is whether it is indeed true that the South is the most anti-Semitic part of the United States. I don't think that most Jews in the South would agree with the findings of the polls and studies, for most Jews live their lives in a placid atmosphere as part of the white majority. It is my view that the studies have never taken into account the special character of the Southerner and the complexity of the South. I'm not sure what such an in-depth study of Southern attiudes toward Jews would show, but I do know that it will take a special sensitivity to the Southern psyche to plan it and a knowledge of Southern Jewish history to interpret it.

SIXTEEN

New Orleans–the Velvet Rut

Because whenever I approach a Jew, the Geiger counter in my head starts rattling away like a machine gun . . . There is nothing new in my Jewish vibrations. During the years when I had friends my Aunt Edna, who is a theosophist, noticed that all my friends were Jews. She knew why, moreover: I had been a Jew in a previous incarnation. Perhaps that is it. Anyhow it is true I am Jewish by instinct. We share the same exile. The fact is, however, I am more Jewish than the Jews I know. They are more at home than I am. I accept my exile.

The Moviegoer,
Walker Percy

I N Hope Valley, the finely manicured, moneyed section of Durham, the new rich built columned white homes around a rolling golf course, and one man even constructed in his front yard a three-foot replica of the plantation manor as a doll house for his little girl. A few Jewish families lived out there, but none of them could belong to the Hope Valley Country Club high on the hill. The Hope Valley sons gravitated to the Durham High tennis and golf teams and the daughters anchored the Christmas debutante season, but the rustling gowns never could conceal the crumbling backdrop of the Durham City Armory where the big debutante ball was held. Desperate for recognition, one of the tobacco wives once pulled strings in New York to have the actress Ann Sothern send her daughter Tish Sterling to touch the ball with stardust, giving the local paper a little historic item to mention every year thereafter.

227

I felt uncomfortable out at the Hope Valley dances the few times I went, only because the girls seemed so familiar with the place, greeting the parent-chaperones with intimate hugs while I always had to ask my date simple questions like where to go to sip our punch at intermission. As Durham's first family, we were finally asked to join, but it was too late by then and my parents didn't want to give them the satisfaction; mostly, my mother hesitated at the idea of my hanging around the pool with the smoothly tanned, shapely Hope Valley girls.

The country club exclusions in cities across the South still irritate the Southern Jews who have overcome almost every other form of discrimination. From the James River Country Club in Newport News to the Carolina Yacht Club in Charleston to the Piedmont Driving Club in Atlanta, the Jews are still outsiders looking into the last symbols of social acceptance, all the more humiliating now that many of them have accumulated a good deal more money and social status than the gentiles they want to play golf with.

Nowhere is the system of exclusion more finely honed than in New Orleans, where social status parades each year in Mardi Gras, advertising class distinctions more blatantly than in any other city in America. New Orleans revolves in a fantasy world of its own creation. Even a new language of social prestige has been invented to signal a guest's arrival into another world, strange-looking words describing organizations called "krewes" and "mistick," and ancient sounds like Momus, Comus, Proteus—gods and goddesses gazing down at the aspiring mortals below.

For German Jews, many of whom trace their ancestors to an earlier date than the leaders in the system which now discriminates against them, Mardi Gras is an annual reminder that they are outsiders looking in. Perhaps in self-defense, and because class distinctions permeate the city, they imitate the attitudes of the gentiles, pretending to be part of them—consumed with lineage and aloof from the Jews of later origin, as proud as the other old families of their own collection of Mardi Gras doubloons dating back to the nineteenth century.

The question that fascinated me, however, was not what Jews suffer looking in, but what the gentile community feels looking out. How do they rationalize it? At what age does it start and how do their children feel about it? Will it ever end? So I went to Mardi Gras to gauge the fragility of the barriers between Jews and

228

gentiles, and perhaps come to understand the nature of social discrimination all over the South. Besides, up in Durham, Mardi Gras always loomed as one of those delicious escapades on the list of essential experiences for every true-blooded Southern boy.

A breathless city awaits the climactic moment of Mardi Gras—the King of Rex with the Queen of Carnival on his arm leaves one side of the Municipal Auditorium to join the court of the Mistick Krewe of Comus at midnight for the final spectacle of Carnival, when the two courts together promenade around the Comus side of the auditorium floor before ascending a double throne to preside over the final event. Rex, a local civic leader at a pinnacle of his life, today has abandoned his gray flannel suit for a resplendent shoulder-length blond, curly wig, a bejeweled crown, and a twenty-five-foot gold cape on rollers. The King of Comus, in glittering silver costume, masked in stylish anonymity (as are all the male members of the elite Comus Krewe), maneuvers his court slowly to the appointed spot; and like astronauts docking in space, the two monarchs bow through the greeting ceremony with tantalizing attention to each superb moment. With fluttering white gloves, the elegantly gowned ladies of Comus applaud the familiar ritual symbolizing the exchange of queens, so that the golden Queen of Carnival joins the silver King of Comus. With a sweeping wave of her scepter she blesses her subjects in the balcony, who, though in white tie and tails, are not allowed on the dance floor; they have come by special prized invitation to watch the costumed revelry below.

It is never lost on anyone, least of all the people who count in New Orleans, that Rex and his queen, who are after all the King and Queen of Carnival, leave their side of the auditorium to come *to* Comus to pay homage, Comus being the oldest and most exclusive of Carnival krewes.

A reporter turns to a feathery woman next to him and asks, "But what of the people who are *not* here?"

"Who cares?" she answers blithely.

In 1970 the *New York Times* carried a story on Mardi Gras by Roy Reed which said, ". . . the city has about 14 leading krewes. The leading krewes exclude Jews, Negroes, and Italians. Negroes and Italians formed their own club. Jews, especially those important

229

in the city's economic structure, traditionally leave town on Mardi Gras." Howard Jacobs, a columnist of the New Orleans *Times-Picayune*, responded with a hot letter to the *Times* (which it didn't print) calling the charge of a mass exodus of Jews at Mardi Gras "a colossal myth," and a "pernicious legend that feeds on its own antiquity."

While pointing to the participation of Jews in some of the lesser Carnival organizations, Jacobs also wrote in the letter, "Three of the top-drawer Carnival krewes do not invite Jewish membership—Comus, Momus, and Proteus. The roster of these elite krewes is composed almost exclusively of old-line New Orleans families of Gallic or Anglo-Saxon derivation. It should be stressed here that the rigid exclusiveness of these groups is by no means confined to the Carnival season, but is a policy extension of the three ultra-social clubs with which the aforementioned krewes are affiliated—the Boston Club, the Louisiana Club and the Pickwick Club. . . . Enlightened Jews have never questioned their inalienable right to restrict their membership to whom they choose."

There is no mass exodus of Jews from New Orleans during Mardi Gras. A few of the top Jewish families do leave town to avoid embarrassment to their friends and to themselves. But most of the 10,000 Jews in New Orleans have learned to live with it; and some like Howard Jacobs defend the right of the clubs and the krewes to discriminate because of their private character. Moreover, the Rex organization, which coordinates the major events of Mardi Gras, opened its doors to a few Jews and tradesmen after World War II (when Rex adopted the "pro bono publico" motto). But the older gentile families kept control through a seniority system that placed them in the "inner circle" of the Rex organization, the key group that selects the king and queen, courts, themes, invitations, and costumes. The character of the evening underwent even further change when the Rex ball emerged as a civic event, abandoning its exclusivity to business customers from New York and a scattering of secretaries from the local bank.

To relieve the pressure for participation, the city has allowed krewes and balls to proliferate, until today there are more than sixty balls scheduled from December 23 to February 23, costing an average of $25,000 each.

The amount of civic energy and money drained off every year from more meaningful pursuits by such a back-breaking planning and financial effort has left the field open to the Jewish community to lead and contribute to the civic organizations that run everything else in town—charities, the opera guild, the symphony, the museums, and organizations like the League of Women Voters. And they have taken up the slack to such an extent that Jews have won the *Times-Picayune* Loving Cup, for "unselfish service to New Orleans" more than one-third the number of times since the award was established in 1901.

Anyone who cares must contend with a preciously short season for civic activity. "If you want to do anything in New Orleans from Thanksgiving to March," an active Jewish woman suggested, "it's always, 'Wait till after Mardi Gras.' And even then, you have to wait till the gentiles get back from their vacations."

Ben C. Toledano, the losing Republican candidate for mayor in the last election and himself from an old-line New Orleans family (his mother was queen of Carnival in 1929), blasted the whole process in a speech in Birmingham in January of 1971. "Mardi Gras," he said, "is probably one of the most depleting and wasteful things we have in New Orleans. . . . In what other city do the men sit down and plan costumes, themes, color schemes and plumage? We in New Orleans do not clutter our minds with information; we are not an intellectual city. If you would look for intellectual activity, you would have to look for it in the Jewish community. They are the angels who support our cultural activities."

In 1968, Calvin Trillin interviewed M. S. Edmundson, a Tulane anthropologist, for an article in *The New Yorker*. Edmundson believed that the exclusion of Jews "expresses one of the normal needs of a 'stable provincial society.' " Edmundson saw New Orleans society as one of the few in America that "refuses to acknowledge the primacy of New York" and to admit Jews would threaten their claims to a society "independent and equal to New York."

But some of the German-Jewish families have been in New Orleans longer than the gentiles who exclude them. The discrimination in the Boston Club, founded in 1852 and linked to Comus, particularly embitters the more prominent members of the Jewish community—lawyers, judges, and business leaders who are not even permitted in the club for lunch as guests (under a general rule barring all guests except out-of-towners).

The Boston Club sits in the midst of Canal Street, a dirty-white building of Victorian design, Old South in character, the white brick set off by a heavy, carved wooden door with shiny brass knobs, not the sort of door one would try to break down by force. It is the only building without display windows on the street, dwarfed by Godschaux's Department Store next door (Jewish owned), looking very out of place among the businesses—like a plantation manor house in a subdivision. One can peer through the windows and see what's going on inside: not Valhalla or Olympus with golden stairways into gossamer clouds, but just another downtown men's club—ordinary, conventional club-fare decor in ersatz Boston taste. There are writing desks and brown leather chairs with lots of pin-striped suits slouching in the stuffing or ordering lunch from black waiters in starched white garb.

I was told that the only Jew ever to walk into the Boston Club was a Jewish baker who delivered bread; and that another Jew did indeed go to Comus every year—by playing in the band.

Mardi Gras day starts at 9:00 A.M. with the Zulu parade, an embarrassing mockery by the least self-conscious members of the Negro community—horned chieftains who toss "soul coconuts" and shuffle and stomp in a mad-cap free-wheeling parade that turns out to be a parody of Mardi Gras itself. The "king" impersonates a comic-strip version of a Zulu chief, regally attired in grass skirt, in minstrel makeup with chalk-white painted mouth, huge earrings, and carrying a scepter with a skull on top. In 1961 a group of prominent black leaders and organizations protested the Zulu parade as a "caricature that does not represent us." They charged in a newspaper ad that "Negroes are paid by white merchants to wander through the city drinking to excess, dressed as uncivilized savages and throwing coconuts like monkeys." The Zulus responded that they were "fighting for our constitutional rights, and if some Negroes don't like the Zulu parade, let them start their own parade."

Then the crowds stir restlessly waiting for the four-hour-long parade (the thirty-fifth in ten days!), children on their father's shoulders, and ten-year-olds atop step ladders with handmade signs that say "throw me a doubloon. . . ." And then you see them—the members of the Rex organization melded into storybook themes atop the floats, throwing trinkets and beads and necklaces to the thirsting crowds. From a distance you can make out only the colorful costumes, but then you notice the faces. Fifteen men on a float and each one is alike. They are masked, not in faces of joy or fantasy but in flesh-colored masks with cutouts for their eyes and mouth, an aristocracy of secrecy, in a plastic mask designed only to hide their identity behind an expressionless, eerie sameness.

One newsman who became a "thrower" on a float wrote an account of the experience. After a morning at the Municipal Auditorium climbing into elaborate costumes while eating slabs of roast beef with various beverages to fortify themselves for the rigors of the day, the throwers, in full dress regalia, stumbled onto the floats for the parade. "And then the business began. I found out why people enjoy going on those floats and throwing those trinkets. There is much more to it than what my float neighbor told me, that most guys just do this so their wives and daughters can enjoy the Carnival balls. It really is an ego trip. It takes a while for you to realize the power you sling from your hands." (There are actually two parades passing by, back to back—the short, elite Rex parade followed without pause by the Elks' club parade, several hundred trucks long, in which any group who wants to can rent a truck, decorate it, and buy beads to sling. Mardi Gras enthusiasts point to the Elks as evidence of the democracy in the celebration, and Jews often ride the floats and join in. But a Jewish woman who did that observed caustically that the Queen of Mardi Gras, who reviews the Rex parade from a box in front of the Boston Club, never stays for the Elks' parade but retires inside to lunch with her king.)

Some Jews think that Mardi Gras discrimination will be overcome only if the black community decides to push its way in, thus opening the way for all minorities. But New Orleans' blacks show no signs of abandoning their current role.

New Orleans somehow has avoided the racial turmoil of other cities, though several years ago a brick whistled over the crowd thudding into the face of Al Hirt, the jazz trumpeter; and while the injury to his lip almost ended his career, city fathers were more concerned that the brick hit someone who was masked, so that whoever threw it, black or white, could not have known the identity of his target. Thus it was interpreted as an attack on Mardi Gras itself—segregated, arrogant, aristocratic, and vulnerable to violence. The brick almost caused the parade to be canceled the following year. When I asked one grande dame to explain the racial calm in New Orleans, she observed, "Well, my dear man, it's too muggy to riot."

Jews in New Orleans like to point out that the first King of Carnival in 1872 was a Jew named Lewis Salomon. Salomon was a clerk to cotton merchants at the time, and was drafted to serve because a local banker, according to Perry Young, a historian of such matters, "preferred to escape the doubtful and conspicuous honor."

Young wrote two florid books on various aspects of Carnival in the 1930's, and he praised Lewis Salomon as the "only Jew yet carnival king, but noble citizen who shouldered an imperious duty that no one else would dare, and carried it to such an amazing success that the circumcised have never had another chance to earn that kind of glory."

He turned his baroque humor to the defense of the exclusion of Jews from Mardi Gras activities, echoing the argument that one hears today: desirable Jews could be invited, but, since it is a religious festival, they should not want to join in. In his book *Carnival and Mardi Gras in New Orleans* (1939), now mercifully out of print, he points out that Jews do take part in that Jewish merchants make money from Carnival.

While Young does not precisely reflect the attitudes of the people of New Orleans thirty years ago, his books were popular, though the language is too ornate to suffer through in more than small doses. In a final tribute, Young uncorked all his talent: "Bless the Jews, we couldn't be gentiles without them; and the ones that we like to see go into the follies of the blest are not those who make a show of wanting it, or turn Christian shoulders into wailing walls for not getting it; and those few whose importunities have fortified the intolerance of carnival societies are never the old-established and long-esteemed Jewish families of Louisiana. (Full many a Christian on the ball night could wish to be a Jew, but— No Cross, no Crown.)"

New Orleans historically was a raucous, unpredictable place caught up in the clatter of trade and intrigues of seaport shenanigans—high pleasure, frontier pomp, and delicious decadence. In 1724, the French imposed the Black Code of 1615, which decreed that Jews would be expelled and that Roman Catholicism would be the only permissible religion.

But Jews were attracted to the potential of the port city, and the laws were either unenforced or made more flexible until France ceded Louisiana to Spain in 1762. The Spanish, with a tradition of Jewish persecution since the Spanish Inquisition in the fifteenth century, took their prejudices more seriously, and a tough military governor named O'Reilly confiscated the property of successful Jewish merchants and drove them out of the colony.

New Orleans really didn't begin to grow until it began trading with the young American republic in the latter part of the eighteenth century. After the Louisiana Purchase, the city exploded in growth—from 10,000 people in 1815 to 100,000 in 1840—providing an extraordinary atmosphere in which daring entrepreneurs could amass fortunes and talented professional men forge public careers.

Judah Touro, the first Jew known to have arrived in New Orleans after 1800, was one of several Jewish merchants and land investors to flourish in this atmosphere. Touro's famous will in 1854, which was published by the *New York Times* because it left $483,000 to charity, established him as America's first philanthropist. Among those benefiting were Jewish congregations, religious schools, benevolent societies and hospitals in nineteen American cities; Catholic, Protestant, and other charities in New England; numerous churches, hospitals, an orphan home, and an alms house in New Orleans. He even left $60,000 for various causes in Palestine and $15,000 to help save the Jews of China. (Touro was a bachelor, and left the bulk of his estate—approximately $500,000 to $750,000—to his life-long friend Rezin Shepherd, who had saved his life at the Battle of New Orleans. Shepherd lived for a time in Massachusetts and was the great-great-grandfather of Leverett Saltonstall; thus Touro provided the early bedrock for a famous Yankee fortune.)

Jews also point with less exuberance to the pirate Jean Lafitte, who supposedly wrote in a family Bible, "I owe all my ingenuity to the great intuition of my Jewish-Spanish grandmother, who was a witness at the time of the Inquisition." Though it is a matter of debate, a number of biographies claim that Lafitte's grandmother "planted a deep hatred of Spain in her grandsons."

Judah P. Benjamin came to New Orleans from Charleston (as a dropout from Yale College) in 1828, and began a meteoric rise in a career that would see him become a United States senator and attorney general, secretary of war, and secretary of state of the Confederacy.

There were other Jews from New Orleans in high office in the antebellum period: Henry Hyams, lieutenant governor of Louisiana in 1859–1860; and Dr. Edwin Warren Moise, who served as attorney general of Louisiana and speaker of the House.

Bertram Korn, who spent years of painstaking research to write his *Early Jews of New Orleans,* said, "There was probably less prejudice against Jews in New Orleans during the antebellum period than in any other important city in the country. . . . . The large-scale acceptance of Jews in almost every nook and cranny of social, political, and cultural life, in addition to the more obvious opportunities of the marketplace, meant that there was no negative pressure upon Jews to create a congregation or to develop an intensive Jewish life. Their energies were directed outward rather than inward."

Korn also points out that Jews were welcomed, and in most instances helped found the exclusive social clubs in New Orleans: "Carl [Kohn] and his nephew Gustave were members of the Boston Club, as were Judah P. Benjamin, Isaac and Samuel Delgado, Benjamin Franklin Jonas, Charles, H. O. and J. M. Seixas, Adolph and Victor Meyer, and Julius Weis, among others. Jonas (who later served as US senator from Louisiana) was a member of the Board of Governors and Vice President from 1894 to 1904."

In addition, "Armand Heine was a founding member of the Pickwick Club; he and his brother Michel actually owned the clubhouse from 1884 to 1894. . . . Edward Barnett and Cohen M. Soria were presidents of the Pickwick Club. Not all of these people were practicing Jews, but they were all born Jews and their fathers were."

Korn muses on the reasons why New Orleans was such a receptive place for individual Jewish accomplishment:

Certain social and economic factors made New Orleans an exceptional American city . . . during this period: the turbulent growth of the city, bringing into its midst people of every kind of background and heritage, and turning it into the most heterogeneous city in the country; the strong rivalry of Creoles and Yankees, both sides eagerly seeking both Christian and Jewish recruits; the absence of a tradition of hide-bound, narrow evangelical Protestants on the one hand, and of defensive, separatistic and suspicious Catholicism on the other; the constant need for men of talent and ability to take leadership in a society where many young men were unambitious, effete dandies; the tremendous economic potential of the city, never really exploited to its fullest, constantly in need of rich imagination and strong direction; the periodic financial crises which shook out the incompetent and the incautious, and made room for new risk-takers. All of these aspects of the city's growth made it possible for Jews to be accepted as human beings, rather than as Jews.

Astonishingly, the Jews of New Orleans, though numbering several hundred by 1830, were so absorbed by the city that they didn't even seek to organize a congregation until 1827. New Orleans was not a pious city, and Protestant clergymen even complained of its godlessness and the "men who regard religion [as] intended only for women and servants." In such an environment, Jews conformed, more caught up in profit, property, and pleasure than in religious practice.

It took until 1840 to take the synagogue seriously, the congregation by default and indifference having fallen prey to the high jinks of a clownish fake rabbi named Rowley Marks, a ludicrous but likable part-time comic actor and fireman who, when a member of the congregation once complained about his conduct during a high holy day service, banged on the podium and screamed, "By Jesus Christ! I have a right to pray!" Finally, after a false start, new leadership moved to New Orleans and convinced Judah Touro to buy and remodel a church into a synagogue, secure a learned rabbi, and form a respectable Sephardic congregation. Touro also loaned money to a growing German-Jewish community for its own temple. Just in time, it seemed; one writer wrote of the condition of the New Orleans Jewish community in 1840: "In only four Jewish homes in town were forbidden foods avoided; in only two was the Sabbath strictly observed; two-thirds of the Jews did not have their sons circumcised; not even fifty of the Jewish boys could read Hebrew."

The New Orleans Jewish community soon was dominated by the new wave of German-Jewish immigration which arrived as the city and the South staggered out of the Civil War to face the humiliation of Reconstruction, and turned to rebuild its burned cities and recapture its dignity.

In 1878, due to another of the recurring epidemics of yellow fever that plagued the growth of New Orleans all through its early history, the German and Sephardic congregations merged. (The epidemic spread through the Mississippi marshlands to Little Rock and Memphis, causing such alarm among Jews all over America that congregations in New York City, Philadelphia, St. Louis, Boston, and Cincinnati raised $60,000 for "the infected region.")

New Orleans then braced for the great wave of Jewish immigration from Eastern Europe in the late nineteenth and early twentieth centuries, bringing fiercely orthodox new Jews into a settled and conservative Reform community that even had experimented with Sunday Sabbath services. But most of them did not stay and since that time, unlike the ratios in most other large cities in America, the Reform Jews there have outnumbered the Orthodox and Conservatives, even today when there are seven different congregations in the city.

Rabbi Julian Feibelman, rabbi at Reform Temple Sinai for thirty-one years, attributes the dominance of Reform Judaism partly to the fear of yellow fever that discouraged the East Europeans from settling in New Orleans, to the mobility of those new immigrants who did come, and to the "vitality of Reform ideas." Feibelman, a complex man who grew up in Mississippi (and who opened the temple to a speech by Ralph Bunche in 1949, the first large integrated meeting in New Orleans history), was a founder of the anti-Zionist American Council for Judaism in the 1940's. This move reflected both his own views and the character of much of the congregation. (Remarkably, his predecessor, Rabbi Maximillian Heller, rabbi at Sinai from 1887 to 1926, was one of the few German Reform rabbis in America who supported Zionism, calling it in 1922 "the most romantic of all movements . . . lending new color and glow to Jewish past, present, and future.")

"I didn't want to see the State of Israel established," Feibelman admitted. "I believed in what Einstein believed; it was good to have a place where Jews could go, but if you had a state, it would mean another army, another navy. I got out of the Council when Truman recognized Israel and never went back. 'You can't argue with history,' I said at the time. 'Now there's a state and we must support it.' "

A former president of Hadassah remembered when Henrietta Szold, the national founder of the Jewish women's organization, visited New Orleans and was asked whether one had to be a Zionist to belong to Hadassah. "She answered, 'Why, certainly,' and the next day, most of the women resigned because they had no ideology. We began to grow again when the news trickled out of Germany and finally there was Israel. When the assimilationist group realized that Israel had become acceptable to the gentiles, they came around."

In New Orleans, the real bitterness over Mardi Gras and the exclusions that accompany it depend on whom you are talking to. The Reform Jews, some of them with historic roots in the community, at one time the very essence of the city, were once blended into its politics, its economy, and its society. Some of them now are several generations into the American experience and indistinguishable in attitude and position from anyone else in New Orleans except at lunchtime and at Mardi Gras. They profoundly resent the parading of position and the flaunting of birth, and perhaps from jealousy are mortified to be excluded from the most visible aspect of the city's social life.

The East Europeans, more conditioned to discrimination by their immigrant parents who were happy enough just to be in America, are more satisfied to face inward to each other. They are committed in their daily lives to a more insular life of Jewish friends, Jewish clubs, and work in Jewish organizations. They raise money for Jewish rather then gentile charities (though they do more than their part as a community obligation). Their goals and values steer them away from the New Orleans social set; they resent more the aloofness of the German Jews, who seem to imitate the gentiles in their obsession with genealogy, than they do the discrimination of the more distant Boston Club and the Comus Krewe.

"What's the big deal?" one of the Orthodox said. "The Reform Jews suffer while we are like the *shvahtsas* at Mardi Gras—we go out and have a good time."

The debutante West Point, the playing fields of Eton, the New Orleans version of Choate-Chapin–Cordon Bleu all rolled into one is a small girls' school in the Garden district called the Louise S. McGehee School. Founded in 1912, with a school coat of arms that contains the words "Noblesse Oblige," the McGehee School still requires each of its girls to draw and display sketches of the long dress she will wear to graduation so there'll be no duplications. For decades McGehee has been the institution by which the elite in New Orleans shield their young women from the blacks, the Jews, the poor, and the different, protecting them from ideas and associations that might lure them from their manifest destiny.

"We started out as a preparatory school for girls who would 'set styles' for the community," said a former teacher at McGehee. "I thought that meant come into contact with ideas in the world—like Jeremy Bentham, Marx, Freud, and John Stuart Mill. Parents began calling the headmistress complaining that I had referred to New Orleans society as upper middle class, instead of upper class; or that I had said aristocracy in the United States is based on wealth instead of inherited ability."

She said that the girls were not empty-headed debutantes, but that they worked hard, were well adjusted, and learned to manipulate their parents, teachers, and the social system itself. "These are steel butterflies," she suggested, "who love to project the image of helpless femininity, but they have wills of iron. They get what they want."

A sixteen-year-old Jewish girl who felt she was better adjusted because she went to a coed school described the girls at McGehee: "They're brought up as Southern belles. They're aloof, they know how to be sweetly snobbish. Most of them are trapped into blind dates all the time with guys from the prep schools in the city, so they learn to snow a guy in one night. Because of the pressure, they are more aggressive in a camouflaged Southern way. It's not relationships they're after, but a good enough time to be asked out again."

A McGehee graduate disputed that view strenuously, stating that "our snobbery was just an act. The truth is that we were terrified of boys."

Jews hesitate to complain about each trivial slight, but the early exclusions teach the children on both sides who matters and who doesn't. A former Comus queen confessed that she knew in the eighth grade at McGehee that she would be either Queen of Carnival or of Comus when she reached the right age. "People from outside New Orleans think the Queen of Carnival is competitive and chosen on beauty, charm, and wisdom. But, because of my father, they would have chosen me if I had two heads; and then they would have put a crown on each head and walked around the ball saying, 'Isn't she a beautiful two-headed queen!' "

One mother gave this caustic summary of how to pick a queen

240

when she responded to a *Times-Picayune* article on "A Day in the Life of a Queen," which said that it was a day "her mother had been working all her life for." "Of course," she added, "it didn't make a rat's ass how hard she worked. It's not decided by hard work."

So at the 1971 Rex Ball, they introduced all of the past queens present by their maiden names to pay tribute to the first families of the city. When a gray-haired, wrinkled regina toddled out on the floor to curtsy to the court, the announcer said "the former Miss . . ." and a woman next to me whispered "the better to tell the players."

It is fashionable for the first families to complain about the deterioration of Mardi Gras, now that the balls and the parades have multiplied so that almost anybody can arrange to have his daughter queen of something or in somebody's court. "The debutante picture has changed," complained the father of a future debutante. "Twenty years ago, there were fifteen girls a season, and now it's more than forty. Anybody can do it . . . it's an outrage."

Moreover, some of the winds of the seventies have reached New Orleans and the girls themselves aren't as enthusiastic about the tinsel world of Mardi Gras as they once were. "My grandmother just didn't realize how much it had gone down," said one girl in jeans who refused to participate. "I told my family that I would much rather have a year in Europe than shoot the money on dresses." The money can amount to more than $10,000 for clothes, parties, and assorted glitter.

Yet the fantasy remains resilient, and many a mother in New Orleans still displays on the coffee table her husband's scepter and her daughter's crown. And if you sit with a group of future debs on the Tulane campus, there will be almost universal agreement as to which queenships matter and which do not. "This is a chicken-shit ball and this is a good one," an acid-tongued blonde volunteered as we went down the list. She explained that a "chicken-shit ball is one at which the men pay to be king and for placing their daughters on the court." A socialite mother put it to her daughter this way: "Remember dear, the butcher and the baker have their own."

And the stories abound of the families who move from New Orleans over the disgrace of a slight to their daughter, the plotting that can influence bank loans and exchange building contracts for

241

queenships inside the Rex Organization. The politics of Mardi Gras seeps down to the girls.

"You can debut either your sophomore or your junior year," a Sophie Newcomb veteran of last year's gauntlet revealed, "and you decide by watching where the sure-shot is." She remembered an argument in senior study at McGehee over a future queen who was aiming too high: "She had a walk-away shot at Momus, but her father just didn't have enough clout to make it in Rex."

A teacher at McGehee chose to send her own children to the Isadore Newman School, the best academic school in the city, because "I didn't want my girls picking up the artificial social attitudes cultivated at McGehee." The Newman School was founded in 1903 as a school for Jewish orphans, and was developed as part of a whole private school system in response to the corrupt era of Louisiana politics. Newman and the Metairie Park Country Day School received large amounts of money from Jewish philanthropies and they became the schools for the children of Jewish families who could afford it and many who could not. Today, Newman is forty percent Jewish, highly oriented to college admission, and as the husband of a McGehee girl from the fifties put it, "Even the dumb society mamas try to send their girls to Newman today." Thus while there are no Jews at McGehee, there are many debs at Newman.

Because of the social patterns in the city, Jewish and gentile enclaves inevitably sprout up inside Newman. For the non-Jews who choose Newman, the pattern of exclusion of their Jewish friends begins with the organization of private dances in the seventh, eighth, and ninth grades. The influential gentile mothers at Newman and McGehee organize the "ice-breakers" for the seventh graders—"Eight O'Clocks" and "Nine O'Clocks"—and slowly edge the girls along into "Younger Set" dances (ninth and tenth grades) and finally into the subdeb category from which they are poised to leap into the real thing.

A former debutante who went to Newman remembered her mother's warning when she submitted the names of two Jewish boys on the invitation lists that the mothers cleared. " 'This is a restriction you will encounter the rest of your life,' my mother told me. When I asked her why, she answered, 'If you can tell me that, you'll answer a question I've always wanted to know myself.' "

A McGehee alumna, on the other hand, confessed that "if you

are at McGehee's the question never comes up. I mean, we just didn't know any Jewish boys. I thought they were like American Indians."

The pattern gets sealed when the teen-agers are selected for Valencia, an all-gentile teen center (a "junior country club for overprivileged children," one member described it) started in the early fifties to bring some of the rowdiness of the high school fraternities and sororities under better institutional control.

Conditioning to Mardi Gras begins to intrude itself early. At the Twelfth Night Ball in January, the Junior Cooks (ages twelve to fifteen) dress in white chef's caps to cut and pass out the cake. Most balls have pages or ladies-in-waiting to help drag the trains of the kings and queens and to ride as cherubic decorations on the floats. It all seems harmless, except that one Jewish woman remembered this comment when she tried to get her sixth grader onto a prestige float as a page. "I was told that the Board said, 'If you let her little boy on, her daughter may try to push on the court soon.' O.K., but my daughter at that time was three years old!"

The Jewish kids respond with a reverse snobbery that tries to laugh at the scrambling for social position while putting pressure on any Jews who venture out into the whirl. "You go to parties, you give parties," complained a fifteen-year-old Jewish girl. "You're never apart from the Jewish crowd; and they resent you if you try to pull away."

The defensive posture of the Jewish kids causes a reaction from the gentiles as the two camps spiral into mutual isolation. "The Jewish kids freeze us out," a Newman girl complained. "All they talk about is the high school Jewish fraternities and sororities like AZA and BBG, while we outlawed that stuff years ago."

A non-Jewish woman who went to Newman in the late fifties recalled the misunderstandings from her side. "There was some cross-dating, particularly if there was a good-looking Jewish girl. But for the most part, the Jewish kids stayed in cliques—they laughed at things only they understood; they were cordial but distant; and they were the smartest kids, so their clannishness always made me feel inferior and left out."

The exclusion of prominent Jewish families from the major balls can cause some painful moments, since some of the kids know each other at Newman and may otherwise be friends. Following the balls, the queens give breakfasts and some of the mothers invite their Jewish friends to these occasions. "You are supposed to stay up until one o'clock," said a prominent Jewish man, "and get your wife and daughter into a gown and pretend you've come from the ball. Why, it's a damn insult."

One Jewish girl remembered when her best friend was queen of a ball she couldn't be invited to, and she was asked over to the house to see her off in her $3,000 dress and "join in" the preball excitement. "I told her I didn't want to go anyway," the Jewish girl recalled, "and in some ways I didn't. Maybe being friends was enough for me—like being Jackie Kennedy's maid." Jewish men who marry into prominent gentile familes are not invited to balls that their wives get invitations to.

Most graduates of McGehee aim for Sophie Newcomb, the girls' school of Tulane, because the debutante season lasts from November to March, and Mardi Gras heavily intrudes itself into college life there. But for years Sophie Newcomb has also been the major school in the South for Jewish girls from all over the South, so much so that the school for a decade has been more than one-third Jewish (and inelegantly nicknamed "Jewcomb").

The organized separations between Jews and non-Jews continue at Newcomb through the sorority system, which is kept exclusive by the girls themselves and the alumnae. Alumnae groups of the older gentile sororities screen girls and recommend them to the current sisters, thus keeping the sorority firmly anchored in Old South values. "If we like a girl from Birmingham they haven't recommended," a president of a major sorority confessed, "we write back and ask. And if they don't like her still, we can't pledge her—so there's just no chance we'd ever pledge a Jewish girl."

Some of the less prestigious sororities pledge Jewish girls but until a few years ago, when the university stopped it, the Jewish freshman girl at Newcomb, before even arriving at school, had to make the choice. "You used to have two rushes—Jewish and non-Jewish," said the former president of a Jewish sorority, "and a freshman went through one or the other. A form would arrive in the mail that summer, and she returned a photo and indicated her preference. Then the school sent copies to the Jewish sororities."

The Jewish fraternities were more indirect. They worked with the Hillel Foundation to get the list of Jewish freshmen; ZBT always went after the Southerners, especially the New Orleans boys. "We never took ghetto-type Northerners," a ZBT of the sixties said. "Most of us went to Reform temples; we once black-balled a guy who asked about keeping kosher and whether we would provide facilities for his own pots and pans."

The Jewish fraternities presented one face to the campus and another to each other. The athletic rivalries between the ZBT and the SAM fraternities were legendary at Tulane, perhaps reflecting the tension between the German Jews and the East Europeans in New Orleans itself. The annual touch football game between the two houses, nicknamed the "Nose Bowl," always drew a crowd of several thousand students.

"It was a blood bath," said a ZBT who played in it before the game had to be suspended in 1964. "Concussions, broken ribs. Of course, when we played the big jock houses like the SAE's or Kappa Sig's, it was never as rough because it would hurt our social standing on campus if we roughed 'em up too much."

While the Jewish students dated freely all over the Tulane campus, female familiarity with Jewish male foibles drew all the Jewish fraternities to the annual skit night at the Raven Bar near campus, in which the pledges at a Jewish sorority would mimic and ridicule the Jewish fraternities. In the middle sixties, the themes were "the usual," said a Jewish girl who helped write them. "We teased them about Gant shirts and weejuns, dating Christian girls, living in the zoo, pawing girls upstairs in the houses, and dropping trou [trousers]."

Another Sophie Newcomb girl of the early sixties remembered the "black and white parties" between the SAE's and Jewish sororities in which "the Jews wore black and the gentiles white—you know, as a joke sort of."

New Orleans may be the only city in the western world in which the men control all of the social life ("where more men own white tie and tails than any other city in the world," any haberdasher will tell you proudly). Thus politics and power are so intertwined with Mardi Gras that some feel the whole process has a paralyzing effect on the progress of the city.

Dr. Charles Y. Chai, an assistant professor of political science at Tulane, is doing research on the power structure and decision making in New Orleans. With extensive personal interviews and questionnaires, he compiled a list of the most influential people in New Orleans, and labeled them the "power elite" (about fifteen percent were Jews). Almost every leader on the list, Jew and non-Jew, expressed the belief that the closed, secret Carnival organizations and the rigid social structure in New Orleans are causes of economic stagnation and civic apathy. But no one said he wanted to do anything about it. "The Jews," Chai observed in an interview, "are as much in the don't-rock-the-boat syndrome as the gentile community."

Chai explained the reaction of the Jews on his list through a substudy he did on power in the Jewish community. He found that the Jews on the "power elite" community list were mostly from "old families raised in the aristocratic tradition with an assimilationist mentality. Curiously, they were not powerful in the Jewish community. In fact, those who were most influential in the Jewish community considered them almost as non-Jews."

So the discrimination in the social clubs and the Mardi Gras organizations continues without public debate or concern. The local Anti-Defamation League has taken no public stand, reflecting the reticence of the Jewish community about making trouble; so while some younger Jews talk of lawsuits to bar use of public facilities for the balls, other Jewish leaders have talked with the membership committees of the clubs and say with a submissive shrug, "There is a waiting list for sons of members, running five to seven years, so how can we ask for preferential treatment?"

"Each generation, Jew and gentile, rails against it," said a younger member of one of the city's most prominent gentile families, "but then you grow up and accept things when you find the bread is always buttered on your side. Here, everybody takes it easy," he continued. " 'The Big Easy'—that's what a magazine called New Orleans. Try to change something and you'll hear it: 'Whoa, man, whoa . . . take it easy . . . eeeeeeeeeasy. . . .' "

For a matronly veteran of years of dragging through the battery of balls and outmaneuvering her friends for the available hairdressers and caterers, Mardi Gras had warped itself from a smothering obsession into a mechanical charade, drained of all gladness and excitement, an empty miasma of thundering boredom. "Discrimination?" she sighed wearily. "I'll tell you why nobody does anything about it. It's all so dull. We're all caught here . . . caught in a velvet rut . . . and we just can't get out."

246

SEVENTEEN

The Burned-Out Cross
of the Klan

"Ku Klux got after some Catholics one time."

*"Never heard of any Catholics in Maycomb either,"
said Atticus, "you're confusing that with something
else. Way back about nineteen-twenty there was a
Klan, but it was a political organization more than
anything. Besides they couldn't find anybody to scare.
They paraded by Mr. Sam Levy's house one night, but
Sam just stood on his porch and told 'em things had
come to a pretty pass, he'd sold 'em the very sheets on
their backs. Sam made 'em so ashamed of themselves
they went away."*

*The Levy family met all the criteria for being Fine
Folks: they did the best they could with the sense they
had, and they had been living on the same plot of
ground in Maycomb for five generations.*

To Kill a Mockingbird,
Harper Lee

W A L K I N G home from junior high school one day, I was stopped
by a man who handed me a pamphlet. "One drop of Jew blood
in your family destroys your white blood forever," it began, and
was signed by the Knights of the Ku Klux Klan. The reaction
I remember most was the blunt shock that the Klan included Jews
on their list at all—the quotes in the newspaper from the rallies out
in Durham County always attacked "the integrationists" and "miscegenation," but never the Jews. "They spoil, corrupt, decay,

247

corrode, debase everything they touch," the pamphlet continued, "and are an alien race in America." I passed it off, on my father's assurance, and heard little more about it.

I have few other memories of the Klan, except once, on a rainy night in Charleston, driving slowly on the outskirts of town, I was jolted awake when my lights suddenly illuminated a Klansman in full regalia square ahead—a ghostly giant in white, distorted into a jagged puzzle by the droplets on the windshield, his arms raised so that the draped sleeves turned him into a human cross. This was no flying apparition; he was engaged in the rather mundane task of directing traffic, motioning cars off the road toward a cow pasture where a cross was burning, dozens of robed figures marching slowly around it in a huge circle. I clutched the wheel, jammed the accelerator flat to the floorboard, and shot into the night.

Until that time, I had laughed at the Klan, just as everyone in North Carolina laughed at "Catfish" Cole, the great Klan-clown who had turned Klansmen into a laughingstock by tangling with the tough, proud Lumbee Indians. The Indians, armed and on horseback, had captured the Klan's Confederate flag with a war whoop and chased them, their sheets pulled knee-high so as to run faster, into ridicule for a decade. But in the swampy perimeter of Charleston that night, I thought I knew what it was to be black— the sure knowledge that out there in the darkness is an intense hatred, insensible and unpredictable, oblivious to individual merit or a lifetime of righteous living, lying in wait or perhaps stalking; and sometime on summer nights over the years, at home restless and alone, could that be footsteps?

Anyone can find Joe Bryan at Bryan's Naturopath Clinic on the outskirts of Charlotte, a plain unobtrusive building with parking places in front. "Just spell my name right and take my picture," he had said when I called. And now he came out into a magazine-cluttered waiting room to greet me—a strapping man, big-shouldered and bull-necked with strong, beefy paws and powerful stumpy thumbs, muscled from crunching sore shoulders and digging deep into the mysteries of aching backs. His stylish clothes surprised me—a sharp brown blazer and wide yellow tie. He seemed the sort of man who might otherwise be wrestling a trailer truck all day, grooving on Roy Acuff and Ernest Tubb, and guzzling a pitcher of beer on Saturday night. A giant Confederate

248

flag drapes an entire wall in his wood-paneled office; with several lines on his phone, and stacks of folders on his desk, it is difficult to imagine him in the white cloak of a grand dragon. The Klan has moved into town and Joe Bryan wants to make a good impression as a professional man—polite, with careful grammar that only rarely slips. This is part of the new image, calling his cross burnings a "convocation," reaching out for "better-type" members, trying to cast off the violent history for a new role in politics, dreaming of power even in the big cities up North, but aiming hard and center for the emerging middle class in the South and the "white people who are fed up" in the nation.

For the past two years Bryan has been locked in a power struggle for control of the Klan in North Carolina with Bob Jones, the North Carolina head of the United Knights of the Klan, which is affiliated with Robert Shelton's South-wide United Klans in Tuscaloosa. Both Shelton and Jones went to jail for a year for refusal to show their membership lists to the House Un-American Activities Committee, and Bryan moved in as caretaker while Jones was away. But the caretaker dug in real tight, and split off into a new group when Jones returned: "We adopted this organization when we couldn't tolerate the misappropriation of funds—to drive their Cadillacs, play nine holes of golf, and drink the finest bourbon. Our people will no longer pay a man to be patriotic."

Joe Bryan has worked up a new line for the press and he starts it by denying he is prejudiced in any way: "I'm not anti-Semitic; I'm not anti-Catholic; and I'm not anti-Negro. I just happen to be pro-Protestant white."

He believes that "the worst thing that ever happened to the Klan was back in the twenties when they came out with being anti-Catholic and anti-Jewish. It hurt the organization in the eyes of the public. We lost prestige. Why, we used to have people elected to office—now all we got is disbarred attorneys and very few people of influence. So we're trying to reform the image in North Carolina to do away with these two parts especially."

The reason for a new impetus to gain Jewish and Catholic membership is the widespread antagonism over busing. "Most people are very upset at the moment about it . . . good friends of mine who happen to be Jewish . . . and Irish and the Italians [he pronounced it "Eye-talians"] up in New York." He was certain that he could draw Jews and Catholics into the Klan because

249

"they've told me many times that they didn't know why we didn't accept them because they believed just exactly as we do."

What kind of Jews does he think will join the Klan?

"Jews like Benjamin Freedman. Maybe you heard of him up in Union, New Jersey. He's about the hardest-hitting, rabble-rousing, anti-Semitic Jew I ever have seen. He really hits 'em hard. I think we could sign up quite a few of this kind." (This description squared with the A.D.L.'s assessment of Freedman.)

He would by-pass the clauses in the Klan charters which require members to believe in Christ, by advocating a system of "degree-working Klan-Kraft as they do in the Masonic lodge." He would draw members from the several organizations which exist just for Jews who accept Christ; for other Jews, under his plan, there would be "a fork at a certain point, one side for those who believe in Christ and the other just for God." (In Tuscaloosa, I asked Robert Shelton, the Imperial Wizard of the United Klans, about Joe Bryan's plan. "If you left it up to Joe Bryan," he said, "he'd have niggers in the Klan.") To illustrate his tolerance, Bryan brags that he even voted for a Jew once.

"I voted for Barry Goldwater. He was a fine and patriotic man. I think he was crucified for nothing really by the news media. We got far worse with what we got than what we would have had with Goldwater."

He blames the media for the Klan's reputation for violence, "especially hanging Negroes." He condemns them for prejudicial reporting, saying, "How can anyone who claims not to be prejudiced say all Klansmen are bad simply because some have committed acts of this sort under the name of the Klan? I don't believe in grouping people, like saying all Catholics are bad because some are connected with the Mafia."

As he rose to show me around the place, I noticed that the walls were full of diplomas (he boasted of a lively degree-and-honorary-certificate printing business on the side). "Naturopaths believe in using only the natural elements—heat, light, massage, steam," he said, pulling the folding doors back on a little massage cubicle. "The medical profession is giving us hell but natural cures are popular with the young." He showed me his buzzer system—to lock the doors automatically and alert the girls in the back to straighten things out. The girls giggle when introduced, all in miniskirted nurses' uniforms, big-busted, teased hair, one of them black. "Just ask her how good I am to work for." He was proud of his place.

I asked him whether his calm language appealed to the membership.

"It would upset you if I called you names—niggers, poor pecks, coons, kikes. It hurts the Klan—all people used to know how to do was to call 'em niggers and burrheads."

I summoned up the courage to tell him I was Jewish, and asked him if he believed that Jews today ought to be blamed for crucifying Christ. He answered with the earnestness of a man who didn't want his own past under too close scrutiny. "I don't think that you should blame me if my great-great-grandfather happened to be a horsethief; and I don't think I should blame you if your great-great-great-grandfather crucified Christ."

Why had the Klan floundered so much in recent years if racial troubles are getting much worse?

"It took a few years for the stench to get around and for the news media to brand us anti-Catholic and anti-Jewish and ever since then, they've been hounding the organization with it and hurting us."

Did he believe that there was a Communist conspiracy to force integration, and were the President and the Supreme Court part of it? "Integration is being widely used by people who have in mind world domination by communism. A lot of people in high places lend passive support by not opposing it." I had obviously asked a question that Joe Bryan was more used to answering.

Historians speak of three Klan periods in American history. The first came during Reconstruction when the Confederate soldiers returning from the battlefields organized to frighten the newly freed Negroes and assault the carpetbaggers who had come to rule the South.

By 1871, the Klan had reached a membership of 555,000 and the most respectable veterans of the War had joined.

Bernard Baruch's father, Simon Baruch, had been a Confederate surgeon for three years in the War, had written a book on the treatment of bayonet wounds, and later, in New York, wrote another book on hydrotherapy. Baruch wrote about an exciting moment in his boyhood in his autobiography, *My Own Story:*

> One autumn day, when I was about five or six, Harty and I were rummaging about the attic of our house. . . . We came across a horsehide-covered trunk which looked promis-

ing. Opening it, we found Father's Confederate uniform. Digging deeper into the trunk, we pulled out a white hood and long robe with a crimson cross on the breast—the regalia of a Knight of the Ku Klux Klan.

Today, of course, the KKK is an odious symbol of bigotry and hate. . . . But to children in the Reconstruction South, the original Klan, led by Nathan Bedford Forrest, seemed a heroic band fighting to free the South from the debaucheries of carpetbag rule. To my brother and me, the thought that Father was a member of that band exalted him in our youthful eyes.

When the Klan turned to violence (in Louisiana, a congressional investigation revealed that two thousand Negroes were killed, wounded, or injured in the few weeks preceding the Presidential election of 1868), Nathan Bedford Forrest ordered the Klan disbanded, and an outraged public opinion crushed the membership; but in the rural South, where men secretly gazed at their tattered robes in the closet and talked of their exploits to their sons, the romantic legend of the Klan lived on.

The influx of immigrants into the United States at the turn of the century revived the Klan, as millions of Americans thrilled to D. W. Griffith's motion picture *Birth of a Nation*, and the organization adopted a severe anti-Semitic and anti-Catholic doctrine. It grew in membership and influence to a position of such power that 40,000 Klansmen paraded down Pennsylvania Avenue in Washington in a show of strength before the Democratic convention of 1924. At its peak in 1925, the new Klan, according to historians, ballooned to between four and five million members. This was the Klan that claimed the membership of aspiring politicians, men like a young Alabama lawyer named Hugo Black.

"There were a few extremists in it," Black explained in a *New York Times* interview in 1967, to which he consented on the condition that it would not be published until his death, "but most of the people were the cream of Birmingham's middle class. It was a fraternal organization, really. . . .

"In fact, it was a Jew, my closest friend, Herman Beck, who asked me to join, said they needed good people in the Klan. He couldn't be in it, of course, but he wanted me to be in it to keep down the few extremists. You know, when I said on the radio that

252

some of my best friends were Jews, they told me later that that was an anti-Semitic remark. Except in my case, it was true."

He told his first meeting, "I was against hate, I liked Negroes, I liked Jews, I liked Catholics, and that if I saw any illegality going on, I wouldn't worry about any secrecy. I'd turn them in to the grand jury."

Rarely were Jews harassed personally by the Klan, but the rough talk and the secrecy frightened the immigrants with fresh memories of the pogroms in Russia. Some made the adjustment rather casually: "I used to sell 'em the sheets," said an old man in Alabama, "and Sam the tailor made them into robes. Let me tell you we had a good business going."

The present Klan had its origins in the civil rights movement, which began to stir just after World War II when so many Southern blacks returned from the service. Many states, in reaction to the burgeoning interest in the Klan, passed legislation outlawing the wearing of hoods or other masks, thus opening up its members to closer scrutiny and forcing open declarations of membership. Unmasked, the Klan never regained its power; moreover, even in the Deep South, the White Citizens' Councils stepped forward as a much more respectable medium of organizational opposition to integration. The Klan was linked with a succession of violent episodes—bombings and emasculations, murders, beatings, pistol whippings and cross burnings, but in comparison to the earlier era, and in terms of members, these were more the acts of a few twisted men than an organized campaign of terror. With a brief flurry of interest during the sit-ins of the early sixties, the Klan drifted into slow disintegration, an alienated group of diehards plagued by internal dissension and financial fraud. Today, the Klan is more a bellwether of racial tensions than a movement, more a social phenomenon than an organization.

After World War II, both the American Jewish Committee and the Anti-Defamation League of B'nai B'rith established regional offices in the South to monitor, report, and, when appropriate, recommend action by the Jewish communities in the South with regard to anti-Semitism.

The A.J.C. had been organized nationally in 1906 for the purpose of preventing "any infraction of the civil and religious rights of Jews, in any part of the world," with a glittering assemblage of eminent German Reform Jews as its leaders—

Adolph Ochs, Julius Rosenwald, Irving Lehman, Jacob Schiff, Oscar Straus, Felix Warburg, Cyrus Adler, Louis Marshall. They were men who generally despised publicity and had access to the halls of power in state and national capitols, and therefore believed in going about their work in a quiet, unobtrusive way—no public attacks, no demonstrations, no press releases, no awareness by the gentile community of their presence. It was a style that would suit the German Jews in the South, too, and would govern the organization throughout its history (though after 1954 a few of its leaders in the South vainly tried to start a "Southern Jewish Committee" because of the national leadership's racial views).

The B'nai B'rith was much older, and founded by Geman Jews in 1843, but taken over by the East Europeans and turned into the major grassroots Jewish organization in America. From the beginning it was based on the idea of a fraternal organization of Jews— with lodges in every city in the nation, sponsors of the Hillel organization on the college campuses, and programs in defense of Jewish rights (the Anti-Defamation League), mutual aid, philanthropy, and social services. While B'nai B'rith would be Zionist from the early days, the American Jewish Committee would be one of the principal outlets for the more aloof, non-Zionist position of the German community, many of whom disliked the American Council for Judaism because it was so vocal, belligerent, and visible in its anti-Zionist views. As Reform Judaism changed, so did the A.J.C., and when both Roosevelt and Dewey forthrightly endorsed Zionist goals in the 1944 campaign, the A.J.C. switched positions to withdraw gracefully from its awkward opposition to American policy toward Palestine. The B'nai B'rith, because of its vast membership and community differences, would remain neutral officially, but many lodges raised money for Zionist causes and helped the Zionist idea politically through the 1940's; all of its national leadership were Zionists, and would participate in the national Zionist organizations and the debates of the era.

In the South, the two organizations would work together but the differences in style would continue to separate the leadership in specific instances of mutual interest. One local leader of the American Jewish Committee described it this way: "Our style is more cerebral, more intellectual, more working behind the scenes for long-range change. The A.D.L. uses the Klan and fear to raise money, and is just more concerned with incidents and fighting fires." An A.D.L. board member dismissed the work of the A.J.C. as "window dressing," saying that the "Reform Jews in A.J.C. never want to get involved. They're embarrassed about anti-Semitic incidents, while we stay on the cutting edge."

The A.D.L. system of informers in the Klan, working with the state bureaus of investigation and the FBI, were and are so ubiquitous that one A.D.L. official could boast that "any bombing is just a failure in our information system." Dwayne Walls, a former reporter for the Charlotte *Observer*, wrote a detailed series of articles for the Race Relations Information Center on the state of the Klan in May of 1970 and reported that the Klan was so infested with informers that when Governor Terry Sanford saw a news story about a meeting and asked if anyone was watching Grand Dragon Jones in North Carolina, an aide said, "We've got someone sleeping with him. Is that close enough?" Walls' series of articles, entitled "The Klan: Collapsed and Dormant," reported that "the nation's third Ku Klux Klan mania has ended," with membership in North Carolina down in four years from a peak in the 1960's of from six to seven thousand in just three cities to fewer than six hundred. He reported also that "rival Klans plunder from one another and . . . the streams of money that once poured in . . . have dried up to a trickle so small it will not pay printing debts for handbills."

The A.D.L.'s undercover work, while hidden from public view through most of the civil rights era, bubbled to the surface on February 13, 1970, in an article by Jack Nelson, a Pulitzer Prize–winning reporter for the Los Angeles *Times*–Washington *Post* news service, uncovering what turned out to be the most embarrassing and awkward incident in A.D.L. history. Nelson wrote in a front-page story that in Mississippi, "the FBI and the Meridian police, bankrolled by an alarmed Jewish community, paid $38,500 to two Ku Klux Klan informants to arrange a trap to catch two young Klan terrorists in a bombing attempt" in which "a Klanswoman was killed, and a Klansman, a policeman, and a bystander were wounded. It also resulted in a thirty-year prison sentence for the wounded Klansman."

The story described how seventeen bombings of Negro churches in the Jackson and Meridian communities in 1967 had culminated in the bombing of the temple in Jackson on September 18, 1967, and of Rabbi Perry Nussbaum's home two months later on November 21, 1967. Rabbi Nussbaum and his wife, both asleep at the time, narrowly escaped injury. On May 27, 1968, a bomb blasted the Meridian synagogue and FBI tape recordings revealed plans to bomb another synagogue with women and children inside. A. I. Botnick, the director of the A.D.L.'s regional office in New Orleans, heard a Klansman say on a tape that "little Jews grow up to be big fat Jews, so kill them while they are young." According to the newspaper story, Botnick "helped raise funds to pay the informers and participated in the original discussion about the trap with the FBI and the local police." Botnick told reporter Nelson that it was "logical" that someone had paid to set up the two Klansmen, and then admitted, "Four guys know I was in on the original planning. It was a trap—you know that. We were dealing with animals and I would do it again."

The deal involved paying informants $69,000 to trap two Klansmen while they were placing dynamite at a Jewish businessman's home in Meridian "if [Klansmen] Thomas A. Tarrants and Danny Joe Hawkins, whom the FBI believed the top two 'hit men,' attempted the bombing." The two of them were suspected of the earlier bombings in Jackson and Meridian. Ultimately, Hawkins did not go; instead Tarrants took a twenty-six-year-old schoolteacher named Mrs. Kathy Ainsworth, who was connected with the White Knights but had no previous record of any crimes. The informants, two brothers, one of whom was convicted and sentenced to ten years for the 1967 lynching of three civil rights workers in Philadelphia, Mississippi, ultimately received $36,500 instead of the full amount because Hawkins was not along.

What happened that night is in some dispute but the article states that "twelve Meridian policemen dressed in black waited in the darkness for the terrorists' arrival. Also stationed at strategic points in the general area—for observational purposes, not for participating in an arrest or gun battle—were eight to ten FBI agents." The informants had called the police to report that a woman, not Hawkins, was with Tarrants.

Tarrants got out of the car carrying a bomb of twenty-nine sticks of dynamite to place in the driveway of the Jewish businessman's house. At the trial Tarrants claimed the police opened fire, but the police claimed that "an order to halt was shouted" and that Tarrants whirled and fired twice in their direction.

Mrs. Ainsworth was killed by a bullet in the spine as she leaned over to open the door for Tarrants. Tarrants sped off in his bullet-riddled car but crashed less than a mile away. He jumped from his car, opened fire with a machine gun on the pursuing patrol car, hitting a policeman and a bystander, tried to flee, and ended up diving into a clump of bushes.

Sgt. L. D. Joyner, who has since been honored by community awards and by the International Association of Chiefs of Police, said, "We figured he still had a machine gun and a hand grenade and we opened up on him. All four of us were firing shotguns from about fifteen feet away. We had in mind killing him, I don't mind telling you. We dragged him out of the bushes and figured he was dead but the son-of-a-gun was still alive." Joyner justified police participation because "they're in constant fear we got somebody set up now. We keep 'em scared to death." He also admitted that one of the informants had cooperated out of fear that "we were going to kill him. We helped him believe it. We acted like we were going to do it."

In its lead editorial, entitled "Law Enforcement Has Limits," the Los Angeles *Times* said, "No matter how great the provocation, the police can never take it on themselves to decide who is guilty, who is innocent; who is to live and who is to die. . . . For a good purpose—to stop terrorism—the police put themselves in the position of acting as Mrs. Ainsworth's judge, jury, and executioner."

The Baltimore *Sun* censured the police, saying that there was "no excuse for an arrangement like this. Even if this were a case of legal entrapment, not an ambush, as some suspect—it is objectionable."

The Des Moines *Register* said, "Black and Jewish residents of the area may breathe more easily as a result. But the incident may have imperiled the future of all of us."

The American Civil Liberties Union and the American Friends Service Committee, two organizations long active in Southern civil rights activities, jointly asked for a Presidential investigation of the FBI actions in the case, charging that law enforcement authorities used questionable techniques "to lure the Klan members into an ambush." The national A.D.L. office issued a statement that they had assisted in the fund-raising only "as a matter of civic responsibility . . . to obtain information leading to the apprehension of the perpetrators of these acts of violence. . . . We had no part in the disbursement of funds nor any contact with informants nor any participation in the police activity. So far as we know, there is no basis for criticism of the law enforcement authorities."

Tarrants pleaded innocent by reason of insanity, but a jury in Meridian found him guilty of placing the bomb and he was sentenced to thirty years in prison. Danny Joe Hawkins, the article said, "has been arrested and tried twice—once for bombing a Jackson real estate office and once for robbing a Memphis bank. The Jackson trial resulted in an acquittal and the Memphis trial in a hung jury and a mistrial."

I saw Hawkins in Mississippi while he was awaiting a second trial for the Memphis bank robbery. Reporters don't usually meet Klansmen at social occasions, especially those sponsored by the Mississippi Council on Human Relations, but Ken Dean, the director of the Council for six years, was leaving his job to return to graduate school. Dean had been identified in the *New York Times* follow-up story on the bombing as one of the sources of the original Los Angeles *Times* news story, and some members of the Council had been deeply upset with him. But now they had come to give his wife a parting gift and say farewell—about a dozen blacks, most of the white liberal community in Jackson, including Hodding Carter III, editor of the *Delta Democrat Times*, and Rabbi and Mrs. Perry Nussbaum, whose home and temple had been bombed, perhaps by Hawkins. Dean had visited Hawkins and Tarrants in prison and had done favors for their families, and Hawkins thought he too ought to come and say good-bye. The reception was held in the rectory of the Episcopal Church in Jackson across the street from the governor's mansion, and we all stood around for an hour or so sipping coffee and punch and nibbling cookies the ladies had prepared for the occasion. Out in the courtyard, six newsmen sat around Danny Joe Hawkins talking.

He was a kid, really, in his early twenties, the kind you see playing pinball machines in beer joints across the South, handsome in the accepted Southern way, his hair combed in early Elvis style, black and wavy on the sides with an intentional cowlick hanging down front, dressed neatly in a tie and short-sleeved shirt. He was soft-spoken and flattered by the attention, but unwilling to mix at all because of the sensitivities of the people inside. He spoke of the fear in the Klan now—the feeling that the police and the FBI could shoot any of them without worrying about arrest or the intricacies of courts and trials. He knew of highway patrolmen and FBI agents "who just love to shoot anything, black and white," and told of his brush with death by the same state trooper who he said had opened fire on the Negro students at Jackson State. He claimed that he was being persecuted by the FBI because they were furious he had not gone with Tarrants that night, and that they were all "out to get me."

Inside, the group presented a gift to Ken and Mary Dean and then quieted down for him to say a few words. Hawkins stood up and walked over to the doorway to listen.

"I've discovered humanity on the left and the right," Dean said to the group, uncomfortably aware of Hawkins at the back of the room. "Lawyers for the Klan and for the civil rights workers tell me that justice isn't truth but only what twelve men say it is. I hope we can strive for the day when justice and truth become the same thing."

None of the Jewish leaders involved in the Meridian case wanted to talk about it. Most felt that it was wrong for the article to have been written; they were greatly relieved when the bombers were captured and were sorry Kathy Ainsworth was dead, but they were very embarrassed by the disclosures. Leaders were certain that most of the members of the Jewish community thought they were raising money to buy information, not to bribe a group of Klansmen into another crime and certainly not to have anyone killed. One stated that "this was a dog-eat-dog situation and you've got to play rough with the Klan"; another said that he had received a call from a Baptist preacher who praised him, saying, "This must be a proud day for you. It's about time y'all fought back"; and one of the leaders confessed to misgivings because he felt that someday the Klan might seek revenge for Meridian.

Away from Mississippi and Alabama, few Jews worry much about the Klan anymore. The laws unmasking the membership shrunk their numbers to just a few bitter-enders; television news mocked their ceremonies and destroyed whatever mystery was left. Now, they are no longer even a symbol but just a remnant of Southern history and a reminder of the sickness that once festered in the Southern soul.

259

EIGHTEEN

The Jewish Mayor of Atlanta

O n the day before the mayoralty election, Vice-Mayor Sam Massell had chosen to hold his final press conference in the living room of his suburban home, surrounded by his wife and three children—a setting calculated for a calm, statesmanlike windup to a bruising campaign. Instead, he called the group supporting his opponent "a small corps of self-appointed kingmakers" and proceeded to name the president of the biggest bank, the president of the Chamber of Commerce, the owner of Atlanta's two largest newspapers, and the current mayor—Ivan Allen, Jr., giving up his job after nine years—as "the power pack . . . who wouldn't let me sit in their clubs and do not want me in the mayor's chair." When a reporter asked if the opposition had stemmed from his religion, Massell fired back, "I don't know any other way to explain it."

Pointed accusations had swept through the Atlanta community since the first days of the stormy campaign; now an election morning headline read: "5 Are Anti-Semitic Vice-Mayor Charges."

The next night, Massell was five thousand votes behind as late as eleven P.M., when the black precincts began to come in.

"The dark horse is starting to move," the morning paper reported that one smartly dressed Negro man said.

"Yea, baby," added another, "and don't forget we've got our Jewish jockey in the saddle."

Assimilation in the South is never just a product of the beckoning hand of acceptance or the ready access to privilege. Fear can mold attitudes as readily as hopes; memories recede but work silently on motivation, and attitudes can be passed on to the next generation even though children aren't always conscious of the reasons why.

Atlanta, in many ways, is a Jewish community molded by trauma. The lynching of Leo Frank in 1913 left a deep and lasting scar on the soul of the immigrant generation; the bombing of the temple in 1958 reconfirmed those fears but at the same time reassured the Jews of Atlanta, since the entire responsible community—the mayor, governor, civic leaders, churchmen, the media —rose as one to condemn the bombing as the act of outlaws.

Today, Atlanta has the largest Jewish community in the South, sixteen or so thousand people out of a population of a million and a quarter, in the metropolitan area. The Jewish community is prosperous, growing, assertive, and involved. One would think that it would be radiating pride over the election of Sam Massell as mayor in 1969 as evidence of its acceptance in the community at large. But Massell was elected in a fiercely controversial campaign and the sounds of it will reverberate around the Jewish community for a long time.

Sam Massell, at the age of forty-two, became Atlanta's youngest mayor in 120 years by putting together a coalition of blacks, white liberals, and working-class whites who wanted to vote against the Atlanta business establishment that had run the city for thirty years. Yet he had come out of that very establishment, grown up in it as the nephew of the legendary builder Ben Massell, and had wheeled and dealed himself into a real estate success in the office of Ben's Allan-Grayson Realty, which was the instrument through which Ben Massell molded the physical backdrop for the modern Atlanta story.

"Sherman burned Atlanta and Ben Massell built it back," said Ivan Allen, Sr., at a testimonial dinner at the end of Ben's career in 1961. Mayor William Hartsfield called him "Atlanta's one-man boom" who "changed the physical appearance of Atlanta more than any one man in the city's long history."

It sounded like high-blown oratory, but in this case, it was true. Ben Massell built more than a thousand buildings in downtown Atlanta, and at one time was the only builder with faith in the downtown. And he reached out, turning the renowned Peachtree Street into a seven-mile-long wandering ribbon of office buildings and shops, a developing corridor to the elegant suburbs in Buck-head and the northeast. He backed architect John Portman's visions for Atlanta, building the Merchandise Mart—the first building in the $100-million Peachtree Center—and aerial walkways connect-ing glass offices and sculpted banks to the 800-room Regency Hyatt House Hotel, with its space needle and its rocket-ship ele-vators shooting through the roof of a twenty-two-story-high lobby to a rotating sky-top café, all glittering symbols of the "New Atlanta" that Ivan Allen never tired of talking about. Ben Massell kept driving hard, putting up office buildings with or without tenants, because he sensed the boom coming to Atlanta, which would turn it into the business and financial center of all the southeastern United States. He gambled on Atlanta and won; it paid off for him and for the city.

It's a daring story, because Ben Massell made one fortune, lost it all in the Depression, and made another one after the war. "His career is like Atlanta's history," said the Atlanta *Journal-Constitu-tion* in a 1959 profile. "Both got burned, then built anew and agreed they had done better the second time than the first." When Ben died in 1962, he was worth an estimated forty million dollars.

There is a legend in Atlanta that the first families pledge their children to public service, assuring their sons a livelihood to go out to rule and contribute. People will point to Ivan Allen, Sr., pushing and supporting Ivan Allen, Jr., into civic work, finally leading to Allen's election as mayor in 1961; and to Ben Massell and his nephew Sam, whom Ben chose (so the legend goes) to carry on the family name when Ben, Jr., abandoned Atlanta for New York City after World War II.

"Nonsense," said an old friend of Ben's, regarding the relation-ship with Sam. "Ben Massell just wasn't that kind of man. I'm sure he threw a few commissions and deals in Sam's direction, but he never sponsored him." Another friend said, "Ben lived pretty much from day to day, and had too much of a sense of humor about him-self to think in terms of a family dynasty."

Sam did not inherit Ben Massell's fortune, contrary to wide-spread rumors in Atlanta. The will filed in the Fulton County Courthouse reveals that Sam received $10,000 on Ben's death in 1962, and that the bulk of the estate went to Ben's wife and his children. But he did inherit a legendary name in the city, which helped a great deal in his efforts at public office. "It was a name," said the Mayor, "that had immediate recognition and respect."

Ben had been born in Lithuania and had come with his parents to the United States when he was two years old. The grocery store in the Negro section on the south side never grossed more than one hundred dollars a week, and with seven children to take care of, Ben grew up worrying about pennies, and whether the rain on Saturdays would cut off next week's income. In an interview in 1959 he remembered "an inferiority complex which so affected him that, even as a young man, he sometimes burst into tears when he entered a bank to borrow money for a project."

When he made his first fortune in the twenties, he began to learn what money could mean. He became one of the few East Europeans that the older and wealthier German Jews invited into their country club; and he joined the Reform temple.

The comeback after the Depression gave him the security he had always wanted. The Massell charities began to give away $200,000 a year. He founded an optometric clinic and a dental clinic for the poor; he broke with the anti-Zionists in the temple and became one of the nation's largest contributors to the State of Israel; and though he didn't live lavishly, he did buy the first sixteen-cylinder Cadillac in Atlanta.

"Ben wasn't a religious man," a friend said. "He got involved in Israel slowly because he was influenced by the old German crowd. But they really never accepted him; he played poker and hung out with the Orthodox boys."

All the Massells named their sons "Jr.," as was the custom in the temple community in Atlanta. "I never knew that it wasn't generally done in Jewish families," the Mayor said, "until ten or fifteen years ago when somebody first told me. There are so many of them here." (He had been known as "Buddy" Massell until college and people still yell it at him when he campaigns.) "I made a special effort not to name my son Junior. . . . I named him Steven Allen Massell, so his initials spell SAM," he said smiling.

Sam Massell's early life history is not much different from that of hundreds of other Atlanta boys. His father had a small law practice but lived mostly in brother Ben's shadow. Sam went to Druid Hills High School and the University of Georgia in 1944, where he was president of the Phi Epsilon Pi House, the fraternity of the Reform Jewish community. He left school to finish at

Georgia State and then earned a law degree at Atlanta Law School. He considered a job as an executive director of the national Jewish law fraternity, Nu Beta Epsilon, but couldn't persuade them to move their headquarters from Philadelphia to Atlanta.

Instead, Massell became chief of publications for the National Association of Women's and Children's Apparel Salesmen, Inc. He drifted until he joined his Uncle Ben in the Allan-Grayson Company after it changed its name from Allan-Goldberg (Sam Goldberg "got tired of people coming in and asking for Mr. Allan," someone said), and his capacity for hard work began to pay off. The Georgia Association of Real Estate Boards gave him the "Most Outstanding Real Estate Transaction of the Year" award in 1955, 1957, and 1959 for three big deals he was in with Ben. The Atlanta Jaycees named him the "Outstanding Young Man of the Year" in 1957; the Atlanta Real Estate Board elected him to membership in the Million Dollar Club in 1959 and 1960. With solid financial underpinning and the respect of the business community, political success seemed destined.

Sam was first elected vice-mayor in 1961, the same year that Ivan Allen, Jr., defeated restaurateur Lester Maddox. Four years later Massell swept to reelection victory over five opponents, without a runoff, carrying all one hundred precincts and seventy-two percent of the vote. The extent of that victory set him up for a future race; and despite the fact that Ivan Allen too had received broad black support in the mayor's race and was a moderate, the two men would never become personal or political friends.

A basic conflict arose out of what Southerners call "upbringing." Ivan Allen, Jr., was born a patrician from one of Atlanta's first families. Once a segregationist by his own admission, he became one of the most courageous and liberal political leaders in the South. "Allen's views on race represented about as dramatic a switch as a public man could make," a longtime observer of Georgia politics remarked. He was the only Southern mayor to support and testify in favor of the Civil Rights Act of 1964. And when the Dixie Hill area broke into racial rioting in 1967, Allen braved a mob and was jostled off the top of a car while trying to calm the crowd. No one in Atlanta would forget his finest moment, the open acts of official and personal sympathy in the tense days after the assassination of Martin Luther King—using the powers

264

and services of his office to assist the King family, meeting the plane that brought the body and the family from Memphis, draping the city hall in black, and helping to transform the funeral into a national day of mourning for black and white America.

Allen gave Massell exposure, allowing him to represent the city at the United States Conference of Mayors, to testify before Congress in behalf of legislation to aid urban areas, and greet dozens of groups visiting the city. Massell worked harder than any vice-mayor in Atlanta's history, obviously aiming at a future race for the top job.

Allen watched Massell for eight years—but personality, style, and ambition divided them. Allen possessed scoutmaster qualities and an old-fashioned morality—stern, correct, precise in personal relations. For Allen, problem-solving was as close as a telephone call to the bank presidents, the Chamber of Commerce, the executive offices of Coca-Cola (founded in Atlanta, and still its home base). He expected absolute loyalty from Massell and didn't get it. Massell didn't enjoy behind-the-scenes successes; he was shaping a constituency for the next mayor's race and wanted to be out front. Moreover, he wasn't sure that Allen might not be his opponent.

For Allen, the mayor's job was part cheerleader and all builder —a stadium, and plans for a coliseum, professional football, baseball, and basketball teams, freeways and airports, downtown development and industry. Massell cavalierly dismissed these achievements as "bricks and mortar," and saw himself as a man more committed to the human problems of the poor and the black.

Allen was a politician of the fifties, new to the issues of race relations, the reconstructed Southerner who thought that an occasional trip to the ghetto and an open door to black leaders was enough. Massell grew to political maturity in the sixties, more issue-oriented than pragmatic.

Over the years, Allen's doubts about Massell's judgment and his ability to unite the city ripened into opposition. In Allen's view (shared by the business minds downtown), Sam Massell just wasn't good enough for the job.

The business establishment selected Rodney Cook, a former city councilman who had won election to the state legislature as a moderate Republican, to run against Massell. Two crucial issues were involved: first, the Chamber of Commerce wanted to consolidate Fulton County with the City of Atlanta to control future growth. With more people living outside the city limits than within (500,000 in the city proper and 1.373 million in the metropolitan area), Ivan Allen felt the facts dictated consolidation, to cut the cost of government and expand tax revenues. But consolidation would dilute the powers of the Negro vote. (The metropolitan area is three-fourths white; the city fifty-fifty.) Massell opposed consolidation. Cook endorsed it. In addition, Allen's latest project, the rapid transit bond issue, had been defeated by massive black opposition, out of a conviction that it was designed more to bring suburban shoppers to the downtown stores than to serve the needs of the black community. Massell agreed with the blacks; Cook did not.

They would face each other directly in a runoff.

In the first primary, Maynard Jackson became the first black in the city's history to be elected vice-mayor. Certainly, if a black could get enough white votes to be elected vice-mayor, a white with black support ought to have a head start in the second primary for mayor. To be sure, there might be a backlash in the white community against any candidate with black votes, but there would also be certain defections from the business community in funds and support just because Massell looked like a winner. The members of the establishment were in trouble and they knew it.

With one week to go, Massell received word that the Atlanta *Constitution* was planning to break a story, backed by affidavits, charging that Massell's younger brother Howard had been accompanied by police detective H. L. "Buddy" Whalen on visits to eleven nightclub owners to solicit campaign contributions. Whalen was a former head of the vice squad who had been assigned to the campaign at Massell's request to protect his family. "Buddy Whalen helped in his off-duty time," Howard said in defense. "He knew so many club owners he could introduce me on a strictly friendly basis." The newspaper would be charging that Howard Massell was using a detective as a threat to shake down campaign funds, and there would even be whispered fears (infuriating the candidate) of "Mafia influences" if Massell won. ("This left you open to charges you were beholden to the underworld," Ivan Allen would say later.)

Howard's reputation in the Jewish community didn't help any. Howard had once owned a nightclub called The Party, not the

266

most respectable of places, and three years before had been arrested for possession of "indecent and obscene photographs and films" in his home, and (according to the indictment sheets on file in the courthouse) was fined a thousand dollars and placed on twelve months' probation without a jury trial.

The story of the campaign funds broke in the *Constitution* on the Friday before the Tuesday vote. Mayor Allen ordered Police Chief Herbert Jenkins to investigate the charges over the weekend; and on Sunday afternoon, Allen scheduled a television appearance in which he suggested wrongdoing and asserted, "If Massell is a man of conscience, he should immediately withdraw from consideration for an office which requires intuitive integrity and instinctive withdrawal from even the suspicion and appearance of evil."

Reporters grabbed for the Mayor's statement and dashed from his office at City Hall to Channel 11, where Massell and Cook were making a joint appearance on the "Atlanta Now" show. One of the reporters sent a copy of the statement up to the moderator, who asked Sam to comment.

"He reacted calmly," reporter Raleigh Bryans wrote the next morning, "but his wife, Doris, standing off-camera, exploded with two angry comments. 'That stupid fool,' said Mrs. Massell. 'Anti-Semitic WASPS,' she then snapped." The story explained for the uninitiated that "WASP is a slang abbreviation for White Anglo-Saxon Protestants."

A news aide begged Massell to hold a press conference in time for the eleven P.M. news but he refused. Weeks before, they had scheduled for the next morning an election eve television appearance in the living room of his home, planning to display a smiling candidate surrounded by his family, for a dignified windup to the campaign. That would be the setting for the answer to Allen. As the advisers began to assemble at his campaign headquarters for a late-night strategy session, calls started coming in from irate voters complaining about Allen's last-minute tactics. Most encouraging, the bulk of the calls were coming from the working-class south side, where any liberal with black votes could not expect to do well. Ivan Allen was turning Sam Massell from a front-running liberal into a scrappy underdog.

The team of advisers plotted into the night the scenario for the next day, which would be the last day of the campaign: statements of indignation and endorsement from respected leaders; a calm but strong television press conference not "stooping" to answer Allen's charge; surprise at the panic of the opposition. Then at eleven that night, the early edition of the Monday paper hit the streets and Sam for the first time must have seen the "anti-Semitic" quotes from Doris.

When I interviewed her, Doris said that she had been shocked to see that statement in the paper.

"I thought nobody but the detective heard it. I was new in this business, and I didn't know they printed everything unless you said 'off the record.' But I was so angry and hurt. It was really a low blow for Ivan to do something like that. But they had tried everything else." Doris, a small-town girl from Hogansville, Georgia, admitted that "I'm Irish. I really have a temper."

The next morning, Massell answered with the calculated fury of a man in control of his language and his ideas, direct but not in bad taste, his cadence measured but his ideas clear when he wanted them to be and vague when he preferred. The syntax of his opening statement was perfect and his words obviously had been weighed beforehand for impact and impression.

"I tell my five angry adversaries," candidate Massell said on his final television appearance, "that they shall not crown a mayor for 500,000 people. Money and power shall not dictate to the electorate."

Asked to name the five, Massell named Mayor Ivan Allen; his opponent, Rodney Cook; Jack Tarver, president of Atlanta Newspapers, Inc.; Mills Lane, president of the Citizens and Southern Bank; and Frank Carter, president of the Chamber of Commerce.

"President Harry Truman once said, 'If you can't stand the heat, stay out of the kitchen,' " Massell continued. "Having been subjected to occasional discriminatory treatment since childhood as a member of a minority group, I have learned how to face the heat. I have learned to work a little harder to forge ahead . . . to overcome."

Cook denied he was behind the newspaper disclosures and called the charges of bigotry "deplorable," regretting the "smear campaign against me and some pretty fine people." Carter of the Chamber of Commerce called the charges "asinine."

Tarver, the owner of the Atlanta *Journal-Constitution*, tried at first to pass it off lightly. "At least," he said, "Massell has injected a refreshing new note, if only in the area of local newspaper criticism. The usual demagogic line is that we are completely dominated by our Jewish advertisers." Then, warming up to the subject, he said, "Isn't it a sad commentary on the caliber of the man that, in the final hours before the election, Mr. Massell seems to be stressing his Jewishness as his outstanding qualification?"

Massell privately had been critical of the newspapers for refusing to look at his opponents' financing, but he backed away from openly charging them with anything but a last-minute blow. He was particularly incensed at the delay—Whalen had originally been assigned as a bodyguard for the family and had complained to the police of Howard's use of him for fund-raising on September 20th, almost four weeks earlier. Massell claimed in an earlier statement that he put a stop to it when he learned about it, but for the television press conference he phrased his criticism of the delay by the newspaper in more general terms. "This mayoralty campaign began ten months ago, but we must ask why they waited until the closing days to fabricate a scandal which can't be fairly answered in the time remaining before the election."

Reg Murphy, editor of the Atlanta *Constitution*, was sensitive on the point of delay and responded carefully in a column on election morning:

> . . . The Atlanta *Constitution* knew of the rumors more than two weeks ago. But there was no solid evidence. . . . We learned last Monday, one week ago today, that one Atlanta nightclub owner had signed a sworn affidavit about the matter. This still wasn't enough. Last Wednesday afternoon, two other nightclub operators signed similar sworn statements and made them available to the Atlanta *Constitution*.
>
> The evidence was in hand, enough for a news story. . . .
>
> One of the candidates chose to interpret the publication of these facts as anti-Semitic. He brought religion into the campaign. We did not. . . . Merely raising the charge as an attempt to discredit reports will not intimidate us, no matter how painful the charges themselves.

Massell saved his most specific remarks for Mayor Allen. "As he goes out of office, it appears he has reverted to some of his original feelings."

269

"What feelings?," a reporter asked, to clear up whether Massell was referring to segregation.

"Not too long ago," Massell replied, "in his office, the mayor met with a group of ministers, including his own pastor. I was the only lay person present. We were discussing human relations problems, when the Mayor [Allen] turned to these people and said, 'Sam Massell does these things because he believes in them; I do them because it's a practical approach.' These men of God wouldn't believe that a man would say that, believe that."

Blacks poured out to support Massell, and he beat Rodney Cook with ninety percent of the black votes and twenty-five percent of the white votes. He ran stronger than expected in working-class districts on the south side, which normally vote against any candidate with black support and where anti-Semitism is probably greatest.

Bill Shipp, a political writer for the *Journal* and *Constitution*, wrote, "Mayor Ivan Allen, Jr., had done what Massell himself had not been able to do. He had cast Massell as the official, ready-to-be-steamrolled, outside-the-in-crowd candidate."

Some black politicians in Atlanta a year later felt that the anti-Semitic charge was a shrewd political move on Massell's part, and not just a burst of temper. "We were apathetic until the Ivan Allen–Massell exchange," said one of them. "Maynard had been elected in the first primary, and there was little interest. The anti-Semitic charge made it real; blacks knew it was true. The joke around Atlanta was that we couldn't have a nigger vice-mayor and a Jew mayor.' "

No one can know what Massell's real motives were in making the accusations which would appear the morning of the election. There was a strong political case to be made for blasting his opposition—that he needed to draw attention from the charges against his brother, undercut the credibility of Ivan Allen, attack the establishment frontally to bring out a bigger black vote the next day. There were personal reasons—to assume responsibility for injecting anti-Semitism into the campaign and thereby cover the embarrassment to his wife for her outburst the day before, to make the best of a bad situation and offset the damage since Doris had made anti-Semitism an issue in the campaign anyway, perhaps even a long-smoldering antipathy to the social slights from Ivan Allen and the downtown business establishment. (The Jewish community was startled that the years of silence had been broken

270

by someone from Southern Baptist stock. Doris converted when she and Sam were married because "I feel you should convert to your husband's religion and I didn't want the children torn between two churches. My mother taught me that as long as I found a man who would treat me right, that was all that was important.")

Mayor Allen, in his book *Mayor: Notes on the Sixties*, confessed that in deciding to ask Massell to withdraw, he "recognized that Massell was ahead in the race and we knew that whatever I might say would have little if any effect on the outcome. . . ."

Then why did he do it?

"I was shocked when I saw the chief's report on Howard's activity," he said in an interview. "It was thorough and shocking. I felt I had always spoken out on what was right and wrong and I had to this time."

Would he have done the same thing if the report had involved Rodney Cook? "If it had been Rodney Cook, I might have gone to him personally and asked him to withdraw. There had been whisperings about Howard, and his general reputation for carrying on wasn't good. Maybe that affected my decision, I don't know." He didn't think his action had any influence on the election, in part because "I failed in making the public understand that privileged licenses require law enforcement approval."

He felt that Massell handled his demand for withdrawal "adroitly and with reasonable poise, except," he added, "for the anti-Semitism part. There was never any indication of my being anti-Semitic, and I never looked on Sam as Jewish, or Christian, or anything else, and his Jewishness never came up. It was the one weak charge in his counterattack."

The anti-Semitic charge stunned the Atlanta Jewish community. "Sam was jumping on men who had been a credit to Atlanta," one long-time Jewish leader complained. "It would have been far better to have said, 'I will not stoop to answer.' He just got very bad advice and it will leave a residue of bad will for years."

Many of the old German Jewish families did not support Massell; some of the leaders, like Dick Rich, the department store president, opposed him openly. (Rich had been close to Allen for years before Allen's election. The Mayor's first real confrontation with blacks came before he was elected during the sit-ins and boycotts at Rich's, where he sat on the board of directors; in addi-

271

tion, Allen appointed Rich to head the Metropolitan Atlanta Transit Authority, lending credence to the attack by the black leadership that the mass transit system was more designed to bring white suburban shoppers to Rich's than take blacks to new jobs.)

The most common comment among the Reform temple Jews was, "If only Morris Abram had stayed in Atlanta to run instead of Sam Massell. . . ." Abram was a promising Atlanta lawyer who had left the city to practice law in New York after he won the landmark Supreme Court case abolishing the county unit system in Georgia. He had run for Congress and been defeated in 1950; close friends felt that in New York he might make his way in politics. In New York he headed up the prestigious American Jewish Committee, and for a short time was president of Brandeis University in Massachusetts; he resigned from Brandeis in 1970 to enter briefly and then withdraw from a campaign for a United States Senate seat from New York.

One political observer noted, "It was as if Sam didn't have the sheen of excellence that Morris had, and they didn't want him to be the first Jew to move out and be elected. Besides, Sam had an image of falling on his face, and they were afraid he would be a millstone around the neck of the Jewish community."

The wife of a leading German Jewish leader put it more strongly: "With all the smart Jews in Atlanta, why did we have to find a stupid one and put him out front where everybody could see him."

In the non-German Jewish community, resentment bristled over the irony of a Jew from a Reform temple, which they regarded as closer to a church, wrapping himself in the cloak of Jewishness at the last minute for what looked like political reasons. "I assure you," said one, "Sam became Jewish that night. He never did much before that."

A frequent visitor to the city saw it this way: "There was a reverse backlash. People here have a high and mighty feeling about Atlanta. There were a lot of whites who voted for Massell because they didn't want it said that Atlanta was anti-Semitic; and there were a lot of Jews who voted for Rodney Cook because they didn't want a loud-mouth as mayor."

A Jewish admirer of the Massells attributed the anger in the Jewish community to jealousy over the fame and success of the Massell family. "In most ways, they are the most exciting family in

Atlanta. Ben was immigrant; he made it, lost it, and made it again. Then Sam comes along. They are an essential part of Atlanta history. That's more than most of us can say."

The Jewish community wasn't ready for an aggressively worded charge against social and political discrimination. This was a community with a tradition of quiet—one generation traumatized by the lynching of Leo Frank in 1913; another shaken by the bombing of the Temple (Hebrew Benevolent Congregation) in 1958. Moreover, in Rabbi David Marx's Reform congregation, no one ever called attention to his Jewishness, but treated it respectably, coolly, and appropriately as the "best" people in Atlanta might expect. Massell broke that tradition dramatically, and because the Jews of Atlanta had avoided notoriety for fifty years, he unsettled them by offending the gentiles and raising old anxieties.

The Frank case had been a nightmare come true for the Jewish South, a wound with deep and extensive psychological implications for the Atlanta Jewish community.

Leo Frank came from a Brahmin German Jewish family in Atlanta, and ran a pencil factory there. On April 27, 1913, fourteen-year-old Mary Phagan was found dead in the factory; Frank was charged with her murder and sentenced to be hanged in August.

"I attended every day of the trial," said Sam Eplan, now in his late seventies but still practicing law in Atlanta. "The yokels lined the streets yelling at the jury every night when they went to the hotel—'Hang the Jew.' You were afraid to walk down the street if you were Jewish."

After the trial, Tom Watson, the agrarian rebel turned sour, part populist, part anti-Catholic, and all demagogue, picked up the Frank case in his *Jeffersonian Magazine* and *Jeffersonian Weekly*. "Over and over," wrote C. Vann Woodward in his biography of Watson, "Watson reviewed the evidence in the case: torn garment 'spotted with virgin blood,' the tuft of hair, the crumpled white form. Rumors, half truths, special pleading, merciless slander, every device known to the skilled criminal lawyer—he employed." Little Mary Phagan would sell papers—in a short time Watson's circulation grew from 25,000 to 87,000, and the price per paper doubled.

Watson stirred the mobs with his stinging rhetoric: "Frank

273

belongs to the Jewish aristocracy, and it was determined by rich Jews that no aristocrat of their race should die for the death of a working girl. . . . While the Sodomite who took her sweet life basks in the warmth of today, the poor child's dainty flesh has fed the worms"; or, "Our Little Girl—ours by the Eternal God—has been pursued to a hideous death and bloody grave by this filthy perverted Jew of New York." And, using a retouched picture of Frank with thickened lips and popping eyes, "You could tell Frank is a lascivious pervert, guilty of the crime that caused the Almighty to blast the Cities of the Plain, by a study of the accompanying picture; look at those bulging satyr eyes, the protruding sensual lips, and also the animal jaw."

When the governor of Georgia, John M. Slaton, believing that Frank had not received a fair trial, commuted his sentence to life, Frank was dragged from the Milledgeville Prison Farm and driven 175 miles over dirt roads to be hanged from an oak near the house where Mary Phagan was born.

Janice Rothschild, the wife of Rabbi Jacob Rothschild, wrote a history of the Temple, containing interviews with some of the old Atlanta Jews about those terror-filled nights:

> One Temple member recalls that his father could not go out in public during this period simply because he bore a resemblance to Leo Frank. Another member of the congregation tells how her father became so discouraged he sold his store and moved away. Many families left town temporarily or went to hotels for safety. Most Jewish homes in downtown Atlanta were boarded up during the summer of 1913.
>
> Another lady remembers the night that Governor John Alston commuted the death sentence of Leo Frank. A teenager at the time, she had gone to a movie with her boyfriend. In the middle of the picture her uncle came down the darkened aisle of the theater with a flashlight searching for them. He had come to take them home. A rumor was abroad that the governor would sign Frank's commutation sometime during the evening, and such was the temper of the city that a young Jewish boy and girl might not be safe downtown when the announcement came.

One would think that the Frank case would have united the old Jews and the new Jews, pushed them into each other's arms out of a common threat to their safety.

"No," said one old man who was Eastern European in origin. "The German community wanted to disappear into the woodwork, and they turned inward to each other as if to have anything to do with us would endanger them. To tell you the truth, we wanted to disappear too, but we couldn't. So we just pulled our wagons in a circle and insulated ourselves from the *goyim* as much as we could." The pogroms of Russia were too fresh in the minds of the immigrants to respond to the Frank case in any other way.

Atlanta is not a city of long tradition or deep roots in Southern history. Unfortunately, little is known of the early Jewish community there because General Sherman burned the records with the rest of the city; but we do know that Jews lived in Marthasville, the original Atlanta, in 1844, just a few years after the Georgia General Assembly decided to build a railroad terminus there; that Jacob Haas came in 1847, when Atlanta was a village of 1,500 people, and that his daughter Caroline was the "first white female child born in Atlanta"; that his nephew Aaron Haas served on the city council and became the first mayor pro-tem in Atlanta history in 1875 (Aaron Haas married Frances Rich, the sister of the five Rich brothers, who were struggling to start a small clothing store in the city); that Solomon Dewald spent three years in the Confederate army making shoes for soldiers, along with Levi Cohen, a master tinsmith, who made canteens; that David Mayer was a devoted Shriner, and when he found out that General Sherman was a Shriner too, he hung his Shriner's apron on the doorpost of his house and the Yankee army "passed over" it, leaving the house as the only structure standing among smoldering ashes for miles around. (Mayer was one of the first advocates of public schools, is often referred to as "the father of public education in Atlanta," and served on the first Board of Education from 1870 until his death in 1890.)

Compared to the swamp towns of Charleston and Savannah, Atlanta was "favorably situated for health" (in the words of a visitor), so Jews migrated there when the city began to grow as a trade center around the railroad. But even though Rabbi Isaac Leeser of Philadelphia tried to urge a handful of "Israelites" there in 1852 to start a congregation, he wasn't successful until 1867, when he returned to Atlanta for the wedding of Abraham Rosenfield and Miss Emilie Baer and took advantage of the community gathered there to plead for a "congregational union." (Abraham

Rosenfield and his brother Louis were celebrities of sorts in Atlanta—they both had been in Ford's Theater that fateful night when John Wilkes Booth leaped from the President's box onto the stage.)

The wedding party agreed to start the Hebrew Benevolent Congregation, but it would adopt the new reforms sweeping American Judaism slowly and reluctantly, hiring and firing rabbis frequently, until 1895 when the trustees hired their first American-born rabbi, thereby winning the approval of the Atlanta newspaper. Even though he was approved by a close 37 to 34 vote, twenty-three-year-old David Marx led the congregation headlong into classical Reform Judaism. In just five years, Marx had abolished the bar mitzvah, changed the age of confirmation from thirteen to sixteen, required the removal of hats in the temple, refused to wear rabbinical garb during services, and adopted the Reform Union prayerbook. He married one of Abraham Rosenfield's daughters, thus associating himself with the very founding of the congregation. Grafted by marriage to the roots of Judaism in Atlanta, he would stay there as rabbi for more than fifty years.

By 1900 Atlanta had already expanded to a city of 114,000 and Marx, growing now into a self-assured and dynamic pulpit personality, the first rabbi in Atlanta to speak English without an accent, saw a new role for himself. "They did not chain me to the pulpit," he would say many years later.

He gave frequent guest sermons in the Protestant churches in Atlanta as well as the little country churches in Fulton County; he was invited to pronounce the opening prayer to the Georgia State Senate; became a guest columnist for the Atlanta *Journal;* and was part of the official delegation that greeted Presidents McKinley, Theodore Roosevelt, and Taft when they visited the city. He was proudest of the joint Thanksgiving worship service in the temple with the ministers of the Unitarian, Presbyterian, Baptist, and Universal churches, an annual event for many years. When members of the congregation said, "He made us proud to be Jews," they were referring not to pride in the teachings of Judaism but pride in Marx's acceptance by the gentile community, which they assumed to represent acceptance for themselves.

Inside the temple, Marx totally dominated the board of trustees. He urged them to pass a resolution "disapproving National Zionism" just after the first Zionist Congress in 1898. He inaugurated

276

Sunday morning worship services in 1904 that drew larger attendance than the Friday night and Saturday morning services combined. (The presence of a gentile choir ultimately forced him to
turn the Sunday morning service into a lecture series, because the
choir members wanted to go to their own churches on Sunday
mornings.)

The East European peddlers were beginning to cluster in Atlanta, a growing center for trade and commerce that looked promising for a man whose greatest dream was to open his own shop. The
Germans, by now an integral part of the Atlanta social scheme
(several were listed in the Social Register), shook their heads at
the newcomers—they wore skullcaps in public, spoke in an embarrassing language called Yiddish, lived on the poor side of town,
and trucked with the Negroes as customers. Needless to say,
neither Marx nor the congregation was anxious to recruit new
members from them; besides, Marx's stand on Zionism and the
overall haughtiness of the membership discouraged new members.
Other congregations more attuned to the philosophy of the immigrants began to spring up—Orthodox synagogues, one the largest
in the South, which ultimately "converted" into an immensely
popular Conservative synagogue which offered some reform—
prayers in English, sermons, families sitting together—but without
the extremes of the temple.

Marx wasn't afraid, however, to step out front when principle
moved him: He was the spokesman for a group of ministers who
successfully fought compulsory Bible reading in the schools in a
highly publicized debate before the state legislature. The vote
defeating the bill requiring Bible reading came a few days before
the trial of one of the members of Marx's congregation—Leo
Frank.

Rabbi Marx visited Frank in prison many times at the request of
Frank's wife, Lucille, and she became more and more dependent on
him for advice. When Frank's throat was cut during an attempted
murder by an enraged fellow-prisoner, Marx sensed the impending
tragedy but was helpless. After the lynching, Marx helped Lucille
smuggle the body onto a train to New York in the middle of the
night, for they feared rioting and incidents if they moved it in the
daytime. The lynching had a profound impact on Marx, a deeply
shattering experience; he reacted the only way he knew, and turned

into a starkly powerful force for assimilation in the German Jewish community and a bitterly controversial figure to the new immigrants.

"He believed," said one member of the temple, "that the closer the temple got to the churches, the better off we were." He forbade the singing of Hatikva, the Jewish anthem of hope, as a "song of looking back"; he attacked Zionism and the idea of the Jewish state from the pulpit; he refused to use wine or a canopy in wedding ceremonies; he abolished the lighting of Sabbath candles and the opening of the ark during adoration; no Hebrew was taught in the temple schools. The stories of his efforts to blame the Orthodox community for the anti-Semitism that led to the lynching (a natural rationale for him, perhaps, since he observed that the German community was rising in status until "they came") still ricochet around the Jewish community. "I don't believe he ever actually said anything like that," Janice Rothschild replied, "but things were so tense between the two communities that it is easy to see how the new Jews would think he said it."

An older woman with an accent said, about the Frank case, "God forbid it should have been a Russian. It's a blessing it wasn't one of our 'schleppers.'"

"Marx was not a 'leave-a-vacuum' rabbi," remarked one woman who grew up in Marx's temple Sunday school with Sam Massell. "He was trying to say to our Christian neighbors, 'Look—we're not the kind of Jews you think we are—we're just like you.'"

Rabbi Harry Epstein, for more than forty years rabbi at Ahavath Achim, the largest Conservative synagogue in the Southeast (1,785 familes today), said that "Marx would have been an excellent Presbyterian minister; he knew little about the Talmud and they taught absolutely nothing in the Sunday school."

One woman dropped out of the temple because "once, when my son came home with Hanukkah candles, he didn't know what to do with them. I heard him in his room—he lit them and sang Christmas carols."

Today, among the older people in the synagogues, one can still pick up the flavor of the resentment against Marx. "Don't be fooled into thinking it was Marx alone who wanted all of this," said one old man at services in one of the synagogues. "He reflected the feelings of the old dyed-in-the-wool *Deiches*." He spit the slang Yiddish word for the German Jews. "They wanted nothing to do with us. They wanted to fit in with the gentiles."

A friend sitting next to him told of a joke popular when Marx was at the height of his influence. "Marx was a Christian with certain peculiar notions of Christ as a deity." When asked whether Marx left any lasting influence, he responded, "He certainly helped the membership in the Unitarian church."

The old German families I interviewed talked mostly of his appearance, his manner, his voice. "He was my father's idol," said one woman, ". . . a wonderful appearance—tall and white-haired—he looked waspish and aristocratic. To us, he was a symbol of God's voice on earth."

The communities sealed themselves off from each other, each looking down on the other. "My parents," said a temple member whose family roots went back into Atlanta history, "in their most liberal moments referred to Russian Jews as 'kikes.' The groups had little to do with each other until after the war."

"Before the war, it was a flat rule," said one woman in the Russian community. "Temple members belonged to the Standard Club; and everybody else divided depending on how long you had been there. If any synagogue members belonged to the Standard Club, they were insurance men and salesmen and everybody said they did it for money.

"After the war, things began to change. The kids were better educated, for one thing. And the Standard Club, when they built that extravaganza way out in North Atlanta, had to go seeking Russian Jews with money. And, with the influx of new Jews from the North and all over, suddenly the Southern Russians didn't look so bad to the Atlanta German Jews. Besides, with the Yankees, who knew who was German and who was Russian anyway? They were what they said they were."

Another man, from one of the oldest Jewish families, remembered Ben Massell, who came from Lithuania but joined the temple and the Standard Club as soon as he made money, bringing the rest of the Massells in with him. "Ben Massell got in on the first move of the Standard Club in the twenties. But we never really accepted Ben, nor did he accept us."

One woman in the synagogue community recalled Sam Massell from his early days: "I was in Sam's age group but I didn't know him. That wasn't unusual; the temple crowd of kids rarely associated with us. I assure you, Sam never set foot in the Jewish Alliance (the Community Center). The temple crowd thought even that was too much identification."

279

The divisions split along social lines for young people. The synagogue community encouraged B'nai B'rith Youth Organization and the temple community sponsored a fraternity called the Top Hat Club. When Top Hat put on an annual dance, called "Ballyhoo," occasionally they invited some Jewish boys from the Conservative synagogue. "Man, it was like becoming a male debutante for a Conservative to be invited," said one man who did go.

"There were a few of us who crossed over to the temple crowd," another man of East European origin said. "But you had to have certain qualities: first, any good-looking girl could make it; second, a boy could be accepted if he didn't look like a stereotype Jew; third, your parents had to establish themselves as not being pawnshop Jews; fourth, you had to live in the new suburbs in the north side, particularly Druid Hills—a southeast Atlanta Jew was unequivocally barred; fifth, you had to master the vernacular and the dress and the mannerisms of the gentile deb-daters."

During World War II, Marx, who was a founder of the American Council for Judaism, denounced the idea of Israel from the pulpit. But the Nazi experience was changing the congregation more than he understood. Ida Levitas grew up in Atlanta's Russian community and could say that "Leo Frank didn't bring us together. It took Hitler to do that . . . to put them down a notch. They knew then that none was better than another, and so did we."

In 1946, fresh out of four years in the army, where he had been the first Jewish chaplain into combat at Guadalcanal, Jacob Rothschild came to the temple to replace Marx. Rothschild was thirty-five at the time, and though his name was synonymous with Jewish aristocracy, he was the child of first-generation East Europeans, had grown up in Pittsburgh, and was broad in outlook. Within three months after his arrival, he married the beautiful Janice Ottinger, the great-granddaughter of the temple's third rabbi (Dr. E. M. B. Browne, whose nickname in 1877 was "Alphabet" Browne), thus repeating what Marx had done within a short time of his arrival in Atlanta fifty years earlier—marry into the German aristocracy whose relationships reached back to the earliest days of the temple.

Mrs. Rothschild remembered a ditty that June Stevens wrote at their twentieth anniversary celebration a few years ago:

> Rothschild, what a lovely name, and what a
> lovely family tree.

He must be related to that charming Baron G.
But this Rothschild took Atlanta like a Jewish
    General Sherman
He wasn't related to Baron G.
He wasn't even German.

"When I came to Atlanta," Rothschild said, "there were just four hundred members. The congregation was anti-Zionist, and there were no bar mitzvahs, no cantor, no Hebrew except the *Shema*, and a minimum of ritual. Marx didn't even oppose Christmas trees."

His wife, Janice, was at home in the higher reaches of Atlanta Jewish society; more important, she was free to be herself and speak her mind. "Janice was Reform," a friend said, "but she recognized the implications of Zionism way before he did, and dragged him to Israel often enough to change him completely. Also, he wanted to move with his congregation; the old German families were dwindling and Israel began to count."

Rothschild began to speak out on social issues, even before the '54 decision. And though he was violating an ancient code in the Jewish South—that rabbis don't speak out on matters of race—the congregation seemed to go along. "However uncomfortable they were, they were just too ashamed not to support him," said one member of his congregation.

Atlanta prided itself on its good race relations—William Hartsfield was a bulldozing, energetic mayor for twenty years who opened up the Vine City area to attractive Negro homes, and Ralph McGill ennobled the front page of the Atlanta *Constitution* with his editorials that created the atmosphere of "The City Too Busy to Hate." Thus, Rothschild's courageous stance on civil rights made the Jewish community more acceptable to the power structure in the city—but not to the rural whites who were leaving the hard Georgia clay for the bright lights in Atlanta.

On October 12, 1958, fifty sticks of dynamite blasted a gaping twenty-foot hole in the side of the Temple, but missed the sanctuary. Eugene Patterson, associate editor of the Atlanta *Constitution*, described the damage:

It buried the little sky blue robes of the children's choir under glass and plaster dust. The white collars lay gray and torn in water from broken pipes.

It blew the vestibule wall and buried a bronze plaque

commemorating men of the congregation who were killed in the military service of the United States flag.

It toppled Menorahs from a broken shelf and left those . . . lying bent and tarnished under the wreckage. . . .

A small record album on one damaged shelf was named "Thank you, God."

Within minutes of the news, Mayor Hartsfield arrived at the temple, and the picture that the wire services sent out across the country showed Hartsfield and Rothschild crouching in the rubble together, examining the damage.

"Looking at this demolition," the Mayor declared, "I cannot help but realize it is the end result and payoff of a lot of rabble-rousing in the South. Whether they like it or not, every political rabble-rouser is the godfather of these cross burnings and dynamiters who sneak about in the dark and give a bad name to the South. It is high time the decent people of the South rise and take charge if governmental chaos is to be avoided."

Georgia Governor Marvin Griffin and President Eisenhower also issued statements condemning the bombing.

"People in other Jewish communities that had had violence asked how we got public officials involved," said Janice Rothschild. "Well, it was spontaneous. Hartsfield was there almost as soon as my husband was. People sent flowers to my daughter because it was in the paper that it was her birthday the next day and Jack didn't have time to be with her."

Ralph McGill weighed in with a forthright Pulitzer Prize–winning editorial:

Let us face facts.

This is a harvest. It is the crop of things sown.

It is the harvest of defiance of courts and encouragement of citizens to defy law on the part of many Southern politicians. . . .

It is a harvest, too, for those so-called Christian ministers who have chosen to preach hate instead of compassion. Let them now find pious words and raise their hands in deploring the bombing of a synagogue.

You do not preach and encourage hatred for the Negro and hope to restrict it to that field.

Twenty-four hours after the bombing, Rothschild announced the topic of his sermon—"And None Shall Make Them Afraid." On Friday evening, the congregation filled the patched-up temple to overflowing for services, despite further threats of violence.

"It was an ingathering of the spirit," recalled Cecil Alexander. "We were all uneasy but it was exhilarating."

Rothschild knew that it would be a sermon long remembered and that many were thinking "I told you so." But he wasn't going to apologize or seek atonement.

"This single act of devastation has taught lessons which all words, all prayers, all pleas had been unable to teach. . . . The curtain of fear has been lifted. Decent men are at last convinced that there can be no retreat from their ideals . . . this despicable act of desecration has turned up the flame and kindled the fires of determination and dedication. It has reached the hearts of men everywhere and roused the conscience of a whole community. . . . With God's help we shall rebuild in pride and gratitude—and create a stronger Home of the Spirit where He may dwell in our midst. Together with an aroused humanity we shall rear from the rubble of devastation a city and a land in which all men are truly brothers—and none shall make them afraid."

The Jewish community of Atlanta was startled at the reaction of the non-Jewish community. More than forty years had passed since the Frank case, but the scars from that painful memory had never fully healed.

"I may be romanticizing it now," said Janice Rothschild, "but the fear from the Frank case didn't end until the bombing. One ended what the other started."

Rabbi Rothschild saw the bombing as a turning point for the city itself. "The temple bombing was the one traumatic event that set Atlanta on its course. It brought the muted moderates out of the woodwork."

Support and contributions poured in from church groups, Protestant ministers, and every religious and political leader of all races in the city and some from abroad; Ben Massell contributed fifty thousand dollars (and a chapel in his wife's name) for the rebuilding.

"It was a great catharsis for the Jewish community," said one leader. "The bombers made a mistake in bombing the temple. The

283

fundamentalists were offended that anybody would bomb an institution where they had religious roots."

Sam Massell never felt inhibited by the temple bombing, for not long after the event he became the outspoken vice-mayor of Atlanta. But when he won the top job in 1969, he began to look forward to the next election, and revise his political profile. In his first two years in office, Massell reversed himself on the major issues in the mayor's campaign, political observers said, because he would face a black opponent in the next election (either Vice-Mayor Maynard Jackson or State Senator Leroy Johnson) and needed the downtown leadership he ran against the first time.

He stood up against a strike to unionize garbage workers, striking black workers charged, to win back the antiunion forces of the Chamber of Commerce. He also proposed a partial merger of the city with Fulton County (through state legislative action rather than referendum), and some black leaders claimed he just wanted more white voters in the city.

His sensitivity to the Mafia rumors caused him to accompany the police on numerous raids, personally to announce the closing of a female impersonation club backed by "out-of-town gangsters." He posed for pictures with a new helicopter and other crime-fighting equipment for the police and asked the Justice Department to "investigate all facets of organized crime in Atlanta."

To court the white middle class, he warned hippies, when Tenth Street in Atlanta was fast becoming a national mecca, "Unless you have bread and a pad, please find your thing somewhere else, or face a bad scene."

To win the support of the edifice-conscious downtown leadership, he switched position to lead the effort to build a sports coliseum, and to pass the mass transit bond issue he had opposed in the campaign.

To remind working-class whites of his sympathy and objectivity, he warned black leaders that turning Atlanta into an "all-black city . . . is political blindness . . . when the economic base of our city is threatened."

Sam's performance in office has been characterized by such a thorough flip-flop on major issues, that even Ivan Allen compliments him now. "In a year's time, his attitude and goals have completely changed," said former Mayor Allen. "He has adopted a progressive program that would have made him acceptable as a candidate to us—the building of a coliseum, moving ahead with rapid transit, the expansion of the city. He denounced it as 'brick and mortar' then; but he's come around to it because it's what makes a city."

Massell supporters point to other achievements during his term of office: Atlanta has had almost no racial unrest since he took office, he has led the city into the first charter revision in half a century, and has brought blacks into supervisory positions in city government. Moreover, they point out, the city is proud that he was selected in 1972 as president of the National League of Cities.

The Jewish mayor of Atlanta sat in his shirtsleeves in his office in city hall—a small man about five feet six, busy, but eager to talk about the campaign and growing up in Atlanta. Mayor Massell recognizes that his name isn't easily identified as Jewish and admits that he makes extra efforts to let people know it.

"I guess I find myself overemphasizing it . . . because I am proud and think I am doing a good job as mayor. I would like this to reflect whenever possible on people who can identify with me." He pointed to plaques on the wall, from the American Jewish Committee, El Al Airlines, and several from the State of Israel. He displayed an artist's wood carving of the word "Shalom"; and holding up his ring imprinted with a Hebrew letter on it, he said, "Even the ring I'm wearing has on it the letter 'hai,' which means 'for life.'" (He confessed he does not read Hebrew.)

Massell had no regrets after the election about his charges of anti-Semitism. "Well, I had regrets that anti-Semitism had become an element, a factor, but I didn't have any regrets at exposing it."

Customarily, the mayor of Atlanta has been invited to join the prestigious Capitol City Club in downtown Atlanta as an honorary member. Massell declined because he felt the cast of the campaign forced him to be consistent.

"And I felt that, hopefully, this might play a small role in changing some policies. I met with the president of the club and just explained that, if I couldn't be a member not being mayor, then being mayor itself was not enough to make the difference. Incidentally, before I would continue my membership in the Standard Club, which is predominantly, or maybe completely Jewish, and where I have been a member for many, many years, I got an agreement from them that they would file a nondiscriminatory statement of policy with the National Conference of Christians and Jews, which locally has been taking an active role in polling clubs as to their position on discrimination. I've got the same procedure in the mill with three other clubs which have offered me honorary memberships."

Massell showed no restlessness talking about the linkage between being Jewish and his politics. "Having been Jewish and raised in a Jewish family with Jewish ideals, I think this might be the reason I'm more liberal and more compassionate about human rights. But I don't decide that, because I'm Jewish, I should react differently to something. I may react differently because I have been Jewish."

He remembered a speaker at the annual banquet of the temple youth group, the Top Hat Club, who "talked about how it had made him a better person being Jewish, because he had to work harder . . . in order to compete . . . so thus he actually became a better surgeon than his peers. I thought a great deal about that and it became a sort of guidepost or a challenge for me, that I would benefit because I was Jewish."

He made his first trip to Israel with a group of mayors the spring after the election. "The most moving experience for me was planting a tree in the Kennedy Forest . . . first, I was so impressed with the amount of farming going on throughout Israel, having been reared to believe that Jews didn't farm . . . and secondly . . . my affection for the Kennedys . . . to be in a place as a memorial to President Kennedy, and then to be able to dig in the ground with my hands in Israel and do something like the Jews were doing there was just very moving to me."

He recalled a meeting with Teddy Kollek, the mayor of Jerusalem, whom he invited to Atlanta. "I told an audience here," he said chuckling, "that he and I had a lot in common; among other things I found out that he and I both had to go to the Jewish community for our campaign funds."

He realizes that being Jewish and Southern projects him nationally to a television audience he might otherwise not command. "I was selected for a *Meet the Press* interview with five other mayors at the U.S. Conference of Mayors meeting. Maybe being Southern was enough, but there were other Southern mayors there. Carl Stokes gets pulled into things because he is a Negro mayor of Cleveland, and I suppose I get asked because I am a Jewish mayor of Atlanta."

286

Sam Massell, having grown up in an atmosphere in which his friends treated Judaism as a social encumbrance, seems to enjoy the reactions to his new style. "I had a friend once who changed his name from Goldberg to Cavalier because he said he wanted to get his foot in the door and prove himself. I'm doing just the opposite. I'm certain that I'm being invited through doors because I am openly Jewish."

The Atlanta Jewish community has a vitality that one doesn't find in any other Jewish community in the South, a self-confidence that comes out of a milieu of growth and civic dynamism. Where the Birmingham Jewish community is ill at ease in a roughneck steel town, Atlanta is relaxed; where New Orleans is stifled under the secrecy of costumes and masks, Atlanta is more open and expansive; where Richmond Jews can be haughty and Old South, Atlanta is more egalitarian and New South. Inside the Jewish community, the Massells were an early example of what prosperity and the spirit of the city would do to the institutional underpinnings that kept the German Jews apart from the East Europeans. Today the differences exist only in the minds of those old enough to remember the early days.

Sam Massell, in a curious way, restores a sense of balance to the Atlanta Jewish community. With all the controversy surrounding his years in office, none of the reaction has set in that the most pessimistic old-timers feared. For those with memories of Leo Frank, Sam Massell was a test for the city of Atlanta. He was everything they thought the first Jew elected to public office should not be—blunt, outspoken, and controversial. Yet, they are seeing him judged as a public figure, not as a Jew; as a politician, not as the public representative of the Jewish community; by his record in office, not by his religion. Perhaps, too, they are relieved that the Jewish community itself is divided over Sam's record as mayor, an indication that the Jewish community is mature enough to judge its own by the same standard as the rest of the city does.

"I don't know what the lesson is," said a young Jewish lawyer who worked for Massell in the election. "Sam is now the darling of the downtown crowd because he's the Great White Hope against a black mayor next time. We've come a long way, though. Now people cuss him as an s.o.b. and not as a Jew-mayor."

287

VI

Jews and Blacks

NINETEEN

The Maids and Black Jesus

"Jews are just like the other people, only more so."
Anonymous

I N the fall, when the leaves were gone, I could see the bus stop through the trees from our front porch. Every morning except Sunday, the six Negro maids who worked on our street got off the early morning bus together and they would walk up the street, peeling off one by one into the houses of my friends, saying good-bye until after dinner, when the phone would ring and they would meet again to go home.

I was raised Southern-style—by the maid. No one can understand the mystery of the South without delving into this murmuring undertone—a relationship primordial, like parent and child, of discipline and need, shadowing every white Southerner throughout the rest of his life.

Mother and I once figured that, if you counted back to the Nachamson family, we had lived with only four maids in sixty years. That wasn't unusual for many of the white families I knew, Jew and gentile. Ethel Benjamin raised my brother and stayed with us for sixteen years; Zola Hargrave raised me and has been with us for twenty-four years. I asked them both where their names came from and they just said, "I don't know, some old slave name, I guess," though Zola thought she was named after a famous ballet dancer; perhaps Ethel from Judah Benjamin's plantation, but she never knew.

291

They are nearly as much a part of me as my parents are: the gentle arms, the stinging switch, bedtime stories, the Jewish dishes they cooked, and the gospel hymns they hummed while sweeping the porch in the white uniforms they picked out in Evans' United Department store.

When Zola made the chopped liver for the Jewish holidays, it was an all-day affair—frying the livers and the onions in the morning; boiling the eggs and setting up the grinder and calling me to stuff some ingredients through, so I could eat it fresh and moist on crackers before she mushed it all together with chicken fat.

I remember how startled I was to discover, as I got older, that my mother really couldn't cook at all. Whenever I came home from camp, college, or the Navy, Zola would fix up a brisket, or some crisp roast chicken, or a perfect corned beef; her matzo-ball soup was as deep a Sabbath tradition in our home as the Friday night candles and the *kiddush*. Zola would also cook up Southern dishes like squash casserole, fried okra, butter beans, and she rolled her fried chicken in matzo meal. (Because my mother never served pork at the table, Zola would pretend to cook bacon for herself when I wanted some.)

Before she worked for us, Zola had learned to cook Jewish food for a family in New York, but she had fled the big city out of loneliness for her family, farm people down in Chatham County. She always said learning to cook Jewish food was a skill that led directly to secure, permanent employment. She once told me that the saying down in Hayti was, "Once a Jew-maid, always a Jew-maid." The reason was, if a family moved away, other Jewish families in town were always eager to hire a cook who knew what gefilte fish was and that Friday night was chicken soup night.

Zola never missed coming in, no matter how bad the weather, because she thought I would dry up and famish if she didn't tuck her special sandwiches in my lunch box. She would remind me to bundle up tight, to be careful crossing the street, to be sure and buy milk instead of Coca-Cola with my lunch money.

She had to tolerate the uninhibited inquisitiveness of a third grader in a Southern grammar school who learned a vacation song one June with the verse:

> I can tell you all about why
> Hans must wear his wooden shoes;

Just why the darkies are not white;
And the Chinamen wear queues.

When I asked her why the "darkies are not white," she answered, "Just born that way, I suppose." Since I spent so much of my early years with Zola, it was inevitable that she would mold some of my moral precepts, and leave me with her own special insights into food, life, and the weather. Once, when I came dashing into the kitchen after a loud crash of dishes, I heard her mutter to herself, "Life is just cleaning up one big mess after another." She taught me that wishing makes it so; that if you do something good, you receive something in return; that someone is always worse off than you; that when it rains while the sun shines, "the devil's beatin' his wife with a hambone"; that "lightning is God doing his work"; that "the hurrieder I go, the behinder I get"; and that when a "weeping willow grows higher than the house, somebody inside is gonna die."

She knew all about the mysterious powers of foods: that "peanut butter and cheese make you constipated"; that "milk turns sour in your stomach when you drink it with fish"; that "if a boy stutters, slap him with raw liver and he'll stop"; that "Jello is called nervous pudding because the shaking makes you nervous."

As the years went by, the role of the Southern maid intrigued me, especially when I discovered that Southern Jewish girls were much closer to their maids than to their mothers in the ease with which they discussed sex problems. The practical advice and love lessons came out of hard experience: "It's easier to keep a man faithful before you're married than after"; "if anybody tries to rape you, kick him where it hurts most"; "if you already have children and get married, a man is just another mouth to feed"; "don't eat sweets when you have your period—it makes you flow more"; "babies don't come out of marriage, they come out of love."

At night when Zola changed out of her white uniform into other clothes to go home, she carried my mother's old pocketbook and wore my mother's hats that were out of style, a painful image to me now, stepping right out of the old pictures in our family photograph albums. Her house, which Dad had financed, was built of brick, because she didn't want "a stick house that would blow down," and it was furnished with the furniture out of the old house we had lived in. A visit there was a dreamlike passage into my boyhood, stirring cowboy memories of skinning my knee while chasing my brother on horseback around her coffee table. She kept clippings of our family under a glass in her living room—the honor roll list at Durham High and the picture of Dad being sworn in after the last election.

Mom never hesitated to leave me with Zola when she and my father went away on trips; life would roll on so steadily, that I cannot even remember missing my parents. Like the legendary maids of Southern literature, Zola had huge soft breasts that she used to nuzzle me in when I was little. And she was eight months pregnant with her son Robert before she thought she ought to let us know. Before he was old enough for school, she used to bring him over to play in our recreation room with my old toys and games, so that she could keep watch over him; and when he got bigger, she would ask me for any worn-out sweaters and socks with holes in them, because "he's growin' so fast I just cain't keep up," and I would sneak her some good socks and underwear, too, when my mother wasn't noticing.

She had high hopes for Robert, to whom she preached about going to college, and she hugged my mother tearfully when Mother said, "Don't you worry about paying for Robert's college, Zola; he's one more son we've got to send through school." When Robert got a football scholarship to the Negro college in Greensboro, Zola told me, "I just pray he don't get hurt; he wants to be a *pro*-fessional so he can make a heap a' money."

In college, since Chapel Hill was only eight miles away, I would sneak over for some of her cooking because she was lonely in the house with "nothin' but the creaks to keep me company," and she missed my "noises." On rare occasions she would write me notes about how lonely the house was—wonderful stream-of-consciousness sentences without punctuation or capitalization. She always signed them with the same ending, a formal "Your maid, Zola Hargrave." When I graduated from college, I decided to drop my nickname Sonny and adopt Eli, my grandfather's name. Zola misunderstood my purpose and thought I was signaling my intention to assume a new role in Southern society. She called me "Mister Eli" for months.

One morning at breakfast, my father asked Zola about integration, and she replied, "Well, it's not for me. It's for the young people. We're too old, but they got their lives ahead."

Robert never joined the movement, but she was deeply affected

294

by his ambition to be something better than his father had been. Once, when Passover came on a Saturday, my mother asked Zola if Robert could come over to help. "I thought we could teach him how to wait on tables," Mother said.

"No thanks," Zola answered without looking up.

"Why not?" Mother asked innocently ". . . pick up some extra money . . . it's a mighty good thing to know."

"Please, Miz Evans. I appreciates it and all, but I don't want him to learn to wait."

One night when I was taking her home, she said, "I been with y'all twenty years today." We both laughed about the time I ran naked out of the bath and she rumbled down the street after me and spanked me harder than I had ever been spanked before. She reflected seriously on the years.

"You know what's meant most to me?"

"What's that?"

"Mr. and Miz Evans always let me come in the front door."

When I flew home from law school after a call from my father saying that Mother had heart pains and the doctors weren't sure about a stroke, I took Zola aside in the kitchen and asked about it.

"She won't rest," Zola reported. "You know her. I tries to tell her."

"Zola," I said, "please take care of her. She needs you so much to keep her still. Now you promise."

"We needs each other," she said.

Sometimes, just a remark would echo through my soul and dredge up all the emotions of the years we spent together—the remorse, loyalty, penitence, and love. "When you going to get married and have babies so I can raise 'em up like I did you?"

Every morning at nine-thirty, after my mother had left the house to join my father at the store, Ethel Benjamin, our maid for sixteen years before Zola came, would turn on the radio to listen to the gospel hymns of the Blackwood Brothers; she would hum along while puttering around the house in her nylon-stocking cap she wore to keep the dust out and I would tag along with her till she shooed me outside to play. When the theme of that program came on, it was time to run into the kitchen to sing along, and maybe help shell butter beans or watch the cake making.

295

Help to cheer the lone and sad
Help to make some people glad;
Make your life so be
That all the world will see
The joy of serving Jesus with a smile.

Psychologically, it was just easier for me to sing hymns with Jesus in them if they were Negro spirituals. My friends didn't seem to see any distinction; black and white Christianity was all mixed up in their minds. They saw the emotion in the black church as "primitive" or "ignorant," a reaffirmation of the supremacy of the white culture. Whites didn't sing Negro spirituals in church on Sunday—even the ones with Jesus in them—which made spirituals even more attractive to me when we sang them in school.

And I got to be pretty good at pushing the singing in that direction at Boy Scout camp-outs, class picnics, and bus trips to the state museums in Raleigh. As soon as the group singing took on religious leanings, I would start right in with:

Nobody knows de trouble I seen
Nobody knows but Jesus . . .

My friends and I as teen-agers did what most other white boys did on the weekends. Occasionally on a Sunday night we visited the rural black churches just to see the holy rollers shake and chant. While the mysteries of the white fundamentalist church churned up resurrection and retribution, the black church conveyed a sense of gentleness and consolation. While the white church twisted and distorted the Old Testament into a prophecy for the New, the black church seemed to take stories of the Old Testament seriously. Somehow I didn't recognize the blood-and-guts Old Testament with the "foreshadowings" of the fundamentalist church: when Abraham started to slay his son Isaac and God sent a lamb to take his place, the fundamentalists prophesied Jesus taking man's place on the cross; when the sailors threw Jonah into the raging sea and the whale swallowed him up for three days, and then spit him out, that was symbolic of the crucifixion, the sepulcher, and the resurrection. The fundamentalist epigram summed it up:

The New is in the Old contained;
the Old is in the New explained.

296

But listen to an old black preacher sing his sermon—about Moses leading the children of Israel out of slavery, of Joshua and the battle of Jericho, or of Daniel in the lion's den. Negroes didn't just read the stories in the Old Testament for signposts to the New; they made them come alive. And the lessons meant as much to them as the parables of Jesus. To me, Negroes and Jews were joined in a union of persecution and hate; we were both children of history, both celebrating a people in slavery and a yearning for deliverance.

Negroes unabashedly picked names for their children like Moses and Mordecai; I even met a man once who told me his middle name was "Nevertheless" because his mother had seen it in the book of Exodus.

Negroes believed in my hero Moses with more passion than I did, and that drew me to them:

Go down, Moses
Way down to Egypt land
Tell ole
Pharaoh . . .
To let my people go.

I remember squeezing the meaning out of each word in "Swing Low, Sweet Chariot," because I had to avoid white Baptist hymns about Jesus or faked them with moving lips and no sounds; but spirituals (especially those that didn't have "Jesus" in them) I could sing out all the way, with ten times the fervor, to make up for what I held back before, and join full-throated in all the Jesus-joy I felt so left out of.

The Negroes flocked each Sunday to the old clapboard churches on their side of town, the women all dressed up in sashes and fancy hats, the little girls in starched pinafore dresses with bright ribbons in their hair. And the fat choir ladies would file in, each a gospel reprint of Mahalia Jackson in a long white robe, singing as they marched to the choir loft, the piano ringing out a mixture of the blues and the gospel, and heads all nodding to the syncopated rhythms of praying in the let-it-all-out style of the black church.

We white boys went to black prayer meetings of the holy rollers just to watch them move, and clap hands, and sing out "Halleluja" and "Amen, brother." We bathed in the "Oh tell it . . . tell it" magic of hypnotic stimulation between preacher and congregation,

297

each driving the other on to mounting excess of singsong sermonizing and jump-up conversions and twitching moments of "cain't-stand-it-no-more" spiritual release and liberation. For us white boys clustered way in the back where we had to stand to see anything, it was more like going to a performance than to a religious service. It was a special experience for me to immerse myself in a kind of Christianity without fear. For one thing, no black preacher-man would try to convert a Jewish boy, because he was white; and there was no chance any of my buddies would get swept away and go down front to be saved, and leave me as the only unwashed outsider at the service. And afterwards, all of us together would imitate the Negro preacher, moaning and crying out the "praise de Lawd" accents of the panting sermons.

The Jesus of the black man and the Jesus of the white man gazed at congregations whose needs and histories molded two distinctly different saviors. While Black Jesus was benign and understanding, White Jesus was strict and unbending. "Sweet little baby Jesus" was black; "Jesus Christ, our lord and savior," was white. Black Jesus passed among the people; White Jesus marched at the head of the crusade. Black Jesus suffered on the cross, to be sure, but He was a comforter looking down to His flock, offering a tranquil hand; White Jesus, "the Son of God," had His eyes turned heavenward to the disappointed Father, asking forgiveness for those who crucified Him. Black Jesus seemed less concerned with drinking and smoking and more devoted to easing the burdens of life; White Jesus seemed stern and self-righteous. Black Jesus would forgive; White Jesus would punish. Black Jesus was more the friendly saint; White Jesus more the awesome soldier.

Zola once invited me to come and watch Robert narrate a Bible story in a Sunday school play. She beamed at me at intermission, and whispered proudly, "No one else here had any white people come and watch them." On the wall, Black Jesus peered down on the little children in starched Sunday dress; His face, of course, was white.

TWENTY

Israelites and the Ex-Slaves

The Jew . . . is a human being—that's enough for me; he can't be any worse.

Concerning the Jews,
Mark Twain

I N 1853 a report by a non-Jew to the American and Foreign Anti-Slavery Society stated, "The Jews of the United States have never taken any steps whatever with regard to the slavery question." Slavery, the gnawing issue tearing the young nation apart and dragging it inevitably into a bloody confrontation, was too explosive an issue for most Jews to speak out on. There is not recorded a single abolitionist among the Jews in the South; for the most part, as in the North, Jews in the South held the views of their neighbors.

Jews owned few slaves, because most of them arrived late in the South and had not yet developed the financial position to do so. In 1850 there were but fifty thousand Jews in America (out of a population of twenty-three million); but from 1850 to 1860, another one hundred thousand came among more than two million Irish, English, and European immigrants fleeing the economic depressions of Europe. Since Jews were forbidden to own land in Eastern Europe, the early settlers headed directly for the cities, a familiar brier patch for traders and shopkeepers, where Jews could share each other's company and practice their religion together. But in the South, only one-seventh of the Negroes lived in the cities; since Jews were not living on plantations (though some

299

Bavarians would settle on small farms) most Jews did not own slaves. There were some spectacular exceptions, however, particularly among Sephardic Jews who had migrated to the South a generation earlier.

Judah Benjamin's plantation near New Orleans had 140 slaves; Isaiah Moses kept thirty-five slaves on his farm in Goose Creek, South Carolina; Mordecai Cohen worked twenty-seven slaves on his plantation in St. Andrews, South Carolina. Many households owned one or two slaves as cooks and housekeepers. (Thirty-four out of seventy-three Jewish families known to be in South Carolina in 1790 owned 150 slaves; in 1840, in New Orleans, fifty-five families held a total of 348.)

Rabbi Bertram Korn's study of this subject, *Jews and Negro Slavery in the Old South*, concludes that "Jewish owners of slaves were not exceptional figures . . . it was only a matter of financial circumstance and familial status when they were to become slave owners." Korn estimates that approximately one-fourth of the Jews in the South owned slaves, the same statistic as for the rest of the white South in the 1860 census.

However, Jews were involved in all the institutions surrounding and supporting the slavery system. In his search into wills, court records, and slave-sale documents, Korn discovered that "Jews participated in every aspect and process of exploitation . . . testifying against Negroes in court, apprehending a runaway slave, inflicting punishment upon a convicted Negro. . . ."

Numerous Jews in major Southern cities had gravitated toward trading as a career—as commission merchants, auctioneers, and brokers—since procuring, advertising, and conducting a sale of all kinds of property was a corner of commerce that required no capital. They were licensed as public officials and, according to Korn, "were expected to deal in slaves as readily as any other sort of merchandise." Jacob Levin, acting rabbi and leader of the Jews of Columbia, South Carolina, advertised in 1852 a sale of "twenty-two likely Negroes, the larger number of which are young and desirable"; Israel Jones of Mobile, Alabama, president of the first congregation in Alabama, also advertised a slave auction: "Man Alfred, 25 years old, field hand; Boy Isaac, 7 years old; woman Judy, 30 years old; and two work horses. Terms cash."

However, almost none of the major slave traders was Jewish, though Harriet Beecher Stowe quotes a letter in her *Key to Uncle*

Tom's Cabin that the Jewish Davis family of Petersburg and Richmond traveled all over the South to "buy them up at low prices (during the summer and fall), trim, shave, wash them, fatten them so that they may look sleek and sell them at great profit."

Korn found only a few instances of miscegenation involving Jews, though he lists a string of Northern Negroes with names such as Hannah Adler, Perry Cohen, Isaac Farber, Richard Levy, Peter Levy, Isaac Nathans, Abraham Stern, and thirteen Negro Tobiases who were likely to have received their names from either Jewish owners or Jewish fathers. In the only case of cohabitation ever brought to court, David Isaacs and Nancy West, "a free mulatto woman," were indicted in 1826 by the grand jury of Albemarle County, Virginia, "for outraging the decency of society . . . by cohabitating together . . . as man and wife, without being lawfully married." A higher court reduced the charge to the lesser offense of fornication.

One of the most distinguished Negroes to hold office during the Reconstruction period was Francis Lewis Cardozo of Charleston (a second cousin, once removed, to the famed Supreme Court Justice Benjamin Nathan Cardozo), the son of either the famous Southern journalist Jacob Cardozo or his lesser-known brother Isaac, through a mixed mulatto and Indian girl named Lydia Williams. Highly educated, with degrees from the University of Glasgow and the London School of Theology, Cardozo returned to South Carolina after the Civil War to serve as a member of the South Carolina Constitutional Convention of 1868, a member of the University of South Carolina Board of Trustees in 1869, secretary of state of South Carolina from 1868 to 1872, and state treasurer from 1872 to 1876. In an era noted for corruption and fraud, his record stands out as capable and untainted, and he is the subject of numerous articles and books.

His brother, Thomas Y. Cardozo, fared less well as superintendent of education in Mississippi in 1874, for he resigned under threat of impeachment, having been accused of embezzling two thousand dollars from Tougaloo College, and was tried for his crime along with the governor and the lieutenant governor, who were also accused of various acts of corruption and graft.

Daniel Warburg, the first member of the distinguished family of bankers and scientists to settle in America, lived in New Orleans in 1821. He claimed revelation of geometric and mathematical secrets beyond ordinary men and offered it ("this genius that governs me") to the nation for ten million dollars or to the British for five million pounds sterling, warning that whoever bought it "will govern the seas of the world." (Neither nation bought it.) Warburg fathered two mulatto sons, one of whom, Eugene, a stonecutter and engraver, left New Orleans to study and work in England, France, and Italy. (The Warburg family in Hamburg acknowledged their existence in the family genealogical charts published in Germany.) Eugene designed bas reliefs illustrating *Uncle Tom's Cabin*, and in 1855 sculpted a bust of the United States Minister to France, John Y. Mason, which today can be seen in the halls of the Virginia Historical Society in Richmond.

Jews seemed to act toward slavery like other white Southerners in their same economic class, and Korn points out that "antebellum Southern Jews were more likely to quote the Talmudic maxim that 'the law of the land is the law [for the Jews]' . . . than they were to evaluate the failings of slavery in the light of the prophetic ethic." He also found no evidence from letters or documents that Jews contrived their acceptance of slavery as "protective coloration" out of fear of anti-Semitism, though no Southerner spoke against the tide of feeling just before the war without reprisal.

Although members of older Southern Jewish families, like Joseph Cardozo, could write articles in defense of slavery, stating that "the reason the Almighty made the colored black is to prove their inferiority," some of the later immigrants were shocked at the treatment of the slaves—the public floggings especially. Others wrote letters revealing that their families bought slaves to free them. According to Korn, however, most would have probably agreed with Aaron Hirsch, who came to America in 1847 and peddled through Mississippi and Arkansas: "The Negroes were brought here in a savage state; they captured and ate each other in their African home. Here, they were instructed to work, were civilized, and got religion and were perfectly happy."

With few exceptions, the American rabbis did not speak out on the slavery issue either, until the war was inevitable. In 1861, during a National Fast Day called by President Buchanan to try to head off the breakup of the Union, Rabbi Morris J. Raphall of New York City delivered a sermon entitled "The Bible View of Slavery" that was to become the most controversial statement ever issued by an American rabbi. The sermon claimed that the "very highest authority—the Ten Commandments" sanctioned slavery, and attacked the abolitionists for distorting the text of the Bible to contend that biblical law made slavery immoral and unlawful: "How dare you denounce slavery as a sin? When you remember that Abraham, Isaac, Jacob, Job—the men with whom the Almighty conversed, with whose names He emphatically connects His own most holy name . . . that all these men were slaveholders, does it not strike you that you are guilty of something very little short of blasphemy?"

Papers throughout the South reprinted the sermon, but other rabbis reacted violently, calling Raphall a "fool," "a knave," and "immoral." Rabbi David Einhorn of Baltimore, the leading abolitionist among the rabbis, and one of the few rabbis who had been condemning slavery from his pulpit since 1856, blasted away at Raphall, asking if God had shown any respect for "historic right" when he emancipated the Hebrew slaves from Egyptian slavery, and arguing that religious principles of freedom and righteousness must triumph over ". . . ancient prejudices and . . . hallowed atrocities." Einhorn's slashing reply received such wide circulation that Southern sympathizers in Baltimore burned his printing press, young men from the congregation guarded him and his home around the clock, and he finally had to flee for his safety to escape the rioting in the city between the secessionists and the abolitionists.

Rabbi Isaac Wise, with a constituency in the South (his daughter married Adolph Ochs of Chattanooga, thus sealing his commitment to the South), rarely mixed political debate with Jewish issues, but this time he attacked the abolitionists as "fanatics, demagogues, and demons of hatred and destruction . . . who delight in civil wars. . . ."

He suspected the abolitionists as political opportunists aimed at conquering the South, and feared they would then turn on the Jews. He found flaws in Raphall's arguments, and discussed them calmly and moderately. But he was still not capable of condemning slavery altogether. "We are not prepared, nobody is, to maintain that it is absolutely unjust to purchase savages, or rather their labor, place them under the protection of the law, and secure them the benefit of civilized society and their sustenance for their labor. . . ."

After the fighting started and national discussion ceased in the rush for battle, Wise despaired for Jews on both sides. He asserted, "Force will not hold together this Union," and declared that he could not choose sides, because "we abhor the idea of war, but also we have dear friends and near relations, beloved brethren and kinsmen in each section of the country, that our heart bleeds on thinking of their distress, of the misery that might befall them."

Wise taunted the abolitionists for their lack of tolerance for the dilemma of Southern Jews. "Go down south," he said "and expound your doctrines to the community; and if you dare not do it, why do you expect the Jews there to stand in opposition to the masses of people?"

From their earliest encounters, Negroes and Jews in the South have had a special relationship, first growing out of a buyer-seller need for each other, and strengthened by a mutual fear of the white society they lived in. The Negro sensed from the beginning that the Jew in the South was not the same kind of white man as other whites—he spoke the language with a strange accent; he would sell his wares to slaves and freedmen when other whites turned from them as lowly and unworthy; he was not a large slave owner nor a farmer, more the salesman in attitude, grateful to customers of whatever color. After the emancipation, just when the second generation of German Jews was growing less distinguishable from other whites, the Negro would hesitantly unlock the door of the shanty to the bent figure of the new peddler from Eastern Europe and experience the Jew all over again.

The affinity of the Negro for the Jew wasn't only economic, it was religious. The slave, bondaged and hopeless, identified strongly with the Israelites of the Old Testament, embraced the legends of Moses and Joshua, and embellished and absorbed them into plantation songs of longing and suffering, of striving for freedom in the promised land.

"The Negro identifies himself almost wholly with the Jews," wrote James Baldwin. "The more devout Negro considers that he is a Jew, in bondage to a hard taskmaster and waiting for Moses to lead him out of Egypt."

A black preacher in Mississippi told me his favorite stories from the Old Testament: "Well, there's Joshua . . . we sing about him, you know."

"Yes, sir," I said. "And what's the lesson?"

"If you keep circling and make enough noise, the walls will come

304

a-tumbling down," he answered. "And then there's Daniel—he would not bow down and the lions stood there looking at him because of his faith. And of course, there's Moses—leading the children of Israel out of slavery into the promised land—that was Dr. King's favorite." To many blacks, George Wallace and "Bull" Connor were the Pharaohs; Selma and Montgomery, the land of Egypt; and Martin Luther King, their Moses. (Sometimes, blacks absorbed Jewish religious attitudes by a kind of strange osmosis. "My grandmother refused to eat catfish all her life," said a black law student at the University of Mississippi, "because she said it was against her religion.")

Gary Marx polled black attitudes toward Jews in his study for the A.D.L. series entitled *Protest and Prejudice*, and found marked differences between the attitudes of Northern and Southern blacks toward Jews.

The polls involved blacks only in Atlanta and, for contrast, a city with a more violent history—Birmingham. Marx found the following. To the statement, "Jews have too much power in the United States," 18 percent in New York and 9 percent in Atlanta answered "true"; to the statement, "Jews are warm and friendly," 71 percent in New York and 85 percent in Atlanta answered "true"; to the statement, "The more contact a person has with Jewish people, the more he gets to like them," 59 percent in New York and 84 percent in Atlanta replied "true"; with regard to negative business practices—statements like "shrewd and tricky," "shady practices"—the percentages were approximately equal, with the Southern Negroes always showing a slightly better attitude toward the Jews. However, to the statement, "Jewish storeowners are better than other white storeowners," 10 percent in New York agreed and 32 percent in Atlanta; to the statement, "Jewish landlords are better than other white landlords," 19 percent in New York agreed and 31 percent in Atlanta.

Marx printed a few quotes from interviewees, both positive and negative, some of which reveal that Southern blacks don't look on Jews as "whites" but as a sympathetic third race, in contrast to the other whites they encounter.

A nurse's aide in Atlanta said of Jews, "They treat you just like you were white or a Jew. I could buy groceries on credit at the Jewish store while some of these white storeowners won't even cash my check."

A housewife in Birmingham said, "Jewish storeowners are better because they will keep cutting the price of an item you want until you can afford to buy it. They do not want you to leave the store without buying. . . . They call you Mrs. or Miss and they also address you properly on the mail that is sent to you."

An unemployed worker in Birmingham saw this difference between Jews and other white landlords: "The Jew automatically kind of gives you a chance to pay. Even if he has a white man collecting. The white man will want to put you out the minute you don't pay or get behind, but the Jew, you can call him, and he will make the white man extend you time."

While the presence of Jewish civil rights activists in the South has, on the whole, embarrassed Southern Jews, Marx found strong evidence that Negroes nationally as well as in the South hold more positive attitudes toward Jews because they perceive Jews as civil rights supporters. North and South, approximately 45 percent of those polled felt that Jews were "more in favor of civil rights than other whites" and only 3 percent said "less"; to the question of Jews being better at hiring Negroes in the North and the South, 69 percent agreed and only 15 percent disagreed.

"We knew as soon as the temple was bombed," said a black leader in Atlanta, "that the whites had done it as a warning to the Jews. Down here, black churches catch it all the time so we identified with the Jews after that."

A black civil rights leader confessed that he always carefully used the phrase "Jewish community," because in the small town he grew up in, "the way the white Southerner said 'Jews' always sounded like 'nigger' to me."

The commitment of Northern Jewish money to equal opportunity in the South also had an influence on the attitudes of Southern black leadership toward all Jews, Southern Jews included. The best example was Julius Rosenwald of Chicago, who, through the Rosenwald Fund, gave away more than twenty million dollars to the cause of Negro education and health in the South. After his death, through his daughter, Edith Stern in New Orleans, the Rosenwald fortune partially shifted to a Southern Jewish base and became one of the few activist sources of money in the South for groups and individuals concerned with civil rights.

Rosenwald saw early the relationship between the peddler-salesman and the mail-order catalogue. So he invested in the mail-order business with Richard Sears and Alvah Roebuck just as

America was coming out of a depression in the late nineteenth century. Rosenwald was never quite sure why he got so rich so fast, but in three years, sales from the dream book in the front parlor rose from one million dollars to eleven million dollars; in ten years, to fifty million; in thirty years, to two hundred million.

The Rosenwald Fund was run by Southern liberals, Will Alexander and Edwin Embree, who guided its programs and projects until the Fund dissolved in 1948. ("Coming generations can . . . provide for their own needs," Rosenwald wrote in the letter of gift.) The Fund built more than fifty-two hundred rural schools for Negroes; invested more than three million dollars in Negro health institutions and health services; and helped revitalize the Negro colleges (with major endowments and building funds to Dillard University in New Orleans; Meharry Medical College in Nashville, Tennessee; Morehouse College in Atlanta; Fisk University in Nashville; Spelman College in Atlanta; Howard University in Washington, D.C.; and Tuskegee Institute in Alabama, where Rosenwald served on the board of trustees).

Rosenwald also believed strongly in investing in people, helping talented individuals at crucial times in their careers, and with Will Alexander's unerring judgment in selecting recipients, the Rosenwald fellowships assisted a glittering array of Negro students like Ralph Bunche in political science; Marian Anderson in music; John Hope Franklin in history; Kenneth Clark in psychology; Gordon Parks in photography; Ralph Ellison, Langston Hughes, James Baldwin, and Willard Motley in creative writing. Later, fellowships for study went to white Southerners like young Ralph McGill in journalism; Lillian Smith and Elizabeth Hardwick in creative writing; and scholars like Rupert Vance in sociology and C. Vann Woodward in history. In total, the Rosenwald Fund provided almost two million dollars for individual fellowships in the South, most of it in the 1930's when money for study was almost impossible to find.

Governor Eugene Talmadge of Georgia lashed out at the "Rosenwald menace to the Southern way of life," but the Fund never wavered in its mission. When Rosenwald's daughter, Edith, married a New Orleans businessman named Edgar Stern, the Stern Family Fund emerged as a major force for change in the region, giving community action grants to minority groups before the term gained acceptance, and providing major organizing grants for the

Voter Education Project of the Southern Regional Council, which ultimately played the central role in registering three million new Negro voters in the South in the 1960's.

In Charleston, a young black named Bill Saunders rose to prominence when he organized first a hospital workers' union and then a strike that attracted national attention and the support of Ralph Abernathy's SCLC in its first major effort after the death of King. He works for the Weil Mattress Company in Charleston, and we took a lunch break together, he sitting on one of the machines with puffs of mattress stuffing clinging to his hair and in the creases of his work clothes. "The Jews are not caught in the middle anymore. They're on their way now."

He founded an organization called the Committee for Better Racial Assurance (with the somewhat ominous initials COBRA), and the Jewish community contributed two thousand dollars to help start it. Some Jews criticized the leadership in the Charleston Jewish community for the contribution, but one of the leaders defended the decision as "not blackmail, just good relationships with the black community."

Saunders complained that "the Jews are Jews when one thing is happening and white at other times. In the long run, they are more sympathetic than other whites but lots of time, their sympathy is an act."

He felt that "Jews want to give the impression that they have suffered like black people, but it's not true. They have a special complexion, to begin with, and they came here voluntarily, not as slaves like we did."

What of the common argument that if blacks worked as hard as the early Jewish immigrants did, they too could make it out of poverty in a generation?

"They came out of the ghettos and knew how to hustle," he replied. "We didn't. Actually, the old men have suffered, but to talk to their sons is like talking to a different race."

Still, Jews knew discrimination, I insisted, right here in Charleston at the country clubs, and they had helped settle the place.

"They shouldn't be so hung up about the Carolina Yacht Club," he said. "It's the only place they can't go. And they can park their yachts someplace else and fish all they want."

He admired Jews for the way they had opened up so many

choices for themselves. "The Jews have it any way they want it here, and that's what we're after. If they want to live in an all Jewish community, they can; if they want to live near a country club, they can; if they want to live in an integrated neighborhood, they can." And then he gave a whistle about the elegance of the homes around Confederate Circle, a new development. "Hot damn, they got some homes over there. And it's all Jewish, man. That's cool. I like that."

The history of the relationship between blacks and Jews forms an important backdrop to an understanding of the painful reactions of Jews to events in the South since 1954. From 1800 to 1850, the scattered number of German Jews in the South were mostly towns-folk with just a few family slaves (though some Jews, but very few, owned plantations with hundreds of slaves). During Reconstruction, the Jew as peddler and the black man as freedman found each other out of economic necessity; and once the thousands of East European immigrants made the transition from peddler to shopkeeper, the black man moved with him to the only store in town that extended credit, addressed him and his wife as "Mr." and "Mrs.," and allowed his family to try on clothes before buying them. Though the black man was as fundamentalist in his religious beliefs as his white neighbors, part of his soul lay with the Israelites of the Old Testament, and so religious anti-Semitism was never a central part of his emotions.

Once the Supreme Court handed down its historic decision, every Southerner faced the moment of choice. For the Jewish Southerner, the decade of racial tension would take on special dimensions.

TWENTY - ONE

Southern Jews in Crisis

T H E desegregation era in the South, from 1954 onward, brought tense times for Jews, caught between determined civil rights organizers and embittered whites, wanting to head for the bunkers until the rocks and the marches and the tear gas stopped. The Anti-Defamation League of the B'nai B'rith and the American Jewish Committee kept a steady watch on the growth and psychology of anti-Semitism. Northern reporters covering the flash points in the crisis were understandably fascinated with the Klan and the psychopathology of hate because of the excitement and passion they generated, but few of them understood the South, and many wrote with little insight into its heart and with some antipathy for the region itself.

Much of what has been written about Jews in the South has come out of crisis situations—after a bombing, during demonstrations, in the midst of a boycott—when tensions were highest and fear greatest. Few observers took the time to look through the clichés to the nuances—the differences between the generations, between the professional men and the shopkeepers, between the German Jews and the East Europeans, and above all, the difference between private views and public acts—the rabbis, who spoke from a religious and moral perspective and yet were necessarily wary of an interviewer, out of legitimate concern for the jeopardy of the Jewish community and the safety of the temple building; and the congregation fixed on economic survival, in the sure knowledge that they must live in a community after the writers and the television cameras pushed on to the next confrontation.

Perhaps there is no "South" anymore, other than the geographical and historical South, but psychologically it is a region of such complexity that sweeping generalizations about it are foolhardy and naïve. Each town, small enough to be responsive to individuals and to fate, deserves its own distinctive history; whole regions, like the Mississippi Delta stretching from New Orleans through Memphis, or the coastal plains sprawling across the Virginias and the Carolinas, superimpose themselves over conventional state groupings. Rural Mississippi and Alabama—for journalists, the bellwether for the region—differ so markedly from the rest of the South that they surely rate special attention; for too long they have distorted the national view of the Southern psyche. The steady departure of Jews from the small towns to the major cities since the Depression should focus any honest appraisal of the Jewish experience on the cities where the majority of the Jews live.

Most Jews in the South have watched the civil rights crisis hoping not to be harmed themselves. It is no longer a shock to the Jewish community in general—in New York City, for example, having watched itself react to rising racial fears—to discover that some Jews are prejudiced. Jews in the South are no exception, but for the most part they are more liberal than other white Southerners while more conservative than Jews in the North. As one rabbi who served in the South for thirty years said, "Sure, there are some biased people, but by and large, Jews are sympathetic. They just don't want to stick their necks out." He then told a joke about an all-Jewish jury accidentally selected for a civil rights trial. When the judge asked the foreman for his verdict, the foreman announced, "Your honor, we've decided not to get involved!"

Southern Jewish logic on civil rights often has a convoluted rationale of its own. Jewish sympathies are with the oppressed; storeowners with black customers treat them with respect, but when trouble starts, fear of the whites overtakes all other emotions. "At first when we were boycotted," said a small merchant in eastern North Carolina, "we were bitter, since we had done so much for the Negro here—the only credit store in town, the first to start lay-aways, the first to hire Negro clerks. But when it actually came, we often thought how frightened we would have been if we had been the only store downtown *not* boycotted."

The key to the sources of those attitudes reaches deeply into Southern custom and Jewish history. Charles Wittenstein, who attended high school in the Bronx, contrasted the Northern Jewish

311

child's fear of blacks with the attitude of Southern Jews whom he has observed in his twenty years as director of the American Jewish Committee regional office in Atlanta.

"For one thing, Jews in the Bronx never had servants of any color, but Jews in the South did, from the beginning," he observed. "Maybe it breeds paternalism but the memories build humanity too, when the barriers break down. Second," he continued, "a Jewish child in the South may have some of the same fear of blacks as Jews in the Bronx, but the Southern Jewish kid knew the black kid wouldn't lay a hand on him. The Southern Jew doesn't have the memory of physical conflict with blacks that we do, and that's bound to make a difference."

The Russian immigrant to the South brought lessons with him in his memories—the pogroms were led by marauding bands of *muzhiks*, the illiterate Russian peasants who guzzled vodka and lay around the countryside, unpredictable and primitive, and who conditioned the Jews instinctively to fear the Southern dirt farmer. It required no effort to transfer those fears to the rednecks. But the Jewish immigrant had never seen black men before; he was more willing to respond out of actual experience with the Negro than out of a twisted history of slavery, guilt, and pathological hate. When the Negro smiled at the Jew, the Jew smiled back.

Harry Golden translated these emotions succinctly in more modern times: "Since the beginning of the civil rights movement, the Southerner has feared the Negro, the Jew has feared the Southerner, and the Negro has feared no one." (Not altogether true, of course; the Negro had good reason to fear the Southerner, too.)

While the Jewish community almost always puts its own safety first, individual acts of courage throughout the civil rights era deserve mention. Ask Hodding Carter, III, editor of the *Delta Democrat Times* in Greenville, Mississippi, about the Jewish storeowners who stayed with the paper when the White Citizens' Council undertook a concerted house-by-house drive to destroy circulation and frighten off advertisers. Ask John Lewis, former chairman of the Student Non-Violent Coordinating Committee and now director of the Voter Education Project, about the Jewish merchant who consistently put up bail money during the entire agony in Selma, Alabama. Ask black leaders in Atlanta about the early commitment of Rabbi Jacob Rothschild, who spoke out in the strongest terms after the '54 decision, was the key organizer in the

312

community tribute by 1,200 leaders to Martin Luther King in 1963, and who never stopped working publicly for civil rights, even after the temple bombing in 1958. Ask the leaders on the Southern Regional Council about the remarkable sixteen years of Rabbi Charles Mantinband in Florence, Alabama, and Hatties-burg, Mississippi, deep in the roughest part of Klan country, who somehow managed to bulldog his way through community threats and congregation pressures, opening his home to Negroes and civil rights workers, speaking out against segregation in the pulpit and at nearby Negro colleges, and remaining always a respected and active member of the board of the Southern Regional Council and the Mississippi Council on Human Relations.

In 1962, Mantinband wrote these words summing up the dilemma of the Jew: "Life can be very placid and gracious in this part of the country—if one runs with the herd. The South is turbulent and sullen and sometimes noisy, but there is a conspiracy of silence in respectable middle-class society. Sensitive souls, with vision and the courage of the Hebrew prophets, are drowned out. Timid souls, complacent and indifferent, seldom articulate their protests."

There were others. Morris Abram, an Atlanta lawyer from Fitzgerald, Georgia, challenged the county unit system in Georgia, by which a white voter in a small south Georgia county was equal to thousands of blacks in Atlanta's Fulton County. In successfully winning the case before the U.S. Supreme Court after ten years of legal wrangling, Abram changed the political history of the state. Sylvan Meyer, editor of the Gainesville *Times* in Gainesville, Georgia—among the first newspapers in the South to support the 1954 Supreme Court decision—steadily advocated compliance through the violent years, winning the national Sigma Delta Chi award for editorials attacking interposition. Meyer also served as chairman of the Georgia Advisory Commission to the U.S. Commission on Civil Rights.

This has not been a proud era for the Southern churches—the photographs of tight-lipped ushers blocking the way of Negro worshipers on Sunday stand as plaintive indicators of the moral distance between the pulpit and the congregation. For the most part, the rabbis, too, have been forced to stay in the background, most of them Northern-born and still Yankees to the locals, even after decades with the congregation. Many rabbis tested the water,

313

some more boldly than others (like Rothschild and Mantinband), but in each case they stepped briefly forward, sometimes into the spotlight, and then retreated to watch and wait.

In 1949, when no large hall in New Orleans could be found where Negroes and whites could hear Ralph Bunche, Rabbi Julian Feibelman opened the doors of Temple Sinai to two thousand people, the first major integrated audience in New Orleans history.

Rabbi Ira Sanders of Little Rock appeared before an open hearing of a committee of the Arkansas State Senate in 1957, at the height of the confrontation between Governor Faubus and the federal troops, to testify in opposition to four prosegregation bills:

> Above my love for Arkansas comes my devotion to America
> . . . I regard the Supreme Court as the final democratic
> authority of the land. . . . Once they pass on the constitu-
> tionality of the law, it should become operative as the law of
> the land. Higher than legal law, however, stands the moral
> law. . . . When Jesus died on the cross, He repeated those
> immortal words: "Father, forgive them, for they know not
> what they do." Legislators! May future generations reading
> the statute books . . . not be compelled to say these words
> of you. . . . Defeat, I pray you, in toto, these four
> measures.

On Yom Kippur eve of 1958, when his temple was packed, Rabbi Emmet Frank of Alexandria, Virginia, unloaded on the Byrd machine and its policy of "massive resistance," which had closed down the schools in Prince Edward County. The speech created a furor unequaled by any other utterance in the South by a rabbi during the whole era:

> Has silence given the Jew of the South security? . . .
> Bombings, economic reprisals have been his reward. . . .
> Let the segregationists froth and foam at their mouth. There
> is only one word to describe their madness . . . Godless-
> ness, or to coin a new synonym—Byrdliness. Byrdliness has
> done more harm to the stability of our country than McCarthy-
> ism. . . . Thousands who in the South were ready to accept
> the law of the land, reject it now because of misguided, false,
> and tyrannical leadership.

The Danville *Register* branded him "not only mad but silly"; the Richmond *Times* was "horrified by Rabbi Frank's theocratic ostracism of the senior senator from Virginia"; and the Arlington chapter of the Defenders of State Sovereignty warned that "friendly relations between Jews and Christians would be damaged" unless the Jews "move quickly to refute and condemn Rabbi Frank." Within a month, however, eleven ministers endorsed the sermon, one of them comparing him to the Old Testament prophets; his board stood by his right to choose a sermon as "solely the province of the rabbi," and he weathered the criticism both within and without the congregation.

In Memphis, the morning after the assassination of Martin Luther King over so simple a matter as a garbage strike, Rabbi James Wax marched beside Reverend Henry Starks, president of the black Ministers' Alliance, and the Very Reverend W. A. Dimmick, who was carrying a giant gold processional cross on a black staff. The three of them led a somber procession of one hundred and fifty black and white ministers and priests through downtown Memphis, past the four thousand National Guardsmen in full battle gear, to the steps of city hall to plead with Mayor Henry Loeb to settle the strike and end the violence in the city. Speaking in "impassioned and bitter tones," according to the *New York Times*, at an "emotion-drenched meeting," Wax as president of the Memphis Ministerial Association shouted at the mayor, who was less than four feet away, "We fervently ask you not to hide any longer behind legal technicalities and slogans but to speak out at last in favor of human dignity . . . [to obey] laws greater than the laws of Memphis and Tennessee . . . the laws of God."

The next day, Billy Loeb, Mayor Loeb's brother, resigned in a rage from the temple. (Henry Loeb had been confirmed there as a boy but had converted to the Episcopal church after he married a former queen of the Memphis Cotton Carnival.) Said Rabbi Wax, who received more than a thousand letters and phone calls in protest, "It was the most right thing I ever did as a rabbi from a moral point of view. But I never realized the depth of feeling in the community."

These were not patterns of leadership but isolated incidents. Deeper in the South, away from the centers of population and modernity, the Jews were intimidated into silence along with other voices of moderation. The extremists would have their turn.

Harry Golden was an exception. Free-wheeling and original, exuberant and perceptive, he came to the South in his late thirties and adopted it as home. The remarkable thing is the extent to which the South adopted him. Harry was pure East Side Jewish in his writing and his humor, but as word spread of the "old imp" (as Jonathan Daniels, editor of the Raleigh *News and Observer*, is fond of calling him), the Southern newspapers gave him exposure and the Northern press gobbled his ideas whole.

I visited Golden once eight years ago in his office at *The Carolina Israelite* in Charlotte. There he sat in his Kennedy rocker, his feet barely touching the floor, a twinkling Jewish Buddha with a cigar. The walls were crowded with books and dozens of autographed pictures of famous acquaintances such as Carl Sandburg, John F. Kennedy, Adlai Stevenson. In the corner stood his celebrated cracker barrel where he threw finished articles for the paper, which would go to press when the barrel was full.

Harry's numerous "Golden plans" infuriated segregationists and delighted Southern intellectuals, not because they were absurd but because they were rooted sufficiently in Southern myth to work perfectly well if anyone was astute enough to try them. My father had used the vertical integration plan long before Harry wrote about it, to keep the lunch counter integrated in our store.

The white and Negro stand at the same grocery and supermarket counters; deposit money at the same bank teller's window; pay phone and light bills to the same clerk; walk through the same dime and department stores and stand at the same drugstore counters. It is only when the Negro "sets" that the fur begins to fly.

. . . instead of all those complicated proposals, all the next session needs to do is pass one small amendment which would provide *only* desks in all the public schools of our state—*no seats*. The desks should be those standing-up jobs, like the old-fashioned bookkeeping desk. Since no one in the South pays the slightest attention to a vertical Negro, this will completely solve our problem . . . in fact this may be a blessing in disguise. They are not learning to read sitting down anyway; maybe standing up will help.

His "White Baby Plan" sprung from his mind when he read of two Negro schoolteachers who wanted to see a revival of Olivier's *Hamlet* in a segregated movie theater and borrowed the white children of two friends to take in with them. They were sold tickets without hesitation:

. . . people can pool their children at a central point in each neighborhood, and every time a Negro wants to go to the movies all she need do is pick up a white child—and go.

Eventually the Negro community can set up a factory and manufacture white babies made of plastic, and when they want to go to the opera or to a concert, all they need do is carry that plastic doll in their arms. The dolls, of course, should all have blond curls and blue eyes.

His strength as a humorist was also his weakness as a chronicler of Jews in the South. He couldn't pass up a good story, and since his audience was in the North, he wrote from the perspective of the peddler's pushcart, relevant for the immigrant generation but less valid for Jews born in the South.

However, Golden punched the paunches of a lot of Southern politicians who were taking themselves too seriously stirring up fears of the Negro. He had no peer when it came to poking holes in Southern segregation and pointing up the South's hypocrisy by manipulating its mores. His latest plan in November of 1971 would solve the problem of busing and prayer in the schools in one grand step:

Why not amend the Constitution to permit prayers on the bus instead of the classroom?

We could have praying buses and nonpraying buses. The constitutional lawyers will be happy because religion will not be invading the classroom; it will be invading the highways (where it can do the most good). The ministers will be happy, and the intransigent parents will of course commit their kiddies to the buses because the kiddies will get a longer time to pray.

For the life of me, I cannot see what is wrong with this plan. It is not only gradual enough to satisfy Southerners, but it will reinvigorate the parishes.

In the cities with a liberal political structure—Atlanta, Norfolk, New Orleans, and Nashville—the Jewish community moved in behind the gentile leadership as supportive though rarely outspoken partisans of the liberal position of the fifties—that the Supreme Court ruling was the law of the land. But in Birmingham, where the steelworkers know a great deal about dynamite; and in

Montgomery, where a candidate for mayor named Admiral John Crommelin, running on a stridently anti-Semitic platform, could get twenty percent of the vote; and in Jackson, Mississippi, where the state association of the White Citizens' Council is headquartered in a beautiful new building near the state capitol; in the smaller towns across the South that had their own footnotes in the history of the region—towns like Bogalusa, Louisiana; Canton, Mississippi; and Williamston, North Carolina—fear silenced any dissenters, and Southern Jews needed no elaborate rationale for their own silence.

In Montgomery: "It doesn't help the Jews or the Negroes for us to leap out in front of the parade and wave the flag for the Negro thing. Why, they'd blow up the parade!" And in rural Virginia: "We are such a small community, all we can do is give anti-Semites additional ammunition." In Mississippi some Jews joined the White Citizens' Councils, unable to resist pressure from the whites, or because the protective coloration of their grandfathers had become their color, or for more complicated reasons, like this man in a crossroads town in the Delta: "It was clear after the '54 decision that here it was either the Klan or the Citizens' Council. We joined with the Catholics here to keep the Klan out. And I joined to keep the Council from becoming anti-Semitic."

James Silver wrote in *Mississippi: The Closed Society* that just after the Supreme Court decision, the white Citizens' Council "built up a card file of the racial views of nearly every white person in Jackson." A Jewish woman remembered that "it was like the Gestapo down here for a while"—neighborhood canvassing, questionnaires. Would you send your child to an integrated school? Why? Whom did you vote for in the last election? How long have you lived in Jackson?

The Supreme Court decision caught the South off guard and the Citizens' Councils had to crank up the propaganda machinery in a hurry. One leader of the Mississippi Jewish community explained, "They started looking around for materials to send out and they went to the old-line hate groups for help. Lo and behold, we started getting anti-Semitic stuff in the mails. And I mean lots of it."

Suddenly, the Jews were tumbling in the cyclone as well, and in the cruel Mississippi Delta some Jews felt it necessary to proclaim their agreement with the white community. Someone, presumably Jewish, authored an anonymous pamphlet entitled "A Jewish View of Segregation," which the Citizens' Council office in Jackson dis-

318

tributes to this day. It criticizes the Anti-Defamation League for filing a friend of the court brief in the 1954 case (listed alphabetically, the A.D.L. came first among a dozen amicus briefs, which caused one Jew to complain to an official, "I don't mind you slipping in a word or two, but why in hell did you have to head the list?"). The pamphlet denies that the Citizens' Councils are anti-Semitic, pointing out in what most Jews considered a not-so-veiled threat, "Where prominent Jewish leaders have enrolled as members and taken an active part in the duties of the Council, there is no chance of anti-Semitism creeping in . . . [but] the Jew who attempts to be neutral is much like the ostrich. And he has no right to be surprised or amazed when the target he so readily presents is fired upon."

James Silver also reported that, "with a few clergymen in modest rebellion against the status quo, the Citizens' Council eagerly grasped to its bosom a strange new reinforcement in the person of Rabbi Benjamin Schultz." Schultz was the rabbi in Clarksdale, Mississippi, who became a director of the American Jewish League Against Communism, charging in 1951 that George C. Marshall was "a fall guy" in a plot to shield pro-Red activities and that Admiral Nimitz had a "bad record on tolerance of pro-Communists" (for which Schultz was denounced by a combined statement of the A.D.L., the American Jewish Committee, the Union of American Hebrew Congregations, the American Jewish Congress, the Jewish Labor Committee, and the Jewish War Veterans of the U.S.A.). His principles for Mississippi stated, "If Mississippi had its way, Castro would not be in Cuba now; Washington would not have installed him there. If Mississippi had prevailed, the Berlin Wall would have been torn down as soon as it went up. . . . If Mississippi had prevailed pro-Communists would be off the college faculties. . . ." The county churches rewarded his leadership by electing him president of the Coahama Ministerial Association in 1964.

Paul Anthony, for ten years director of the Southern Regional Council, said that "in the period from 1956 to 1958, the Jewish merchant had no choice of whether to join the White Citizens' Council. It was a real blackmail deal."

The Councils did not consist of rag-tag whites on the fringes of society, like so many of the Klan groups of the same era; these were the most respected members of the white financial and business establishment, joined together in what started as a respectable community effort to fight integration. "The money dried up at the banks and loans were called in," said a Jewish storeowner who finally joined because of the pressure. "If you had a restaurant, linen wasn't picked up; if you owned a store the local police could play havoc with you on the fire laws."

"Respectable" efforts soon disintegrated into violence, not openly organized by the Councils but released through the atmosphere of defiance that the demagogues created and nurtured. According to Anti-Defamation League statistics, in the period from 1954 to 1965, there occurred some 227 bombings of Negro churches, homes, and other places of worship, and fifty-six suspects were arrested; there were over a thousand reported instances of racial violence, reprisal, or intimidation, and forty-three deaths of individuals concerned with the civil rights movement. Temples or other Jewish structures were bombed in Atlanta, Nashville, Jackson, and Jacksonville, Florida, and undetonated dynamite sticks were found on the steps of synagogues in Birmingham, Charlotte, and Gastonia, North Carolina.

Harold Fleming, a former director of the Southern Regional Council, told Allen Krause, a young rabbi interviewing for a doctoral thesis on the role of the Reform rabbis in the desegregation crisis: "I'm not sure the more defeatist rabbis were not right, in practical terms, that there were very stringent limits on how much direct or unilateral action by rabbis could have changed the situation in those days . . . a whole predominantly WASP region . . . had to be moved on this."

Alfred Hero's 1965 study of *The Southerner and World Affairs* contains a chapter on Southern Jews which is astute in its hunches while acknowledging the need for a much larger sample before he could make any final conclusions. It is, to my knowledge, the only effort at polling Southern Jewish opinion on a variety of matters, although it represents a cross-section of only two hundred interviews.

Hero found small-town Jews particularly elusive, and couldn't decide whether they were more careful (and conservative) with strangers or less honest (and therefore more liberal) because they simply wanted to appear more worldly to a university researcher asking them opinions for an academic study. He did note that the same couple would answer more conservatively when there were other Jews around than they would in a private interview; and that most admitted that they projected a more conservative public image than their true opinions warranted during periods of increased racial tension.

He observed that "Jews throughout the South have been on the average better off, better educated, more concentrated in elevated social and occupational groups, and more urban than gentiles—all factors associated with greater interest, knowledge, and exposure to world affairs." One out of seven read publications like *The Atlantic* or the Sunday edition of the *New York Times*, and three-fifths read weekly magazines like *Life, Time* or *Newsweek.* "The proportion of Jews accepting isolationist or neo-isolationist thinking," he reported, "was roughly half that among gentiles of similar education and occupation in the same communities."

On race: "The informants were more than twice as likely as the Southern Protestant white average . . . to feel that desegregation is both inevitable and, in general, desirable in the long run, and only about one-third as inclined as the latter to believe that Negroes are constitutionally inferior. . . . Only a handful of Jews were actively racist beyond the conformity apparently required for maintaining their business and professional careers in strongly segregationist communities."

He noted that "the smaller and more homogeneous the backgrounds of the local Jewish community, the more conservative its international attitudes," and that new converts to the Episcopal, Methodist, and Presbyterian churches (he found that Unitarian converts were more liberal) "have been even more careful to adopt the more conservative attitudes prevalent in the gentile power structure." He added that "many of these prosperous Jews married above their social origins. Insecurity about acceptance among the gentile elite is probably at work in a number of cases."

He observed an ambivalence in attitudes toward the liberal national Jewish organizations like the Anti-Defamation League, the American Jewish Congress, and the National Council of Jewish Women. "While wanting to separate themselves in the local gentile mind from them and their egalitarian pronouncements and accusing them of generating anti-Semitism among segregationists, they have wanted the support of these agencies in case of anti-Semitic developments in the region."

Through most of the civil rights era, at least until the urban riots in the North polarized white opinion, Northern Jews formed the bedrock support for liberal causes in America. When the

321

differences between good and evil in the South were easily defined, Northern Jews assumed that Southern Jews could tell the difference too—Bull Connor, Ross Barnett, Sheriff Lawrence Rainey, Leander Perez—such clear-cut symbols of evil, how could any Jews remain silent?

The era would witness several classic confrontations between Northern and Southern Jewish values on race: the civil rights lawyers who served in the South during the sixties; the civil rights workers in Mississippi during the summer of 1964; and the events surrounding the tension-packed days in Birmingham when Bull Connor's police dogs and fire hoses shocked world opinion.

In the period between May 1 and July 1 of 1963, Bull Connor made good his pledge to "fill the jails" in Birmingham by arresting more than ten thousand people, mostly blacks of less than eighteen years of age, and herding them into makeshift detention centers. In the full presence of network news cameras, on May 4, while Martin Luther King and the Reverend Fred Shuttlesworth were in jail, over five hundred blacks gathered in Kelly Ingram Park to protest police brutality; Connor ordered them to leave, and then ordered his police to disperse them with billy clubs and dogs, backed up by powerful gushes of water from fire hoses. Reporters heard him screaming gleefully, "I want to see the dogs work. Look at those niggers run!" Newspapers all over the world carried pictures of black students huddling together to protect themselves from the force of the water, and snarling dogs ripping the clothing of fleeing people.

At that moment, sharing in the dismay, the Conservative Rabbinical Assembly of America was holding its annual meeting at Kiamesha Lake in the Catskill Mountains, and during the discussion over a resolution condemning the violence at Birmingham, a number of the rabbis gave impassioned speeches, saying, "The time has come, not for lip service, but for action." A delegation of nineteen volunteered to go to Birmingham and join the protest; they raised the money for the trip right in the Assembly meeting hall. When the wire services picked up the story, the Birmingham Jewish community called an emergency meeting and selected a delegation to meet the plane at the airport and urge the rabbis to return home. Needless to say, the rabbis who were coming to the South out of moral commitment were astonished.

Two of the rabbis met with the group until dawn. What they heard was the story of a Jewish community in panic. For months

322

King had led an economic boycott on the downtown which had all but destroyed the Jewish storeowners, effectively blocking Negro trade and frightening off the whites from the most elegant stores— Pizitz's, Loveman's—not to mention the less fancy shops selling work clothes and pegged pants, all being driven out of business. In addition, several sticks of dynamite with a faulty fuse had been discovered on the steps of the synagogue, and the leadership was asking the rabbis to return home before they involved the Jewish community any deeper in turmoil. But the rabbis were determined and one of them tried to calm the townsfolk: "We are committed; this has nothing to do with you so do not worry." (One of the community leaders told me, "We couldn't convince them; they knew all about it.")

The rabbis stayed at the Negro motel owned by A. G. Gaston, which was the Reverend Dr. King's headquarters for the entire campaign. They spoke in the black churches and taught some of the students "Hava Nagila" to sing in the marches, but the Birmingham newspapers did not report their presence. The next day, they refused to meet with any of the Jewish community leaders again. But news leaked out that the rabbis were planning to march at the head of a demonstration planned for Friday morning, and the local leadership, in another frenzy at so public a display of Jewish involvement, demanded another meeting.

They met with eight rabbis in Karl Freedman's law offices, until three o'clock in the morning. Freedman started the meeting off with a determined plea to the rabbis that ended with, "You'll kill my wife and daughters"; at one point, a participant remembered that one of the rabbis said, "The Jews have too long been passive; we know the risks; we may be shot at, but it is time." Dora Roth remembers telling them, "You will go back on the plane heroes and leave us to gather the wrath. I hope your convictions are strong enough to carry the blood of my children on your hands."

"The contact was an aching one," wrote Rabbi Andre Ungar of Westwood, New Jersey, who sat in on that meeting. "What seemed to stun them most agonizingly was the realization that we were at the call of the Negro leadership rather than vice versa. It appeared to outrage the natural order of things."

A break in negotiations canceled the march and the rabbis returned to their congregations in the North on Friday, in time for Sabbath services that evening. Later, when the motel was bombed, the Jewish community would blame it on the audacity of the rabbis who they claimed affronted Southern custom by staying in a black motel; but with King headquartered there, Birmingham extremists needed no further provocation.

When I graduated from Yale Law School in 1963, Northern Jewish law students looked to a few years in Mississippi as a major career option, rivaling clerkships, the Justice Department, and Wall Street law firms as the most romantic, exciting, and worth-while way to dig in on the firing line, to matter for the first time in their lives, helping the black man to win the only battle that seemed important. One civil rights leader in Mississippi estimated that in the decade since 1960, "as many as ninety percent of the civil rights lawyers in Mississippi were Jewish"—the best students in their classes at Harvard, Yale, and Columbia law schools, ready to summon the Bill of Rights against the last frontier of officially sanctioned injustice in America.

They were an intense, brooding, brilliant group who worked fifteen hours a day in the cluttered law offices of the NAACP Legal Defense Fund, the American Civil Liberties Union, or the Lawyers' Committee for Civil Rights Under Law, analyzing the welfare standards, the bail system, the arrest procedures, the justice of the peace rulings—racing up to Greenwood to seek a parade permit for a group of demonstrators, dashing over to Tupelo to gather evidence for a complaint for the Justice Department on jail beatings or intimidation. It was a heady, engrossing time, when the law and the state met point-to-point and a man was as good as the quickness of his mind, the wellsprings of his energies, and the courage he could muster.

Most of them arrived without any commitment to the South, with a strong sense of service to the concept of equality, with no knowledge of the poverty, deprivation, and desperation of the rural Southern blacks, but somehow ready to hand themselves over for a back-breaking day-and-night challenge for the experience of it. Many of them came to lose themselves in the passion of the movement, until they found their way and decided what they really wanted to do with their lives.

The Mississippi Negroes came to know and trust them, for they were ubiquitous and talented, and the very term "Jew federal lawyer" came to mean a sympathetic, hard-headed man with the tools to help when the trouble started. The trust for the Jewish lawyers spilled over into trust for the Southern Jews as well.

324

The civil rights activists—lawyers, organizers, and black leaders—stayed to themselves and rarely mixed in the white community. "We were all pretty much isolated," said Armand Derfner, a friend from Yale days who spent three years in Mississippi. "Your friends were all in the movement and when we got together, it was hard to talk about anything else. The problems were so overwhelming and the pressure so intense that it was an all-consuming experience." Annually, they would gather together for a freedom seder at Passover, but no local Jews ever came.

"It was a terrible period," recalled Marian Wright Edelman, the first black woman lawyer in Mississippi, who headed the NAACP Legal Defense Fund office for four years. "There was a time when bombs were going off in Jackson twice a week—one day a friend's house, one day the temple. We were all anxious."

The Jackson Jewish community had little contact with them, except to invite them occasionally to a Sabbath meal at home when a young couple new in town showed up at the temple. "The Jackson Jews were hospitable at first," said one of the lawyers there in the middle sixties, "wanting to respond nicely to outsiders. Later, they were just too frightened to have anything to do with us. I remember one lawyer and his wife, new in town, who were casually invited to a party at the temple and then were asked to sneak out the back door when the host found out what they did for a living."

A handful of the lawyers transformed themselves into Southerners, or at least embraced the more superficial aspects of the Southern style. To begin with, it was easier to deal with rural sheriffs and judges if they blended in a little, so they developed Southern accents to cover their Bronx roots, and an easier manner to mask their taut nerves, and they learned to stand around with hands in their hip pockets and scratch themselves in just the right place when talking to a deputy. Perhaps they themselves were tasting the pressure the South puts on outsiders to conform. I knew one who dated an Ole Miss majorette and lived just off fraternity row in Oxford; another who went out with the Queen of the Natchez Pilgrimage; and a third who married (or "stole away" as one of the Jackson Jews put it) the daughter of the leading segregationist attorney in town. In short, they became Mississippi as all hell on the surface, just to try on a new up-front identity for a few years. But they were not Southern enough to reassure the Mississippi Jewish community. "It was just too dangerous to be friends with them," said one Jewish woman. "They were too well known as troublemakers, and when they came to dinner on Friday night, all they wanted to talk about was civil rights. It was unpleasant to be with them."

The civil rights workers who flooded into Mississippi in the summer of 1964 had neither the protective cloak of the law nor the relative safety of the major cities to save them—committed, middle-class youth, more than sixty percent of them Jewish, from Northern schools, products of the Kennedy era of the hero in politics, looking to the Peace Corps and service to the poor as outlets for their energies, ready to move, in James Silver's words, "in the shadow of . . . death."

A Jewish couple in Jackson, Mississippi, for twenty-five years ("newcomers," they said), remembered that "the young civil rights workers were easier to get to know than the lawyers. They were polite and idealistic and just down for the summer to help and learn. But when we heard they would be living with Negroes, without adult supervision, out in the sticks—even the girls—well, we knew there'd be trouble."

Michael Schwerner and Andrew Goodman were two of those students, working under the aegis of the Council of Federated Organizations (COFO), a confederation of the major civil rights organizations working in Mississippi at that time. The two of them would share a common grave with a slim, twenty-year-old black named James Chaney, while trying to register black voters near Philadelphia and Meridian, Mississippi. "Sure I felt sorry for those boys," said an old German Jewish merchant, the fourth generation in Mississippi. "But nobody asked them to come down here and meddle with our way of life."

The Jews in Mississippi were alarmed after the death of the civil rights workers, and concerned over the publicity in New York and Mississippi. "The local papers liked to call attention to the fact the boys were Jews," one Jewish leader said. "That way, they could explain it all away as outside agitators who got what they deserved."

After the murders, the federal law enforcement activity in the state of Mississippi was strengthened, the FBI opened up a concerted effort to break the back of the Klan, and the Voting Rights Act in 1965 would pave the way for more enduring changes. Fittingly, as Mississippi became a better place for blacks, it would become a better place for Jews as well, both Northern and Southern.

EPILOGUE

The Changing Provincials

*It's important for me to be a Southerner generally
in the same way as it's important for a Jew to be a
Jew, or whatever else a man might be. . . . I was
born into it—the South—and rather than repudiate it,
it seems better to me to try to realize the positive
benefits there are from the life-situation I grew up in.*

Self-Interviews,
James Dickey

T H E death of the three young men in Mississippi led directly to
the passage of the Voting Rights Act of 1965, which brought a
special kind of revolution to the South—political gains for the
blacks, to be sure, but along with it a revolution in atmosphere, in
tone, and in hope. Whereas in 1965 there were fewer than fifty
black elected officials in the South, by 1972 there were more than
eleven hundred. In Mississippi in 1965 the figures on registration
of blacks rose from less than five percent of the eligible black voters
to more than sixty percent. The South was changing, and in the
process, so was the definition of what it meant to be a Southerner.

This book has been a personal journey for me, struggling
through the web of childhood memories, to reconcile what I
thought were unresolvable conflicts of growing up Jewish in the
South. But the definitions are changing in a South that is booming
economically, a South with a larger percentage of school integration than the North, with black sheriffs and school board members,
with voices of moderation more firmly rooted than at any time in its
history. The passions of the past are still present and can explode

329

into violence at any moment; the bitter memories cannot be erased quickly on either side. But, in so many ways, the South of today is the most optimistic section of America.

The provincials are changing too, for the small-town era that molded so much of the culture of Southern Jews in this century is vanishing, as the Jews follow the rest of America to the cities and the suburbs.

"There used to be two or three Jew stores in every one of these towns," said the leathery old man in a rocking chair at an eastern North Carolina crossroads hotel. "Since the chains came, every one of these towns looks alike."

In the last thirty years, the Deep South has been losing population and the cities in the border states have been growing (though slowly; see Appendix D). Because of military bases, the numbers increased dramatically during the war but, omitting the explosive Jewish immigration to Miami, the overall number today is about the same as it was in 1948 (about 250,000). With the rest of the South growing, the ratio of Jews to the rest of the population has declined in every Southern state (the total in all the South is less than the number of Jews in the state of New Jersey). The big growth today is in Dallas, Houston, and Atlanta, and to a lesser extent in Richmond, New Orleans, and Charlotte.

The future of Jews in the South then is tied to the future of the *urban* South, and there is every indication that the region will continue to prosper, that the rate of out-migration for Negroes and presumably other Southerners will continue to decrease, and that Jews will remain a small but constant presence in the major Southern cities. Their future culturally and religiously is another matter, though not any more pessimistic than the future of the American Jewish community as a whole. It is wrapped up in the extent to which cultural and educational institutions grow and reach for the young; it will be influenced by the future of the State of Israel, and how young people in the South respond culturally to its fascinations; and it will be touched by world politics—the future of the three million Jews of Russia, who might migrate to Israel or even America to replay the drama of the last century and renew Jewish life. When Ernest Van Den Haag, in his book *The Jewish Mystique*, predicted the complete assimilation and disappearance of Jews in America within a hundred years, he cautioned that "history abounds with unforeseen elements which . . . can make nonsense of the most rational prediction. Who could have predicted Hitler in 1920—fifteen years before he started killing Jews? . . . Who therefore would be presumptuous enough to predict the fate of the Jews from now on?"

My father and I talked recently about the old arguments among Jews concerned with dual loyalty at the time the State of Israel was established. "There's not so much patriotism in the South anymore," he said. "The fifties was the high point of it in our lives, when Jews were afraid their friends would think they were less of an American if they supported Israel. People today are learning to live with dual loyalties—racial pride, state pride, religious pride. And it's easier now. For one thing, the South isn't as demanding of its people as it used to be."

The superpatriotism in the South, with its particular regional intensity, was so absorbing that it tended to block out other loyalties. Now, with the end of isolation and the arrival of the South into the nation, it is easier to be Jewish in the South just as it is easier to be black, Catholic, or hold minority views there.

I have written this book to capture the texture of growing up Jewish in the South, to uncover the linkages between Southern Jews and the wrenching drama of Southern history. I also hoped to create a new prism to cast fresh light on the conventional view of the South. I love the South and that's the hell of it. It frightens me and inspires me, it excites me and threatens me. I am bloated with its memories and haunted by its devils.

But events have overcome the three-hundred-year contest for the soul of the South. For me, a reconciliation of these conflicts goes to the nature of my being. It is as if the New South has released the Jewish instincts inside me, and drawn me closer to the roots of each in the process. They cannot be unraveled, I have learned; together, they are the home I seek and the man I am.

331

Appendixes, Bibliography, Acknowledgments, and Index

APPENDIX A

Jews Elected to Office in the South, 1800–1920

THIS is a partial list of Jews elected to office in the South who are mentioned in the literature:

David Emanuel, the sixth governor of Georgia in 1801;

Jacob Henry, elected to the North Carolina legislature in 1808 (his eloquent speech in defense of his seat in the face of a constitutional provision requiring belief in the New Testament was one of the first statements on Jewish rights in America);

Joseph Darmstadt and Benjamin Wolfe, on the Richmond (Virginia) Common Council in the early nineteenth century;

Solomon Jacobs, acting mayor of Richmond, Virginia, in 1815;

Gustavus A. Myers, elected to the Richmond, Virginia, city council in 1829 and reelected twenty-six consecutive times;

Isaac Herbert Kempner, Adrian Levy, and Michael Seeligson, all of whom served as mayor of Galveston, Texas, in the antebellum period;

Phillip Phillips of Mobile, elected to the Alabama legislature in 1844 and to the United States Congress in 1853;

David S. Kaufman and Adolphus Sterne, elected to the United States Congress from Texas in the 1840's (Sterne once addressed the Texas state legislature in the Choctaw Indian dialect);

Jacob De Cordova of Houston, elected first to the Texas House of Representatives and to the Texas Senate in 1847;

Judah P. Benjamin of New Orleans, Louisiana, United States senator and attorney general, secretary of state, secretary of war to the Confederacy; Henry Hyams of New Orleans, lieutenant governor of Louisiana in 1859; Edwin Moise of New Orleans, attorney general of Louisiana and speaker of the Louisiana House;

N. Greenwald, alderman in Brownsville, Tennessee, in 1860;

Jonas Levy, mayor of Little Rock, Arkansas, from 1860 to 1865;

Rabbi Jacob Peres of Memphis, Tennessee, elected president of the Board of Education in 1865;

Paul Schuster, alderman in Memphis, Tennessee, in the late 1860's; William Lovenstein, member of the Virginia House of Delegates and the Virginia Senate in the 1870's;

Aaron Haas, elected to the city council in Atlanta, Georgia, in the 1870's (he was the first mayor pro-tem in Atlanta history in 1875);

Samuel Weil of Atlanta, Georgia, state legislature in the 1870's;

Jacob Ezekiel, a member of the Richmond, Virginia, city council in 1871;

Franklin Moses, Reconstruction governor of South Carolina in 1872 (nicknamed the "robber governor");

Mathias Cohn, member of the Arkansas state legislature and of the first Board of Trustees of the University of Arkansas in 1877;

Henry Nachman, mayor of Lake City, South Carolina, around 1880 (when he insisted he couldn't serve because he was not yet a citizen, the city council passed an ordinance saying the mayor needn't be a citizen);

David Mayer, founder of the Atlanta school board in 1870 and a member or officer of the board until 1890. Walter H. Rich, Oscar Pappenheimer, and Mrs. Victor H. Kriegshaber also served on the school board in the early 1900's;

Max Gunst, elected to the Richmond, Virginia, city council in 1896, served forty consecutive years;

Jacob Haas, elected to the Atlanta, Georgia, city council in the 1890's, and Joseph Hirsch, elected to the Atlanta city council and as mayor pro-tem in 1896; Aaron Elsas and Max Kutz to the Atlanta city council in the early 1900's;

L. S. Ehrich as mayor and Mark Moses to the town council of Georgetown, South Carolina, in the 1890's;

Henry Alexander, a member of the Georgia state legislature at the turn of the century;

Benjamin Franklin Jonas of New Orleans, United States senator from Louisiana in the early 1900's;

Victor Hexter to the city council in Dallas, Texas, in the early 1900's;

Sol Bloomberg, Barney Bowman, and Joseph Wallerstein, members of the Richmond, Virginia, city council in the early 1900's;

Joe Levy, alderman in Galveston in early 1900's; I. H. Kempner, mayor of Galveston, 1917; Mrs. I. H. Kempner, Galveston school board, 1920's;

Charles Cohn, on the Nashville, Tennessee, city council in the 1920's;

Edmond Kalmon, mayor of Albany, Georgia, in the 1920's;

Harris Newman of Wilmington, elected to the North Carolina senate in the 1920's.

APPENDIX B

Jews Elected to Public Office in the South since 1945

THIS is a list I gathered informally as I traveled through the South, and is in no way comprehensive. Florida is omitted because the Southern half of the state makes it so atypical (see Appendix D).

ALABAMA

Bessemer: Bennet Cherner, state legislator
Birmingham: Ben Erdreich, state legislator
Demopolis: Jerome Levy, city councilman
Florence: Harold May, chairman of Board of Education for 24 years
Mobile: Mayer "Mike" Perloff, state legislator
Sulligent: Aaron Fine, state legislator
Tuscaloosa: Bert Banks, state legislator

ARKANSAS

Eldorado: I. L. Pesses, mayor
Pine Bluff: Sam Levine, state legislator

GEORGIA

Albany: Harry Goldstein, county commissioner
Alma: Nathan Cohen, mayor
Athens: Joel B. Joel, state legislator
Atlanta: Joel Fryer, Superior Court judge; Harold Klein, member of the Board of Education; Elliot Levitas and Sydney Marcus, state legislators; Sam Massell, mayor and vice mayor

337

Augusta: Leopold Mothner, city council; Nolman Simowitz, county commissioner; Harry Stein, city councilman
Brunswick: Joe Isenberg, state legislator
Camilla: I. Macey, city councilman
Carollton: Ted Hirsch, mayor
Fitzgerald: Abe Kruger, vice mayor and city councilman
Greensboro: Don Lacoff and Ben Weinstein, city councilmen
Louisville: Herman Rashkin, mayor
Macon: Robert A. Berlin, state legislator
Savannah: Leo Center, Benny Garfunkel, and Jay Shoob, city aldermen; Alan Gaynor, state legislator; Sol Clark, appointed by Governor Jimmy Carter, then elected Court of Appeals judge
Savannah Beach: George F. Schwarz, city councilman
Sparta: Charles Friedman, city councilman

LOUISIANA

Baton Rouge: Alvin Rubin, federal judge
Natchitoches: Sylvan Friedman, state senator
New Orleans: Peter Beer, Walter Marcus, Eddie Sapir, city councilmen; Jerome Winberg, Criminal District Court judge

MISSISSIPPI

Alligator: Saul Klein, mayor
Cleveland: Louis Kaplan, alderman
Hazlehurst: Paul Kemp, alderman and mayor
Louise: William Sklar, mayor
Rolling Rock: Sam Rosenthal, mayor for 42 years (until 1969)
Rosedale: Mickey Dattel, mayor and city councilman
Sunflower: Harry Dattel, alderman; Samuel Labovitz, alderman
Yazoo City: Harry Applebaum, state legislator and mayor

NORTH CAROLINA

Chapel Hill: Steve Bernholz, city councilman
Charlotte: Arthur Goodman, state legislator; Elliot Schwartz, solicitor
Durham: E. J. Evans, six terms as mayor; Jack Preiss, city councilman
Fayetteville: Monroe Evans, two terms as mayor
Gastonia: Marshal Rauch, state legislator; Leon Schneider, mayor
Goldsboro: Lionel "Sloppy" Weil, city councilman
Greensboro: Ben Cone, city councilman and mayor
High Point: Fred Swartzberg, city councilman
Lumberton: Bob Weinstein, city councilman
Wilmington: Hannah Block, city councilwoman; B. D. Schwartz, mayor and state legislator

SOUTH CAROLINA

Abbeville: Joe Savitz, mayor

Barnwell: Solomon Blatt, speaker of the South Carolina House; Herman Mazursky, mayor

Charleston: Arnold Goodstein, state legislator; Lenny Krawcheck and Samuel Rittenberg, state legislators; Irvine Solomon and Dr. Gordon Stine, aldermen

Columbia: Isadore Lourie, state legislator; Hyman Rubin, state senator

Eutawville: Harry Marcus, mayor

Georgetown: Sylvan Rosen, mayor; Meyer Rosen, state legislator; Cecil Schneider, city councilman and mayor pro-tem; Irving Schwartz, city councilman

Greenville: Max Heller, mayor and city councilman

Manning: Julian Weinberg, mayor

Spartanburg: Matthew Poliakoff, state legislator

St. Matthews: Murray Linnett, town councilman

Sumpter: Morris Mazursky, city councilman

Walterboro: Isadore Bogoslow, state legislator

TENNESSEE

Chattanooga: Arvin Rheingold, state legislator

Knoxville: David Blumberg, city councilman

Memphis: Eugene Beerman, state legislator; Josie Berson, first woman (and Jewish) member of governor's cabinet, state Commissioner of Employment, Security, and Manpower; Marvin Brody and J. Alan Hanover, state legislators; Philip Perel, city councilman

Nashville: Leon Gilbert, state legislator; Dan May, city councilman

TEXAS

Austin: Jeffrey Friedman, city councilman

Bellaire: Ben Bronstein, city councilman

Corpus Christi: Albert Lichtenstein, mayor

Dallas: Mrs. Jan Bromberg, trustee of Dallas Independent School District; Irving Goldberg, federal judge; Joe Golman, state legislator; Ted Harris, city councilman; Adeline Harrison, city councilwoman; Abe Meyer, city councilman

Dublin: M. Hoffman, mayor

Galveston: Henry Clark, Galveston school board; Joseph Ginsberg, councilman; David Greenberg, district court judge; Mrs. Ruth Kempner, city councilwoman; Edward Schreiber, mayor; A. R. Schwartz, member, House of Representatives and state Senate

Hearne: J. "Jake" Abrams, mayor

Houston: Rex Braun, state legislator; Mrs. Gertrude Barnstone, board

of Houston Independent School District; Dick Gotlieb, city coun-
cilman; Dr. Leonard Robbins, president of Houston Independent
School District; Mrs. Ruby Sondock, judge, Court of Domestic
Relations
Richmond: Peter Oshman, city councilman
Sherman: Joe Kaufman, mayor; Myer Shosid, city councilman

VIRGINIA

Arlington: Leroy Benheim, state senator
Lynchburg: Abe Cohen, city councilman and vice mayor; Elliott
Schewel, city councilman
Newport News: Alan Diamonstein, state legislator
Norfolk: Bernie Levin, state legislator; V. H. "Pooch" Nusbaum, city
councilman; Stanley Sachs, state legislator
Portsmouth: Lester Schlitz, state legislator
Richmond: Nate Forb, city councilman

APPENDIX C

Threats and Violent Acts against Jewish Institutions, 1950–1970

SUBMISSION BY ANTI-DEFAMATION LEAGUE OF B'NAI B'RITH
BEFORE THE U. S. SENATE SUBCOMMITTEE ON
INVESTIGATIONS OF THE COMMITTEE ON GOVERNMENT OPERATIONS
AUGUST 4, 1970

ANTI-DEFAMATION LEAGUE—EXHIBIT A

BOMBINGS, ATTEMPTED BOMBINGS AND BOMB THREATS AGAINST
JEWISH INSTITUTIONS—BACKGROUND 1950–1970

Actual and attempted bombings—and bomb threats—directed against Jewish religious institutions, so far as is known, have taken place only within the last 20 years. The first such manifestations took place in Miami during 1951 when a series of five bombings or attempted bombings were directed against four Jewish institutions between June and December of that year. Of the five episodes, three were abortive—unexploded dynamite sticks being discovered before they went off. In the other two episodes, a partly completed Jewish Center was damaged by a dynamite explosion and a Temple and its school were partly wrecked by a blast that shattered 44 windows.

The five episodes were part of a general campaign of terrorism in Miami during 1951 during which eight other actions took place, some aimed at Jewish institutions, some at public buildings, some at a Negro housing project.

A second series of bombings or attempted bombings was aimed at seven Jewish houses of worship and other institutions in various Southern states between November 11, 1957, and October 12, 1958. These episodes took place at Charlotte and Gastonia, N.C.; at Miami and Jacksonville, Fla.; at Nashville, Tenn., Birmingham, Ala., and Atlanta, Ga. The Charlotte and Gastonia attempts were abortive.

In a report published at that time, the Anti-Defamation League noted several patterns in the 1957–58 bombings and attempted bombings. In all cases, an apparent attempt was made to avoid injury to human life and to time the explosions so that they could only cause property damage—an apparent attempt to intimidate the local Jewish communities in the cities mentioned. Almost identical zippered satchels were used to conceal the dynamite in the Gastonia and Birmingham cases. The Miami and Nashville episodes took place on the same day. The Jacksonville and Birmingham episodes took place on successive days. In all cases, with the possible exception of Birmingham, the dynamite used was reported to be of a common variety, readily available for sale or easily stolen.

In four cases—Nashville, Miami, Jacksonville and Atlanta—telephone calls were placed to prominent local individuals by anonymous persons identifying themselves as members of a so-called "Confederate Underground." It was generally believed by law enforcement authorities that one group of individuals was responsible for all seven of the episodes.

The ADL said in its report that the similarity of the dynamitings indicated that these bombings and bombing attempts were part of a criminal conspiracy cutting across state lines. So far as we know, no arrests were made, except in the case of the blast at the Temple in Atlanta on October 12, 1958. In that case, five men were indicted—all of them affiliated with the racist, anti-Semitic organization called the National States Rights Party. One of the defendants was tried, his first trial ending in a hung jury and a mistrial, the second trial in an acquittal. So far as is known, none of the other defendants was ever brought to trial.

The National States Rights Party is still active, with headquarters in Savannah, Ga. One of its long-time leaders is an announced candidate for Governor of Georgia this year. The party publishes a monthly propaganda paper called The Thunderbolt with a paid circulation, reported to the U.S. Post Office in the Fall of 1969, averaging 32,589 for the 12 months preceding filing date, and 49,655 for the issue nearest filing date. These circulation figures are believed to be far higher than the actual membership of the NSRP, although the group has small, scattered units in a number of states, both in the South and elsewhere around the country.

The decade of the 1960s reveals the following picture:

In 1960, there were 30 bomb threats and four actual explosions—the latter including the following: A molotov cocktail thrown at a temple in Los Angeles, a dynamite bombing at a synagogue in Kansas City, Mo., one explosion at a temple in Springfield, Mass., and a firebombing at a synagogue in Gadsden, Ala. The bomb threats took place in various states—California, Florida, Texas, Tennessee, Illinois, Wisconsin, Rhode Island, New York and the District of Columbia among them.

In 1961, there were dynamite blasts at two synagogues in Chicago, and a molotov cocktail was tossed at a synagogue in New York, a total of three bombings. There were two abortive attempts and five threats.

In 1962, a bomb exploded in a box containing religious garments at a temple in Philadelphia, and in Miami, dynamite sticks were found by police in front of a temple. The year saw half-a-dozen bomb threats.

In 1963, there was only one episode—a bomb threat against a synagogue in Gloucester, Mass., while in 1964, there were no recorded bombing episodes of any kind. There were two bomb threats recorded in 1965—one in Dallas, Texas, the other in Springfield, Mass., while in 1966, there were no recorded bombings, attempted bombings or bomb threats.

In September, 1967, a temple was bombed in Jackson, Miss., and two months later, the home of its rabbi was bombed.

In 1968, there were three actual bombings. A dynamite blast at a temple in Meridian, Miss., in May caused considerable damage to a religious school attached to the temple, and blew out one wall of the temple itself. In June, the Hebrew Theological College at Skokie, Ill., was the target of a home-made pipe bomb that was thrown five feet short of the building itself and caused damage to windows only. In August, a small cherry-bomb was thrown outside a temple in Whittier, Calif., injuring students in front of the building. In October, a fire-bomb was thrown at a Hebrew school in Brooklyn, N.Y. Earlier in the year, fire-bombs and anti-Semitic signs were found outside the offices of a Jewish Educational and Vocational Services agency in St. Louis; the unexploded bombs were made from liquor bottles filled with gasoline and cloth wicks. The wicks had not, apparently, been ignited.

During 1969, there were one dynamite explosion, four fire-bombings and two bomb threats. The dynamite explosion took place on January 11, 1969, at Shaare Tikvah Synagogue in Temple Hills, Prince Georges County, Md., and damage was heavy, being estimated at $150,000. The four fire-bombings took place as follows: On March 15, 1969, at a Hebrew day school in Plainfield, N.J., on April 29 at the Hebrew Shelter Home in Hartford, Conn., and on May 6 and September 12 at two different synagogues in Brooklyn. The September episode took place during a break in the Rosh Hashanah high holiday services, as worshipers were leaving the building. The bomb threats during 1969 took place at the Sunday school of a reform temple in Shreveport, La., while classes were in session. After the phone call, children were evacuated but no bomb was found.

For the year 1970, through July 15, there has been one dynamite blast, one episode involving explosive devices described in one report as "noise-makers," two fire-bombings, and one bomb threat. In February, the doors of a Seattle synagogue were splintered by a dynamite explosion. The "noise-makers" episode took place on March 25, when two explosive devices were tossed at a Jewish Center, in the Bronx, N.Y. The two fire-bombings took place on June 18 at a temple in Elizabeth, N.J., and on July 7, when two fire bombs were thrown at a temple in Rockaway Beach, Queens County, N.Y. The one bomb threat so far this year took place on March 18 and was received, via mail and telephone, at a temple in Springfield, Mass.

Appendixes

The pattern of recent years—especially 1969 and 1970—appears to show a tentative trend toward more frequent use of fire bombs and molotov cocktails, easily made from bottles, gasoline, and cloth wicks.

ANTI-DEFAMATION LEAGUE—EXHIBIT B

BOMBINGS, ATTEMPTED BOMBINGS, AND BOMB THREATS
AT JEWISH INSTITUTIONS

	Dynamite explosions	Other explosions	Fire bombings	Attempted bombings	Bomb threats	Totals
1960	2		2		30	34
1961	3			2	5	10
1962	1			1	6	8
1963					1	1
1964						
1965					2	2
1966						
1967	2					2
1968	2	[1] 1	[2] 1	1		5
1969	1		4		2	7
1970 (½ year)	1	[3] 1	2		1	5
Total	12	2	9	4	47	74

[1] Cherry bombs.
[2] Unignited fire bomb.
[3] Noise maker.

ANTI-DEFAMATION LEAGUE—EXHIBIT C

BOMBINGS AND BOMB THREATS AT JEWISH INSTITUTIONS,
JANUARY 1, 1969–JULY 15, 1970

1969

January 11, 1969: Temple Hills, Prince Georges County, Md., Shaare Tikvah Synagogue bombed. $150,000 damage. Dynamite used; heavy damage.

February 2, 1969: Shreveport, La., Bomb threat by telephone at Sunday school of reform temple.

March 15, 1969: Plainfield, N.J., Fire bomb attack on Hebrew day school.

April 29, 1969: Hartford, Conn., Fire bombs at Hebrew Shelter Home.

May 6, 1969: Brooklyn, N.Y., Fire bomb at Congregation Yetev Lov D'Satmar Synagogue.

September 12, 1969: Brooklyn, N.Y., Kehilath Yakov Synagogue fire bombed during Rosh Hashanah (just after services).

November 13, 1969: North Hills, Long Island, N.Y., bomb threat at Temple Judea. No bomb found.

1970

February 6, 1970: Seattle, Wash., Synagogue doors splintered by dynamite.

March 18, 1970: Springfield, Mass., Bomb threat received by telephone and mail at Temple Kadimah.

March 25, 1970: The Bronx, N.Y., two explosive devices thrown at Mosholu Jewish Center.

June 18, 1970: Elizabeth, N.J., Temple B'nai Israel fire-bombed.

July 7, 1970: Rockaway Beach, Long Island, N.Y., two fire bombs at Congregation Derech Emunoh.

ANTI-DEFAMATION LEAGUE—EXHIBIT D

FIRES AND ARSONS AT JEWISH INSTITUTIONS

	Arsons	Attempts	Threats	Total
1960	2			2
1961	6	1	1	8
1962	4			4
1963		1		1
1964	2			2
1965	3	1		4
1966	4			4
1967	2			2
1968	7			7
1969	15	1		16
1970 (½ year)	10			10
Total................				60

ANTI-DEFAMATION LEAGUE—EXHIBIT E

FIRES AND ARSONS AT JEWISH INSTITUTIONS,
JANUARY 1, 1969–JULY 15, 1970

1969

January 1–2, 1969: Brooklyn, N.Y., Series of three small fires set at Manhattan Beach Jewish Center.

January 3, 1969: Far Rockaway, Long Island, N.Y., Fire destroyed Shaaray Tefila Synagogue. Cost to replace synagogue estimated at $1,000,000.

January 20, 1969: Brooklyn, N.Y., "Suspicious" fire at Yeshiva Magen David Synagogue. Student received summons for criminal mischief.

January 23, 1969: Far Rockaway, Long Island, N.Y., Fire at Hebrew Institute of Long Island.

January 30, 1969: Brooklyn, N.Y., Fire at Yeshivath Torah Vadaath of Crown Heights. School supplies and texts destroyed.

February 16, 1969: Brooklyn, N.Y., Three-alarm fire, destroyed gymnasium at United Lubavitcher Yeshiva.

March, 1969: Philadelphia, Pa., Fires set to mail placed in door at Congregation Beth Zion Synagogue.

March, 1969: Manchester, N.H., Arson attempt at Jewish Community Center.

May 15, 1969: Newark, N.J., Fire at Temple B'nai Abraham. Arson suspected.

July 8, 1969: Manchester, N.H., Vandals set fire to rabbi's office at Temple Adath Yeshurun. Valuable records and book manuscript destroyed.

July 14, 1969: Brooklyn, N.Y., A "deliberately" set fire damaged a room at the Yeshiva of Flatbush.

October 5, 1969: Los Angeles, Calif., Fire at Hillel Building at University of Southern California. Damage estimated at $10,000.

November 28, 1969: Brooklyn, N.Y., Fire gutted Yeshiva Marbestse Torah. $100,000 damage estimates.

December 7, 1969: Queens, N.Y., Fire set at Woodside Jewish Center. Three teenagers charged with setting fire.

1970

January 19, 1970: The Bronx, N.Y., Fire damaged Congregation Ahavath Torah Synagogue. Scrolls and religious objects destroyed. Arson charged by City Fire Marshal's office.

January 28, 1970: The Bronx, N.Y., Fire set at Minsker Congregation. Prayer books and lobby area damaged. Synagogue also smeared with swastikas.

February 9, 1970: Brooklyn, N.Y., Fire at Congregation Kasser Torah. Ark containing sacred scrolls damaged.

February 12, 1970: Brooklyn, N.Y., Fire caused extensive damage to Yeshiva of Flatbush. Arson suspected.

May 6, 1970: Dorchester, Mass., Vandals set fire to sacred scroll in Chezra Shas Synagogue.

May 27, 1970: Dorchester, Mass., Vandals set fire to sacred scroll in Chezra Shas Synagogue for second time.

May 27, 1970: Dorchester, Mass., Two fires set in Agudath Israel Synagogue.

June 2, 1970: Dorchester, Mass., Fire of suspicious origin damaged Congregation Chai Odom Meeting House.

June 19, 1970: Dorchester, Mass., Fire of undetermined origin at Hebrew School of the Congregation Agudath Israel. $1,500 damage estimated.

June 19, 1970: Washington, D.C., Fire at Yeshiva High School for Boys in Rockville, Md. Arson suspected. $30,000 damage estimated.

ANTI-DEFAMATION LEAGUE—EXHIBIT F

EXAMPLES OF VANDALISM AND DESECRATION AT JEWISH
INSTITUTIONS, 1969 AND 1970

1969

January 10: Shreveport, La., Swastika painted on a synagogue.

January 23: Far Rockaway, N.Y., Vandalism at Temple Emanuel.

February 4: The Bronx, N.Y., Windows smashed and locks broken at a synagogue.

April 2: New York, N.Y., Temple Rodeph Sholom defaced: "33,000 GI's Dead" painted in orange letters 18 inches high. Episcopal church nearby similarly defaced.

April 3–4: Springfield, Mass., Three Jewish institutions smeared with swastikas.

July 15: Woburn, Mass., Seventy headstones overturned at a Jewish cemetery.

July 22: Massapequa, Long Island, N.Y., Congregation Beth-El vandalized.

July 29: Rockaway, Queens, N.Y., Rocks thrown at Young Israel of Queens.

August 24: Waterbury, Conn., Beth Israel-Sharis Israel synagogue vandalized. Holy Ark damaged.

September 1: Glen Cove, Long Island, N.Y., Temple Tifereth Israel desecrated. $10,000 damage. Obscenities on walls, holy scrolls damaged, furniture smashed, office ransacked.

September 3: Derby, Conn., 200 gravestones overturned at Jewish cemetery.

September 26: Brooklyn, N.Y., Crown Heights Yeshiva vandalized.

October, 1969: Brooklyn, N.Y., Synagogue vandalized twice this month.

October 31: Queens, N.Y., One synagogue and two Jewish centers smeared with swastikas.

November 1: Cheyenne, Wyo., Swastikas painted on front door of Mount Sinai Synagogue.

November 3: Brooklyn, N.Y., Anti-Jewish slogans and swastikas painted outside Congregation B'nai Jacob.

November, 1969: Rumson, N.J., One Jewish cemetery desecrated. Congregation B'nai Israel desecrated four times in one year. Cemetery chapel also desecrated. Alleged KKK activities being investigated by Monmouth County prosecutor.

November 19: Lynn, Mass., Robbery and desecration at synagogue.

December, 1969: Indianapolis, Ind., Three Jewish cemeteries recently reported vandalized.

December 24: Canton, Mass., Temple Beth David desecrated by swastikas and anti-Jewish slogans.

December 26: Wanamassa, N.J., Congregation B'nai Israel cemetery desecrated.

1970

March 12: Bangor, Me., Beth Israel Synagogue damaged by vandals.

April 5: Brooklyn, N.Y., Vandalism at synagogue.

April 13: Springfield, Mass., Swastikas smeared during recent days at two Jewish synagogues.

April 20: San Francisco, Calif., Congregation Knesseth Israel vandalized for second time in two weeks.

June 1: Hartford, Conn., 100 tombstones overturned in recent days in two Jewish cemeteries.

APPENDIX D

Shifts in Jewish Population in Southern States, 1937–1970

I. STATES LOSING POPULATION

	1937	1948	1970
Alabama	12,148	16,290	9,465
Birmingham	*5,300*	*4,200*	*4,040*
Arkansas	6,510	11,320	3,065
Little Rock	*2,500*	*1,143*	*1,200*
Louisiana	14,942	18,320	15,630
New Orleans	*8,700*	*7,500*	*10,150*
Mississippi	4,603	4,210	2,500
Jackson	*235*	*350*	*420*
Tennessee	25,811	28,190	16,710
Chattanooga	*3,800*	*2,200*	*2,250*
Memphis	*13,350*	*6,500*	*9,000*
Nashville	*4,200*	*2,900*	*3,700*

II. STATES GAINING POPULATION

	1937	1948	1970
Florida	21,276	41,000	189,280
Miami	*7,500*	*40,000*	*140,000*
Georgia	23,781	25,311	26,310
Atlanta	*12,000*	*10,217*	*16,500*
Savannah	*3,900*	*4,000*	*3,500*
North Carolina	7,333	8,850	9,450
Charlotte	*720*	*770*	*2,100*
South Carolina	5,905	3,780	7,285
Charleston	*2,540*	*1,892*	*2,850*
Texas	49,196	53,020	65,520
Dallas	*10,400*	*10,000*	*22,000*
Houston	*13,500*	*14,000*	*20,000*
Virginia	25,066	26,142	37,350
Newport News	*1,950*	*1,600*	*2,300*
Norfolk	*8,500*	*7,500*	*8,550*
Virginia	*7,500*	*7,500*	*9,600*
TOTALS	196,571	236,433	382,565*

* Excluding 140,000 in Miami, the figure is 242,565.

BIBLIOGRAPHY

I. Books

Adorno, T. W., et al., *The Authoritarian Personality*. New York: W. W. Norton & Co., 1950.

Allen, Jr., Ivan, *Mayor: Notes on the Sixties*. New York: Simon & Schuster, 1971.

Allport, Gordon W., *The Nature of Prejudice*. New York: Addison-Wesley, 1954.

Baruch, Bernard, *My Own Story*. New York: Henry Holt and Co., 1957.

Birmingham, Stephen, *Our Crowd: The Great Jewish Families of New York*. New York: Dell, 1968.

————, *The Grandees: America's Sephardic Elite*. New York: Harper and Row, 1971.

Boyd, William Kenneth, *The Story of Durham: City of the New South*. Durham, N.C.: Duke University Press, 1927.

Brotz, Howard, *The Black Jews of Harlem*. New York: Free Press of Glencoe, 1964.

Burgess, M. Elaine, *Negro Leadership in a Southern City*. Chapel Hill: University of North Carolina Press, 1960.

Cahnman, Werner J., *Intermarriage and Jewish Life: A Symposium*. New York: Herzl Press and the Jewish Reconstruction Press, 1963.

Caldwell, Erskine, *Deep South: Memory and Observation*. New York: Weybright and Talley, 1966.

Cash, W. J., *The Mind of the South*. New York: Alfred A. Knopf, 1941.

Cauthen, John K., *Speaker Blatt: His Challenges Were Greater*. Columbia, S.C.: R. L. Bryan Co., 1965.

Clark, Elmer T., *The Small Sects in America*. New York: Abingdon Press, 1939.

Dabbs, James McBride, *Haunted by God*. Richmond, Va.: John Knox Press, 1972.

David, Jay (ed.), *Growing Up Jewish*. New York: William Morrow, 1969.

Dinnerstein, Leonard, *Jews in the South*. Baton Rouge: Louisiana State University Press, 1973.

350

Embree, Edwin, and Waxman, Julia, *Investment in People: The Story of the Julius Rosenwald Fund.* New York: Harper and Bros., 1949.
Faulkner, William, *The Town.* New York: Random House, 1957.
Frady, Marshall, *Across a Darkling Plain.* New York: Harper's Magazine Press, 1971.
————, *Wallace.* New York: Meridian Books, 1970.
Frank, Fedora S., *Five Families and Eight Young Men: Nashville and Her Jewry 1850–1861.* Nashville, Tenn.: Tennessee Book Co., 1962.
Galphin, Bruce, *The Riddle of Lester Maddox.* Atlanta, Ga.: Camelot, 1968.
Glazer, Nathan, and Moynihan, Daniel Patrick, *Beyond the Melting Pot.* Cambridge, Mass.: M.I.T. Press, 1963.
————, *American Judaism.* Chicago: University of Chicago Press, 1957.
Glock, Charles Y., and Stark, Rodney, *Christian Beliefs and Anti-Semitism.* New York: Harper & Row, 1966.
Golden, Harry, *A Little Girl Is Dead.* Cleveland: World Publishing Co., 1965.
————, *Forgotten Pioneer.* Cleveland: World Publishing Co., 1963.
————, *Enjoy, Enjoy!* Cleveland: World Publishing Co., 1960.
————, *For 2¢ Plain.* Cleveland: World Publishing Co., 1955.
————, *Only in America.* Cleveland: World Publishing Co., 1958.
————, *The Right Time: An Autobiography.* New York: G. P. Putnam's Sons, 1969.
————, and Rywell, Martin, *Jews in American History.* Charlotte, N.C.: H. A. Stalls Printing Co., 1950.
Greenberg, Mrs. David J., *Through the Years: A Study of the Richmond Jewish Community.* Richmond, Va.: Richmond Jewish Community Council, 1955.
Gordon, Albert I., *Intermarriage: Interfaith, Interracial, Interethnic.* Boston: Beacon Press, 1964.
Halperin, Samuel, *The Political World of American Zionism.* Detroit: Wayne State University Press, 1961.
Heller, Rabbi Max, *Jubilee Souvenir of Temple Sinai 1872–1922.* New Orleans: Congregation Temple Sinai, 1922.
Hero, Alfred O., *The Southerner and World Affairs.* Baton Rouge: Louisiana State University Press, 1965.
James, William, *The Varieties of Religious Experience.* From the Gifford Lectures at Edinburgh, 1902. New York: Random House, Modern Library, 1902.
Kaplan, Benjamin, *The Eternal Stranger: A Study of Jewish Life in the Small Community.* New York: Bookman Associates, 1957.
————, *The Jew and His Family.* Baton Rouge: Louisiana State University Press, 1967.
Karp, Abraham (ed.), *The Jewish Experience in America*, Vols. I–V. Waltham, Mass.: American Jewish Historical Society, 1969.
Katz, Shlomo (ed.), *Negro and Jew: An Encounter in America.* New York: Macmillan, 1967.
Key, Jr., V. O., *Southern Politics: In State and Nation.* New York: Alfred A. Knopf, 1949.

351

Korn, Bertram W., *American Jewry and the Civil War*. (Copyright Jewish Publication Society.) New York: Temple Books, Atheneum, 1970.

———, *The Early Jews of New Orleans*. Waltham, Mass.: American Jewish Historical Society, 1969.

Lee, Ernest (ed.), *Our First Century: 1854–1954*. Memphis, Tenn.: Temple Israel, 1954.

Lee, Harper, *To Kill a Mockingbird*. Philadelphia and New York: J. B. Lippincott Co., 1960.

Marcus, Jacob Rader, *Early American Jewry: The Jews of Pennsylvania and the South 1655–1790*. Philadelphia: Jewish Publication Society of America, 1955.

———, *The Colonial American Jew 1492–1776*. Detroit: Wayne State University Press, 1970.

———, *Memoirs of American Jews 1775–1865*. Vols. I, II, and III. Philadelphia: Jewish Publication Society of America, 1955.

Marx, Gary T., *Protest and Prejudice: A Study of Belief in the Black Community*. New York: Harper Torch Series, Harper & Row, 1969.

Meyer, Isidore S. (ed.), *The American Jew in the Civil War*. New York: American Jewish Historical Society, 1962.

Morris, Willie, *North Toward Home*. New York: Houghton-Mifflin, 1967.

Nathan, Anne, and Cohen, Harry I., *The Man Who Stayed in Texas: The Life of Rabbi Henry Cohen*. New York: Whittlesey House, 1941.

Nugent, Walter T. K., *The Tolerant Populists*. Chicago: University of Chicago Press, 1963.

O'Connor, Flannery, *Mystery and Manners*. New York: Farrar, Straus, and Giroux, 1969.

Olson, Bernard, *Faith and Prejudice*. New Haven: Yale University Press, 1963. (See particularly Chapter 8: The Crucifixion: The Jews and the Christians.)

Percy, Walker, *The Moviegoer*. New York: Alfred A. Knopf, Inc., 1961.

Percy, William Alexander, *Lantern on the Levee*. New York: Alfred A. Knopf, 1953.

Porter, Earl W., *Trinity and Duke 1892–1924: Foundations of Duke University*. Durham, N.C.: Duke University Press, 1964.

Postal, Bernard, and Koppman, Lionel, *A Jewish Tourist's Guide to the U.S.* Philadelphia: Jewish Publication Society of America, 1954.

Reznikoff, Charles, *The Jews of Charleston: A History of an American Jewish Community*. Philadelphia: Jewish Publication Society of America, 1950.

Rothschild, Janice O., *As but a Day: The First Hundred Years 1867–1967*. Atlanta, Ga.: Hebrew Benevolent Congregation, 1967.

Rountree, Moses, *Strangers in the Land*. Philadelphia: Porrance and Co., 1969.

Rubin, Louis D., *The Golden Weather*. New York: Atheneum, 1961.

Sachar, Howard M., *The Course of Modern Jewish History*. Cleveland and New York: World Publishing Co., 1958.

Sanders, Ira E., and Palnick, Elijah E., *The Centennial History of Congregation B'nai Israel*. Little Rock: B'nai Israel, 1966.

Selznick, Gertrude, and Steinberg, Stephen, *The Tenacity of Prejudice: Anti-Semitism in Contemporary America*. New York: Harper & Row, 1969.

Shankman, Sam, *The Peres Family*. Kingsport, Tenn.: Southern Publishers, Inc., 1938.

Sherril, Robert, *Gothic Politics in the Old South*. New York: Ballantine Books, 1968.

Silver, James W., *Mississippi: The Closed Society*. New York: Harcourt, Brace & World, 1963.

Styron, William, *Lie Down in Darkness*. New York: Bobbs-Merrill, 1951.

Sklare, Marshall, *The Jews: Social Patterns of an American Group*. New York: The Free Press, 1958.

Stern, Malcolm, *Americans of Jewish Descent*. Cincinnati: Hebrew Union College Press, 1960.

Talese, Gay, *The Kingdom and the Power*. New York: World Publishing Co., 1969.

Temple Sinai: The First 100 Years. New Orleans: Temple Sinai, 1970.

Tilley, Nannie May, *The Bright Tobacco Industry 1860–1929*. Chapel Hill: University of North Carolina Press, 1948.

Tumin, Melvin M., *An Inventory and Appraisal of Research on American Anti-Semitism*. New York: Freedom Books, 1961.

Van Den Haag, Ernest, *The Jewish Mystique*. New York: Stein and Day, 1969.

Watters, Pat, *The South and the Nation*. New York: Pantheon Books, 1969.

Winkler, John K., *Tobacco Tycoon: The Story of James Buchanan Duke*. New York: Random House, 1942.

Woodward, C. Vann, *The Burden of Southern History*. New York: Vintage Books, 1961.

———, *Tom Watson: Agrarian Rebel*. New York: Macmillan, 1938.

Yaffe, James, *The American Jews: Portrait of a Split Personality*. New York: Random House, 1968.

II. Articles, Pamphlets, Speeches, Documents, Family Histories

Adler, Selig, "Zebulon B. Vance and the Scattered Nation," *Journal of Southern History*, VII (August, 1941), 357–77.

Bloom, Jack, "Journey to Understanding," *Conservative Judaism*, XIX, 4 (Summer 1965). Published by the Rabbinical Assembly.

Clark, Thomas D., "The Post-Civil War Economy in the South," *American Jewish Historical Quarterly*, LV (1966), 424–33.

Cleghorn, Reece, *Radicalism: Southern Style—A Commentary on Regional Extremism of the Right*. Published by the Southern Regional Council and the American Jewish Committee, December, 1968.

Citizens' Councils of Mississippi, *A Jewish View of Segregation.* Anonymous pamphlet published in 1954.

Cohen, Oscar, "Report on Five-Year Study of Anti-Semitism." Paper delivered by the National Program Director of the Anti-Defamation League of B'nai B'rith to the National Community Relations Advisory Council, June 23, 1966.

——, "Public Opinion and Anti-Jewish Prejudice in the South." Paper delivered to the National Executive Committee Meeting of the Anti-Defamation League of B'nai B'rith, September 25, 1969, New Orleans, La.

Dawidowicz, Lucy S., "Can Anti-Semitism Be Measured?" *Commentary*, L, 1 (July, 1970), 36–43.

Dinnerstein, Leonard, "A Neglected Aspect of Southern Jewish History," *American Jewish Historical Quarterly*, LXI, 1 September, 1971, 52–68.

——, "A Note on Southern Attitudes toward Jews," *Jewish Social Studies*, XXXII, 1 (January, 1970), 43–49.

Fein, Isaac M., "Israel Zangwill and American Jewry: A Documentary Study," *American Jewish Historical Quarterly*, LX, 1 (September, 1970), 12–36.

Fichter, Joseph H., and Maddox, George L., *"Religion in the South, Old and New."* From *The South in Continuity and Change*, edited by John Clifford McKinney and Edgar Thompson. Durham, N.C.: Duke University Press, 1965.

Fishman, Joshua A., "Southern City," *Midstream*, VII (September, 1961), 39–56.

Forster, Arnold, and Epstein, Benjamin R., "Report on the Ku Klux Klan," *Facts*, XVI, 3 (May, 1965). Published by the Anti-Defamation League of B'nai B'rith.

Friedman, Murray, "Virginia Jewry and the School Crisis: Anti-Semitism and Desegregation," *Commentary*, XXVII (January, 1959), 17–22.

Gaba, Morton J., "Segregation and a Southern Jewish Community," *Jewish Frontier*, XXI (October, 1954), 12–15.

Geffen, Joel S., "Jewish Agricultural Colonies as Reported in the Pages of the Russian Hebrew Press Ha-Melitz and Ha-Yom," *American Jewish Historical Quarterly*, LX, 4 (June, 1971), 355–82.

Golden, Harry, *Harry Golden on Anti-Semitism, Jews, Christians, Race Relations, Negroes, Whites, Civil Rights, States' Rights, the South, the North, Social Action and Some Other Matters* . . . New York: Anti-Defamation League of B'nai B'rith, 1966.

——, "Jewish Roots in the Carolinas," *The Carolina Israelite*, 1955.

Greenberg, Mrs. David, *The Richmond Story: A Selective Chronology of the Richmond Jewish Community, 1870–1924.* Published by Richmond Jewish Community Center, 1955.

Harris, Ray Baker, "Eleven Gentlemen of Charleston," *Founders of the Supreme Council, Ancient and Accepted Scottish Rite of Free Masonry.* Published by the Supreme Council, October 1, 1959.

Hertzberg, Steven, "The Jewish Community of Atlanta from the End of the Civil War until the Eve of the Frank Case," *American Jewish Historical Society Quarterly*, LXII, 3, (March, 1973), 250–285.

Korn, Bertram W., *Jews and Negro Slavery in the Old South 1789–1865.* Elkins Park, Pa.: Reform Congregation Knesreth Israel, 1961.

Krause, Allen, "The Southern Rabbi and Civil Rights." Doctoral thesis, Hebrew Union College, Jewish Institute of Religion, 1967.

Krause, P. Allen, "Rabbis and Negro Rights in the South 1954–1970," *American Jewish Archives*, XXI, 1 (April, 1969), 20–47.

Lowi, Theodore, "Southern Jews: The Two Communities," *The Jewish Journal of Sociology*,VI, 1 (July, 1964), 103–17.

Mantinband, Charles, "Rabbi in the Deep South," *ADL Bulletin*, May, 1962, p. 3.

———, "The Horns of a Dilemma," *Central Conference of American Rabbis Yearbook*, LXXIV (1964), 242–49.

———, "In Dixieland I Take My Stand." First Annual George Brussel Memorial Lecture, Stephen S. Wise Free Synagogue, New York City, April 16, 1962.

Miller, Alexander F., "Safety and Security of Southern Jewry," A Digest of Reports submitted by ADL Field Representatives following visits to 143 Southern Communities from Virginia through East Texas from May 20, 1958, to June 16, 1958. (Unpublished.)

Nussbaum, Perry, "Christian Love for the Jews," *The Jewish Digest*, XV, 9 (June, 1970), 61–63.

Peskin, Allan, "The Origins of Southern Anti-Semitism," *Chicago Jewish Forum*, 1954, 83–88.

Reissman, Leonard, "The New Orleans Jewish Community," *The Jewish Journal of Sociology*, IX, 1 (June, 1962), pp. 110–23.

Roth, Philip, "The New Jewish Stereotypes," 1961. Reprinted in *Zionism Reconsidered*. New York: Macmillan, 1970.

Seiger, Rabbi Chaim, *Immigration, Settlement and Return: Jews of the Lower Mississippi Valley 1865–1880.* Paper presented at Anglo-Jewish Historical Society in England, 1970.

Silberman, Lou, "American Impact: Judaism in the United States in the Early Nineteenth Century." The B. G. Rudolph Lectures in Judaic Studies, Syracuse University, April 29, 1964.

———, "Jewish Communities in the Changing South." Address at the 26th General Assembly of the Council of Jewish Federations and Welfare Funds, November 14–17, 1957, at New Orleans, La.

Stern, Malcolm H., "Some Notes on the History of the Organized Jewish Community of Norfolk, Virginia," *The Journal of the Southern Jewish Historical Society*, I, 3 (November, 1963), 12–36.

———, "New Light on the Jewish Settlement of Savannah," *American Jewish Historical Quarterly*, LII, 3 (March, 1963), 169–99.

———, "Monticello and the Levy Family," *The Journal of the Southern Jewish Historical Society*, I, 2 (October, 1959), 19–23.

Sutker, Solomon, "The Jews of Atlanta: Their Social Structure and Leadership Patterns." Unpublished Doctoral thesis, University of North Carolina, 1950.

Tobias, Thomas J., "The Cemetery We Eradicate," *American Jewish Historical Society Quarterly*, LIII, 4 (June, 1964), 353–69.

———, "Joseph Tobias of Charles Towne: 'Linguister,'" *American*

Jewish Historical Society Quarterly, XLIX, 1 (September, 1959), 33–38.

Twain, Mark, "Concerning the Jews," *How to Tell a Story and Other Essays*. New York: Harper and Bros., 1899.

Ungar, Andre, "To Birmingham and Back," *Conservative Judaism*, XVIII, 1 (Fall 1963). Published by the Rabbinical Assembly.

Viener, Sol, "Surgeon Moses Albert Levy: Letters of a Texas Patriot," *American Jewish Historical Society Quarterly*, XLVI, 2 (December, 1956), 101–13.

Walls, Dwayne, *The Klan: Collapsed and Dormant*. Race Relations Information Center, Nashville, Tennessee, May, 1970.

Williams, Roger, "Two Old Men: Solomon Blatt and Edgar Brown," *South Today*, II, 8 (April, 1971).

Acknowledgments

T H I S book could never have been written without the assistance, guidance and affection of many people.

Since it is the story of several generations of our family, it required long hours of interviewing my parents. They are remarkable people, and whatever else comes from this experience, it will have been worth it to rediscover them as friends and to communicate with them on the most profound levels. I especially want to acknowledge the unique contribution of my brother Bob, whose perceptions into our lives in our hometown reverberate through the book. In addition, Helen Rowan read the manuscript at a crucial stage and criticized with her customary brilliance and unerring taste. There is a great deal more of her in this book than she ever realized.

I will always be grateful to Willie Morris, the editor of *Harper's* magazine, for his enthusiasm for this idea and for agreeing to send me through the South under the auspices of the magazine. At Atheneum, Herman Gollob, editor-in-chief, and Pat Irving were invaluable in shaping the manuscript; Jack Fisher, the former editor of *Harper's*, urged me to be more personal than I had originally intended and he was right; Pat Myrer at McIntosh and Otis was far more than just another agent in arranging the finances for the project.

For reading the manuscript and adding their insights, I want to thank Avery Russell, Jack Nessel, Elizabeth Drew, Nancy Ehle, Walter and Ann Dellinger, Frederick Mosher and Barbara Babcock. In addition, one of the finest scholars on this subject, Rabbi Malcolm Stern of the Central Conference of American Rabbis, gave me dozens of research and interviewing leads to start me off, and spent hours at the end peppering me with detailed questions to check for accuracy; Dr. Eric Meyers, director of the Cooperative Program of Judaic Studies at Duke University and the University of North Carolina, read an early draft and opened my eyes to the larger questions; Sigmund Meyer was kind enough to share his lifetime of interest in the history of the Durham Jewish community.

For many courtesies and assistance all along the way, I will always be grateful for the reception and the openness of the hundreds of people I talked with across the South. They made researching the book a deep and lasting personal experience. I want to thank especially Jack Bass, Ginger Slaughter, Dwayne Walls, Dr. Cecil Slome, Mrs. Miriam Kroskin, Herbert Newmark, Lois Farfel, Mrs. Josie Berson, Mel Rashkis, Betsy Hegeman, Sol Viener, Eden Lipson, Steve and Dottie Bernholz, Mrs. Ann Colvin, Carol and Harry Stein, Gail H. Evans, Joel Fleishman, Ken and Mary Dean, Hodding and Peggy Carter, Marian Wright Edelman, Naomi Kaufman, Mary Canada in the Duke Library, Ciba Vaughan, Honey, Mike and Lolly Brener, Robin Pinkham and Anne Queen. Mr. and Mrs. Frank Strong and Caro Mae Russell allowed me to live in their lovely homes in the Chapel Hill woods, Jimmy and Nina Wallace their cottage on the outer banks of North Carolina, and Dr. and Mrs. Nicholas Georgiade their tree-top house at Beech Mountain. They all enabled me to live a North Carolina boy's dream of writing his book in the fantasy places. I also would like to thank Oscar Cohen at the Anti-Defamation League for the use of his research memos and background papers; Charles Wittenstein at the Atlanta office of the American Jewish Committee for his advice and contacts; and the regional officers of A.D.L.—Sherman Harris in Richmond, A. I. Botnick in New Orleans and Ted Freedman in Houston—for their cooperation.

Finally, I should like to add a personal note of appreciation to a number of people who helped through the years: first, to my three uncles who were also mayors of their towns for letting me sit in on their political discussions when the family got together— Mayor Monroe Evans of Fayetteville, North Carolina; Mayor Leon

Schneider of Gastonia, North Carolina; and Mayor Harold Frankel of Huntington, West Virginia; to my uncle and my seven aunts (especially Ethel for her summer of note-taking with her mother thirty-five years ago) for sharing memories of Jennie and Eli Nachamson.

Second, I will always be grateful to Alan Pifer, president of the Carnegie Corporation of New York, for giving me the opportunity to roam across the South these last five years for the foundation. The experience tossed me into the crosscurrents of the civil rights movement in ways that influenced me deeply.

And last, no book writes itself. Carol Sloane and Rue Canvin somehow interpreted my scribbling and typed up two years of notes, interviews and musings. They know how far we've come.

359

INDEX

Eli N. Evans

Eli N. Evans was born and raised in Durham, North Carolina. He graduated from the University of North Carolina in 1958, and spent two years in the Navy, stationed in Japan. After graduating from Yale Law School in 1963, he worked as a White House aide from 1964 to 1965 and was a speech writer for political candidates in North Carolina. From 1965 to 1967, he worked at Duke University on a nationwide study of the future of the states that was headed by former North Carolina Governor Terry Sanford. Since then he has traveled extensively in the South as a grants officer for the Carnegie Corporation of New York and has administered other programs in minority problems, governmental affairs, and public television. Mr. Evans currently lives in New York City.